Zion and State

For my parents, with love

ZION and STATE

Nation, Class and the Shaping of Modern Israel

MITCHELL COHEN

Basil Blackwell

First published 1987

Basil Blackwell Ltd
108 Cowley Road, Oxford, OX4 1JF, UK

Basil Blackwell Inc.
432 Park Avenue South, Suite 1503
New York, NY 10016, USA

British Library Cataloguing in Publication Data

Cohen, Mitchell
Zion and state—nation, class and
the shaping of modern Israel.
1. Zionism   2. Israel—Politics and
government—1948–
I. Title
320.95694   JQ1825.P3
ISBN 0–631–15243–1

DS
149
.C627
1987

Library of Congress Cataloging in Publication Data

Cohen, Mitchell, 1952–
Zion and state.
Bibliography: p.
Includes index.
1. Zionism—Palestine—History.   2. Labor Zionism—
Palestine—History.   3. Revisionist Zionism—Palestine—
History.   4. Right and left (Political science)
5. Israel—Politics and government.   I. Title.
DS149.C627   1987   956.94'001   86-23235
ISBN 0–631–15243–1

Typeset in 10 on 12pt Sabon by
Opus, Oxford
Printed in the USA

Contents

Preface:
The Vision of Zion and the
Realities of Statehood

May 1958 marked ten years of Israeli independence. The re-establishment of Jewish sovereignty in Palestine, some two millennia after the violent end of the Second Jewish Commonwealth there, represented a veritable revolution in Jewish life. A dispersed and persecuted people had reclaimed political self-determination successfully. From the perspective of its first decade, the fledgeling Jewish state's leaders could view its progress with considerable satisfaction. Although born in war shortly after the greatest catastrophe of Jewish history, and while still facing fierce enmity from its neighbors, Israel was increasingly stable and confident. Its army was strong, its economy was consolidating and its gates had been opened to hundreds of thousands of Jewish refugees from Hitler's carnage and from the Arab world.

In that month David Ben-Gurion addressed the conference of Mapai, the socialist party which dominated both the Zionist struggle for independence and the politics of the new state. The prime minister pressed themes he had long articulated: In the diaspora the Jew was a being divided against himself, a minority figure who lived in two milieux, that of his own people and that of an external, hostile world in which he was never at home, yet on which he was always dependent. In Israel, however, this 'cleavage between the Jew and the man' was 'healed'. Here, Jews were 'subject to a Jewish state framework and it is they themselves who mould it and determine its character'. Here, everything was 'a hundred percent Jewish and a hundred percent human'.

Here had been created 'a new Jew' and 'a new man' whose most notable quality was that he had 'completely emerged from the distorted environment of the diaspora and its painful complexes, that of degrading inferiority as well as that of fancied superiority'. This new Jew was 'rooted in the soil of the homeland, confident in himself and master of his fate', an integrated being, equally at home with his 'distant, Biblical characteristics'

and as a citizen of the contemporary international community.¹ In the
Jewish state, the Israeli premier was telling his audience, an existential crisis
inherent in diaspora existence was resolved; the new Jew knew who he was
and what that meant. This contrast between old and new Jew was, in a way,
epitomized by a comment one of Ben-Gurion's protégés made to a meeting
of Mapai's Young Guard some two years later. According to Shimon Peres,
the problem facing his, the new, generation in Israel was 'not to know what
we want to be, but what we want to do'.²

In 1962 a story entitled 'The Way of the Wind' was written by a young
member of a kibbutz, one of the communal farms that long symbolized the
practical achievements of Israeli socialism. Amos Oz's short work of fiction
was set in an imaginary kibbutz, Nof Harish, in the Jezreel Valley, where
once the winter capital of ancient Israel stood, and where, in the twentieth
century, some of the pioneering projects in collective settlement, regarded as
heroic exemplars by Zionist socialists, began. The title came from
Ecclesiastes: 'As thou knowest not what is the way of the wind/ Nor how
the bones do grow in the womb of her that is with child;/ Even so thou
knowest not the work of God/ Who doeth all things'.³ In Hebrew, 'The Way
of the Wind' is *Derekh ha-ruakh*, the word 'ruakh' having numerous
meanings including wind, spirit, mind, intellect and ghost.⁴

The narrative takes place during a *khamsin*, a wave of sweltering winds
which originate usually in the Arabian peninsula. The youthful Gideon
Shenhav is to participate in a parachute display in honour of Israeli
Independence Day. His 75-year-old father, Shimshon Sheinbaum, a
kibbutznik renowned for his role in the labour movement, will watch.
Shimshon, who has never been able to communicate with his son, is a man
rigid in his world-view, punctilious in his daily habit, 'a single complex of
vision and execution'. He is also decidedly disappointed in his progeny, who
as a child was 'slow of speech and no doubt of thought', hardly what
Zionist revolutionaries hoped to behold in their offspring.⁵

Gideon enlisted in the paratroopers to prove his mettle to his father. With
the kibbutz watching, he proudly joins his comrades in their jump into the
Middle Eastern skies. But Gideon begins to drift and drift in the wind, the
ruakh. And he drifts until caught in electric cables. Sparks flying, he cries,
'Tell them to switch off the current quickly', while his father calls him
coward and orders him to cut his straps. Gideon severs all except one and is
caught upside down, dangling in the wires, with the kibbutz children
laughing at his awkward position. Gideon, too, laughs – before finally
throwing himself on the cables. In the meantime, 'The hot wind continued
to tyrannize the valley'. Gideon Shenhav, who should have epitomized the
new Jew, an integrated being preoccupied not with who he was but with
what to do, dies of shock hanging upside-down near his kibbutz, with the
torrid *ruakh* blowing through the Valley of Jezreel. *Izreel*, the Hebrew for
Jezreel, means 'May God give seed'.

It is a truism that no successful political movement, however self-conscious its practice, finds in its achievement the full embodiment of its founders' purposes. This is especially so with Zionism, an endeavour with revolutionary intentions, and progenitors and protagonists of great imagination and aspirations. The tensions between their visions of Zion and the realities of state-building and statehood were often enormous. The obstructions – often unanticipated – encountered in realizing their aims were frequently surmounted in circumstances and with means adverse to their original animating spirit. This book is concerned, among other things, with the fate of that spirit, and particularly with that of the Zionist Labour movement, and its chief component, Mapai. The reason is simple enough: it was due to the Labour movement's leadership that Zionism attained its goal of Jewish statehood.

A multiplicity of factors was, of course, at play. None the less, in difficult circumstances, and with a remarkable outburst of political, social and economic inventiveness and energy, Zionist Labour, and especially its leader David Ben-Gurion, fashioned a formidable political strategy that embedded a synthesis of national and class concepts in the material process of re-creating a Jewish community in Palestine in the 1920s and 1930s. This built the material foundations not only for Jewish sovereignty, but for the spiritual hegemony of Labour as well. However, in the process of achieving its revolution, Labour's own character and politics changed in decisive ways. It will be suggested in these pages that those transformations significantly helped ensure Labour's greatest achievement – a sovereign Jewish state – and, paradoxically and dialectically, the eventual subversion of Labour's own political direction and spiritual dominance. This turn of Zionist political history may be represented by the contrast between the self-assurance projected by Ben-Gurion and Peres on one hand, and Oz's picture of the hapless Gideon dangling amidst the wires on the other.

The Zionist endeavour aimed not only to place Jewish existence on a new (safer) physical basis, but to restructure its symbolic universe so that it might survive and flourish in a new and changing world of nations. Consequently, Zionist and Israeli politics must, to a very significant extent, be understood as a struggle to define an emerging political culture. Zionism implied a refocusing of Jewish identity so that its territorial dimension – always implicit in the orientation of Jewish religion to *Erets Israel*, the Land of Israel – was renewed. This reorientation, in turn, brought with it the possibility of a *national* Jewish culture, instead of the predominantly religious one that characterized 2,000 years of diaspora life. As a result of the pogroms of 1881, the authority structure of Russian Jewry, already under challenge, temporarily failed to sustain itself and, consequently, new players were thrust on to the political stage, and new structures of consciousness were generated. The memoirs of an early Russian Zionist leader poignantly captured this restructuring by observing that 'The people of the book . . . became the people of newspapers. Of old they had been wont to turn everyday to the pages of the Talmud to find out what the sages had to say. Now they turned to the editorial pages'.[6] This was expressive of the rebirth of an explicitly political dimension in Jewish life in the late nineteenth century, the emergence of what one scholar has called a new Jewish politics.[7] Although there were 'cultural' and religious Zionists who would object to this characterization, it is not inaccurate to speak of Jewish nationalism as a whole as an attempted transvaluation of the Jewish symbolic universe.[8]

The first turn in this development is the subject of the opening part of this book, that is, the emergence of a modern Jewish politics, or more specifically, its nationalist variant. Part one begins with an exploration of the concepts of nation and nationalism, and the historical transformations that yielded modern Jewish politics and Zionism. Then the ideological and organizational world of early Zionism is examined. This serves as a prelude to part two which is an extended analysis of the rise of the Zionist left and the Zionist right, and the fierce struggle between them to dominate the political culture of the future Jewish nation.

Zionism aspired to reset the boundaries and categories of Jewish existence. The formative historical events in a nation's history – 'the process by which the legal and physical boundaries of a nation are set' – may be the decisive determinants of the national identity of its members, as one political scientist notes. Major crises, he continues, especially violent ones such as war and revolution, set the 'psychological boundaries' of a nation and can shift identification from one political unit (e.g. a village) to another (e.g. a nation). Such crises can be viewed 'in terms of the inferences individuals draw from them about their fellow citizens'.[9] Be it eastern European Jewry following the violence of 1881, or Theodor Herzl in the aftermath of the virulent anti-semitism he witnessed in the Vienna and Paris of the 1890s, a set of historical circumstances radically reshaped the inferences those Jews who became Zionists drew about the world surrounding them. The contest between the left and the right may be seen as a struggle to dominate and define this reshaping process.

That contest, the focus of the second part of this book, pitted the Zionist Labour movement, led by Berl Katznelson, Itshak Tabenkin and especially David Ben-Gurion, against the 'Revisionists' led by Vladimir Jabotinsky. The latter classified his outlook as 'monistic' because be claimed to espouse 'pure' nationalism; there could be but one set of categories to dominate the modern Jewish consciousness and that was of the nation-state. Labour, on the other hand, recognized two sets of categories, nation and class, and sought to transcend any contradictions between them by positing an identity in interests of the emerging Jewish working class in Palestine, and of the Jewish nation as a whole. For reasons that will be discussed at length, Labour's victory in this struggle enabled it to become the primary architect of the Zionist state. However, with Labour's triumph came a self-transformation which, in my view, was critical in shaping the future of Israeli politics to this day. It represents what I call the reification of Zionism under Labour dominance, and is the subject of the final third of this book.

Reification is a term I have expropriated for my own purposes from Georg Lukács' classic *History and Class Consciousness*. In its simplest form, reification occurs when relations between human beings and the products of their activity appear to them as relations among things beyond them. Lukács drew from Marx's discussion in *Capital* of 'the fetishism of commodities', that is, the tendency of producers in capitalism to perceive their products – commodities – not as embodiments of their own social activity but as things.[10] The worker himself functions as a commodity since he sells his labour power to the capitalist for a wage. Lukács took these concepts and generalized them, making use of Max Weber's projection of the continuing rationalization of modern society, that is, the increasing dominance, in all aspects of life, of formalistic, quantifying reason and calculability as expressed in the modern capitalist enterprise, bureaucracy, the role of science, the formalism of the modern legal order and the 'disenchantment of the world'.

For Lukács, the nature of capitalism – its entire system of human, social, and economic relations – was thus to be discerned in the 'commodity-structure', which, in concrete form, is taken from the hands of those who produce it (the workers) and placed on the market (by its owner, the capitalist) where it 'acquires a "phantom objectivity", an autonomy that seems so strictly rational and all-embracing as to conceal every trace of its fundamental nature: the relation between people'.[11] Human beings find themselves in a 'pre-existing and self-sufficient' world, and become increasingly passive, unable to imagine themselves as its creators, let alone masters.[12] The means of human life appear as ends, while the real end – human beings and the satisfaction of their needs – becomes the means, integrated into the productive system. For Lukács, following Marx, achieving socialism meant that the self-conscious proletariat was both the subject (or active agent) of the revolutionary process and its object, since by creating a classless society it abolishes itself as well as the ruling class. As the 'identical subject–object of history', the proletariat overcomes reification.

It is a central contention of this book that in the process of its realization, Zionism reified. More specifically, it was socialist or Labour Zionism that reified since its right-wing opponents fetishized the state from the outset. The premise of Jabotinsky's 'monism' was that any 'ism' – such as socialism – when synthesized with Zionism, polluted and, ultimately, misdirected and distorted the effort to establish a nation-state for the Jews. Labour, in rebuttal, argued that since no state is an abstraction, the type of society being constructed was as fundamental as the state itself; and since within all states there are social systems, why should capitalism be less a pollutant than socialism?

The process of reification can be seen in the changing role of the state – or the state-in-genesis before 1948 – in Labour movement ideology and politics. From being an essential means to the liberation of the Jewish people, the state increasingly became a thing unto itself. Since the quest for statehood and the re-creation of Jewish political culture were at the heart of the Zionist enterprise, the changing relations between state, nation and class within this project were fraught with consequences. We can summarize this evolution as follows. For socialist Zionism, as it crystallized by the 1920s, the emerging Jewish working class in Palestine was both the subject, that is, bearer, of the Zionist revolution, and its object. Labour posited the creation of 'am oved', a working (classless) nation in its own state, as its goal. The working class was proposed as the identical subject–object of Jewish history because its interests were deemed to be universal – i.e. the embodiment of those of the nation as a whole – in contrast to the bourgeoisie whose profit-seeking individualized interests were, of necessity, particularistic. In the process of state-building and re-entrenching a Jewish community in Palestine, the Zionist capitalist had to invest his energy and resources where it would give him adequate returns; the worker, owning nothing but his labour power, could invest his energy where the Jewish nation needed it. For Zionist socialism, the Jewish national project was, therefore, a collective project by definition. The vehicle for the Zionist socialist revolution was the Histadrut (the General Confederation of Jewish Labour in Palestine) which was founded in 1920. The Histadrut aimed to be a Jewish workers' state within the state of Mandate Palestine, as well as the harbinger of a future, sovereign, socialist Jewish state. It was not merely a trade union federation, but a vast public sphere of the working class which included a co-operative economy, agricultural settlements and an elabourate social welfare structure under its umbrella. Its internal governance was determined by elections in which various labour and socialist parties competed.

A variety of pressures led the Labour movement, in the late 1920s, to seek to translate the dominance it was then establishing in the Yishuv (the Jewish community of Palestine) into dominance of the world Zionist Organization (ZO), the general structural framework of the Jewish national movement. Founded originally by Herzl in 1897 and seated later in London, it was controlled by middle class elements who, in turn, determined its priorities. Labour successfully 'conquered' the ZO, though only after a bitter and at times violent competition in Palestine and in the diaspora with the Revisionists, who were then also bidding for the Zionist leadership. The defeat of the extreme right led to its marginalization in Zionist and Israeli politics in the ensuing crucial decades. Labour, or more specifically its chief component, Mapai (founded in 1930), did not accomplish this through gaining electoral majorities in elections to the biennial world Zionist

Congress or to the Yishuv's institutions. It was never able to do so (apart from in the Histadrut). It achieved its goals through coalitions with other (usually bourgeois and religious) parties, coalitions in which it was, however, the largest party and the dominant factor. My argument is that in the process of capturing the mantle of Zionist leadership by means of such coalitions – the sole way available to it – the Labour movement's politics fundamentally reoriented. Specifically, and a good deal of its own rhetoric aside, Mapai jettisoned the identity of national and working-class interests as an operative premise of its politics. Instead it accepted the principle of 'segmented pluralism', in which various segments of the Yishuv, based on ideological and religious cleavages, would construct their own socio-cultural, economic and political 'pillars', that is, extensive networks of institutions encompassing all aspects of the lives of their adherents. This was, in general, a type of vertical social segmentation in contrast to the horizontal one of class.[13] Consequently, the Histadrut, conceived originally as a class-based institution, became only one, though the largest, of many pillars of the future society, rather than the embodiment of that society.

This meant in fact that Labour represented a particular rather than a universal interest; the nation-state, as something that 'seems so strictly rational and all-embracing', standing above all classes, came to represent the universal. The state, as an operative concept, became a thing unto itself, and the Labour movement increasingly became a statist movement, seeking to identify itself with the state, rather than identifying the nation's interests with those of the working class. In so doing, it accepted an essential aspect of Revisionist political culture, the idea that the nation and the state were and should be entities above class, and that working-class institutions were particularistic. Whereas Labour Zionism once sought to synthesize the universal – socialism – with a particular – nationalism – the universal category now became the state as embodiment of the nation, and socialism and socialist institutions became the particular, at best 'helpers' of the state. This took concrete form in Ben-Gurion's policies of 'mamlakhtiyut' in the first decade-and-a-half of statehood. *Mamlakhtiyut* (derived from *mamlakha*, kingdom in Hebrew) may be roughly rendered into English as statism, and was translated into policy as the subordination of all 'particularist' institutions, be they of the left or right, to the state.[14]

With this came the subordination of the Labour movement to the state *qua* state, and the nationalization of many of its key institutions and functions, formerly under the auspices of the Histadrut. As will be evident in the second and third parts of this book, many of these same institutions and functions were those that the Revisionists, in the 1930s, insisted belonged in 'national' rather than 'class' hands. Israeli Labour may be the sole historical example of a socialist movement that, in power, nationalized and subordinated its *own* institutions, thus, ultimately, undermining itself. Jewish messianism, the state and the army – always important components in Ben-Gurion's political vocabulary – increasingly displaced the socialist idea, and the notion of *am mamlakhti* (a statist nation) eclipsed that of *am oved* as his operative political principle. A generation of young Mapai adherents emerged for whom the state and its mechanisms, and especially the military, were the primary frames of reference; the questions they posed were not those of class or socialist community, but rather of efficiency and what became known as *bitsuism* (activism), which they contrasted with ideology. They represented the end of Labour Zionist ideology. Their concern was, to quote Peres again, who along with Moshe Dayan symbolized the *bitsuistim* ('activists', or 'doers'), 'not to know what we want to be, but what we want to do'.

In the 1950s a mass immigration of Jews from Arab lands arrived in Israel. These were people with no roots in the Labour Zionist tradition or in the environment that nurtured it. *Mamlakhtiyut*, however, did not seek to socialize them into the Labour Zionist symbolic universe – the Histadrut educational system was abolished in 1953 and replaced by a 'mamlakhti' system – but rather into one whose primary categories were nation and state. The state institutions on which the new immigrants were dependent were dominated by the Mapai establishment, and almost half the Israeli economy was in public (i.e. state or Histadrut) hands. Consequently these immigrants later identified the Labour movement as the class that ruled them, rather than a bourgeoisie. Their resentments were, in turn, tapped eventually by the party of political *ressentiment*, Herut, led by Menahem Begin, Jabotinsky's successor. This development was facilitated too by the unremitting hostility of Israel's neighbours, the negative experiences many of these immigrants had had in the Arab lands of their birth and the consequent appeal of an ultra-nationalist party like Herut, with its forthright belligerence towards the Arabs. Furthermore, while the Revisionists themselves had been compelled to seethe powerlessly during long years in the Zionist political wilderness, the spirit of reified Zionism fostered by Ben-Gurion was in significant ways closer to their political culture – which fetishized the state and the army – than to that historically associated with the Labour movement, which had once championed, and built its power on, the vision of the Histadrut, the kibbutz, and social experimentation. The state, rather than the voluntaristic activism of the Labour movement, was canonized by *mamlakhtiyut*. In short, the seeds were planted for Labour's future unravelling and eventual defeat by the right in 1977; the pressures of national emergency – in particular the wars of 1967 and 1973 – could only strengthen extreme nationalists, and this intensified at a time when Labour's younger generation, which finally came into its own in the mid-1970s, was composed either of technocrats or of people unable to sort out the ideological wires amidst and from which they, like Gideon Shenhav, were dangling.

This book is a critical interpretative analysis with a particular focus. Zionism's principal concern was neither big power politics nor the Arab world, but rather the increasing distress and persecution of the Jews. It therefore sought – and achieved – a revolution in *Jewish* life, and my questions in this book address themselves strictly to that revolution. As such, these pages are concerned primarily with a dynamic internal to Zionist and Israeli politics and their preoccupations are purposefully selective. 'No inquiry', as Lucien Goldmann observed, '. . . is ever exhaustive . *It only poses certain questions to reality and chooses facts in light of these questions.* Moreover, in the image it constructs, the importance ascribed to the different facts it takes into account is proportionate to what the problems represent for the researcher or inquirer'.[15] My aim, consequently, is not a general political history of Zionism and Israel. I intentionally do not devote substantive treatment to various matters such a history would of necessity encompass such as Zionist foreign policy (the struggles with the Mandatory authorities, Palestinian Arabs and the Arab world in general), or the evolution of the religious and some left-wing parties. This is not to belittle their importance. Their proper due should – and is to – be found in studies with other foci;[16] herein they will be of concern in as much as they help to illuminate the questions to which I do address myself.

The origins of this book go back to the spring of 1973 when, as an undergraduate spending a year at the Hebrew University of Jerusalem, I wrote a paper on Lukács for one course, while concurrently enrolled in another which was an admiring appreciation of *mamlakhtiyut*. As I studied Ben-Gurion's policies, *mamlakhtiyut* struck me as a form of reification and this led me to probe questions pertaining to the place of the state as a means and/or end of Zionism.[17] I tried to raise the theme of Zionism's reification in various articles published over the following decade, although until the research for this book was done (1983–5) I assumed its roots to be in the actual transition to statehood (in other words, largely a post-1948 phenomenon) and I thus did not, as this book seeks to do, take sufficient account of the changes that came with Mapai's assumption of leadership in the Jewish national movement in the 1930s.[18] Inevitably, this required especial focus on Israel's first prime minister. While I reject 'great person' theories of history, it is perhaps appropriate to note here that despite my critique of him, I am convinced that Ben-Gurion will be recorded as the towering figure of modern Jewish history. As this book I hope makes evident, he was, more than any other individual, responsible for Jewish statehood, and simultaneously for the undermining of the chief tool he used to achieve it, the Israeli Labour movement.

As I have been politically active as editor of *Jewish Frontier*, the American Labour Zionist journal (1979–85), and as a supporter of the Israeli Labour and peace movements, it would be disingenuous for me to suggest that this work is 'scientifically objective', something I have, in any case, never believed possible in the study of politics or history. As such, my ambition here is not pseudo-neutrality in treating my material, but fairness and proportion. Again following Goldmann, it strikes me as preferable to be explicit about the fact that certain categories of thought influence my analyses, rather than to pretend to repress them; thus frank criticism of my own work is more easily and properly facilitated.[19]

Acknowledgements

In writing this book I was fortunate to receive the assistance and friendship of numerous individuals. I can only begin to express my appreciation to them. Several scholars and friends, in Israel and in the United States, gave critical readings to sections of the manuscript, and the result is, undoubtedly, a better book thanks to them: Myron J. Aronoff, Jonathan Frankel, Yosef Gorni, Ben Halpern, Lori Lefkovitz, Robert M. Seltzer, Eli Sha'altiel, Marie Syrkin, Michael Walzer and Bernard Wasserstein. Rabbis Miles Cohen and Leonard Gordon kindly shared their expertise by reading the parts that make biblical and Rabbinic references. Conversations I had with Dan Horowitz, Anita Shapira and Shabtai Tevet in Israel in the summer of 1985 were helpful in clarifying some of my thoughts. To Steve Zipperstein, whose knowledge of Jewish history has enriched my own endlessly, I must express especial appreciation, both for his encouragement of this book and for his invaluable criticisms of it. I am deeply grateful to Nicole Fermon and Karyl Weicher, whose friendship, loyalty and patience have been very important to me.

In the past quarter of a century there has been a remarkable outpouring of scholarly research, particularly in Israel, on Zionist and Israeli politics and history. Believing that knowledge is in fact a collective enterprise, I wish to acknowledge a general, but great, debt to these efforts (many of which are cited in the footnotes) in my own work. I am also pleased to acknowledge, with gratitude, the assistance of several institutions which facilitated the completion of this book. My colleagues in the political science department of Bernard M. Baruch College of the City University of New York consistently encouraged my work. I wish to thank the Oxford Centre for Postgraduate Hebrew Studies for hosting me as a Visiting Scholar in the summer of 1984. I am grateful to the Memorial Foundation for Jewish Culture for a Fellowship-Research Grant, and to the Research Foundation of the City University of New York for a PSC-CUNY Grant. The financial generosity of the latter two institutions allowed me to travel to Israel to do essential research in the summers of 1983 and 1985. I made use of numerous libraries and archives, and while they are all listed in the bibliography, I would like to express particular appreciation to the Zionist Archives and Library in New York, and its director Esther Togman, for their kindness and assistance. Thanks are due to Eyal and Lilakh Inbar, Harriet Lewis and Nancy Wellins for research assistance in Israel. Tamar Ben-Vered has been both generous and excellent as my Hebrew tutor for several years; I am appreciative of her both as a teacher and for examining the transliterations in the manuscript. My thanks as well to Sean Magee and Claire Andrews of Basil Blackwell for their encouragement and for being a pleasure to work with. Finally, several friends aided me in various ways as this manuscript came to completion, and I wish to express my gratitude to them as well: Andrea Eptor, Nusi Sznaider, Florindo Volpacchio.

Mitchell Cohen
New York City

Note on Transliterations
and Abbreviations

The system of Hebrew transliteration in this book is a modified version of that used in the *Encyclopaedia Judaica*. In addition, diacritical marks are not used and several names and terms have been left in spellings that have become familiar in English. The body of the text has been rendered consistent, but not the notes so as to facilitate reference to an original source using other forms of transliteration.

The following abbreviations are used for archival and other materials in the references:

CZA   The Central Zionist Archives (Jerusalem)
ZAL   The Zionist Archives and Library (New York)
JIA   The Jabotinsky Institute and Archives (Tel Aviv)
LA   The Labour Archives/Lavon Institute (Tel Aviv)
LPA   The Labour Party Archives (Beit Berl/Kfar Saba)

A full list of archives and libraries used may be found in the bibliography at the end of the book.

Part One
Foundations

1
Nations

Forgetting, and I would even say historical error, are essential
factors in the creation of a nation . . .

Ernest Renan[1]

I

A report on nationalism published in 1939 by a study group of the Royal
Institute of International Affairs remarked that as a consequence of varied
historical conditions the Jews assumed 'at an exceptionally early date, some
of the characteristics which have since become associated most closely with
the modern concept of a "nation" '.[2] The key words in this observation
were 'early date' and 'modern concept', for nation and nationalism
generally are regarded as phenomena that appeared in a stage of world
history that long postdated the development of Jewish peoplehood. In
significant regards contemporary Jewish nationalism, and especially Zionism, represented a reinvention of fundamental elements of Jewish 'nationality' that were present since antiquity: culture (in terms of language and
especially religion), land, the aspiration for political independence and a
deep historical consciousness of peoplehood. Yet, while the longing to
'return to Zion', to return to *Erets Israel* (the Land of Israel), had been an
essential motif in Jewish history since the end of the Second Jewish
Commonwealth some two millennia ago, Zionism emerged and succeeded
at a specific juncture of general and Jewish history.

This book is concerned with the politics of those Jews, children of the late
nineteenth and early twentieth centuries, who sought to rebuild and
reinvent Jewry as a nation in an era of nationalism, revolution and
anti-Semitism in Europe, both east and west. However, its point of
departure differs from that of most other studies of the politics of Zionism
and Israel, which usually note that the growth of European nationalism
provided the setting within which Zionism arose, but do not attempt to
frame Zionism within that context. 'Judaism has been preserved, not in

spite of history, but by history', Karl Marx correctly noted in an essay otherwise distinguished, ironically, by its misconstruing of Jewish history.[3] Similarly, Jewish peoplehood was preserved within history, not despite it. Therefore, before examining in the next chapters what nation and nationalism meant for Zionists, and the extent to which the evolution of Zionism followed patterns similar to other nations and other nationalisms, we turn first to the broader significance of these terms for their era.

As a symbol and as a historical reality, 'nation', like 'class', has been one of the most potent of modern political forces. It is also, again like class, one of the most elusive of concepts, apparently simple but complex at the same time. Political scientists, philosophers, historians, sociologists and nationalist leaders inevitably find themselves in contradiction with each other when trying to define or specify 'nation' and 'nationalism'. In a recent study of *Nations before Nationalism*, John A. Armstrong criticized nationalist thought for seeking 'essences' of national character rather than 'recognizing the fundamental but shifting significance of boundaries for human identities'. Consequently, he urged a focus on 'attitudinal boundary mechanisms' of self-exclusion which distinguish groups from each other:

> the conception of the ethnic group or incipient nation as a group defined by exclusion implies that there is no purely definitional way of distinguishing ethnicity from other types of identity. The boundary approach clearly implies that ethnicity is a bundle of shifting interactions rather than a nuclear component of social organization.[4]

Another scholar, Hugh Seton-Watson, declared himself 'driven' to the conclusion that a scientifically precise definition of a nation was an impossibility, and that at best this phenomenon can be said to exist when 'a significant number of people in a community consider themselves to form a nation, or behave as if they formed one'. He qualifies this by saying that it need be only a significant part of the population, so long as it has 'national consciousness'.[5]

It may be that the most one can intelligently demand in defining 'nation' is the delineation of sets of somewhat permeable characteristics, which individually or in different combinations, gain or diminish in importance depending on the historical case, and which compose a collective, generally self-identified human entity to which we have given this name 'nation'. Such a definition is somewhat unsatisfying; an examination of the historical uses of the term 'nation' may, at least partially, yield a more concrete sense of the phenomenon. The word 'nation' is derived from the Latin verb *nasci*, to be born,[6] and *natio* first indicated a human collectivity whose members were linked by origin, and which was bigger than a family, though not sufficiently large to compose a clan or people (*gens*). The Romans did not classify themselves as a *natio*, but did refer, usually in a derogatory sense, to groups of foreigners living together within the Roman empire – sometimes in cities, at other times within colonies – as *nationes*.[7] Roman law distinguished *ius gentium*, usually translated as the law of the peoples (or, sometimes, nations) from *ius civile* (civil law). The latter referred to that which was distinctive to the Romans. As the jurist Gaius put it,

> Every people that is governed by statutes and customs observes partly its own peculiar law and partly the common law of all mankind. That law which a people establishes for itself is peculiar to it, and is called *ius civile* . . . , while the law that natural reason establishes among all mankind is followed by all peoples alike, and is called *ius gentium* . . . as being the law observed by all mankind. Thus the Roman people observes partly its own peculiar law and partly the common law of mankind.[8]

The various peoples of the Old Testament are interchangeably called *gentes, populos* and *nationes* in the Vulgate, indicating, in Huizinga's words, 'a fairly indefinite interrelationship of tribe, tongue, and region'. Eventually, Bretons and Bavarians, as well as English, Germans and French, came to be called nations as relations of dependence developed among their populations, although this originally carried no political or administrative significance. However, 'the emotion embodied in *natio* was the same everywhere: the primitive in-group . . . felt passionately united as soon as the others, outsiders in whatever way, seemed to threaten or to rival them. This feeling usually manifested itself as hostility and rarely as concord'.[9]

The term made significant, though varied, appearances in the Middle Ages. In major trading centres, merchants of common geographical origins grouped in 'nations'.[10] Foreign students at medieval universities were frequently aggregated in *nationes*. Although these were exclusivist neither in composition nor language, their formation represented in miniature an important contraposition that would later be replicated on a pan-European scale. Medieval universities, as church institutions, had a universalist character with Latin as their language and the clergy of the Church Universal directing studies and teaching; *nationes* of students represented an organizational counter-principle to Christendom as a universal empire – an inkling, one might say, of the future world of jurisdictional differentiation and clashes between nations, states and the Church. It is important to bear in mind, however, that in medieval universities such *nationes* were not in fact nations in any modern sense. Rather they emerged as self-help unions for foreign students, and also in some cases as 'communities of opinion' tied to teachers.[11] Such developments can be seen in Bologna in the twelfth century. At the University of Paris there were *nationes* of France, Normandy, Picardy and Germany, each with students of varied origin. Eventually administrative and political divisions of *nationes* appeared in Europe as well. For example, the Diet of Transylvania in the fifteenth century was composed of representatives from Hungarian, Szekely and

Saxon '*nationes*'. When the Great Schism of the Church, with its competition between popes in Avignon and Rome, was resolved at the Council of Constance, the foreign delegates, in a parallel to the case of university students, composed *nationes* based partly on common vernaculars, as well as on allegiances to secular princes in their lands of origin. (Such phenomena already were present at the Council of Lyon in 1274.) At Constance, these *nationes* had a representational function.[12]

'Natio' thus underwent a somewhat inconsistent evolution, as Seton-Watson notes. Other words, such as *populus*, people and *peuple*, were used to describe entire populations. Later, in eastern and central Europe, as assorted influences derived from the Enlightenment and Romanticism spread, terms like *Volk* in the German or *Narod* in the Russian came to imply both 'natio' and 'populus' at once, and the employment of the words *Nation* in German and *natsiya* in Russian became infrequent.[13] When Count S. Uvarov, later Tsar Nicholas I's education minister, propounded what became known as the doctrine of 'Official Nationality' – the trinity of 'autocracy, orthodoxy and nationality' – the word he used for the latter was *narodnost*. In eighteenth-century France, *peuple* usually described the population in general, and *nation* referred to an elite.

Use of the term national*ism* is generally dated to the late eighteenth and early nineteenth centuries. Seeking to trace its French origins, along with those of socialism and liberalism, G. de Bertier de Sauvigny suggests that their emergence as recognizable ideological terms corresponded, more or less, with their adoption by a social or political group. Eventually an 'entity' composed of 'ideology plus people' had sufficient impact to provoke a response, usually hostile, from within the surrounding society.[14] The first such usage in French was apparently in *Mémoires pour servir à l'histoire du jacobinisme* published by Jacques Barruel in 1798. This exiled priest attributed the following words to the head of the Masonic 'Illuminati' sect: 'The moment in which men unite in nations ... they will cease to be recognizable under a common name. *Nationalism*, or national love, will replace general love'.[15] One cannot love the nation and humanity at once; nationalism, in his view, is *l'égoïsme* of the nation. Metternich regarded 'nationalisme' as a term denoting scorn. When Larousse first entered the term in the pages of its dictionary in 1874 it defined it as 'Blind and exclusive preference for all that which is of one's own nation [*Préférence aveugle et exclusive pour tout ce qui propre à la nation à laquelle on appartient*]'.[16]

According to de Sauvigny, 'nationalisme' became part of common French parlance after the 1830s, and thus only after nationalism had made a substantial impact on France and Europe. A significant earlier usage occurred, however, during the Napoleonic era when one Rudolf Zacharias Becker was taken into custody for attempting to create a 'Deutscherbund' in the French empire. He explained to the authorities that the Germans, not composing a single state themselves, ought to be distinguished from the

English, the French and other nations which did. He insisted that since Germans were divided among several states, his own call for the cultivation of German 'national virtues' carried no political implications. A German's 'nationalism', that is, his loyalty to his nation, was distinct from, and entailed no conflict with, loyalties owed to the state of which he was a citizen. The assumption was that the demands made by nation and state were not necessarily congruent, and in this Becker anticipated a distinction later frequently made between (German) *Kulturnation* and (French) *Staatnation*.[17]

In part, the contrast between the philosophers Herder and Rousseau in the eighteenth century also anticipated this distinction. Herder's concept of nation rested on *Volksgeist*; nationhood was constituted on the basis of the cultural spirit of a people, especially as expressed in its language. Human diversity had as a 'natural corollary' the development of different national languages, and 'every distinct community is a *nation*, having its own national culture as it has its own language'.[18] He apparently originated the German term *Nationalismus*; his nationalism, however, was not political for his concern was with cultural self-definition and cultural self-determination. For him, 'Nature creates nations, not states'.[19] States were not unnatural, but they were derivative from, and secondary to, a nation conceived as a unit bearing culture, a people bearing a *Volksgeist*. 'The state can give us many ingenious contrivances; unfortunately it can also deprive us of something far more essential: our own selves'.[20] On the other hand, by insisting on the inalienable, indivisible sovereignty of the people, expressed in its General Will, Rousseau thus anticipated the notion of nationalism as *political* community, as something which engenders the demand for political self-determination as a fundamental principle.

The revolutionaries of 1789 spoke of themselves as 'patriots'. *Patria*, or fatherland, is ancient Greek in origin (*patris*) and denoted a place to which one was loyal; in its Latin form *patria* was linked to devotion to the Roman republic and its virtues.[21] Beyond defence of *la patrie*, 'patriotism' had little content *per se* for the French revolutionaries.[22] However, that the revolution engendered substantial changes in what these words implied, can be seen, first of all, in the 'Declaration of the Rights of Man and the Citizen'. Following the author of *The Social Contract*, it proclaimed that sovereignty resided in the people, and that France was now composed of *citoyens*, not *sujets* of a king. This was expressed actively two months before the 'Declaration' was issued when, on 17 June, 1789, the Third Estate, representing some 97 per cent of the French population, proclaimed itself the National Assembly of France, thus usurping sovereign prerogative on behalf of the French people as a whole, and thus challenging the prerogatives of the monarch, the nobility and the clergy. This vividly contrasts with Montesquieu's reference to nation in *The Spirit of the Laws* as 'the lords and the bishops', adding that 'the commons were not yet thought of'.[23] What was significant about 1789 for the concept of nationalism was this reconceiving of political relations; loyalty was now owed to France, not just a French king. Asserting the sovereignty of the people meant, in principle, that the people would determine its own fate, and no longer permit the king and the other two Estates to do so. Concurrently, it also meant that there was an entity known as France, made up of citizens known as Frenchmen, which ought to determine its fate *vis-à-vis* the rest of the world.

It was earlier, in January of that year, that this impulse was articulated most forcefully by the Abbé Emmanuel Joseph Sieyès in his incendiary Rousseauist pamphlet 'What is the Third Estate?'. In fact, the revolution itself was the answer to his question. Be that as it may, he identified the politically underprivileged 97 per cent of the population that composed the Third Estate with the nation as a whole. Indeed, *he identified what had previously been regarded as one segment of the society with the whole of the society* by naming his first chapter 'The Third Estate is a Complete Nation'. Hence his provocative formulation: 'What is the Third Estate? *Everything*. What has it been until now in the political order? *Nothing*. What does it demand? *To be something*'.[24] Virtually all public and private activities required for a nation's survival and prosperity, he asserted, were in fact carried out, almost entirely, by the Third Estate. The nobility was a parasite living off political and civil prerogatives, defending private, particularistic – not public – interests, in other words its own.[25] And all this, of course, while pretending to be France, along with the king. 'What is a "nation?" ' Sieyès asked. 'A body of associates living under a *common law* and represented by the same *legislature*'.[26] In fact he meant that a nation ought to be such, for otherwise, by his own definition, the French were not yet a nation. However, while this definition seems to be a strictly political or legal one, it is not one of a *Staatnation*, as he made it clear that a nation, ultimately, could not be defined by its positive law-making capacity alone since 'The nation is prior to everything [*La nation existe avant tout*]; it is the origin of everything. Its will is always legal; it is the law itself'.[27] In other words, the nation alone may make positive law and is the rightful legislator; only natural law stands above it. The nation is composed of equal individuals who, making up a whole and only as that whole, has the right to legislate a constitution. The nation's origins are in natural right, the government's origins in positive right (*droite*). 'Power belongs solely to the whole [*l'ensemble*]. When a part protests [*réclame*], the whole no longer exists'.[28]

Hence the individual should be citizen, not subject, because he is part of the sovereign whole, the French nation. While the rise of nationalism is usually historically linked to that of liberalism in the nineteenth century, herein, it should be noted, were also to be found the roots of illiberalism often feared in nationalism; the individual will is regarded as a mere element. However, at the same time, as if by dialectic, a fundamentally democratic and participatory impulse was at work too. Before 1789 French subjects were just that, *sujets* of a monarch and thus but objects in the world of politics. They were equal solely in Christ. But when the banner of the nation is carried aloft, the citizen appears as a member of the sovereign, an individual who ought, at least theoretically, to be equal with all others before the law, and as an author of the law. Membership in an estate no longer defines political rights and status. This turning signified a revolution not only in France but in the nature of collective and political identity and obligation – and the rest of Europe knew this, as the two-and-a-half decades following the revolution demonstrated.

A recent Marxist analysis posits nationalism as a gateway of Janus, a historical opening above which sits the Roman god, one face to the future and one to the past.[29] The French revolution might be viewed as the flood that flung wide that portal, the threshold marking transformation after centuries in which the medieval world of feudalism, empire and church succumbed to the rising tide of liberal capitalism, the long-term impact of centralizing monarchies and the emergence of political and cultural entities composed of populations increasingly expressing what later was called national consciousness. It was the rise of these factors – capitalism, centralizing states and the emergence of more defined political–cultural entities/populations – that undermined the old world, and gave birth to the concepts of legitimacy we find expressed in Rousseau, Sieyès and the Declaration of the Rights of Man.

The banner of popular sovereignty was held aloft especially by the commercial classes, by the bourgeoisie. This effectively meant that 'the people' was deemed the political sovereign, but only part of them, a particular class, was economically sovereign. It was not a Rousseauian political community that would be established, but a framework in which individuals – theoretically all of them – could compete for profit. In contrast to the world of mercantilism, which assumed a certain coincidence between the political and the economic, the world of liberal capitalism and nationalism reserved to the political and the economic spheres, respectively, their own activities. The crudest ideological justification of capitalism was that of what can called benefit-inducing egoism; the pursuit of individual self-interest was deemed to yield public good, and vices were expected, somehow, to cancel themselves out in the end. Ironically, this ideology – created in the liberal image in which men are conceived as atomistic suppliers and demanders on the market, balancing each other out – was paralleled in notions of the interrelations between nations. Nationalism seemed like a natural extension of the individual's insistence on self-determination. It was hoped that a balance of powers would produce an equilibrium, rather than a war of every nation against every nation. It made sense for those social classes which championed liberalism to view nationalism as a common cause.

The linkage between rising liberalism and nationalism was partly disrupted following the revolutions of 1848. Napoleon's invasions had stimulated struggles for national independence in the first half of the nineteenth century; where processes of stabilization and reconsolidation took root after 1848, more conservative nationalisms ensued. However, some scholars, such as Lewis Namier, have emphasized the 'radical' nature of post-1848 nationalisms; since they were linguistically rooted, it was claimed, they almost naturally saw themselves as unbounded by borders. The belief that all speakers of a tongue should be politically contiguous easily led, in turn, to racism and radicalism embodied in particular in the notion of *Volksdeutsche*.[30] Of course this was not only a post-1848 phenomenon. Nor is it necessarily to be viewed as radical. Conservative elements are markedly present in what has been called the 'German "organic version" of nationalism', which combined notions of 'national will', the natural division of humanity into linguisitically based nations, national expression through political self-determination and the absorption of the individual into an organic state.[31] Fichte's *Addresses to the German Nation*, delivered at the Berlin Academy beginning in late 1807, declared that 'to have character and to be German [*Charakter haben und deutsch sein*] undoubtedly mean the same', and that 'the first, original and truly natural boundaries of states are beyond doubt their internal boundaries. Those who speak the same language are joined to each other by a multitude of invisible bonds by nature herself'.[32]

Namier contraposed linguistic nationalism to what he classified as a more conservative territorial nationalism such as in Britain and Switzerland. In those lands, he claimed, a type of territorial nationalism existed that was more conducive to constitutionalism, which itself requires territorial and political stability; consequently it permitted the growth of liberty.[33] Linguistic nationalism, he thought, could only breed intolerance, and the will to homogeneity. Whether one characterizes these factors as conservative or radical, the late nineteenth century did give birth to nationalisms with just these characteristics. Such, however, were not the only nationalisms championed.

II

In 1862, at a time when the struggle for Italian unity both stirred and frightened the European imagination, the question of nationalism was treated by two very different authors, each with assumptions and temperaments radically at odds with the other, each arriving, not surprisingly, at the most disparate of conclusions. A slender tract entitled *Rome and Jerusalem* was published in that year by a German Jew named Moses Hess. This self-proclaimed disciple of Spinoza had, some years before, penned the first socialist tract in the German language, and was a sometime comrade, sometime foe of Marx and Engels; he is often credited with converting the latter to communism.

However, while Marx and Engels had proclaimed in *The Communist Manifesto* that as a consequence of the internationalization of capitalist relations of production nations were, daily, vanishing more and more, that workers had no fatherland, that capitalists and proletarians had more in common with their class compatriots in other nations than with their patriotic co-nationals of opposed classes, Hess's booklet asserted that the contemporary epoch was one of nationalism. The great French revolution of 1789 had ushered in an age which would be marked by 'a simultaneous upheaval of all suppressed races ... in order to challenge the ... prerogatives and arrogance of the ruling races in the name of a higher justice.'[34] In such times, he proposed, Jerusalem should be liberated along with Rome; his own people, from whom he had been estranged during some two-and-a-half decades of utopian socialist agitation, ought to seek its future in a socialist Jewish commonwealth in Palestine, a 'new Jerusalem' that might be a light unto a world of nations, built according to a 'Mosaic constitution', which he equated with socialism.

In moments of enormous suffering induced by major social transformation, speculative minds tend to seek solutions in utopia. So declared the essay 'Nationality' by the Victorian historian Lord Acton. The greater speculative minds, like Plato and Thomas More, chastised their worlds but their warnings never passed from literary proposal to practical politics. Indeed, a philosopher's plans may compel 'the practical allegiance of fanatics only, not of nations', for a 'new notion of happiness' must be linked to 'the sense of present evil' in order for a 'settled purpose and plan of regeneration' to mature.[35] Abstractions, he continued, respond to a multiplicity of evils generally susceptible to no single solution. The grievances may indeed be just, but response by confused impulses could lead but to false and arbitrary principles. The most dangerous and subversive of them in the modern era were equality, communism and nationality: 'Though sprung from a common origin, opposing cognate evils, and connected by many links, they did not appear simultaneously. Rousseau proclaimed the first, Baboeuf the second, Mazzini the third ...'[36]

While Hess extolled the historical potentials unleashed by 1789, Acton was an admirer of Edmund Burke's famous critique of the French revolution. In the demand for the Republic One and Indivisible, Acton saw the demand for a sovereign whose authority and legitimacy rested precisely in being a whole. Popular sovereignty engendered nationality and with it a rejection of the legitimacy of past authority, indeed, of the past itself. Acton believed that there was no more potent a contemporary political doctrine than nationalism, and that it was inherently illiberal. In a world of nations demanding self-determination, pluralism within them was inevitably threatened. He averred that the 'rights of nationality' were jeopardized by 'the modern theory of nationality' which made state and nation commensurate, thus undermining the possibility that several nationalities might coexist within a given state. Liberty, for Acton, a Catholic liberal in Anglican England, meant protection from just this, from 'the influence of authority and majorities, custom and opinion'.[37] Nationalism could but provoke his deepest distrust; what he admired in Britain and Austria was the acceptance of a multiplicity of national groups within their borders.

John Stuart Mill, an English liberal of another sort, declared in his *Considerations on Representative Government* of 1860 that free government required coextension of nationality and territorial boundaries. The existence of any forceful 'sentiment of nationality', he wrote, constitutes 'a *prima facie* case for uniting all members under the same government, and a government to themselves apart'. In fact, 'One hardly knows what any division of the human race should be free to do if not to determine with which of the various collective bodies of human beings to choose to associate themselves'. Mill, whose liberalism reflected a concern for pluralism of individuals in contrast to Acton's for groups, was closer to the general spirit of nineteenth-century liberalism which tended to be identified with nationalism, often, as in 1848, with great force. Assumed was a parallel between the individual, his ability and right to determine his own fate, and that of a nation to do likewise. This would be consummated, in Namier's words, by a 'peaceful fellowship of free nations' in each of which individuals lived in peaceful fellowship.[39]

To conceive of the 'nation' as an individual is to pose the question of what demands 'the sentiment of nationality' – or a concretized form of it such as the state or a nationalist movement – may make of its members. Liberalism, which generally assumed as its starting-point the individual as an abstract, ahistorical entity (particularly in social contract theories based on positing a state of nature), must therefore have inherent problems with defining what ties a nation's members together. (Acton's pluralism was rooted in a corporatism more medieval than modern liberal in character.) 'Nation' assumes some notion of community going beyond the individual – indeed in its most radical and reactionary forms it assumes the total eclipse of the individual. Yet the word community, if it is to have any meaning, must go beyond ahistorical individuals contracting to live civilly with one another, just as it must certainly exclude a vision of individuals who 'make themselves' out of themselves, as if they were Robinson Crusoes wandering in the world of men and women. For a coherent liberal concept of nation to emerge, the irreconcilable must be reconciled; the individual as a thing unto himself must somehow be part of a trans-individual entity. Nations, like classes, are not individual enterprises.

Socialists would seem to have had an advantage in understanding nations since their assumptions were, in the first place, trans-individual. Marx's theory rested on the notion of the 'social individual', a being who individuates himself in and through society and in interrelation with his fellows.[40] Marxism, however, was particularly – though not singularly – remiss in understanding nations and nationalism. It preferred to regard them as epiphenomenal and ephemeral, part of a passing historical stage, comprehensible at best as frustrated responses to repressed aspirations, at worse as obfuscatory tools of the bourgeoisie. Marxism, in contrast to most nationalist theorists, was right in insisting that like all social formations, nations were and are historical, not eternal phenomena. However, the tendency of Marxists to class reductionism, to ascribing ultimately most or all of fundamental human realities to class, made it virtually impossible for them to comprehend nationalism adequately. The worker's identity and fate, Marxists insisted, were determined by class and *in reality* he had no nation, however he might conceive himself, and whatever conflicting identities he might think he had. If progress was to be born of the liberating power of a *universal* class, the proletariat, what place could Marx posit for such a thing as a nation? In this sense the projected future 'socialist man' was often as abstract as the being liberals began with.

For Marx, nationalism would vanish; Hess envisioned a communist–nationalist future; Acton contraposed liberalism to nationalism; Mill's view was the converse of that of Acton. The history of nationalism presents these three doctrines – nationalism, liberalism, socialism (or communism) – in relations much more complex and elusive than those suggested by any of the nineteenth-century thinkers. Certainly these ambivalences were reflected in the movements that actually claimed to carry them forth. In this Hess and Acton were in agreement: looking at their age they saw intrinsic ties between nationalism, with its equalitarian assertion of popular sovereignty, and revolutionary socialism. Acton saw the legitimacy of the existing order most threatened by the 'subversive' and linked notions of equality, communism and nationality, each of which, as noted above, he believed was derived from common sources.[41] It was precisely in this threat that Hess placed his hopes.

While the direct impact of an Acton, Hess, Mill, or Marx on contemporary national movements was negligible, the same can hardly be said of Giuseppe Mazzini. His foe Cavour, aristocratic liberal and diplomatic manipulator of Italian unification on behalf of Piedmont, may have been the successful politician of the Risorgimento, but the visionary Mazzini was its intellectual incendiary. Though hardly a great thinker – few nationalist theoreticians have been – it was Mazzini who understood, as others did not, the problematic relations between liberal individualism and nationalism. He asserted that his goal was not just Italian unification but the creation of a certain type of united nation, and he insisted on linking a universalist vision with the particular needs of the Italians. The individual's first duty was not to the nation, wrote this nationalist ideologue, but to humanity: 'You are *men* before you are *citizens* or *fathers*'.[42] The individual, the family, the nation, the state and humanity stood in mediated relations to one another. In the age of nationalist rebellion, Mazzini the idealist believed his programme linked a response to a present evil (foreign domination in Italy's case) to a vision of the good – not to a notion of happiness.

What defined this good? Mazzini was convinced that liberal individualism was an incomplete and historically *passé* vision. But his argument was not that of German organic nationalism; to the contrary. He saw the 'Declaration of the Rights of Man and the Citizen' of the French revolution as a great step forward for humanity; however, he believed it gave men their rights only as egoistic individuals, as ethically utilitarian beings who were anarchic moral agents. The struggle for such rights was an essential one since it was against an old order that ought to have been destroyed. However, 'The theory of *rights* enables us to rise and overthrow obstacles, but not to found a strong and lasting accord between all the elements which compose a nation. With the theory of happiness, of *well-being*, as the primary aim of existence we shall form egotistic men, worshippers of the material.'[43]

His 'liberal' nationalism, as such, rested on premises incongruent to Mill's philosophy; Mazzini saw before him the age of peoples, not individuals. *Duty*, not solely rights (let alone the utility contraposed by utilitarians to natural rights), had to be taught, for the good was to be found in human betterment, not only in human happiness, even in Mill's sophisticated formulation of what happiness means. Furthermore, while material well-being was not to be dismissed, it was to be situated as a *means* in Mazzini's scheme of things; it was not an end unto itself.[44] A 'Patria' is 'a fellowship of free and equal men bound together in a brotherly concord of labour towards a single end ... [It is] not an *aggregation*, it is an *association*.'[45] The nation has a moral end which is the same as the family, 'the *Patria* of the heart'. This end is the moral betterment of humanity, and ultimately all is subordinate to this. Mazzini went so far as to suggest that while the family is an eternal characteristic of human behaviour, 'The *Patria*, sacred today, will perhaps some day disappear, when every man shall reflect in his own conscience the moral laws of humanity ...'[46] Indeed, Mazzini felt compelled to distinguish legitimate national identity from its chauvinist distortions, and thus blamed the failure of the 1848 revolutions partly on the replacement of the legitimate 'sentiment of nationality' by its debasement, which he then called nationalism.[47]

This willingness to admit the historicity of the nation on the part of a nationalist ideologue is striking, but Mazzini saw no contradiction in advocating Italian national unity *and* insisting that, for him, humanity was the ultimate end. '*We believe in humanity, the sole interpreter of God's law on earth*'.[48] But this humanity was a social and differentiated species, not something abstract. This, again, may seem odd for a man whose philosophical underpinnings were idealist; but his idealism was concretized in as much as he argued that as the individual is 'too weak' and humanity 'too large' the nation is a mediator between them.[49] He may have set humanity as an ideal, but this sense of the complexities of human identities was strikingly realistic. He poured scorn on those who saw the world in terms of simple dichotomies and who radically opposed the individual and the collective:

> *Authority* and *Liberty*, conceived as we state them are equally sacred to us, and should be reconciled in every awaiting settlement. *All things in Liberty and for Association:* this is the republican formula. Liberty and Association, Conscience and Tradition, Individual and Nation, the 'I' and the 'We' are inseparable elements of human nature, all of them essential to its orderly development.[50]

The age of individualism was over; that of humanity was dawning, that of the 'individuals of humanity', nations. For Mazzini the mission of a united *republican* Italy was to bring about the moral unity of Europe. A Third Roman Temple – the first being Rome of antiquity, the second of the papacy – would arise. It would be a Rome of the Italian people and it would lead the way to a pacific European federation of republican nations. Like many of his nationalist contemporaries – Hess, Mickiewicz, Dostoyevsky as well as Michelet and (earlier) Fichte – Mazzini imagined his own nation as the bearer of a special task in the world, as a light unto other nations.

If we take Mazzini's themes and replace, respectively, republicanism and Italians with communism and Jews, we find ourselves in Moses Hess's *Rome and Jerusalem*, a booklet whose foreword declares that 'With the liberation of the Eternal City on the Tiber, that of the Eternal City on Mount Moriah commences too; with the renaissance of Italy also begins the resurrection of Judea'.[51] Born in 1812 in Bonn, Hess came of a Jewish family which – unlike the father of Karl Marx – declined conversion to Christianity after Napoleon's defeat led to the resurrection of European ghettos and restrictions on the Jews. He received a traditional Jewish upbringing from his grandfather, a non-practising rabbi who instructed him in the Bible, Talmud and Hebrew. However, he then opted, not for the family business, but for a career as a revolutionary; this took him into the world of European radicalism where he met and mingled with the Young Hegelians, Marx, Engels and Lassalle among others. Following the failure of the 1848 revolutions Hess turned from politics to study, but while immersed in anthropology and the natural sciences he began to pay attention to events in Italy and to link his anthropological readings with the rise of nationalist movements. This, in turn, led to a renewed interest in – he called it captivation by – the fate of the Jews and what the times implied for them.[52]

In the year of Italian unification he set his pen to *Rome and Jerusalem*, stating at the time in the Geneva newspaper *L'Espérance* that 'After the liberation of Italy will come the turn of the Eastern nations, and among them even the ancient people of Israel'.[53] *Rome and Jerusalem* pointedly tells us that in his two earlier books, *The Holy History of Mankind* (1837) and *The European Triarchy* (1841) – neither of which have Jewish concerns – he in fact had advocated the 'realization' of Jewish Messianic belief [*jüdischen Messiasglaubens*]'.[54] The link between the convoluted messianism of Hess's youthful writings and his later proto-Zionism has been explained by Shlomo Avineri as a search for self through pursuit of the socialist vision. The author of *The Holy History of Mankind* was listed anonymously as 'a Young Spinozist' and in Spinoza Hess sought the means to a 'socialist synthesis' of Judaism and Christianity.[55] He divided history into three periods, the biblical, the Christian and that of the future. Spinoza, he proposed, was herald of the third, an era whose birth pangs were to be seen in the French and American revolutions, and whose realization would take form in a socialist world, the ultimate sanctification of human history. Herein religion and state would be united, in contrast to the Christian separation of the two spheres. This separation, he claimed, encouraged tolerance of injustice by emphasizing the distinction between this and other-worldliness. 'Christian dualism', he wrote in a later essay, yielded 'the rupture between theory and praxis, Godliness and worldliness'.[56] The socialism of the future, for Hess, became a return to the ancient Jewish synthesis of religion (or moral vision) and the state.[57]

When he wrote his early works, Hess believed the Jews had no future; the 'new Jerusalem' of which he then spoke would be a European phenomenon synthesizing French revolutionary politics, German *Geist* and English industrial progress. It would be a classless society in which individual and community were reconciled on a basis of social and sexual equality, and the abolition of property and inheritance. It would be built on the foundation of human solidarity, and the state, with a representative regime, would be responsible for welfare, education and health services. Where Christianity mistakenly contrasted the 'materialism' of Judaism to its own 'spirit', for Hess, a socialist world would be the true embodiment of Judaism which, he argued, sought to make *this* world holy, through the monistic synthesis of the material and the spiritual.[58] Hence the greatness of Spinoza who was 'the first who understood the Kingdom of Spirit [*das Reich des Geistes*] as an actuality [*als ein Gegenwätiges*]'.[59] The 'Communist Rabbi', as Arnold Ruge once called him, declared in *Rome and Jerusalem* that, 'from the beginning the Jews recognized and grasped . . . that their world historical vocation was to sanctify not only the individual . . . but also the social life of humanity, to actively foster the evolution of mankind, and to prepare it for a Messianic kingdom [*messianisches Reich*]'.[60]

In *Rome and Jerusalem* there *was* a real place and future for the Jews; while the end of days was not at hand, he imagined the Jews as historical catalyst for social regeneration, for creating a world in which 'the holy spirit of our people will become the common property of humanity'.[61] Animating that spirit was a vision of community, not of the egoism of capitalism.

Where Marx saw a world of class struggle, Hess saw a world of racial and class struggles, and the latter were secondary. He believed that an end to racial conflicts would engender the cessation of class conflict. His use of the word 'race' is less than clear and this reflects its uses in his time. At times he seems to identify race with nation, while elsewhere he sees race as the factor behind nationalism; Hess's was not a systematic or careful mind. His intent, however, was clear: The struggle for the equality of races/nations was *the* issue of the century, and would not be resolved by means of the class struggle alone. Oppressed races/nations had specific problems unto themselves.

Neither Hess nor Mazzini were formidable thinkers, yet they both understood something about their epoch that far finer minds missed. And they both were engaged in quests for community. Egoistic individualism repelled them and they saw the individual in a series of mediated relations with the family, the nation and humanity. Hess, like Mazzini, refused to admit an opposition between the universal and the particular, insisting instead that 'the national essence [*das nationale Wesen*] of Judaism not only does not exclude humanitarianism and civilization [*Humanität und Zivilisation*], but rather, they are its necessary consequence'.[62] For Mazzini and Hess, having a state was bound up with what type of state it would be. For Hess, this was a matter of socialism, for Mazzini, for most of his political life, of republicanism.[63] Mazzini, however, was a bitter foe of socialism and believed that property was a reflection of human nature. He did exhort Italian workers, telling them they had a special role to lead the way to 'republican progress and self-emancipation', while at the same time chastising French socialists for advocating class struggle. He advanced a somewhat muddled concept of an 'Association of Labour' which brought together assorted socialist-like notions of co-operative organization with liberal ideas.[64]

Thus for both Mazzini and Hess, the state to be created was not an end unto itself; nor was it simply a mechanism to allow capitalists to compete safely, or to protect individual rights, or to serve as a shield from 'the influence of authority and majorities, custom and opinion', as Acton put it. The state was a means for purposefully re-creating human lives in the form of a national existence, and this existence, and those lives, were the end, not the state.

III

A glance at some of the varied characterizations given by scholars and others to nation and nationalism in the twentieth century shows a continuing preoccupation with whether a nation is defined through a state or a culture. In other words, the issue of *Staatnation* and *Kulturnation* abides. In Elie Kedourie's celebrated study, nationalism is presented as a nineteenth-century European doctrine which, on the one hand, assumes nations to be natural divisions of humanity and, on the other, seeks to establish the criteria by which a people can legitimately insist on its own state.[65] According to Hans Kohn, nationalism entails 'in fact or as an ideal' a centralizing state over a territory; he emphasizes that nationalism represents a 'process of integration' of the masses of the people into a common political form.[66] Karl Deutsch sees in the nation a 'coming together' of a 'state' and a 'people'. A nation, he writes, is 'a people who have hold of a state or who developed quasi-developmental capabilities for forming, supporting, and enforcing a common will. And a nation-state is a state that has become largely identified with one people'.[67]

Each of these definitions assumes the political fulfilment of a nation's aspirations in state form. John Plamenatz, however, chooses a different emphasis, and, more reminiscent of Herder, speaks of a nationalism which is

> the desire to preserve or enhance a people's natural or cultural identity when that identity is threatened or the desire to transform or create it where it is felt to be inadequate or lacking. I say natural or cultural, for what distinguishes a people from other peoples in their own eyes consists of ways of thinking, feeling, or behaving which are or which they believe to be, peculiar to them. Thus nationalism is primarily a cultural phenomenon, though it can, and often does, take a political form.[68]

Here the key would seem to be the objective reality of subjective factors; a nation and a state are not, nor ought they to be, in necessary historical correspondence. Nation and state are also separated by the Austro-Marxist Otto Bauer who, writing in the multinational Austro-Hungarian empire shortly before the First World War, provided one of the few serious Marxist treatments of the national question. He characterized a nation as '*the totality of men bound together through a common destiny into a community of character*'.[69] These definitions allow for the coexistence – at least theoretically – of different nations within one state. Seton-Watson distinguishes between the state as 'a legal and political organization with the power to require obedience and loyalty from its citizens' and the nation, as 'a community of people, whose members are bound together by a sense of solidarity, a common culture, a national consciousness'.[70] In Seton-Watson's schema (some) nations predate the French revolution, while national*ism* dates from it and, among other factors, is rooted, as we saw earlier, in the emergence of concepts of popular sovereignty.

If European nationalism tends to be linked not only to such concepts but, more broadly, also to the replacement of the feudal by the liberal capitalist world, and if nationalism was often carried forth by the bourgeoisie, what then of the relation between class and nation? Deutsch emphasizes nationalism's successful role as a tool of political integration beyond class; hence he views the constitution of nations as the 'coming together' of a state and a people. A 'people' is defined by him as 'a community of shared meanings . . . a group of people who have interlocking habits of communication. When a man receives a message from another member of his country it clicks with him'.[71] Indeed, a Gaullist or a French communist, he proposes, will concur on 'elegance, beauty, good cooking, and whether one should spend one's money on a truly good dinner or a magnificently furnished bathroom.'[72] While a community of shared meanings, a commonality of culture, language, and interlocking habits of style and communication are undoubtedly essential to what structures a nation, this is simplistic. Such a definition of peoplehood can equally describe other social or political groupings (like class) and ignores the internal structural complexities of a people or a nation. Assuming that this communist does not spend afternoons at the Bourse and is, as is more likely, a worker in the red belt around Marseilles, the actual concerns and 'meanings' that structure his daily life may be much better communicated, but for the difference in language, to an industrial worker in northern England. His primary quotidian needs are unlikely to be focused on magnificent bathroom furnishings, and the capacity to dine at the best of restaurants is unlikely to be assumed. Indeed, what commonality did Cavour, a liberal aristocrat who was at home more in French language and culture than Italian and who, besides his native Piedmont, spent more time in England and France than in the rest of the Italian peninsula, have with the peasants in the unified Italy he did so much to create?

Deutsch's claims are the inverse of those of many Marxists; where he speaks of an integration subsuming class, the latter – or at least most of them – only understood class, and discounted such integration, especially in cultural and linguistic terms. Perhaps the most radical expression of this Marxist failure was Rosa Luxemburg's opposition to all forms of nationalism because they merely obfuscated the class struggle. 'For Social Democracy', she averred, 'the nationality question is, like all other social and political questions, primarily *a question of class interests*'.[73] While Lenin supported the self-determination of nations, he did not view national cultures as ends in themselves, and, following Kautsky, saw the national state as the capitalist norm and the multinational state as regressive.[74]

The failure to explain and to grasp the import of nationalism is certainly one of the most weighty indictments against Marxism. Some, like Tom Nairn, explain this by claiming that past 'historical conditions' were not ripe for even 'a tolerable [Marxist] theory about nationalism'.[75] In view of Marxist claims to 'scientificity', this is unconvincing; indeed, it is something like hiding behind the owl of Minerva. What a Hess or a Mazzini had to say about nationalism certainly pales in depth and rigour compared with what Marx had to say about class; but these lesser minds grasped something fundamental about their epoch and human behaviour that the greater one – who in fact announced the forthcoming extinction of nations – did not. Certainly, both Luxemburg and Lenin ultimately hoped for a nation-less world, despite their differences on the national question in their time. The Austro-Marxist Karl Renner, on the other hand, went so far as to declare in 1917 that the 'process of the formation of nation states can be regarded as the political law of motion of the nineteenth century'.[76]

Fruitful Marxist analyses tend to assume that the place of nation in Marx's general theory is problematic; hence they seek a flexible, or perhaps it would be more accurate to say more dialectical, approach to the relation of base and superstructure as it pertains to nations and nationalism (and other matters as well). The definition of the nation cited earlier from Otto Bauer's *Die Nationalitätenfrage und die Sozialdemokratie* (1907), with its emphasis on community of destiny and community of character, exemplifies this; the conditions structuring that destiny and character, and their interrelation, become all-important. Bauer sought to characterize the nation in non-statist and non-territorial terms while recognizing the deleterious effects of spatial separation of elements of a nation. He wrote that, 'the spatially distinct parts of the nation which carry on their struggle for existence in isolation from each other, also differentiate their originally unitary culture, and in the absence of intercourse between them the original unitary culture dissolves into a number of diverse cultures'.[77] Territory is therefore a 'condition' but not an 'element' of the nation; the nation is constituted through 'common history as the effective cause, common culture and common descent as the means by which it produces its effects, a common language as the mediator of common culture, both its product and its producer'.[78] Clearly, then, such entities, and conflicts among them, will not be abolished if class society is negated. Consequently, as resolution to both class and national conflicts, Bauer proposed a federal socialist state in which each nationality would have cultural autonomy, and in which membership in a nationality would be defined on a personal, not residential or territorial, basis.

The conditions of a nation's 'struggle for existence' were central to Ber Borokhov's 1905 essay on 'The National Question and the Class Struggle'. Here the author, a Marxist theoretician of Zionism, sought to extend and transform the terms of Marxist discourse so as to account for nations and nationalism. He took Marx's notion of 'relations of production', i.e. that which structures society's economic base, and supplemented it with his own concept of 'conditions of production'. For Marx, one's place in the relations of production determined one's class; one was a bourgeois or a proletarian depending on whether one was an owner of the means of production – those means by which society produced and reproduced itself – or only the owner of one's own labour power, which, in turn, one sold to the owner of the means of production for a wage. Marx saw technological advance in each stage of history and, in the famous formula articulated in his preface to his *Critique of Political Economy*, he argued that conflict generated between the developing forces of production and the society's existing relations of production was the source of revolution. According to Borokhov this was broadly true, but insufficient to explain nations; he suggested that since production is dependent on different conditions in different times and places, one must speak not only of relations of production, but of geographic, anthropological and historical 'conditions of production' which, he claimed, give rise to nations. The *'feeling of kinship, created as a result of the visioned common historic past and rooted in the common conditions of production is called* nationalism'.[79] National conflicts occur, he went on, when the conditions of production block the development of the nation's forces of production, thus compelling it to seek other conditions and leading to confrontations with other national groups. Under normal conditions of production, e.g. when a nation can develop unhampered in its own land, class antagonisms naturally intensify, as the Marxist model proposed. However, under abnormal conditions of production, an obfuscation of class and national interests tends to occur. Consequently, there was a Marxist criterion to distinguish progressive nationalism, in which an oppressed national proletariat seeks normal conditions of production, from the reactionary kind.

Each in its own way, these varied explications and definitions of nations and nationalism seek to delineate how, and under what circumstances, collectivities – in this case nationality – form and take on identity in contradistinction to others. Their different emphases, however, ought perhaps to lead to the conclusion that instead of seeing nations as precisely definable, possibly homogenous, wholes, it might be better to regard them both historically and also metaphorically, not as 'individuals' or as organisms, but in a way similar to Freud's view of the psyche. That is, it is possible to think of nations as collective entities of human beings that *are* entities, but which are shaped in historical interaction with the outside world while concurrently divided within and at times against themselves, taking on different general forms depending on the integration or lack of integration, and the balance or imbalance of various elements and factors, both subjective and objective, internal and external; the *nationalisme intégrale* of Charles Maurras is nationalism, but it is of a character significantly different from the synthesis of socialist and very French republicanism espoused by a Jean Jaurès. Yet both remain expressions of national identity and nationalism.

In short, this is to suggest that a definition – if such is possible – of nations or nationalism must be divided against itself on many levels. This may be unsettling to anyone insisting on a strict, which sometimes means simplistic, scientific definition of political phenomena. However, more than half the world's nations today were unrecognizable as such a century-and-a-half ago. What may be the primary formative impact of language on one nation may be that of foreign exploitation on another; a revolution linked to the overthrow of one social order may be essential in yet another case. As Benedict Anderson perceptively points out, while almost all nations are objectively modern formations, they tend to be subjectively ancient.[80] For nationalists, their own nations inevitably have the longest of histories, roots are sought to prove this, mythologies embraced to reinforce it, identities moulded to believe it, children educated to and for it. However, though the Greek city-states fought together in the Persian wars of the fifth century BCE as 'Hellenes' against the *barbaroi*, they could hardly be considered a nation in any modern sense; certainly they were not struggling for a united state of Greece. And when Socrates chose hemlock rather than escape, it was out of loyalty to Athens. We are told in the *Crito* that Socrates could not imagine going elsewhere – *even to another Greek polis*. Along with Huizinga, we may call this a type of patriotism, but hardly nationalism.[81] None the less, the heritage of those wars and the heritage of Thermopolae are part of Greek national identity today, just as the pharaohs are for some Egyptian nationalists. (The Jews, as we suggested at the beginning of this chapter and will show at more length in the following chapter, do not fit this pattern in significant regards.) Most modern nations do not even have such historical records to use – or misuse – and must resort more to the imagination. Consequently, Anderson gives us a particularly suggestive concept of the nation as an 'imagined political community', which conceives itself as limited in membership and as sovereign. The identity is 'imagined' because the members of a nation never know most of their compatriots, but still believe themselves in a 'communion' with them. It is 'limited' because a nation sets boundaries and does so virtually by the act of defining itself as a nation.[82] Mazzini and Hess may have seen their respective nations as catalysts of world *national* liberty, but there can hardly be a universal nation in the sense that Marx spoke of the proletariat as a universal class, i.e. one which abolishes itself in the process of abolishing all other nations/classes.

These imagined communities, it could be said, took on certain forms at particular historical junctures, especially the death of one world and the birth of a new one; hence Seton-Watson's claim that the French revolution marked the rise of national*ism*, even though nations had long existed. He distinguishes 'old nations' – those whose identity was forged before the arrival of nationalism and the events of 1789 – and 'new nations' in which a national consciousness and a national movement were concurrent developments. 'Old nations', like Britain and France, clearly had begun to take shape as nations by 1600, even though four centuries earlier they were not entities recognizable as such. In his classic history of the English language,

Otto Jesperson commented that 'As the language is, so also is the nation'.[83] Until the thirteenth century French-speaking monarchs occupied thrones on both sides of the Channel, and it was not until the fourteenth and fifteenth centuries that 'England' was sufficiently formed for one to speak of the existence of a national consciousness. Norman French was replaced by Middle English in the courts and in the ceremonial opening of parliament in 1362.[84] Centralization of the state under the Tudors spelled the beginning of the end of the fragmented world of feudal loyalties, and created the possibility of a new, broader loyalty (although this was, at first, more to blue blood than to the colours of a flag). France, according to Seton-Watson's chronology, was the first modern nation, its emergence, along with that of the French state, from the early 1500s after a long period of gestation. François I made French the sole official language in 1539.[85]

In Kiev Rus, the first Russian state, several languages were spoken by the largely Slavic population.[86] These dialects later yielded Russian, Ukrainian, and Byelorussian. The dominance of the Russian language *per se* in an entity known as 'Russia' was a product of prolonged development linked to the rise of Muscovy's primacy in the two centuries following the Mongol invasions (in the thirteenth century). By the end of the reigns of Ivan III and Ivan IV, in the fifteenth and sixteenth centuries, a centralized autocratic state apparatus was in place in Muscovy, had integrated the Orthodox church into itself and imagined itself to be the Third Rome (after Rome itself, and Constantinople). The journey had been made from Caesar to Tsar. The 'Westernizer' Peter the Great completed the integration and subordination of the Church and, thanks partly to his conquests, Muscovy had become Russia by the eighteenth century.

Yet among Peter's successors were German princesses, and French and German were the languages of discourse in the society's upper echelons. Interest in the Russian language *per se*, as well as in the birth of a secular Russian literature, emerged in the late eighteenth century, and with them came disputes between modernists and traditionalists concerned with the future of Russian culture. A Russian Academy was formed in 1783 and dictionaries and grammars soon followed. The modernists emphasized the contemporary spoken tongue rather than the Church Slavonic which originally developed in the Bulgarian church and had come to Kiev Rus following its conversion to Christianity in the ninth and tenth centuries. The new stress on language came at a time of victorious Russian military exploits, especially against Napoleon. Upper-class officers who had been to western Europe were infected by new ideas that they had come into contact with there, and in the upper classes in general, as well as in the peasantry to some extent, a national consciousness of sorts began emerging in the first decades of the nineteenth century. In 1832 Count Sergei Uvarov asserted that Russia's foundations ought to rest on the three principles of autocracy, Orthodoxy and nationality, known together as the doctrine of 'Official

Nationality'. The use of the third element represented something new in Russian political vocabulary, although, while many of its proponents were developing historical concepts of Russia and championing the Russian language as an expression of the Russian people, the actual role that they projected for 'the people' was, at best, limited. (After all, until 1862 half the population were serfs.) Only a few of the advocates of 'Official Nationality' thought of nationality in Western terms; by and large the doctrine sought to reinforce the dynasty in an era of revolution in western Europe.[87] By the reign of Alexander III (1881–94) the government, for various reasons, was pursuing a 'Russification' process. Indeed, it was only then that the Russian language became the official tongue in all diplomatic correspondence.[88] Seton-Watson goes so far as to characterize the 1905 revolution as an upheaval that was 'as much a revolution of non-Russians against Russification as it was a revolution of workers, peasants and radical intellectuals against autocracy'.[89]

In the three 'old nations' briefly discussed above – England, France, Russia – we have seen an unevenly developing mixture of several elements leading to modern nationhood and national consciousness. As centralization of authority and administration occurred, language, as a representative and medium of culture and communication, played a crucial role. So, too, did religion in the formation of national political cultures, as can be seen in the politics of the development of Anglicanism at the time of Henry VIII, the impact of Catholicism on the unity and disunity of France, and the integration into and influence of Orthodoxy on the developing state apparatus of Holy Mother Russia. The elements of language/culture, territory and state, as well as their uneven development, were also fundamental in the formation of 'new nations'. Victory for the Risorgimento meant a unified state over a peninsula that previously was politically *and linguistically* fragmented. The Italian nationalist movement's forerunners vigorously debated the value of modern Italian in relation to that of Dante, as well as to French and Latin.[90] Herder's emphasis on language has already been noted; by the time the most virulent German nationalism appeared in the form of Hitlerism, the linguistic element had been mediated in German nationalism by the questions of unified statehood, territorial aspiration and then racism.

The linguistic component was essential as a conditioner of the subjective components of nationalism. The emergence of England as England required the supplanting by Middle English of the French that had supplanted Old English. The literary flowering of the Elizabethan age came some two centuries later, after the Tudors unified the English state. By the sixteenth century the French language had been established and the French state, disrupted by the religious wars of that century, fully emerged under Louis XIV in the seventeenth century. In this time-span comes a flowering of French literature in the persons of Molière, Racine and Corneille. The foundations of Russia were created in the sixteenth, seventeenth and eighteenth centuries, with a flowering of literature in the nineteenth, not long after the role of the Russian language in the life and affairs of the empire became a new matter of concern. One can see a further development of the tie between culture and national community in the nineteenth-century emergence of the historical novel as a literary form in which 'the individuality of character' derives 'from the historical peculiarity of the age'.[91] The French revolution and Napoleon's invasions, by ushering in an age of nationalism and mass politics, led to a broader consciousness of the social world as historically, not naturally, given, as Georg Lukàcs points out.[92] As subjects of the French king were made into citizens of the French nation, a sense of nation and national history was engendered, and in the aftermath of Napoleon's fall, so too was the historical novel.

Anderson argues that the pre-modern 'great sacral cultures' of Christendom, Ummah Islam and Buddhism were self-conceived as all-encompassing communities rooted in a sacred language and a sacred script. Of course only a tiny portion of the population actually knew how to read the script, but upon learning it, an outsider could be admitted to the community. In the European case, since most of the nobility were illiterates, living in a Christian universe mediated by an organized 'trans-European Latin-writing clerisy', the power of the written word – in fact the written Word – was a foundation of the Church's power in the disunified world of medieval feudalism.[93] The processes of state centralization, the 'discoveries' of the world outside Europe, the Renaissance with its humanism (which turned man's eyes to the here and now and rekindled a republican civic spirit), the Reformation (which brought with it Luther's translation of the New Testament into the German of sixteenth-century Saxony, his practical alliance with German princes and the theological emphases on justification by faith alone and the priesthood of all believers), and the emergence of capitalism as a driving force in the midst of these factors – all these contributed to the subversion of the medieval Christian world as one with universal pretensions and authority (embodied in the Roman church), as well as the weakening of the bonds, both utilitarian and religious, of the sacred language.

In seeking to reconstruct Marx, Jürgen Habermas has argued that what leads to 'the specifically human form of reproducing life' first occurred 'in the structures of labour and language'.[94] Modern nations emerged in protracted processes in which an old world failed to reproduce itself; an old system of production and an old system of communication and meanings broke down. The structure of labour and language was refunctioned. Capitalism supplanted feudalism and thus brought forth, at least formally, standards of individualism and equality before the law, as well as urban, and then industrial, civilization; all these spread education and literacy, all these were the antithesis of the agrarian, privileged, decentralized world of feudalism in which a written culture (and language) was the property of a privileged few. 'Printing', declared Thomas Carlyle in 1848, 'which comes necessarily out of Writing . . . is equivalent to Democracy: invent Writing, Democracy is inevitable. Writing brings Printing; brings universal extempore Printing as we see it at present. Whoever can speak, speaking now to the whole nation, becomes a power . . . The nation is governed by all that has tongue in the nation: Democracy is virtually *there* . . .'[95] Printing, too, helped bring nationalism, and is of necessity linked to the linguistic factors mentioned above. And like all capitalist enterprises, printing had to seek expanding markets. In the Middle Ages the populations were illiterate, the intelligentsia clerical, the medium of communication Latin. Before the sixteenth century, for example, most books printed in Paris were in Latin but by the end of that century most were in French. The Latin-reading market was saturated and new horizons were needed.[96] It was at this time that new technical means of communication developed along with centralized monarchies, and, significantly, a secular intelligentsia; Latin's decline was part of a broader process in which the medieval world was splintered and then restructured on a territorialized basis. In uneven sequences, as the commercial classes grew, so did literacy. Importantly, vernaculars became both the languages of intellectual discourse and the languages of centralizing state administrations. Diverse print-languages appeared in different lands. While by the mid-nineteenth century half the populations of the European states, including France and Britain, were still illiterate (and 98 per cent of Russia),[97] this entire process also engendered the spread of education, and the more education became centralized, particularly in the state, the more linguistic and cultural homogeneity spread in given territories. 'In the beginning was the Word', declares an inebriated character in a D. J. Enright novel, 'in the end shall be a public library . . .'[98] National communities become imaginable consequent to 'a half fortuitous, but explosive interaction' between capitalism, print technology and linguistic diversity, as Anderson puts it.[99]

The nationalism of the nineteenth century, with the French revolution as its midwife, demanded for the product of this 'explosive interaction' a self-determining independence and, generally, statehood. While a Hess or a Mazzini articulated such aspirations in universalist visions, the nationalist movements that appeared in the era after them tended more often than not to be preoccupied with matters of inclusivity and exclusivity, sometimes on behalf of self-defence, sometimes on behalf of imperial yearnings or chauvinist vitriol; their dreams of a global fraternity of nations, and their hopes that the national impulse would be oriented to a humanist universalism rather than to radical particularism, were hardly realized in the century after they wrote.

All of these transformations in Western history provide the backdrop both for the emergence of Jewish nationalism in the late nineteenth century and the problems it sought to confront. Zionism was born in the era of nation and class in Europe. Indeed, most of the issues raised within, and by the birth of, nationalism and capitalism were also integral to the birth and evolution of modern Jewish nationalist movements. However, as we have indicated, the creation of modern Israel also represented a re-formation, reconsolidation and reinvention of elements of Jewish 'nationhood' that were present since antiquity: culture (in terms of language and especially religion), land, independent statehood and a historical consciousness of peoplehood. It is to the process by which a once independent but then long-scattered people re-created itself as a national political entity that we must now turn.

2
Historical Crucible

The tragic feature of our history is that we can neither die nor live.

Leo Pinsker[1]

I

After their forcible expulsion from Palestine some 1,900 years ago, the Jews became the prototype of a diaspora people. Although there were substantial Jewish diasporas concomitant with the First and Second Jewish Common-wealths, it was after Rome's destruction of the latter that the Jews constituted a diaspora people, that is, one lacking a territorial base and spatial contiguity, dispelled to various portions of the globe. The word 'diaspora' comes from the Greek for dispersion; Zionists would later prefer the Hebrew word *Golah* (exile), indicating not just a scattering but a dissipation from a specific place. Little comparative scholarship has been dedicated to diaspora nations or peoples, but that which has been done tends to find various parallels among Jews, Armenians, overseas Chinese and Indians.[2] Minority, dispersed status generally engenders a host of legal, economic and sociological debilitations along with conditions of vulnerability; such factors inevitably intensified in an age of nation-building and nationalism.

For the Jews, modern nationalism was indeed a gateway of Janus, a looking-forward and a looking-backward from the vantage-point of an unacceptable, precarious present. Theodor Herzl entitled his novel depic-ting a Zionist utopia *Altneuland*, old–new land. The title was appropriate because, as noted in the previous chapter, while Zionism sought to create something modern, the longing to return to *Erets Israel*, the Land of Israel, was ancient, a central motif of Jewish religio-cultural and collective identity throughout the millennia of dispersion. As a consequence of the events of the late nineteenth and early twentieth centuries the effort was made to actualize, and not just pray for, a return to Zion. It was a specific historical moment – the nineteenth was the century after the French revolution; it was the epoch of nationalism, and the period in which the modern state system of Europe was taking shape. In the midst of this boundary-setting process for European nations, the Jews were forced to reset their own, and to redefine their own existence and status. In so doing they found themselves faced with many of the issues and transformations that their hosts confronted in the process of being nation-alized. Zionism was not the sole Jewish response to these circumstances, but it was certainly one of the most, if not the most, radical of replies. And it was, among other things, a reaction to an accumulated history of persecution and inquisitions. A partial list would include the eleventh-century Crusader slaughters, expulsion from England in the thirteenth century, from France in the fourteenth, from Spain in the fifteenth, the 1648–9 Chmielnicki massacres in the Ukraine (leaving tens of thousands dead), the pogrom in Uman (in 1768, again in the Ukraine), the pogroms throughout southern Russia in 1881. The twentieth century brought the Kishinev pogrom of 1903, the more general Russian pogroms of 1905, the pogroms in the Ukraine leaving approximately another 100,000 dead in 1919–20, and finally the murder of 6 million Jews by the Nazis.

This was a record of continuity and a discontinuity. Auschwitz represented the culmination of the dehumanization of the Jew in Western history on the one hand, and the Jewish fate in the specifically modern era of nationalism and capitalism on the other. In the late eighteenth and in the nineteenth century a fundamental transformation began in the status of European Jews. They faced a metamorphosis of the conditions in which they lived, and this engendered fundamental changes in their modes of response to their environment. An essential aspect of this was the transmutation of Jew-hatred from its religiously based medieval forms into a modern national–racialist doctrine. Although the medieval Jew was branded Christ's killer, he could, by conversion, shed this original sin and hope to integrate into the Christian world. However, for a decidedly distinctive people to convert to a nation in an era of rising nationalist passions was a substantially different question, especially since nationalism presented itself as an almost totalizing form of political and/or cultural integration and identity, demanding, as well, a definitive object of loyalty. The Jew, theoretically, ought to have been able to become the citizen of a nation, but acceptance as such was another matter, particularly if a Jewish community wished to retain a communal identity. Complicating this further was the fact that medieval Jews had been restricted in the socio-economic roles they could play, and were visible in the 'middleman' occupations and commerce scorned by Christianity. They thus became competition for the emerging native bourgeoisies on the one hand, and a despised scapegoat for those social strata left behind or kept below by the rising class on the other.

The word 'Semite' is derived from Shem, Noah's son in the Bible, from whose progeny some two dozen Middle Eastern peoples claim descent according to their various traditions. In modern times it was first used in the late eighteenth century by A. L. von Schlözer as a linguistic term, and some ethnologists employed it to define the varied racial characteristics ascribed, in particular, to Jews and Arabs.[3] The expression 'anti-Semitism', however, was coined specifically as an anti-Jewish term in 1879 by a German, Wilhelm Marr, to emphasize that his hostility to Jews was based not on religion but on social and economic justifications, and especially their 'foreignness'. In little over half a year his book expounding these themes, *The Victory of Judaism over Germany*, became 'the first anti-semitic best-seller', going though a dozen editions.[4] Anti-Semitism since then has become used as a more generic expression for all forms of historical and contemporary anti-Jewish prejudice.

Zionism sought to provide a coherent answer to the questions raised by the historical context that produced anti-Semitism as a term of racial/ national hatred. At the same time, it was rooted in a historical memory of Jewish peoplehood, and a corresponding corporate existence and self-conception, beginning in the world of biblical mythology. In the Bible God tells Abram, 'I will make thee a great nation [*goy gadol*]', and the Jews are described as 'a people [*am*] that shall dwell alone,/ And shall not be reckoned among the nations [*goyim*]'.[5] The biblical patriarch Jacob was renamed Israel, and his sons were the founders of the 12 tribes of the people of Israel. Their status as God's 'chosen' eventually became, of course, a constitutive myth for the ancient Hebrews, was essential to their self-definition and reinforced group self-consciousness.

The Jewish sense of corporate peoplehood – as evidenced in its concrete political embodiment in the First and Second Commonwealths – preceded the development of the Rabbinic tradition and the writing of the Talmud, so it is fair to say that it preceded the maturation of Judaism as a religion. Indeed, membership in the Jewish 'people' was not determined by belief, but by descent (or by conversion). This was also part of the Rabbinic tradition for in the Talmud one is still regarded as a Jew even if one apostatizes. The very term 'Judaism' apparently originated in the first century CE among Greek speaking Jews. In the earlier classical Jewish texts it is *torah* (teaching) that is used, not the Hebrew equivalent of Judaism (*yahadut*). The latter appears only in some writings of the Middle Ages. The Hebrew word for Jew (*yehudi*) was first used for a member of the tribe of Judah, and then for those who lived in the southern biblical kingdom of Judah after the ancient Hebrew monarchy split at the time of Rehoboam, Solomon's son. (The northern realm was called Israel.) 'Jew' came to English via Greek and Latin forms, respectively *Ioudaios* and *Judaeus*, and can be found in early English *circa* 1000 CE.[6]

In biblical Hebrew, several terms were employed to indicate the peoplehood of the ancient Hebrews, terms which are often translated as 'people' and 'nation'. Besides being referred to as *Bnei Israel* (members of Israel, often translated as 'the children of Israel') they are called an *am*, *umah, goy* and *leom.* Nationalism in modern Hebrew is *leumiyut,* and has no biblical equivalent. From the perspective of theories of nationalism, it is notable that the early use of *am* in the book of Genesis is not only generic for the human race but is linked to language. 'Behold', says the biblical God as the tower of Babel is built, 'they are one people and they all have one language [*am ehad ve-safah ahat*]'.[7] Universal language is linked here to universal humanity. The association of language and 'nation', in this case using *goy,* is found earlier in the description of 'the generations of the sons of Noah', where we read, 'Of these were the isles of the nations [*ha-goyim*] divided in their lands, every one after his tongue [*lilshono*], after their families, in their nations [*be-goyyeihem*]'. Cognates of, and words comparable to, *am* are found in other Semitic languages, including Aramaic, Akkadian and Arabic; Hammurabi's Code uses *am-mi* for peoples. Its original root probably meant 'to join, to unite, to be inclusive'.[9]

Terms such as *am, umah, goy* and *leom* often have parallel usages in the Bible, and all of them are employed to describe the ancient Hebrews. We read in Genesis, 'Let the nations [*amim*] serve thee/ And the peoples [*leumim*] bow down to thee', and in Isaiah, 'All the nations [*ha-goyim*] are gathered together/ And the peoples [*leumim*] are assembled'.[10] When Moses tells the pharaoh to 'let my people go', the word used is *am* ('*shalah et-ami*'), and when the Israelites are told that they will be 'a holy nation', it is *goy* (*goy kadosh*).[11] One modern dictionary partly defines *am, umah* and *leom* by one another.[12] However, *am* and *goy* do not have solely Jewish referents and are employed in the Bible to describe non-Jewish peoples also.[13] (The use of *goy* as a term for non-Jews is a later phenomenon, of the Talmudic period,[14] when, we might note, the Jews had lost political independence. The parallel between its subsequent derogatory utilization, and that of *natio* in Rome for a foreign community, including the Jews, merits linguistic and anthropological comparison.)

Whatever the terminology, the Bible portrays the Israelites as a group with a strong sense of peoplehood and, generally, there was a corresponding objective situation. This was carried over into the post-biblical period. Whether this is properly called 'nationhood' is debatable, especially since 'nations' and 'nationalism' are generally viewed by historians as later phenomena, as we have seen. Zionism emerged in the nineteenth century, not before. Yet by subjective and objective criteria – that is, in terms of self-consciousness, separateness and territorialization of the Jews in a formative historical stage of their peoplehood – we must come to a conclusion close to that cited in the previous chapter by the study group of the Royal Institute of International Affairs in 1939: early in their history the Jews clearly had characteristics identified with later notions of nationhood. The Hebrew word *am* is frequently rendered as 'people', although in translations of some passages of the Bible and in some modern usages it is very often rendered as 'nation'. Thus one of David Ben-Gurion's most important collections of speeches and essays – one in which he articulated the essential strategy of the Zionist Labour movement he headed – was called *Mi-maamad le-am* (From a Class to a Nation), and he often spoke of *am oved* (a working nation) and *am mamlakhti* (a statist nation). Whether 'nation' or 'people' is most appropriate here is sometimes difficult to establish, and I have generally translated *am* as 'nation' in Ben-Gurion's usage, although this is with the necessary qualifications which I have indicated.

Zionism must also be regarded as a consequence of the autonomy that characterized the centuries of diaspora life; during them Jewish communities maintained their own structures of authority as well as their own cultural/religious separateness. This was due partly to external coercion and to the corporate nature of the medieval world. The Jews had the additional burden of religious sanctions. On the other hand, Jewish autonomy had roots in institutional factors tied to the nature of the ancient Jewish polity and the substantial experience Jews had in fact had with diasporas before the collapse of the Second Jewish Commonwealth in 70 CE.

The transition to diaspora entailed a decentralization of Jewish life and communal authority on two linked levels. The Land of Israel ceased to be the physical centre of Jewish life, and its religious centre, the Temple cult, was gone too with the destruction of the Temple by the Romans. The reconstitution of Jewish life was partly eased by the fact that from its early development the ancient Jewish monarchy in Palestine was relatively weak, thus allowing for a certain self-reliance, and autonomy in local communities within the kingdom.[15] During the Babylonian exile, a circle of elders emerged together with the priests as a communal leadership concerned both with religious and more general matters. This represented an important organizational adjustment by placing emphasis on the assembled congregation rather than the place of worship. The Jews, writes Salo W. Baron,

> thus emerged from the great crisis of [the First Exile] in the possession of a new institution of national survival. The new type of congregation, meeting in any locality, could be adopted to changing environments in the subsequent millennia of history. The synagogue, having early underground roots in the crucial evolution of the last decades of Judean independence . . . sprouted into the focal institutions of an ethnic-religious group living outside its own land.[16]

'Synagogue', from the Greek for 'collection', came to mean a gathering of Jews, as opposed to a specific place of worship, and it thus took shape as a general and not just a religious institution.[17] Its development reflected conflicts over authority that divided Pharasaic Judaism, which stressed the synagogue as a communal–religious institution, from the Sadducees, who supported the priests in charge of the Jerusalem Temple cult, during the period of the Second Temple. After the temple's destruction and the expulsion of the Jews from Palestine, a foundation for continued organized – non-political – existence had thereby already been created. Following the defeat in 135 CE of Bar Kokhba, leader of the last Jewish rebellion against Rome, Rome allowed the creation of a *Nasi* (patriarch) to serve as official head of the Jews within the empire. The patriarchate obtained substantial secular power at first, but it declined and vanished by the fifth century, partly in consequence of the establishment of Christianity as the empire's religion, and an ensuing deterioration of the situation of the Jews. Parallel to the Patriarchate, there existed in Babylon an officially recognized Exilarchate, or, as it was known in Aramaic, *Resh Galuta* (head of the Exile), a 'sort of hereditary monarchy' which claimed Davidic descent, and which influenced and was supported by the government.[18]

From the Middle Ages to the early modern period in Europe, the Jews were at once severely restricted and significantly autonomous. The one factor fortified the other. Jews were delimited in places of residence and proscribed from a wide range of occupational pursuits. This engendered concentration in various economic roles, something reinforced by the Church's prescriptions and proscriptions concerning the proper place for Jews and activities acceptable for Christians. The foundation of Jewish autonomy was in local communal organization, the *Kahal* (or *Kehilah*, community), which concerned itself with a vast array of secular and religious communal needs, had its own system of taxation and was responsible for relations with non-Jewish powers. It generally had a hierarchy of officials with diverse responsibilities. Supra-communal organization developed as well, especially in the fifteenth and sixteenth centuries. Perhaps the most important example was the Council of the Four Lands (the *Vaad arba aratsot*), on which sat some 30 communal leaders and rabbis from Lesser and Greater Poland, Russia and Lithuania (Lithuania later formed its own organization in 1623 and Volhynia took its place).

The foregoing synopsis illustrates that forms of self-government and local autonomy were a continual feature of Jewish history, both in antiquity and after. Furthermore, while religion was dominant in structuring Jewish life, particularly in the diaspora, autonomy and communal existence was by no means purely religious in character, and was reinforced by external circumstances over which the Jews had no or little control. The internal character of Jewish life played an important role in reinforcing autonomy because it placed a great emphasis on community, requiring among other things a minimum of ten men (a *minyan*) for fulfilment of collective devotional obligations. Even if theoretically possible at times, it was implausible, but temporarily, for a Jew to live as a Jew apart from a Jewish community in the Middle Ages. Hence, for the Jews as a people, communal autonomy 'served as a fairly effective substitute for their state, just as their segregated living quarters, sporadically recorded in antiquity but become permanent features in the Muslim and Christian Middle Ages, gave them the approximation of self-contained territories'.[19]

It is this world that was shattered with the rise of capitalism and nationalism in Europe where, at the beginning of the nineteenth century, 90 per cent of the world's 2.5 million Jews then lived. As Jacob Katz notes, in roughly a century, from 1770 to 1870, the Jews, like the peoples of Europe, found their basic patterns of social life, their legal and economic statuses, and their cultural and religious existence dramatically changed. A configuration emerged in the West that would be replicated elsewhere.[20] Feudalism's corporate order, in which each soul had his place in this world and the next, was replaced by a world of competing nations and competing individuals. The 'free market' view of the world, which imagined human beings as self-contained atoms clashing with others of their kind, brought paradoxical consequences for Jews. In the medieval world the economic role of the Jew was largely restricted; he found himself visible in commerce, especially international trade, moneylending and crafts. In an agrarian Christian universe he was isolated and defined. Between the sixteenth and eighteenth centuries this pattern began to diversify,[21] but this was a product of changes occurring in the European economies as a whole; as a result, Christians, long trained to disdain the Jews and their occupations, were now competing with them in the emerging capitalist world. The ideology of the newly developing economic order assumed individuals, at least theoretically, to be equal before the laws of politics and economics. On the market there were only buyers, sellers and investors. Thus Voltaire, in the famous sixth of his *Lettres philosophiques*, cast his eyes on the London Stock Exchange and was enraptured by the interaction of Christian, Jew and Moslem, as if they were of a single faith. That faith was, of course, profit, and they were abstract *individuals* operating within the market system, not Christian, Jewish and Moslem believers restricted by their corporate status.

In short, the capitalist market universalized what Marx called a Robinson Crusoe image of man, a being who entered civil society out of nowhere, solely 'as an individual', a being whose roots were 'self-made' and not in any communal or social identification. By positing this as the embodiment of human nature, capitalism denied its own historicity and the historical and social embeddedness of human beings; it thus deprived men and women of historical reality, qualitative wants, attachments, loves and hates. This vision of the world was particularly crystallized in Jeremy Bentham's utilitarian philosophy in which human happiness is quantifiable, as if composed of units of marketable goods added and subtracted from a ledger of abstract human desire. Market Man was hardly compatible with the hierarchical and corporate Christian universe of feudalism, whose socio-religious totality denied the reality of independent human individuality apart from the realm of personal salvation. Liberal capitalist ideology revolted against that world, and posited the rights of man against the privileges (or lack of privileges) of estate. The Enlightenment imagined a world of individuals equal in their access to reason. '*Enlightenment*', wrote Kant in a famous essay, '*is man's emergence from his self-incurred immaturity. Immaturity* is *self-incurred* if its cause is not lack of understanding, but lack of resolution and courage to use it without the guidance of another. The motto of enlightenment is therefore: *Sapere aude*[Dare to be wise]'.[22]

In a world being remade in such images, where was the place of the Jew? In Lessing's *Nathan the Wise* the friar tells the title-character, a Jew, 'You're a Christian soul! By God, a better Christian never lived'. Nathan replies, 'And well for us! For what makes me for you a Christian, makes yourself for me a Jew'.[23] The tolerance championed here is based on similarity; in the age of *Aufklärung* the play's title was *Nathan the Wise*, not Nathan *the Jew*. In fact it was the acceptance of difference – historically, culturally, or otherwise created – and not just the assertion of human commonalities that posed the real challenge to ideologies of capitalism with their abstract individualism. As Max Horkheimer and Theodor Adorno noted, 'Bourgeois society is ruled by equivalence. It makes the dissimilar comparable by reducing it to abstract quantities. To the Enlightenment, that which does not reduce to numbers, and ultimately to the one, becomes illusion . . .'[24] The one of religion became that of reason or the individual or the nation. Medieval Europe was a totalizing civilization in which, at least in principle, religion merged with all aspects of life. In the modern world of capitalism, this totality is splintered and religion, along with all other facets of existence, is assigned a given place or niche. Nationalism, in significant regards, sought to recapture the whole, though generalized in a particularized, rather than universal, community. Marx, in contrast, tried to do so by means of a universal class.[25]

The Jews, by the turn of the nineteenth century, were placed, consequently, within a dual bind, that of the individual and that of the nation; this duality, when embodied in historical forces, was one root of their undoing in the modern era.[26] Indeed, the Jews were not considered simply as individuals. As Seton-Watson observes – and as Zionist theoreticians often insisted – diaspora peoples, living as minorities within a host population, frequently have distorted social structures. Not only Jews, but Armenians, overseas Indians and Chinese as well as others, are often found concentrated in certain social and economic roles, such as commerce. Local native populations view them suspiciously as possessors of a 'sinister monopoly' of various occupations. Antagonisms intensify in times of broad social change, when these local populations, or part of them, seek out new economic roles for themselves.[27] Thus the emergence of indigenous commercial classes leads inevitably to conflicts with the 'aliens', who are often pushed out. At the same time, declining aristocratic classes use the prominence and visibility of such minorities in 'middleman' positions for scapegoating, deflecting the anger of the rising classes as well as that of those kept below. The rise of nationalism impacts on this situation dramatically.

Armstrong has developed a useful typology of diaspora nations which distinguishes, first of all, between 'proletarian' and 'mobilized' diasporas. Post-Second World War immigrant workers in Western Europe are examples of the first type, 'a nearly undifferentiated mass of unskilled labor' who lack general communication skills as well as the prospects for social and economic improvement, and are a 'disadvantaged product of modernizing polities.' A 'mobilized diaspora', on the other hand, lacks, in its place of residence, 'a general status advantage . . . yet enjoys many material and cultural advantages compared to other groups in a multi-ethnic polity'.[28] The Jews, Armstrong suggests, were an 'archetypal' mobilized diaspora since their dispersion was more widespread and complete than 'situational' mobilized diasporas which are temporary and partial. Examples of the latter would be Chinese in South-East Asia or Germans in eastern Europe, both of which were 'fragments of far larger, compact ethnic masses constituting two of the world's great societies'.[29] The Jews, by contrast, did not, at least until the late nineteenth century, imagine an imminent reconstruction of their civilization in their homeland. Most mobilized diasporas, in Armstrong's typology, occupy an intermediate position between the archetypal and the situational, Armenians being one example.

Elsewhere Armstrong, having emphasized the subjective nature of boundary-maintaining mechanisms between ethnic groups over extended time periods, suggests that ethnic symbolic communications, linking the past and present for a group, can comprise a 'mythomoteur', a constitutive myth that defines identity 'in relation to a specific polity'. A *mythomoteur* also 'sustains a polity and enables it to create an identity beyond that which can be imposed by force or purchased by peace and prosperity'.[30] Fundamental to Armstrong's distinction between two types of mobilized diasporas – the archetypal and the situational – is their varied use of what he calls 'ethnic myths', a 'border maintaining mechanism' defining the group's relationship to its homeland. The situational diaspora ethnic myth entails a type of nationalism and a sense of superiority founded on its ties to a great, and currently territorialized, civilization (e.g. overseas Chinese). Lacking this, the archetypal diaspora's myth tends to focus on the group's religion. Both Jews and Armenians sustained, and were sustained by, religious myths even though they both retained a 'significant territorial focus', respectively the Land of Israel and the Gregorian Catholicosate of Echmiadzin (site of the consecration of the head of their church since the fourth century). The religious myth 'defines a substitute homeland'.[31] In the case of the Jews, we have already noted how intensely religious myth was supplemented and sustained by communal self-organization.

Finally, Armstrong argues that the crucial factor which threatens mobilized diasporas is 'social mobilization in the society as a whole with its attendant populism; the diaspora nation becomes a convenient scapegoat especially as its usefulness to ruling elites – a usefulness which was often the reason they were invited into these societies in the first place – becomes less and less significant'.[32] If we translate this into the terminology we have used, our point is similar to Armstrong's: fundamental socio-economic transformation from one order to another, encompassing the rise and decline of various social classes and the emergence of national entities, tend to jeopardize diaspora nations, especially those with well-defined socio-economic roles in the old order. They are caught in the middle, as it were. This can be seen both in the transition from feudalism to capitalism and in the transition from colonialism to independence. An extreme example of the latter was the expulsion of Asians, who had played prominent business and commercial roles in the past, from Idi Amin's Uganda in the mid-1970s. At the turn of the century Ber Borokhov, commenting on the status of Jews in colonial North Africa, suggested that when the Moroccan masses revolted against their French masters, they would also vent fury against the Jews, who fitted neither into the category of alien dominator nor into that of native dominated.[33] While this prognosis was historically unfulfilled, at least as concerns Moroccan Jews, similar patterns did afflict Western Jewry in the era of the transition from feudalism to capitalism and nationalism, and also in eastern Europe. With the freeing of the serfs in 1861, the beginnings of a capitalist sector, and threats to the tsarist old regime, came too the undermining of miracle, mystery and authority, if we may borrow from Dostoevsky's Grand Inquisitor. As traditionalist anchors were unhinged, the alien, demonesque Jew became an easy target for the venting of anger, fears and frustrations.

Within this framework it is evident why the impact of the French revolution for understanding modern Jewish history is so essential. This great upheaval vividly illustrated the vice produced by a world projecting itself concurrently and paradoxically as one of competing, autonomous egos and one of competing, clashing, supra-individual entities. Nationalism posited a source of loyalty beyond the individual in the midst of the development of capitalism, whose logic ultimately denied such loyalties. While old ruling classes had made use of national sentiments for their own purposes, this was especially convenient for that class, the bourgeoisie, now that was consolidating its dominance; for whatever legitimate national cultural sentiment might emerge amongst a nation's masses, loyalty to nation and state helped to maintain order – bourgeois order, that is, once it had been established. The individuals within the nation would, theoretically, be partaking in their own sovereignty, but obeisance would be rendered to its incarnation in the state, which helped assure the sanctity of private property and the pursuit of profit. Consequently, rights were proclaimed of man *and* citizen, and the latter was of a republic on the soil of a particular nation. Count Stanislas de Clermont-Tonnerre, in a famous statement, told the French National Assembly in 1789: 'One must refuse everything to the Jews as a nation but one must grant them everything as individuals; they must become citizens'.[34] This was Emancipation. The Jews would be free as *individuals* but not as a corporate community. Clermont-Tonnerre brought this even more sharply into focus by suggesting that the only alternative to his proposal was expulsion. Slightly less than two decades later Napoleon assembled Jewish notables in a 'Grand Sanhedrin', named after the ancient Jewish court, which placed the communal institutions of members of the 'Mosaic faith' under a central Consistory in Paris, and pronounced the political aspects of that faith invalid.

A famous story has Hegel, as he watched Bonaparte enter Jena, comment that the spirit of world history had just ridden through town on horseback. After the emperor's armies swept across Europe, the continent was never the same. And where the tricolour triumphed, the ghetto walls surrounding the Jews fell. It appeared to be the dawn of a new age, one bringing with it all the hazards and possibilities symbolized by the revolution itself. The Restoration temporarily dimmed the skies, for after Napoleon's defeat the victors sought to re-create the old world, including its restrictions on the Jews. It would be some decades before it was clear that that world had been irrevocably crippled. The monarchs of the Holy Alliance had within their kingdoms the overwhelming majority of European Jews. Thus after Waterloo, in much of the west, the Jews faced a choice of return to a restricted existence or conversion. The parents of Moses Hess did the former, and Karl Marx's father opted for the latter. However, not only had the death knell of the *ancien régimes* been struck, despite their temporary resurgence: so too had that of the ghetto. In most of western and central Europe, Jewish legal emancipation was a fact some five decades after the Congress of Vienna.

II

Eastern Europe presented a radically different picture. Napoleon's armies were defeated in Russia, and there was no upheaval in Jewish life commensurate to that in the West. In the tsarist empire the Jewish condition was one of harsh oppression, poverty and degradation. As Muscovy began to consolidate in the sixteenth century, it had excluded Jews from its territories. In the late eighteenth century Russian expansionism, in particular the Polish partitions, led to the incorporation of large numbers of Jews within the tsar's domains. During the reign of Catherine the Great Jewish residence was restricted to the western and south-western portions of the empire, an area which, in the following century during the reign of Nicholas I, became known as the Pale of Settlement.

Throughout most of the nineteenth century the tsars, with occasional respite, utilized assorted means to dispose of what they saw as their Jewish problem. As the leading historian of Polish and Russian Jewry put it, the Jews were 'subjected to various experiments' which, 'supplemented by blood libel and medieval persecutions', turned their existence 'into stark tragedy'.[35] These measures included efforts at coerced conversion and assimilation – military conscription in Russia was for for 25 years and Jewish youth were seized at the age of 12 – the abolition of Jewish communal autonomy and attempts to 'reform' the Jews by means of government schools. Jews were prohibited from residence outside towns and cities, were restricted in occupational pursuits and were forbidden to own rural lands. In sum, the social, economic, political and legal position of the Jews was both vulnerable and visible. All of these factors, combined with the distinctiveness of their religious and communal life, enhanced the impression that the Jews were not merely an alien population, but an Other.

The pogroms of 1881–2 marked a turning-point for Russian Jewry. The Zionist response to this widespread outburst of anti-Jewish violence consisted, at its most radical, of the claim that only the end of the diaspora and the creation of an independent Jewish existence could save the Jews. In less extreme formulations, the Zionist programme sought to transform Jews from an archetypal into a situational diaspora. Homologously, the Zionists would secularize the Jewish ethnic myth, shifting from the religious to the national in conception of Jewish life. The pogroms themselves served to galvanize historical developments well under way. The Jewish political movements, especially nationalist and socialist ones, that burst forth on to the Jewish street in the two decades after 1881 were partly the consequence of an ongoing subversion of traditional authority within the Jewish community, thus opening possibilities for new forms of politics, new leadership, and new political actors. 1881 was the latest in a series of blows against a traditionalist society subjectively 'based on a common body of knowledge and values handed down from the past'.[36] Since the seventeenth century, this Jewry had been progressively disrupted, beginning with the rise and fall of the eschatological revival associated with the false messiah, and then apostate, Sabbatai Sevi (Shabtai Tsvi). The Sabbatian movement appeared in the third quarter of the seventeenth century, not long after Polish and Ukrainian Jewry had been victims of large-scale massacres. With its roots in mysticism (Palestinian Kabbalism to be precise), Sabbatianism's impact was great throughout the entire Jewish world. Its mysticism and messianism, its expectations of a redeemed and restored world in which the Temple would be rebuilt in Jerusalem, clearly threatened the rationalist tradition of rabbinical Judaism, and hence its keepers, the rabbis. The positive reception Sabbatai Sevi received among many Jews indicated the extent of discontent within Jewry, and his conversion to Islam was the source of great disillusionment. In the following century Hasidism was born in the Ukraine and Poland, and this also posed a threat to the traditional authority structure. Hasidism, too, was a mystical movement, but it differed from Sabbatianism in that its followers, *Hasidim* ('pious ones'), did not anticipate immediate eschatological redemption. Their focus was on 'the revival of the Jew in exile . . . It conquered in the realm of inwardness, but it abdicated in the realm of Messianism'.[37] By its emphasis on spontaneous prayer and (moderate) religious ecstasy, and in its reverence for charismatic leaders ('rebbes'), this popular religious movement represented a challenge to rabbinical leadership's stress on Talmudic expertise and traditional forms of Jewish study. The conflicts between the two camps were often bitter.

While Sabbatianism and Hasidism can be broadly characterized as having endogenous roots, the same cannot be said of the *Haskalah* (Enlightenment) movement among the Jews, which began in the late eighteenth century. Its adherents, the *maskilim* ('enlightened ones', singular, *maskil*) sought to reconcile Jewish life with modern European culture. They took substantial reform of traditional Jewish life as a necessity. The *Haskalah* played an essential role in the formation of a secularized Jewish intelligentsia that was responsive to European thought, seeking nourishment from it and, as a partial consequence, capable of understanding and responding to historical and political events around it in a way previously not possible among Jewish leaders. The existence of this intelligentsia was one prerequisite for the emergence of a modern Jewish politics, and also for the transformation of the Jewish religious myth into a secular national one, especially by the Zionists, in the late nineteenth century. By then events, particularly the pogroms, had dashed many a *maskil*'s most cherished hopes. However, as the French Enlightenment helped prepare the way for nationalism by challenging miracle, mystery and authority in the *ancien régime*, so too would Jewish nationalism come after the impact of the Jewish Enlightenment was felt.

The *Haskalah*'s origins are to be found in the journey of the ideas of the French and German Enlightenments – progress, reform, reason, education, tolerance, science – through Jewry in Prussia and Galicia to its Russian co-religionists. The philosopher Moses Mendelssohn (1729–86) is generally credited as its father because of his programme of reconciling religion and reason, the Jews and Enlightened Europe. Early *maskilim*, looking favourably on the experience of Frederick the Great, hoped that by means of a combination of enlightened monarchy and Jewish self-reform (especially through secular education) Jewish emancipation and integration might be fostered. While Russian *maskilim* did incorporate such notions into their own programmes, they also recognized that enlightened government was at best a distant prospect in backward Russia. What *Haskalah* seemed to offer was a place for Jews 'caught between an inaccessible larger cultural world and an unacceptable Jewish one'.[38] Isaac Ber Levinsohn, 'the Russian Mendelsohn', argued in 1839 for reform of schools and the rabbinate, for the opening of 'modern' schools for both sexes with secular subjects in the curricula, and for new *yeshivot* (religious seminaries). He emphasized the importance of the Hebrew language, and also the need to change the occupational structure of Jewry so that Jews would enter handicrafts, agriculture and other economic roles.[39] As a matter of course Levinsohn praised the tsar.

In the previous chapter we saw how the dominance of Latin as the intellectual, administrative and political lingua franca of the European Middle Ages declined concurrently with the rise of national communities whose vernaculars became those of both the mind and the state. This represented the undermining of what socio-linguistics calls diglossia, the use of a 'high' language (in this case Latin) and a 'low' one (such as French or English, or any other tongue employed for the daily discourse of a given population).[40] Linguistic transformation was a fundamental aspect of the emergence of Zionism, although in this case the pattern reversed that of most of Europe. For most European nationalisms, the decline of diglossia led to the replacement by spoken, and then written, vernaculars of the upper language (which, in turn, was relegated to the church and the university). Zionism, on the other hand, succeeded in making Hebrew, previously an 'upper langauge', used primarily for religious and literary purposes, into a tongue of daily discourse for a national community. As such it sought to make Hebrew *the* national language of the Jewish people; it was the only language to which Jews, be they in Vilna or Istanbul, had common ties.

The *Haskalah* movement emphasized Hebrew language and literature, and many of the early Zionists were *maskilim* or the children of *maskilim*. A new stress on Hebrew, in turn, could only enhance the centrality of the Land of Israel in Jewish consciousness; it was there that the Jews once lived as an independent community speaking Hebrew. With the emergence of national-ist ideas within Jewry, Hebraism provided a unifying element linking a land, a language and a people. Like other national movements, Zionism came to see language, in this case Hebrew, as a critical element of cultural authenticity linking the modern people to its progenitors in antiquity as a speech community.[41] Hence, Hebraists tended to negate the lands, languages and culture of the diaspora. In eastern Europe Yiddish was the vernacular of most Jews. Though disdained by *maskilim*, it was the source of a modern, flourishing culture and literature by the late nineteenth century which served as a pillar for various types of diaspora nationalism, such as that of the anti-Zionist Jewish Labour Bund. Such nationalism played down the status of the Land of Israel in Jewish life and culture, and aspired to a Yiddish-based cultural autonomy in the diaspora.

While Yiddish was the vernacular for eastern European Jewry, it was Hebrew that most Jews first learned to read and write, even if they did not know the language well. It has been estimated that in the late 1870s about a quarter of world Jewry (50 per cent of males) could understand the Bible and daily prayers in Hebrew, and about 10 per cent were capable of reading a book in Hebrew. Such knowledge of Hebrew tended to be proportionately much higher in eastern Europe than in the West.[42] As a language of religion, and as that of a substantial literature created between the third and the eighteenth centuries, Hebrew in the nineteenth century was not a 'dead' language, despite frequent epitaphs for it. The Hebrew literary revival of the nineteenth century was substantially engendered by the _Haskalah_ and, in turn, this nurtured the possibilities of a Hebrew-based nationalism. The literary revival tended to employ a neo-biblical, as opposed to rabbinic, Hebrew, since the former was viewed as purer, having been the tongue once used by Jews in ancient Palestine. Increasingly, the dissection of eastern European Jewish life became a theme in Hebrew literature, and this encouraged a critical confrontation between Enlightenment values and both the traditionalism and the debasement of eastern European Jewish life. Among the incongruous results are novels like those of Avraham Mapu in which _Haskalah_ themes are propounded by Lithuanian Jewish characters in neo-biblical Hebrew.[43] Mapu profoundly influenced an emerging generation of _maskilim_ and his fiction, much of which was set in ancient Palestine, was especially popular. It is notable that in one of his novels, _The Hypocrite_, the protagonist visits modern Palestine and from there writes letters home advocating Hebrew revival.[44] David Ben-Gurion, son of a devoted Hebraist from Plonsk, in Russian Poland, recalled in his memoirs the lasting impact of two novels on his youth in the 1890s: Mapu's _Love of Zion_ (published originally in 1853), and the Hebrew translation of Harriet Beecher Stowe's _Uncle Tom's Cabin_. 'Mapu's biblical stories', he wrote, 'breathed life into the holy texts I had studied and strengthened my yearning for the Land of Israel. _Uncle Tom's Cabin_ made me a resolute foe of every form of slavery and subjugation'.[45] (Tolstoy's _Resurrection_ influenced him as well.)

Hebraist intellectuals lived a problematic existence; they were a minority both in a traditional Jewish world and in a backward tsarist empire. Furthermore, they wrote, but did not speak, in Hebrew. They were flowers in a foreign soil. Or at least so thought Eliezer Ben-Yehudah, one of their number, who by 1880 was insisting on the tie between the rebirth of both written and spoken Hebrew and a rebirth of the Jewish nation in its original homeland. In order to flourish, he claimed, Hebrew literature needed a Hebrew environment; hence land, language and enlightenment together would be the salvation of the Jews in an era of nationalism. In his 1879 essay entitled 'A Weighty Question' he insisted that nationalism had not only radically changed the world but that its impact was just beginning to be felt. Born of rebellion against oppression, nationalism represented a justified desire of peoples to sustain their own distinctiveness.[46] But what place would there be for the Jews in a world governed by this principle? The next year Ben-Yehudah prophesied – in language echoing the Passover Seder in which Jews are reminded that they were once liberated from bondage in Egypt to journey to the Land of Israel – that 'Today we may be moribund, but tomorrow we will surely awaken to life; today we may be in a strange land, but tomorrow we will dwell in the land of our fathers; today we may be speaking alien tongues, but tomorrow we shall speak Hebrew'.[47] He went on:

> [We] will be able to revive the Hebrew tongue only in a country in which the number of Jewish inhabitants exceeds the number of gentiles. Therefore, let us increase the number of Jews in our desolate land; let the remnants of our people return to the land of their fathers; *let us revive the nation and its tongue will be revived too.*[48]

While Ben-Yehudah's writings often entail perceptive political observations, the driving force behind them is primarily a national cultural vision. He was both a *maskil* and a critic of the *Haskalah*; his agenda was that of enlightened Hebrew culture, but its development, as he saw it, could not be predicated on the liberalization of Russia and the transformation of the Jewish community there, as many others hoped, but rather on the re-creation of a national Hebrew-speaking community.

III

Ben-Yehudah moved to Palestine before the storm of 1881 broke. The shock inflicted on Jewry by the pogroms of that year cannot be overstated. This was especially the case for enlightened intellectuals who hoped for liberalization and/or the possibility of assimilation. It transformed the nature of Jewish politics; indeed, one could say that it politicized Jewish politics, and in so doing gave a new role to the intellectuals. 1881 served as a formative trauma for Jewish nationalism, one that led to a resetting of Jewish political and psychological boundaries. New inferences were drawn by the Jews about their neighbours and their future relations with them.

The anti-Jewish riots began in Elizavetgrad in the midst of the Russian Eastern celebrations, some six weeks after Tsar Alexander II was assassinated by populists. By the year's end, and sporadically over the next three years, Jews were murdered, beaten, raped, their homes and shops pillaged and their lives ravaged in some 200 towns, especially in southern Russia. Much of the Russian press viewed these outbursts as the virtually inevitable product of simmering resentments against the foreign 'exploiters'. The radical populists of *Narodnaia Volia* (the People's Will) issued a statement 'To the Ukrainian People' in August 1881 praising the violence against the Jew 'who drinks your blood' and who was accused of being the cause of Ukrainian suffering. 'You have begun to rebel against the Jews', it declared. 'You have done well. Soon the revolt will be taken up across all of

Russia against the tsar, the *pany* (aristocracy), the Jews'.[49] The sentiments of many Jewish intellectuals were captured by Shmarya Levin, a future Zionist leader, whose memoirs provide a vivid first-person account of the changes in eastern European Jewish life in the late nineteenth and early twentieth centuries. He believed that 'the government was instigating the pogroms and using them as a safety-valve. It hoped to divert the attention of the populations of Russia from the dissatisfactions born of [its] reactionary policy'.[50] Even in towns like Levin's Swisliwitz, which was spared violence, an atmosphere of fear pervaded, for expectation and dread were 'suspended almost visibly over our heads. There were times when we envied the cities that had already suffered the pogrom. "Better an end with terror than a terror without end" '.[51]

The world of those intellectuals who hoped for change within Russia seemed to come down around them, their aspirations for reform, reconciliation, liberalization and Russification shattered. It was similarly traumatizing for Jewish youth. Haim Hissin, who was 17 when the pogroms began, wrote in his diaries that before them he had looked forward to life as 'a devoted son of Russia. I lived and breathed . . . every new creation of Russian literature, every victory of Russian imperial power, everything Russian filled my heart with pride'. But now he found himself ceaselessly 'hounded by the cruel, pointed question: "Who are you? Identify yourself — if you can" '.[52] This was not just his question or that of his generation; it was the question now posed to the entire Jewish community of eastern Europe.

The aftermath of 1881 reshaped how Jewish political options were perceived, how they were acted on and who Jewry's political actors were. It represented the beginning of a resetting of Jewish political boundaries and the undermining of traditional authority patterns, as well as a reshaping of Jewish political culture. Traditional Jewish leadership, especially religious authorities, proved incapable of confronting the dire circumstances in which Russian Jewish life seemed to have been fundamentally called into question. Particularly significant was the (temporary) subversion of the authority of the *shtadlanim* (interceders), generally conservative and wealthy Jewish notables who took it upon themselves in the past to intervene with the government on behalf of Jewry, presenting themselves as its representatives. Haim Weizmann, the Russian-born Zionist leader and later first president of Israel, described them in his memoirs in these terms: 'Theirs was, even in the best of cases, a class view, characterized by a natural fear of disturbing the status quo or imperiling such privileges as they enjoyed by virtue of their economic standing'.[53] In short, the old Jewish politics, as Jonathan Frankel has shown, was elitist and plutocratic, with all eyes focused on these notables and towards St Petersburg, in the hope of reform from above. Jewish politics *as Jewish politics* was something 'purely auxiliary'.[54]

The response to the pogroms by the *shtadlanim*, especially in the Russian capital, combined meekness, confusion and hesitation. After all, they had, in Levin's words, 'believed wholly in the omnipotence of the government, and not at all in the power that lies in the inner forces of the oppressed . . . They were faithful servants of the government, not simply as a method but by psychological necessity. Their watchword was "Patience and passivity" '.[55] Consequently, new and more properly political forces were galvanized out of the ranks of the traumatized intelligentsia, especially among writers for the Russian and Hebrew press, and within the student population. After 1882 'the concept, if not the practice of open and mass organization took hold'.[56] The change in the political–psychological boundaries of the Jews was perhaps best captured by the title of Leo Pinsker's proto-Zionist pamphlet of 1882, 'Autoemancipation'. In it a *maskil* argued that the Jews could no longer wait until others – the government or their own 'leaders' – acted, but rather had to do so on their own. It was at this time that the proto-Zionist Hibat Zion (Love of Zion) movement began to organize itself; two decades later, a plethora of Jewish political parties and movements had appeared. Levin recalled that 'The old epoch of Jewish passive resistance was coming to an end; it was being replaced by a new epoch of organized effort, of planned activities, having as its goal more tolerable human conditions . . . The new epoch [was] characterized by the organized representation of the Jewish masses'.[57]

In a pattern similar to the development of bureaucracy, which evolved as a consequence of the inability of a ruler's family and/or court to administer expanding government functions, political parties took shape when the recruitment of political leadership and the making of policy 'could no longer be handled by a small coterie of men unconcerned with public sentiments'.[58] An additional contributing factor is often the narrowing of paths available for political expression. In eastern European Jewry a parallel process took place; small coteries of communal leaders faced displacement in the aftermath of 1881 as newly politicized elements within Jewry brought forth an array of new political formations, especially nationalist and socialist ones, that crystallized at the turn of the century. In addition, some two to two-and-a-half million Jews fled from Russia in the next three decades. Whatever the options chosen – emigration to the New World or to Palestine, or participation in the struggle to change Russia – it was clear that a new, and autonomous, Jewish politics was taking form with a new, more national and democratic, political style and content.

'Autoemancipation' was published anonymously in September 1882 and subtitled 'An Appeal to His People by a Russian Jew'. Its author, Pinsker, was an Odessa physician formerly active in the local chapter of the 'Society for the Promotion of Culture among Jews'. He had been an advocate of Russian education and general modernization for the Jews, although doubts had already entered his mind about the efficacy of the *Haskalah* programme after an earlier pogrom in Odessa in 1871. The bloodshed of 1881 led him to reconceive the Jewish problem, a reconceptualization embodied in his use, as an epigram, of part of a renowned teaching of Hillel the Elder: 'If I am not for myself, who will be for me? If not now, when?' Emancipation would only be autoemancipation, an act done by the Jews themselves. His analysis was bold, radical and straightforward. Efforts to change how Jews were viewed and treated by the government and the population clearly hadn't succeeded; whether traditional, 'reformed', or 'modernized', Jews were condemned to be the victims of the same prejudice:

> The essence of the problem . . . lies in the fact that, in the midst of the nations among whom the Jews reside, they form a distinctive element which cannot be assimilated, which cannot be readily digested by any nation. Hence the problem is to find a means of so adjusting the relations of this exclusive element to the whole body of the nations that there will never be any further basis for the Jewish Question.[59]

Jew-hatred, insisted the doctor, was a 'disease', a 'psychic aberration', something 'incurable'. The medicine of reason had failed to vanquish it; so too would legal measures. The Jew was perceived as frightening and ghostly, 'like one of the dead walking among the living'.[60] His neighbours saw him as the source of all evil: 'for the living the Jew is a dead-man, for the natives an alien and a vagrant, for property holders a beggar, for the poor an exploiter and a millionaire, for patriots, a man without a country, for all classes, a hated rival'.[61]

Pinsker's pamphlet prescribed an internal and external reconstruction of the Jews. They needed to re-emerge in national guise, and cast aside the belief that their suffering in the diaspora was part of their fate, a component of a divine plan. They needed to re-enter history and free themselves by creating an autonomous and independent national existence for themselves. He proposed a congress of Jewish notables to lay the foundations for this task. Unlike Hess, with his projections of the sanctification of history heralded by a Jewish socialist state in Palestine, Pinsker, facing the immediacy of anti-Jewish violence, made his goal simple and political: the Jews needed self-determination and all other issues were beside the point, including where this would take place. He went so far as to warn against dreaming of a return to Palestine because 'The goal of our present endeavors must not be the "Holy Land" but a land of our own'.[62] The society to be created in this land was not his central concern, even less were visions of the Messiah. He was a physician, he diagnosed the ailment, he prescribed what was needed for physical survival. The tastes and inclinations of the patient after recovery could be dealt with then.

Pinsker's represented perhaps the earliest sustained formulation of a political Zionism. Its conclusions and programme were not primarily economic or cultural in nature. To gain control over their lives Jews needed

a land of their own, pure and simple. This orientation would be that of
Herzl a decade-and-a-half later. Nonetheless, Pinsker's politics – like all
politics – were not devoid of a socio-economic tinge. The bedrock of Jewish
nationalism, he believed, would be the middle class for, as he wrote in a
letter in October 1883, it 'is our most wholesome, most reliable, element. It
always cherished the interests of our people. In it there still lives the
consciousness of national dignity, and it alone is capable of single purpose
and pursuit'.[63] In striking contrast to this remark, Pinsker, a little over a
year later, presented the following diagnosis of the diaspora to the
Kattowitz Conference, a meeting to co-ordinate the emerging proto-Zionist
groups in Russia:

> We have turned from the normal pursuits of life. We are eliminated
> from the land and overactive in commerce, industry, and similar fields
> to an extent which has obstructed both our mental and physical
> development. The tendency to overemphasize mental activity has
> brought about physical deterioration, and the Jewish people has
> forgotten the meaning of physical labour.[64]

For two millennia Jews had been middlemen and traders. Now it was time
to return to lives of labour and lives on the soil, for 'Everyone realizes . . .
[that this] is the proper basis of society'.[65] The need to change the Jewish
occupational structure was a theme in the *Haskalah*, in which, as we noted,
Pinsker was well tutored. However, that which he now rejected as
obstructing 'the mental and physical development' of the Jews was precisely
the substance of the life of the middle class he had championed.

The organizational expression of proto-Zionism was at first modest. The
various groups that sprang up, known collectively as the Hibat Zion (or as
Hovevei Zion, lovers of Zion), united in Kattowitz (upper Silesia) under the
leadership of Pinsker, who by then was converted to establishing Jewish
autonomy in Palestine. His efforts, and those of Hibat Zion, were very
practical in orientation, concentrating on educational work in Russia along
with promoting settlement in Palestine. The Hibat Zion's Odessa Committee became the centre of Russian Zionism, and a committee was established
also in Warsaw. Despite the 'political Zionism' of Pinsker's 'Autoemancipation', the Hibat Zion came to represent 'practical Zionism' because its
focus was not on obtaining political guarantees for the Jews in Palestine –
Herzl's later preoccupation – but rather on the tedious and difficult effort to
get Jews to settle there. At this time a first wave of modern Jewish
immigration to Palestine commenced. Known as the First Aliyah (Aliyah –
'to go up' in Hebrew), it encompassed about 25,000 Jews from Russia,
Romania and Yemen.

  Among the Russians was a small but notable group of settlers known as
the 'BILU', an acronym for the biblical Hebrew phrase 'House of Jacob, let
us go' (Isaiah 2:5). The BILU was founded by veterinary students at the

University of Kharkov and appears to have gained 525 adherents by the autumn of 1882.[66] Admittance was permitted solely to youth who were personally committed to settling in Palestine, although only about 10 per cent actually got there. Armed with radical and populist ideas imbibed from their Russian environment, they imagined themselves as vanguard pioneers who would create a new foundation for Jewish national life in preparation for the future arrival of the masses. This could best be done, they believed, though communal settlements and the sweat of their own brows; self-emancipation required 'self-labour', not exploiting others to build their homeland.

Within the BILU there occurred a dress rehearsal of one of the central strategic debates of the later Zionist movement. The question was whether the first priority should be actual settlement in Palestine and the establishment of a community there, or pursuit of official recognition for Zionist efforts by the less than friendly Ottoman empire which governed the country. One group of BILU members went to Constantinople hoping to secure recognition by the Sublime Porte, but, precursing Herzl's failure when he tried to do the same some two decades later, they were rebuffed. They eventually went on to Palestine where another group, convinced of the efficacy of concrete work in Palestine, had already gone.

As a self-styled vanguard, the *Biluim* were prepared with a vision. They were not prepared, however, with resources, agricultural expertise and an adequate estimation of the difficulties of Palestine and its climate. Mapu gave a generation romances about ancient Israel, and later generations made romance out of the BILU legacy, but what these youth actually found themselves facing in an Ottoman Palestine run by corrupt and lax administrators was, as expressed by one of their number in his diaries, a 'land of lawlessness, where swindling and chiseling, theft and deceit, are considered a form of bravery'.[67] The local Arab population was hostile, finding them alien (undoubtedly the feeling was mutual) and threatening, and the same was the case with the 'Old Yishuv', the largely orthodox community of Jews who for centuries constituted a quietistic Jewish presence in Palestine, dependent largely on *Halukah* (a system of charity from diaspora Jews). The Old Yishuv found these self-styled 'pioneers', with their modern ideas and hopes, thoroughly blasphemous.

The Hibat Zion became increasingly preoccupied with philanthropic efforts to sustain the struggling colonies in Palestine including the BILU's. The financial drain on the meagre Russian Zionist resources was severe, success was limited and Pinsker, in between struggles with rabbis who sought to impress religious orthodoxy on the movement, was forced to beg assistance from the Rothschild family. Edmond de Rothschild, who over the following decades engaged in substantial philanthropic endeavours in Palestine, insisted that his own administrators direct the settlements. This seemed less and less like autoemancipation, and more and more like a new form of dependence, especially to the demoralized young pioneers of the BILU. 'When shall we see an end to all this?', bemoaned one of them:

> For the time being we bear everything without grumbling, for the sake of something higher, but my heart trembles with fear that this 'higher' something may soon deteriorate and disappear. Is it possible to preserve the purity of one's aspirations, to keep one's soul guiltless, one's self unspoiled, to remain decent when the soul is constantly demeaned by the need to fawn and to stretch out one's hand?[68]

Deterioration did come on the heels of demoralization and dependence, for the First Aliyah as a whole and the BILU within it. Increasing numbers left the country, or, abandoning their idealism, relied on Rothschild and became farm owners hiring inexpensive Arab agricultural workers to labour for them. Although a new Jewish presence was consolidated, it was but a small, modest foundation for a future Jewish national society. By the early 1890s it was evident that this effort at 'practical Zionism' was floundering, as was the Hibat Zion in Russia. The latter did find within its ranks in Odessa a particularly forceful intellectual presence in the person of Ahad Ha-am; but Zionist revitalization would come from the West in the person of Theodor Herzl.

3

Kernel and Shell

In profane matters the instrument derives its worth from the end, and is valued for the most part only so far as it is a means to that end; and consequently we change the instrument as the end demands, and finally when the end is no longer pursued the instruments automatically fall into disuse. But in sacred matters the end invests the instrument with a sanctity of its own. Consequently there is no changing or varying of the instrument; and when the end has ceased to be pursued the instrument does not fall out of use, but is directed towards another end; in the one case we preserve the shell for the sake of the kernel, and discard the shell when we have eaten the kernel; in the other case we raise the shell to the dignity of the kernel and do not rob it of that dignity even if the kernel withers, but make a new kernel for it.

Ahad Ha-am[1]

I

'At Basle I founded the Jewish state'.[2] So declared Theodor Herzl, a man not prone to modesty, in his diaries after the first world Zionist Congress in Basle, Switzerland, in the summer of 1897. 'At Basle, I sat solitary among my friends, like a mourner at a wedding-feast'.[3] So wrote another participant in that Congress, Ahad Ha-am. Implicit in these contrasting responses to the same event were opposed concepts of the Jewish nationalist project, and opposing strategic perspectives on the resetting of Jewish national boundaries. A classic study of Zionism notes that

> any of the three nationalist aims, land, language, or sovereignty, could be made the primary value and the most general end [of Zionism] from which all the others were logically derived. Each of these aims, in turn, was valued because it was conceived as the logical means for dealing with the intolerable situation which lay at the roots of the Zionist myth and idea: the Jewish problem as it became acute for a generation of moderns.[4]

In Herzl and Ahad Ha-am we find a Zionist version of the distinction between *Staatnation* and *Kulturnation*. This chapter endeavours to understand some of the critical formative elements of Zionist politics, first by examining the clash between Herzl and Ahad Ha-am, and then by examining the structural framework of Zionist politics as it emerged in the pre-state period. In ensuing chapters we will look at the evolution of those politics.

Born in 1856 to Hasidic parents in Skvira (Russian Ukraine), Asher Ginsburg, sometimes called the 'agnostic rabbi', became the dominant intellectual presence in Russian Zionism following Pinsker's death in 1891. Ginsburg joined the Hibat Zion in 1886 after moving to Odessa and after an upbringing that mixed intense traditional Jewish learning with a personal quest for Russian and European culture. Like many of his contemporaries, he was especially impressed by the positivism of Comte and Pisarev. His first article, 'The Wrong Way', was an incisive critique of the failings of Hibat Zion, published in 1889. He signed this essay, which rapidly became a classic of Zionist literature, by the pen-name by which he was henceforth known, Ahad Ha-am ('One of the People'). Although it launched an impressive career in Hebrew letters, he later insisted that he chose his *nom de plume* in order 'to make clear that I was not a writer, and had no intention of becoming one, but was just incidentally expressing my opinion on the subject about which I wrote as "one of the people" who was interested in his people's affairs'.[5]

Ahad Ha-am was a man drawn temperamentally more to literary than to public affairs. None the less, his impact on both was substantial, and in neither was he but 'one of the people', not in his haughty personal demeanour nor in his influence. His Zionism placed national cultural revival at its centre. What Armstrong calls the religious ethnic myth – which, we may recall, functions as a substitute homeland – became in his hands a national cultural myth anchored in the proposition that a spiritual centre for the Jewish people ought to be created in the ancient Jewish homeland. We see this transformation in the opening to his first essay:

> For many centuries the Jewish people, sunk in poverty and degra-
> dation, has been sustained by faith and hope in the divine mercy. The
> present generation has seen the birth of a new and far-reaching idea,
> which promises to bring down our faith and hope from heaven, and
> transform both into living and active forces, making our land the goal
> of hope, and our people the anchor of faith.[6]

Faith was to come from heaven to earth. If we may borrow the phrase Max Weber borrowed from Schiller, Ahad Ha-am thus disenchanted the ethnic myth, and re-enchanted it at the same moment by replacing religion with national culture. The most forceful illustration of this was in his remarkable essay on 'Moses' (1904), often considered his finest piece of writing. Here he made clear that his interest was not in a historical figure who was a religious lawgiver, but rather in the incarnation of a Jewish version of Herderian *Volksgeist*. Ahad Ha-am did not care if Moses, 'a walking and talking biped', actually lived; his interest was in 'what manner of thing is the national ideal which has its embodiment in Moses'.[7]

Moses was, for Ahad Ha-am, a prophet first and foremost, and only secondarily a lawgiver, a statesman, or a military hero. As a prophet Moses embodied the extremist's unflagging devotion to truth and righteousness; and Ahad Ha-am, mourner at the feast of the first Zionist Congress, insisted that Israel's salvation would be accomplished by prophets, not diplomats.[8] Prophets embodied the *Volksgeist* and Ahad Ha-am was one of the *Volk* in the sense that raising questions about his own identity as did so many of his intellectual contemporaries was as meaningless as asking 'why I remain my father's son'.[9] The nature of his Zionism was consequent to this, as was what separated him from Theodor Herzl, for Herzl played the diplomat and had lived through precisely those sorts of questions. This Budapest-born journalist, who did more than any single individual to galvanize Zionism as a political movement, was also a man who, before his Jewish nationalist career began, penned in his diaries, 'If there is one thing I should like to be it is a member of the old Prussian aristocracy'.[10] In that same year, 1895, he recalled a bizarre notion he once held; he would propose to the pope that in return for a struggle by the Church against anti-Semitism, he, Theodor Herzl, would personally lead a mass conversion of the Jews on the steps of St Stephen's in Vienna, 'with solemn parade and the peal of bells'.[11]

The product of a middle-class family, he received a doctorate in law before becoming a reasonably prominent writer, authoring essays and plays as well as journalism. Herzl matured as a bourgeois intellectual, strongly attracted to German culture and enlightened hopes. The collapse of those hopes, more than anything else, led to his Zionism; the Dreyfus affair brought but the culmination of a process of redrawing his personal Jewish boundaries, a process he began as an observer of the rising tide of anti-Semitism in Vienna and then in Paris. As correspondent for the Viennese *Neue Freie Presse*, Herzl stood at the Ecole Militaire in Paris on 5 January, 1895 observing the public degradation of the hapless Captain Alfred Dreyfus, who, having been falsely condemned for treason, declared his innocence and swore his fidelity to France while a crowd outside the gates shouted 'A mort les juifs!' Reflecting on this four years later, Herzl starkly captured what the affair implied both for enlightened liberalism and the Jewish future. The following passage illustrates all that brought him to Zionism:

> The Dreyfus case embodies more than a judicial error; it embodies the desire of the vast majority of the French to condemn all Jews in this one Jew. Death to the Jews! howled the mob as the decorations were

being ripped from the captain's coat ... Where? In France. In republican, modern, civilized France, a hundred years after the Declaration of the Rights of Man. The French people, or at any rate the greater majority of the French people, does not want to extend the rights of man to Jews. The edict of the great Revolution has been revoked.[12]

Both Herzl and Ahad Ha-am believed that the legacy of Enlightenment liberalism would betray the Jews, but for Herzl, in contrast to Ahad Ha-am, this belief entailed a rejection of his former self. After a meeting with the philosopher Max Nordau, he noted in his diaries that they both agreed that 'only anti-semitism had made Jews of us'.[13] (None the less, Herzl remained a man of the West, both in his patterns of thought and in his cultural orientation; he was never at ease with the eastern European Jews – the *Ostjuden* – who were to be the backbone of the Zionist movement.) Ahad Ha-am, in contrast, found in Zionism a logical culmination of his *Jewish* development, rather than a radical reorientation of his life.

In his essay on 'Politics as a Vocation', Max Weber distinguished between the person who lives 'for' and the person who lives 'from' politics. In one case the individual seeks to make politics his livelihood, and in the other he 'makes politics his life, in an internal sense. Either he enjoys the naked possession of the power he expects, or he nourishes his inner balance and self-feeling by the consciousness that his life has *meaning* in the service of a "cause" '.[14] Both Herzl and Ahad Ha-am lived for Zionism; neither found a livelihood in it. As if anticipating Weber, Herzl declared in a letter: 'to me Zionism is neither sport nor a business. I am not living on it but for it'.[15] (He wrote in his diaries on his forty-first birthday, 'It is almost six years since I started this movement which has made me old, tired, and poor'.[16]) However, while Herzl lived for Zionism as a political solution to the Jewish problem, Ahad Ha-am lived for it as the concrete source of a rebuilt Jewish national culture. Herzl, as it has been frequently observed, addressed himself primarily to solving the political crisis of Jews – walking and talking bipeds – in a world of failed emancipation, while Ahad Ha-am's Zionism addressed, first and foremost, the question of Judaism in the modern world. One was a *Staat* Zionist and thus the father of 'political' Zionism, the other was a *Kultur* Zionist and the father of 'spiritual' (or 'cultural') Zionism.

Ahad Ha-am did not negate the political dimension of Zionism, but made it a partial element of a whole. The survival of Jewish *Volksgeist*, as opposed to solving the problem of individual Jews facing a crisis, was his preoccupation. In 'The Wrong Way' he asserted that the Law of Moses had the single object of the good of the 'nation as a whole in the land of its inheritance', and that the individual was to be seen as a limb to a body, whose well-being was to be sought *in the body as a whole*, i.e. in the community, not apart from it.[17] He repeatedly castigated any effort to focus on individual needs as opposed to those of the national community. More than this, however, divided him from someone like Herzl, for whom conclusions drawn from personal observation and dislocation were, we might say, a starting-point. What Ahad Ha-am opposed in Herzl was his simplistic *etatism*. It was a question of means and ends. For Ahad Ha-am the shell and the kernel of Jewish nationalism were interdependent; the goal, therefore, had to be the establishment of 'a state that will be a *Jewish* state, and not merely a state of the Jews'. Herzl's classic *Der Judenstaat* considered the possibility of a Jewish state in Argentina, and when the British informally offered a Jewish refuge in East Africa ('the Uganda Plan') to the Zionist Organization (ZO), Herzl anxiously pursued the idea of such a *Nachtasyl* (night-shelter), as his friend Nordau called it. Herzl's novel *Altneuland* (Old–New Land) depicted a Palestinian Zionist utopia barely recognizable – at least culturally – as a *Jewish* state. Similarly, Herzl was apprehensive lest Hebrew become the language of a future Jewish state and create a 'linguistic ghetto'.[18] In Ahad Ha-am's view, Herzl's projected commonwealth was in danger of being 'a state of Germans or Frenchmen of the Jewish race'.[19] The cultural Zionist, who authored a blistering review of Herzl's novel, fretted that a night-shelter might become home, and considered the revival of Hebrew culture the heart of Jewish national revival; he himself played an important role in the development of the modern Hebrew essay and in the modernization and Westernization of Hebrew style.

For Ahad Ha-am the Herzlian statist shell threatened to squeeze the Jewish national kernel empty of that content which gave it spiritual greatness – its cultural heritage. There was grave danger in seeking 'the path of glory in the attainment of material power and political dominion, thus breaking the thread that unites us with the past, and undermining our historical basis'.[20] That foundation, however, was not religious orthodoxy. Ahad Ha-am, in the final analysis, was a modernizing conservative, if we take this literally to mean someone who wanted to be modern but also to conserve. While orthodox traditionalists found him heretical, and even revolutionary, because of his emphasis on national culture (as opposed to religion *per se*), his Zionism was less a rebellion against the Jewish past than an effort to adapt it to and find a way for it in a changing world. Zionism, for him, would restore the 'equilibrium between the old and the new, by clothing both in a single new form'.[21] Jewish culture, and hence the Jews as a people, could not survive without a spiritual centre in Palestine.

For Herzl, on the other hand, the primary issue *was* the shell; the kernel was for him neither a passion nor a pressing concern, despite his designs for a relatively enlightened regime and society in a Jewish state. And liberal and secular though he was, Herzl had no qualms about cultivating alliances with orthodox religious Zionists when, at the turn of the century, he was faced with a challenge within the ZO by a group calling itself the 'Democratic

Faction', led by Haim Weizmann and Leo Motzkin, and composed of an assortment of other young Zionists including Martin Buber. The Democratic Faction, many of whom were Ahad Ha-am followers, wanted the Zionist movement to engage in national cultural education, and opposed Herzl's often authoritarian and high-handed style of running the Zionist Organization. In a pattern replicated in later Zionist and Israeli politics, Herzl obtained support from the orthodox on political questions – even the Uganda Plan – and in return allowed them leverage in their own concerns, one of which was opposition to Ahad Ha-amism.

Herzl, the father of 'political Zionism' – which he insisted superseded the 'practical Zionism' of the Hibat Zion era – was preoccupied with 'grand diplomacy', the effort to gain a charter and support from a great power on behalf of a Jewish state. In the age of imperialism, this seemed to him the most natural of routes; without such a charter, he feared, any effort at Jewish settlement would be unprotected and inevitably undermined by resistance from the resident population. Furthermore, to a man with legal training, a charter appeared the obvious way to secure legitimacy for his endeavour under existing international laws and practices. A 'practical Zionist' strategy of slow work and immigration, of 'gradual infiltration', was 'pointless unless it is based on our guaranteed sovereignty'.[22] Herzl was not especially well informed about Hibat Zion's activities in Russia and Palestine, but he was unimpressed and impatient with its step by step approach, which had clearly proved unsuccessful, as demonstrated by the decline of the First Aliyah. Practical Zionists, he complained in an article in 1900, sent '*settlers for show*', and 'want to start going to Erets Israel even before it belongs to us. The political Zionists . . . say: First it has to belong to us and then we will go there'.[23] However, by the time of Herzl's premature death in 1904, his diplomatic efforts too had failed, as he was rebuffed by the emperors, sultans and ministers he sought out. The imperial powers found little to attract them in the proposals he audaciously advanced. Dramatic though his air was, and despite his brash appearances at various European courts as if he were the head of vast Israelite armies with wealth and power at his disposal, he in fact was a journalist heading an organization with precious little to offer politically or economically.

Yet it was in its weaknesses that the real strength of Herzlian Zionism lay. True, his unsuccessful diplomatic strategy was the product of his liberal European *Weltanschauung*; but it was his own maturation within that European world and his lack of preoccupation with the fate of Judaism *per se* that allowed him to see with remarkable clarity that his people faced a historical crossroads. He was possessed by a sense of urgency and a recognition of the physical precariousness of the Jewish situation in the post-Enlightenment world in a way that Ahad Ha-am was not. The latter may have grasped the impact of a changing world on Jewish culture, but not that on the daily existence of the Jews, something required, of course, if there was to be any Jewish culture. The existence of Jews, who were in fact walking and talking bipeds and not only the embodiment (or potential embodiment) of a *Volksgeist*, was *sine qua non* of Jewish spirituality. Ahad Ha-am's aversion to the 'material' world of politics contrasted with the dark foreboding Herzl felt about what that world might yet have in store. Having watched the Dreyfus affair and the rise of anti-Semitism, Herzl was obsessed with the consequences of Jewish 'material' powerlessness – to such an extent that all else was epiphenomenal.

II

Ironically, both men were elitists of the first order. Neither had faith in the masses. However, their own organizational efforts illustrated, again, their different Zionisms. Ahad Ha-am engaged in a cultural and Herzl in a political elitism, though Herzl's was combined with the effort to construct the infrastructure for a popular national movement. Believing the hope for mass immigration to be a fantasy, Ahad Ha-am stressed spiritual preparation as the paramount task for Zionism, a theme he first presented in 'The Wrong Way'. He became the moving force in a semi-secret society within the Hibat Zion called the 'Bnei Moshe' (Sons of Moses). Its membership was open only to 20-year-old individuals who knew Hebrew and were willing to commit 2 per cent of their annual income to the organization. They conceived of themselves as a vanguard dedicated to their own spiritual and cultural regeneration, and preparation of their people for a new future.

Bnei Moshe spread to several countries and perhaps reached 160 in number before disbanding the year before the first Zionist Congress. It could boast only modest achievements. None the less, and undoubtedly to his satisfaction, Ahad Ha-am's teachings did have a lasting and profound impact on the activities of his followers. This was especially the case within the ranks of Russian Zionism, notably on Weizmann as leader of the Democratic Faction and Menahem Mendel Ussishkin, who became the head of the Odessa Committee in 1896, and emerged as one of the most implacable foes of Herzl on the Uganda issue and many others.

Herzl's combination of liberalism and etatism reflected contemporary currents in Germany, and is manifested in the nature of his organizational efforts, his 'grand diplomacy', and his general political outlook. His diaries are particularly revealing in this respect. Two years before the first Zionist Congress he can be found recalling how he argued vociferously against democracy and socialism with the former *communard* Leo Franckel. Herzl averred that 'one can only govern aristocratically . . . the state and its needs cannot be comprehended by the people'.[24] His predilection was clearly for a paternalistic 'elective aristocracy' which he imagined would have the wisdom to care for the people's needs through a fairly advanced welfare state that would nationalize important sectors in the economy, while at the same time encouraging entrepreneurialism. In *Der Judenstaat*, published a year before the first Zionist Congress, Herzl proposed forming a 'state-creating power' in the form of a 'Society of Jews' which would 'scientifically and politically' plan for Jewish sovereignty and negotiate for a homeland. This endeavour would, in turn, be carried to fruition by means of a chartered 'Jewish Company', a type of joint stock venture for land acquisition, organization of trade and commerce in the designated country, and the disposal of Jewish interests in the lands of emigration.[25]

Unlike Bnei Moshe, the world Zionist Organization that Herzl actually created had an ongoing, visible and overtly political presence. It survived both Herzl's physical demise and the failure of his diplomacy. This was partly because Herzl, as an intuitively political animal, knew that political power could be pursued only through political organization. Herzl was particularly cognizant of public appearances; his journalistic background undoubtedly induced this. The first Congress was intended to be a 'public demonstration'.[26] The delegates were very much like Herzl: educated, middle class, generally modern in political, social and religious views. The old 'notables' were noticeably absent.[27] Of the radicals and socialists who later dominated the Zionist project in Palestine, there were few. In all these respects, the birth of organized Zionism was similar in social and class background to that of other European nationalist movements. This, too, suited Herzl's *Weltanschauung*; he believed that 'Businessmen are best suited for conducting political affairs'.[28] One of the few socialists attending, Nahman Syrkin of Mohilev, wrote that at the first Zionist Congress 'Zionism assumed a reactionary bourgeois character in keeping with the social group which was its protagonist . . .'[29]

The term 'Zionism' – derived from Mount Zion, a hill in Jerusalem – was first used by the Austrian Jewish nationalist Nathan Birnbaum in 1892 and gained general usage with the Zionist Congress in 1897. The latter's 'Basle Declaration', drafted by Max Nordau, proclaimed that 'the aim of Zionism is to create for the Jewish people a home in Palestine secured by public law'.[30] The Congress mandated the creation of institutions to carry this out and the Zionist Organization that emerged, pyramidal in structure, reflected both Herzl's predilections and the organizational imperatives of co-ordinating nationalist activities for a diaspora people. Power tended towards the centre and it could indeed be characterized as an 'elective aristocracy', or as a form of democratic elitism since while it created a hierarchy, it also established a forum for democratic debate, and the means by which a sense of participation might be elicited among the Jewish masses, significant numbers of whom, though by no means a majority, increasingly responded to the Zionist appeal. (This was due, partly, to the enormous impact of Herzl himself, his booklet *Der Judenstaat* and the meeting of the Zionist Congress itself). Local Zionist organizations were delegated substantial autonomy in daily activities, and the Zionist Congress was mandated to be the supreme organ of the movement; it met at first annually and then, after 1901, biennially in Europe. Delegates were elected and the franchise was obtained by payment of an annual membership due ('the Shekel'). The Congress voted on major policy issues and elected an 'Actions Committee'. Also known as the General Council, it was composed originally of 18 members selected to represent various countries, and its responsibility was to run affairs between congresses. Appointed too was a smaller Executive of five which sat in Vienna with Herzl at its head.[31] Plans for dissemination of information and propaganda soon took form, including the launching of a Zionist newspaper *Die Welt*.

The ZO thus took on a multiple nature. On the one hand, it sought to be the framework of a national movement. Its Congress functioned – or presumed to function – as a Jewish national assembly in exile presided over by Herzl, its president. On the other hand, its overall structure resembled that of a political party and its representatives and local organizations frequently acted as if they were parties in Jewish communal politics. The call went out for Zionism to 'conquer the communities'. The first Zionist Congress had some 200 delegates and the second had twice that number.

Soon afterwards factions appeared, and within two decades they turned into political parties seeking through elections to control the Congress, and thereby policy, resources, and, importantly, the Executive, which evolved into something like a Zionist Cabinet. Maurice Duverger, in his study *Political Parties*, delineated how, in Europe, political parties emerged on territorial and programmatic bases in processes internal and external to legislatures. Some grew out of factions within assemblies and then were compelled to create formal mass organizations as suffrage was extended. The classic examples of these were the British Liberal and Conservative parties, respectively descendants of the Whig and Tory parliamentary factions which crystallized, in part, due to members' opposition to (or support of) the prerogatives of the monarchy. Others formed externally to the legislature and then entered into it, having competed successfully in elections (e.g. the British Labour party).[32] Similar patterns may be discerned in the history of Zionist politics, though with this important distinction: the Zionist factions and parties sought control of a non-sovereign organization with limited resources, not a government.

The first faction, to which we have already referred, was the Democratic Faction, founded in 1901. Harsh as many of its criticisms of Herzl were, it regarded itself as the most faithful of foes. 'Before you stands His Majesty's most loyal opposition' – thus did Weizmann, in meeting with Herzl, present himself and his backers.[33] The birth of the Democratic Faction stimulated, in turn, religious Zionists to form – with Herzl's encouragement – Mizrahi (literally 'Easterner', it is derived from the Hebrew *merkaz ruhani*, spiritual centre) in 1902, and it also engendered the ironically named 'United Faction' of Ussishkin. Despite his own differences with Herzl, Ussishkin believed factionalism to be inherently deleterious to the Zionist Organization. As he wrote to Weizmann in the autumn of 1903, 'I want you to know that I am opposed . . . to the [Democratic] Faction, to Mizrahi, and every factionist principle which kills our general orientation'.[34] He thus articulated one of the essentials of what became known as 'General Zionism'. However, as parties emerged, General Zionists, too, would have to organize themselves, even while they protested their non-partisan character. Indeed, at the same time as Ussishkin wrote the aforementioned letter to Weizmann, he was busy organizing the 'Zion Zionists' to oppose Herzl on the Uganda Plan.

The implications of the process of factional differentiation were captured by Weizmann himself. Writing in *Voshkod*, a liberal, non-Zionist, Russian journal, in the spring of 1901, the leader of the Democratic Faction argued that to be truly representative, delegates to Zionist Congresses had to reflect different perspectives and not merely the prerequisites of organizing a territorially dispersed people:

> We are too afraid of controversies that are supposedly academic, but the clarification of which is in fact an urgent necessity to put an end to many misunderstandings and would be of immense educational value to every Zionist. It is true that clarifying all these issues would separate Zionists into separate camps, but this is precisely what we ought to be demanding. If Zionists with different outlooks exist – and they do – they should be grouped accordingly. This would make the work easier, and many issues that today seem blurred and vague would gain by exact definition and delimitation. Zionists cannot build a party but only a league, to be composed of 'fractions' united by a common initial program.
>
> Grouping Zionists according to their place of origins makes sense only for the discussion of purely technical and organizational problems, but it is completely absurd when hammering out questions of principle. These have so far been given very little attention, but they must inevitably be brought to the fore if we wish Zionism to gain in depth and not merely to spread out and vanish on the surface like ripples of water.[35]

At the fifth Zionist Congress, which met in Basle in December 1901, it was decided to make important structural changes in the ZO so that not only territorially based Zionist organizations (e.g. the Russian Zionist Federation) could participate, as had been the case, but ideological groupings as well.[36] The Democratic Faction itself functioned for a only short period, but other factions and parties were to emerge and survive through Israeli statehood.

In a study of *Parties and Party Systems* Giovanni Sartori suggests that 'it is probably no fortuitous coincidence that Western party systems had no part in building the nation-state and became operative only when the crisis of legitimacy – i.e., acceptance of constitutional rule – had been resolved'.[37] The case of the Jewish nation-state and the party system of Zionism are exceptions to this rule: the parties themselves and their systems of interaction were fundamental in the nation- and state-building processes, and the standards of legitimacy that took shape. In short, they were essential to the character of the political structures and political culture on which the state of Israel was founded. State-building was one fundamental role played by legislatures as they developed historically.[38] European legislatures originated as monarchs, limited in power by the decentralized nature of feudalism and its system of privileges, summoned and consulted notables from various localities to obtain consent to and ensure the implementation of policies. The evolution of the British parliament provides one example of this process. Similar factors were at work in Zionist politics since Herzl, by establishing the ZO at a congress of delegates from some two dozen countries, aimed not only to create a nationalist organizational framework but also to establish a constituency for himself as he pursued his Zionist diplomacy. Since the ZO at first had few resources and no coercive powers, its Congress was essentially a means of consultation and consent, although after it attained an official status under the British Mandate, and as its fund-raising institutions achieved some success, control of it carried with it more than symbolic powers.

By the 12th Zionist Congress in Carlsbad in 1921 there were three identifiable blocs. The dominant group were the 'General Zionists', who were bourgeois centrists and claimed, as did Herzl, to express the general interest of the Jewish nation as opposed to those who sought to synthesize Jewish nationalism with any other 'ism'. The Religious Zionists were concentrated in Mizrahi. Finally there were the Labour Zionists, who were as yet minor actors in ZO politics. Many of the factions within these blocs eventually developed party organizations. 'Just as all men bear all their lives the mark of their childhood', writes Duverger, 'so parties are profoundly influenced by their origins'.[39] He notes that 'externally created' parties – those that emerge outside a legislature and not originally as a faction within it – tend to be more coherent, disciplined and centralized than their internally created counterparts. Externally created parties also do not tend to emphasize their parliamentary activities.[40] This was certainly the case in Zionist politics with particularly important consequences as we shall see; the General Zionists, created internally, were organizationally especially weak during the pre-state period, whereas the externally created Labour parties tended to develop strong organizational infrastructures and at first concentrated more on building their own communal and class base in Palestine than on politics within the ZO's institutional framework.

This would be one key to Labour's later rise to dominance; whereas European assemblies developed in the context of existing, (at least loosely) territorialized social orders, the Zionist effort, focused as it was on establishing a Jewish society in Palestine through immigration, had to construct the very base on which political institutions could be sustained. Consequently it was inevitable that the gravity of Zionist politics would increasingly shift to Palestine rather than remain in Europe – irrespective of Hitler – and it did so decisively by the 1930s. Since Palestine was the object of the Zionist endeavour, Palestincentrism inevitably implied that whoever was most successful in building a base there would be politically dominant. Labour was not only most successful at this, it essentially defined the Yishuv (the Palestinian Jewish community) as it was being built, and translated the power it developed there into dominance of its institutions and then of the ZO.

Under Ottoman rule the religiously orthodox pre-Zionist Jewish settlement in Palestine, known as the 'old Yishuv', relied largely on charity (the 'Halukah' system) from Jews abroad for its sustenance, and had no extensive structure. It did have a certain autonomy by virtue of the 'millet' system in which the Sultan allowed each millet, or religious community, significant self-control of its own internal affairs. Palestine at the time was not an entity in itself and was divided administratively, the north being part of the *Vilayet* (province) of Beirut, the south of the *Sanjak* (district) of Jerusalem and the east (mostly within today's Jordan) of the *Vilayet* of Damascus. Under Ottoman suzerainty, which lasted until Allenby's armies occupied the country in 1917, a chief rabbi (the *Haham Bashi*) served as the religious/political leader of the Sefardi Jews in the empire, by the grace of the Sublime Porte. (Since this rabbi was Sefardi, he was not recognized by the Ashkenazi Jews of Palestine who, by and large, were an alien enclave under the aegis of capitulations.) Important aspects of the millet system were later carried over into the administration of the British Mandate.

There were several attempts to establish a self-governing or representative authority for Palestine Jews. One of them was at the initiative of Ussishkin and the Odessa Committee in 1903. Plans were made for an elected congress (a 'Knessiyah') of Palestinian Jewish representatives who would be entrusted with creating an over-arching organization. Ussishkin wanted one structured like the ZO.[41] The effort failed, largely because of Herzl's opposition to creating a political institution before the Jews had established legal rights to the country, and also because of his own disputes with Ussishkin, to which we shall return shortly. With the British occupation of Palestine at the end of the First World War, the 1917 issuance of the Balfour Declaration affirming Whitehall's support of a Jewish national home in Palestine, and then the advent, in 1922, of the Mandate awarded to London by the League of Nations to create that home, self-organization became imperative. The first Asefat ha-Nivharim (Elected Assembly) of Palestinian

Jews was elected in 1920, and in turn it created the Vaad Leumi (National Council) as its executive arm. Here, as in the ZO, various factions and parties struggled for control and contested elections, which, as in the ZO, were conducted by means of party lists and proportional representation.

In 1927 the Mandatory authorities gave official recognition to the organization of the Yishuv as a whole (known as 'Knesset Israel'), and the Asefat ha-Nivharim in particular, 'as a religious community' on the basis of the Religious Community Ordinance of 1926. The Asefat ha-Nivharim was deemed 'representative of the community . . .' and given the right 'to levy upon its members a rate or rates' for educational and other social welfare purposes. However, the 'Jewish Community Regulations' also stipulated that a registrar for Palestine Jewry be established, and that anyone could, by a relatively easy method of requesting that his name be struck off, opt out of membership in the 'recognized community'. This practice was undertaken by significant segments of the orthodox and Old Yishuv communities who objected to participation for numerous religious and political reasons.[42] This demonstrated pointedly the non-sovereign character of the Asefat ha-Nivharim which, like the ZO, had no coercive capacities or means by which to guarantee discipline or unity in support of its decisions. Critics could simply secede. On the other hand, many secular Zionists were profoundly uncomfortable with the religious designation, a product of the millet tradition, of the Palestine Jewish Community Organization. However, they were willing, by and large, to take whatever autonomy they could achieve and to build on it. Thus they hoped to broaden its scope and nationalize its character so that it would be increasingly responsive to their own long-term goals.

Article 4 of the Mandate called for the creation of an 'appropriate Jewish Agency' to serve as 'a public body for the purpose of advising and cooperating with the Adminstration of Palestine in such economic, social, and other matters as may effect the establishment of the Jewish national home and the interests of the Jewish population in Palestine, and, subject to the control of the Administration to assist and take part in the development of the country'.[43] The Zionist Organization was designated as that Agency; however, by the end of the 1920s its president, Haim Weizmann, created an extended 'Jewish Agency' which left the ZO intact, but also allowed for the participation of well-to-do and prominent non-Zionist diaspora Jews, particularly through financial aid, in building the homeland. Thus, politically speaking, two parallel bodies, the ZO/Jewish Agency and the Asefat ha-Nivharim, had been established, with parallel structures. The former, however, by virtue of its status within the Mandate and its increasing command of wider resources, was the more powerful. A working arrangement developed whereby the Zionist Executive was responsible for general affairs pertaining to the creation of a Jewish national home in Palestine, and particularly relations with London, while the Vaad Leumi of the Asefat ha-Nivharim concerned itself primarily with the local issues of the Yishuv.[44] Tensions were none the less inevitable, but effective co-ordination was achieved in particular through the role of political parties within them, especially after Mapai came to dominate both institutions.

In addition, both institutions played important roles in shaping a political culture that facilitated a democratic Israeli political system. The general patterns of Israeli politics – the party system, an electoral system of proportional representation, coalition governments – were all established in the pre-state period. A national political leadership was also formed that had experience in administration as a result of running Zionist institutions. Various scholars have noted the impact of Russian political culture – which was anything but democratic – on the development of the Zionist leadership.[45] There is much truth in these observations. At the same time it should be noted that in the Zionist Congress and in the Asefat ha-Nivharim, Zionist leaders underwent substantial preparatory experience for democratic, legislative politics. The Israeli experience is partly comparable to that of the United States in that by the time of American independence a generation of leaders had been formed who were already well practised in legislative (though, unlike Israel, not party) politics in local assemblies.[46] The latter were, in fact, 'the only institutions of the colonial government which American settlers controlled'.[47] It was in these assemblies that 'the political interests of the colonists were advanced with increasing success against royal governors.'[48] Similarly the ZO and the Asefat ha-Nivharim were used to further Jewish interests and self-government in conflict with a British administration, while at the same time giving a generation political training.

III

Had the ZO followed Herzl's political Zionist strategy exclusively after his death, we can almost surely say in historical retrospect, it would not have attained its goals. This is not to say that his concept of a charter was entirely misconceived. The Balfour Declaration was a sort of charter. It was concretized by the establishment of the Mandate which, albeit only in its early years, greatly facilitated the Zionist project. The Declaration's architect, however, was Haim Weizmann, a foe of Herzl and disciple of Ahad Ha-am, who believed that a 'charter' was only part of the Zionist task, and that without practical effort in Palestine its promise might well not be fulfilled.

Zionism's success was significantly due to the strategic reformulation known as 'synthetic Zionism', a union of political, practical and cultural efforts. At the eighth Zionist Congress in August 1907 synthetic Zionists began their ascendancy, and one of them, Arthur Ruppin, was dispatched to Palestine to open a ZO colonization office there. Weizmann told the

Congress that, for him, political Zionism was 'a synthesis of activities in all fields of practical work, as a means towards achieving the political end – the Charter – which will be the result of practical work'. He added: 'We must strive for the Charter, but as a result of our exertions within the country. If the governments issue us a Charter today, it is merely a scrap of paper. But if we work in Palestine, then it is written in sweat and blood, and bound together with a cement that will never lose its hold'.[49] At the ninth Zionist Congress in Hamburg in 1909 there were still intense conflicts between political and practical Zionists. None the less, it endorsed a proposal by the German Jewish sociologist Franz Oppenheimer to commence a program of co-operative agricultural settlements in Palestine. Finally at the Congress of 1911, again in Basle, David Wolfsohn, Herzl's much weaker successor as president of the ZO, resigned and the era of political Zionism came to an end.

Although Weizmann in his autobiography, *Trial and Error*, took credit for the term 'synthetic Zionism', and although he was its most prominent champion, the idea had been in the air for some time. At the Helsingfors conference of Russian Zionists in 1906 one delegate, Simon Weissenberg, suggested a Hegelian triad: Hibat Zion's practical Zionism was the thesis, Herzl's political was the antithesis, the programme of the future would be that of synthesis.[50] An especially influential presentation of synthetic Zionism appeared in a 1904 pamphlet by Ussishkin, the irascible and forceful Russian Zionist leader. 'Among the closer friends of Herzl', writes Shmarya Levin, '[Ussishkin] was regarded as an opponent of the latter because he symbolized the old days when Zionism was centered more on Palestine than on the political setting, the days when – so it was said – a goat in Palestine counted for more than the promise of a chancellery'.[51] The practical differences between their approaches – which in fact reflected long-standing differences between Herzl and the Russian Zionists – can be seen in their 1903 controversy over Ussishkin's unsuccessful effort to create a communal infrastructure for Palestine Jewry.

At the time that Ussishkin was chairing the meeting of the *Knessiyah* in Palestine in August 1903, the Uganda Plan was debated in Basle by the sixth Zionist Congress. At Herzl's behest the Congress voted to send an exploratory commission to East Africa.[52] Ussishkin, a 'Zion Zionist', was an ardent foe of the Uganda Plan. Unable to be at the Congress to oppose it, he published a letter the following October in *Die Welt* addressed to the Congress delegates denouncing Herzl's effort. By agreeing to send the exploratory committee, he fumed, the Congress betrayed Zionism. He pointedly declaimed that 'all the majorities in the world ... will not dissuade me from Erets Israel ... [O]nly those who were so blinded by diplomacy and extravagant political talk failed to notice in their naiveté that the decision of the Zionist Congress to send an expedition to any other country constitutes a renunciation and abandonment of Palestine'.[53]

Stung by this, Herzl in his reply focused not on the Uganda Plan but on Ussishkin's recent activities in Palestine which, in his view, were doomed to failure. (They did fail, but partly because Herzl's prestige was so great among Palestinian Jews – despite Uganda – that his opposition to the *Knessiyah* was sufficient to undermine it.) Herzl chastised what he called Ussishkin's 'utter inexperience in politics', and criticized him for having 'convened a small secret assembly' which would inevitably induce adverse Turkish reaction: 'I cannot imagine that the Turkish government will permit the Jews in Palestine, of all peoples, to have an independent representative assembly when it does not permit such independence, even under military pressure from all the Great Powers, to other peoples, that is to Mohammedans and the Christians within its realm'.[54] In Herzl's mind Ussishkin's effort represented all the misconceptions of practical Zionism. A land could not be obtained by purchasing parcels of it and moving step by step; rather, the key was 'acquisition under civil law and under international law'. Referring to the town in which Ussishkin resided, Herzl declared that a 'first-year law student' knew that 'Even if he were to buy every existing parcel of land in Yekaterinoslav, Yekaterinoslav politically will not belong to him but to the Russian sovereign, and woe to Mr. Ussishkin if he were to take it into his head to do anything on land acquired under civil law that was against the laws and regulations of the empire'.[55]

This demonstrated a certain ignorance on Herzl's part of the efficacy of law in the provinces of the Ottoman empire. (It was also hardly a fair representation of Ussishkin's position.) Most of Herzl's foes were not opposed to diplomatic activities *per se*; they simply did not have great faith in the prospects for their success. Even those with a more optimistic prognosis believed that beginning to rebuild Jewish Palestine was prerequisite to the establishment of a Jewish national home; if political Zionism did not succeed, at least a basis would exist for further struggle. Ironically, it was among the Russian Zionists like Ussishkin, representatives of the most embattled Jewish community, that the most fervent foes of a refuge outside Palestine were to be found.

The Zionism Ussishkin articulated particularly impressed Russian Jewish youth. (I use 'articulated' in a qualified sense since, though a forceful orator, Ussishkin, a man renowned for his stubbornness, had a penchant for mangling the several languages he knew; 'Ussishkin's obstinacy', a friend commented, 'went so far that he refused to yield even to the laws of grammar'.[56]) In 1902, at the Russian Zionist conference in Minsk, at which anti-Herzl forces sought to marshal themselves, Ussishkin called for a resurrection of the BILU idea. Two years later, in the same year as Herzl's death, this was placed within a broad strategy in his pamphlet entitled 'Our Programme'. While it emphasized practical work in Palestine, Ussishkin called for a three-pronged effort that would simultaneously be practical, political and cultural.

The failures of Zionism in the past, he insisted, were due to one-sided approaches; Hibat Zion's focus was practical, the ZO's was diplomatic and cultural Zionism's was spiritual renaissance. The three had to be brought together. However, he was particularly adamant against a policy entirely predicated on obtaining a charter. For a people to make a land its own ultimately required not the grace of princes, potentates and ministers, but the building of a national community in the land, a mixing of the people's sweat with its soil: 'Long before a state is established the territory must actually belong in an economic and in a political sense to that people which desires to form a center in it. Its whole life must be dependent upon this people, which must be possessor *de facto*, even though not as yet *de jure*.'[57]

Ussishkin called for co-operative Jewish agricultural settlements in Palestine, following Oppenheimer's suggestions. In such communities, Ussishkin warned, the principle of 'self-labour' must reign; hiring inexpensive Arab labourers to work for Jewish farmers would corrupt the entire enterprise of re-creating the Jews as a nation. The Jews could only reclaim the land of Israel by working it and rooting their lives in it. Otherwise the new Jewish society would be on top of a volcano, for inevitably the Arabs would resent *their* sweat building the future of another people. What was needed, he proclaimed, hoping to inspire a new generation, was a neo-BILU vanguard, a 'Jewish Universal Society of Workmen' composed of single, strong youths, each willing to go to Palestine for three years 'in order to perform his military duty to the Jewish people, not with musket and sword, but with plow and sickle'.[58]

The year in which Ussishkin's pamphlet appeared marked the beginning of the Second Aliyah. In the decade before the First World War a new wave of Jewish immigration came to Palestine that was to have a decisive impact. It was influenced by the revolutionary winds then blowing strong in the eastern Europe of its origins, as well as by Ussishkin's call for a new BILU. The Second Aliyah brought to Palestine rebellious Jewish youth who had visions of linking socialist universalism to nationalist particularism; this would take concrete shape, as will be shown in the next section, in experimental social institutions and communities – experiments that laid the foundations for the creation of the state of Israel, and which originally developed outside the political battles of the ZO, though with the ZO's aid.

To Moses Hess, that sanctifier of history who called for a Jewish socialist state as one link in a chain of human redemption, a friend wrote, in response to the publication of *Rome and Jerusalem*: 'you world reformers are really strange saints, you take the stages of development of your personalities and your momentary thought processes very easily for the development of the actual period and the real world'.[59] The young radicals of the Second Aliyah did just that: they took the development of their personal crises as Jewish youth in a world of oppression, revolution and failed hopes to be that of their people, because they believed these crises to be one and the same. If we may borrow from Acton, they linked 'the sense of present evil' to a 'new notion of happiness', and in so doing fashioned the Zionist Labour movement and its strategy of state-building. It is to these strange saints that we now turn.

Part Two
Struggle

4
From a Working Class
to a Working Nation

Our urge for life whispers hopefully in our ear:
Workers' Settlements, Workers' Settlements.
Workers' Settlements – this is our revolution.
The only one.

Y. H. Brenner[1]

I

The Abbé Sieyès identified the Third Estate as 'a complete nation'. Hegel characterized the bureaucracy as the 'universal class' because he saw the state as the embodiment of the universal, and civil servants as that class which, in pursuing the interests of the state, pursued the interests of the whole. For Marx, the proletariat was bound by 'radical chains' because in its oppression all oppression was to be seen. By its liberation – through the creation of a classless society in which each would contribute according to his abilities and receive according to his needs – all would in fact be liberated; the proletariat was the class whose interests were universal interests, and whose victory would usher in a new age, that of socialism. The Zionist Labour movement in Palestine was built by youthful 'strange saints' of the type of which Moses Hess's correspondent wrote; they identified their personal crises and development with those of their people, and envisioned the emerging Jewish working class in Palestine as the universal class of the Jewish nation. This class was not only the vanguard of a Jewry being re-created, but, they believed, the nation would be reborn in its image. In the decade before the First World War, radical young immigrants of the Second Aliyah sought to lay the foundations for such a future.

'The interests of the workers', declared one of their number in 1911, 'and the general national interests – are one and the same'.[2] Eighteen years later the same individual, David Ben-Gurion, told the Council of the Histadrut (the General Confederation of Jewish Labour in Palestine), of which he was now Secretary-General, that 'The question of Hebrew labour in the Land of

Israel is not a class question, but a Zionist question . . . The economic value of labour in the nation's existence determines the social value of the worker in the nation's life. The actualization of Zionism conditions and obliges the working class in Palestine to greatness'. The worker had a 'decisive responsibility for actualizing Zionism' and this determined his 'character, thought, and hierarchy of values'. In contrast to the wretched status of the Jewish proletarian in the diaspora, in Palestine he/she exemplified the historical values of the nation. The Jewish working class was not just a vanguard of a beleaguered people; its purpose was to enact a revolutionary metamorphosis in Jewish life through its self-transformation 'from a working class to a working nation'.[3]

This meant, at least theoretically, that the working class ought to be the leading, if not the ruling, class in the Zionist movement. However, this was not how the Zionist left, at the turn of the century, originally projected the development of a Jewish national home. In fact the Zionist left at first assumed that the Jewish bourgeoisie would direct, activate and dominate the colonization process much as the European bourgeoisie had built European capitalism; and indeed, as we shall see in the following chapters, once Labour attained hegemony within the ZO, it retreated from the identification of class and national interests – although it was this identity which allowed it to establish its spiritual and organizational dominance. And it is this development that created the system of Zionist, and then Israeli, party politics.

In the 1920s Zionist Labour assumed along with Marx and Engels that 'The ideas of the ruling class are in every epoch the ruling ideas: i.e., the class which is the ruling *material* force of society is at the same time its ruling *intellectual* force . . .'[4] Labour successfully created the means by which it would define and dominate the material organization of immigration and the developing Yishuv in the decade after the First World War. The centrality, for the Zionist movement, of the absorption of immigrants into the country and the apparatus Labour constructed were critical to this process, as was the fact that the first major wave of postwar immigration, the 'Third Aliyah', was peopled, once again, by eastern European youth who were inspired by revolutionary fervor in the wake of the Bolshevik revolution. Marx and Engels had also argued that 'the existence of revolutionary ideas in a particular period presupposes the existence of a revolutionary class'.[5] In Palestine, such a class hardly existed in the Jewish community; the Zionist Labour movement saw itself building it. As a result, a peculiar constellation emerged whereby a barely existing class came to be posited as the universalizing agent of national liberation for a particular people. This position, however, was consequent, not anterior, to the organization of the Zionist left.

Zionist politics was a fervently articulated politics, in part because many of the early eastern European Zionists were children of both *maskilim* and an era of revolution, nationalism, and anti-Semitism. Strongly ideological politics was also a function of the very project of Zionism – the redrawing of political, psychological, economic and of course physical boundaries of the Jewish people. Early Labour Zionism, as we have noted, was not preoccupied with Zionist Congress politics, even though Nahman Syrkin served as a lonely voice of socialist opposition to Herzl. More importantly the dynamic and visionary Syrkin sought, in the years after the first Congress, to articulate a coherent synthesis of socialist and Zionist ideas, a project in which he was considerably more successful than in his efforts at organization. His 1898 pamphlet, 'The Jewish Question and the Socialist Jewish State' mixed utopian socialist and populist notions with nationalism in order to assert that 'A classless society and national sovereignty are the only means of completely solving the Jewish problem'.[6] He posited a perennial tension between Jews and non-Jews that had reached a critical point with the emergence of bourgeois society, which he characterized as *bellum omnium contra omnes*. The religious Jew-hatred of the Middle Ages, he perceived, had been replaced by a racial anti-Semitism. This, in turn, was especially potent in the middle classes, which were being undermined by big capitalists, and in the peasantry, which was being exploited or undermined by the big landowners. As Syrkin argued:

> The more the various classes of society are disrupted, the more unstable life becomes, the greater the danger to the middle class and the fear of proletarian revolution ... the higher the wave of anti-semitism will rise. The classes fighting each other will unite in their common attack on the Jew. The dominant elements of capitalist society, i.e., the plutocrats, the monarchy, the church, and the state, seek to exploit the religious and racial struggle as a substitute for the class struggle.[7]

While Jews may once have served useful economic functions in their host societies, these roles had become a general liability with capitalist development and the emergence of indigenous elements seeking now to displace them. All around him Syrkin saw forces at work subverting the Jewish future and requiring a new basis for Jewish life. A socialist Zionist state was what he proposed, and he called on the Zionist movement to commence a programme of socialist colonization based on communal settlements. In this way, 'from the outset' the Jewish state would 'avoid the ills of modern life'.[8] Class struggle had no place in such a programme; socialist development would preclude the need for it. In a powerful 'Call to Jewish Youth' in 1901 he vigorously denounced 'reactionary bourgeois Zionists' for advocating programmes of capitalist colonization, which he insisted doomed Zionism by introducing 'those class interests and social conditions which will destroy Zionism'.[9] If the narrow, profit-oriented interests of the bourgeoisie dictated Zionist strategy, it would of necessity provoke class war and the undermining of the Jewish national project, in Syrkin's view. 'When class-hatred and bankruptcy will come instead of liberation and rebirth', he declared, 'the reactionary Zionists will be adjudged guilty before the tribunal of history'.[10] His alternative was a Jewish commonwealth built from the outset on co-operative foundations. While not insistent on Palestine as the site for this state – and later, from 1903 to 1909, Syrkin thought that the dire Jewish straits demanded a state in *any* available territory – he saw it as the best option in 1898, and he envisioned Zionism struggling 'in alliance with other oppressed nationalities in the Turkish empire through a common stand against the Turks'.[11]

The emergence of an organized Zionist left came between 1897 and 1906, a period in which Jewish political formations, especially in eastern Europe, were galvanized. It was the youth that tended to take the centre of the political stage. If the impetus for mass Jewish politics and organization came in the early 1880s, it was now that it crystallized. In 1897 both the Zionist Organization and the Jewish Labour Bund were formed, respectively in Basle and Vilna. The Bund was a socialist (anti-Zionist) organization that came to espouse national cultural autonomy in the diaspora and grew into the most potent force in the eastern European Jewish left. In contrast to the Zionists, its cultural orientation focused on Yiddish, the daily spoken language of the east European Jewish masses.[12] In addition to the Bund, an entire spectrum of leftwing Jewish groups came on to the scene and Jewish participation in general politics grew as well; at times almost a third of the political arrests in the Tsar's empire were of Jews.[13] Also, the Russian General Zionists were mobilized under Ussishkin's leadership and non-Zionist liberals organized.

The situation took on a character of urgency after eastern European Jews were traumatized by more pogroms, beginning with the murder of 47 Jews in Kishinev in 1903. 'For the Jewish people', proclaimed Syrkin, 'the Kishinev pogrom is the finger of history'.[14] There would be new outbursts in the revolutionary years of 1905–6 leaving well over a thousand dead. The Jewish response to these events was, however, significantly different from that of the 1880s. There was now an organized Jewish politics, there were publicly articulated Jewish political ideologies and programmes, and there were armed Jewish self-defense groups that arose spontaneously or were organized by Jewish political parties.[15] A Union for Equal Rights, composed of liberals and Zionists, was formed in 1905 and advocated civil equality for Jews and the convening of a Jewish national assembly. The third Congress of Russian Zionists, meeting in Helsingfors (Helsinki) in December 1906, endorsed *Gegenwartsarbeit* (work-in-the-present), the principle that Zionists would not only focus on Palestine but would also struggle on behalf of Jewish needs and rights in the diaspora, as well as for a democratized Russia in which all nationalities would have autonomy. Amidst these events a young Odessa Jew named Vladimir Jabotinsky, one of the architects of

Helsingfors, became especially prominent for his opposition to class politics and for his advocacy of the convening of a Russian Jewish national assembly.

All the parties presented themselves on the Jewish street as champions of its future, especially concerned to capture the hearts of the young. The Zionists feared that the Bund would carry the day for socialist revolution, the Bund feared the Zionists would lead Jews astray to Palestine. 'The party', as Frankel writes, '. . . provided an organizational outlet for long pent-up energies now released; a fraternal brotherhood in which the youth could merge with the workers; a romantic world of self-defense and combat units; and an ideological map showing the way step by step from present distress to future salvation'.[16] One such path was charted by the Zionist left, which first emerged in the form of scattered groups identifying themselves as socialist and Zionist. As early as 1897 a group called the 'Poale Zion' (Workers of Zion) was founded in Minsk and in the five years after the turn of the century other Poale Zion groups appeared in various parts of the Pale, in the Austro-Hungarian empire, in the United States and in Britair. However, these hardly composed a movement, were disunited and tended to fragment over pressing – and sometimes not-so-pressing – issues. Of particular dispute was whether Poale Zionists should concern themselves with Russian revolutionary politics or solely the Zionist endeavour. On this question 'Blues' (particularly the Minsk group), who favoured the latter course, were divided from the 'Reds', who supported involvement in Russia.

To complicate matters, the British government's offer to Herzl of a possible Jewish homeland in East Africa (the 'Uganda Plan') led to further splits, as it did within the Zionist movement as a whole. 'Territorialists', which on the left meant primarily the Zionist Socialist Labour party (the ZS), which Syrkin joined, argued that romantic yearnings for Palestine ought to be disregarded because of the actual dangers the Jews faced. The Jews needed a territory sooner rather than later – *any* territory. The ZS was opposed by the 'Zion Zionists' who insisted that only Palestine could be a Jewish national home. Yet another group, the *Vozrozhdeniye* (Renaissance), supported a territorial solution to the Jewish question, but saw this as a long-term prospect and therefore struggle for Jewish autonomy in the diaspora had to be primary in the meantime. The influence of *Vozrozhdeniye* went beyond its small numbers because of its influential journal, and in 1906 it became part of a new party, the Seimists (or SERP, the Jewish Socialist Workers' party) which, based in the Ukraine, advocated national autonomy on a personal rather than a territorial basis, and projected a future Russia in which a multitude of nationalities would each have its own Seim (parliament) in a confederal framework. Combined with the Bund, this plethora of political parties offered numerous possibilities for leftist Jewish youth to find political expression.[17]

It was within this context that Ber Borokhov's impact was felt. A radical young intellectual from Poltava in the Ukraine, Borokhov came from a

Hibat Zion family and was influenced by Marxism, philosophical empirio-criticism and the attempt to bring these two together by the eclectic theorist and later rival of Lenin, A. A. Bogdanov. Borokhov was briefly an organizer for – and then expelled from – the Russian Social Democratic party in Yekaterinoslav, where he also founded a short-lived Zionist socialist group in 1901. He spent several years working closely with Ussishkin and the General Zionists, and was a fervent foe of the Uganda Plan.[18] In late 1905 and early 1906, with the encouragement of Ussishkin, Borokhov sought to pre-empt the other forces on the left by creating a united Poale Zion party that would be wedded to Zionism and Palestine (as opposed to terri-torialism) while simultaneously advocating autonomy for the Jews in Russia and their participation in the revolutionary struggles there. The Jewish Social Democratic Workers' Party-Poale Zion (henceforth Poale Zion) was formed in the winter of 1906. At the centre of its founding conference in Poltava was Borokhov and his close friend Itshak Ben-Tsvi (the only participant who had actually been to Palestine). The party's organizational success in Russia was limited and severely handicapped when Borokhov and other leaders were arrested in June 1906 after the tsarist police found an arms cache in the Ben-Tsvi home. As Ben-Tsvi, who managed to escape the round-up, put it, 'the Poltava period of our movement ended in total rout'.[19]

The impact Poale Zion did have was due to the synthesis of Zionism and Marxism that composed the party programme. This was primarily the work of Borokhov, developed first in a late 1905 essay on 'The National Question and the Class Struggle', and then in 'Our Platform', written for the new party early the next year. Borokhov not only provided an ideological formulation attractive to radical Russian Jewish youth, but he sought to give, within a Marxist framework, a justification for Zionism and a strategic perspective on its fulfilment. That strategic perspective was to have an important role within left Zionist politics in Palestine as well as in Russia.

'Proletarian Zionism is possible only if its aims can be achieved through class struggle', declared Borokhov. 'Zionism can be realized only if Proletarian Zionism can be realized'.[20] Borokhov, as discussed in chapter 1, supplemented Marx's notion of 'relations of production' with his own concept of geographical, anthropological and historical 'conditions of production'. By this he sought to explain the birth of nations and national conflicts through the fact that production is dependent on different conditions in different times and places. He distinguished normal conditions of production – wherein a nation inhabits a particular land and there are increasing class antagonisms according to the Marxist paradigm – from abnormal ones in which a scattered nation lacks a territory as its own strategic base, leading to an obfuscation of national and class consciousness. Consequently Borokhov – with the Jews clearly in mind – saw the need for a progressive nationalism of an oppressed proletariat which seeks to create normalized conditions of production. 'Our national consciousness is negative in that it is emancipatory. If we were the proletariat of a free nation which neither oppresses nor is oppressed, we would not be interested in any problems of national life'.[22]

He went on to argue that as part of an abnormal nation the Jewish proletariat was characterized by its economic marginality in its host countries and that it was compelled to follow its employers, chiefly the Jewish middle bourgeoisie, as they were constantly squeezed out and compelled to migrate by the linked forces of anti-Semitism and domestic national competition. In a later essay Borokhov sought to demonstrate on the basis of Russian census statistics what he called 'the prevailing law of Jewish economics, namely that the concentration of Jewish labour in any occupation varies directly with the remoteness of that occupation from nature'.[23] The general economic and class realities of diaspora existence, as such, were inherently vulnerable and were inevitably undermined, leading to what Borokhov called a 'stychic' or spontaneous migratory process which, he thought, would inevitably lead the Jews to Palestine. In Palestine Jewish petty capital and labour would be directed towards basic industry and agriculture, and thus the economic structure of Jewish life would begin to be normalized. Socialism, by means of the class struggle, was the Poale Zion's 'maximum programme', while its 'minimum programme' or 'immediate aim' was Zionism:

> The necessity of territory in the case of the Jews results from the unsatisfactory economic strategic base of the Jewish proletariat. The anomalous state of the Jewish people will disappear as soon as the conditions of production prevailing in Jewish life are done away with. Only when the Jews find themselves in the primary levels of production will their proletariat hold in its hands the fate of the economy of the country. When Jews participate in those sectors of economic life wherein the social fabric of the whole country is woven, then will the organization of the Jewish proletariat become free and not rely on the proletariat of the neighboring peoples.[24]

Normalized in their own land, occupying all levels of economic production, the Jewish proletariat would wage class war on its own grounds like – and in solidarity with – all other national proletariats.

Palestine, according to this theory, would evolve along capitalist lines as conceived by classical Marxism; it would be built through the initiative of capital, and class antagonisms and conflicts would ensue as a typical capitalist class structure took form. The development of the forces and relations of production would be in the hands of the Jewish bourgeoisie. 'Colonization methods' in a capitalist era were not the concern of the proletarian movement, for those methods were 'part of the creative sphere of capitalist activity, of the organization of production'. As a good Marxist, Borokhov posited that 'The bourgeoisie regulates the creative factors of the spontaneous process; the proletariat regulates the liberating factors'.[25] The strategic conclusion is clear: the task of Poale Zion as a class party was class organization in Palestine in anticipation of the future class war for socialism, not settlement projects or collabouration with the bourgeois Zionist Organization.

Ironically, while these theories played a critical role as a mobilizing ideology for the Zionist workers' movement, Labour's actual development and its rise to power in Palestine were in the end a result of its rejection of Borokhov's programmatic conclusions. This Marxist Zionism, whatever its brilliance, was formulated in the diaspora and it very quickly ran aground on Palestinian reality. That reality compelled its transcendence.

II

In 1905 two Zionist Labour parties were founded in Palestine. They both believed that socio-economic 'normalization' was essential to the Jewish future, that is, in their own national society the Jews would play all economic roles in contrast to their restricted and vulnerable occupational structure in the diaspora. This goal was fundamental to how Labour Zionism envisioned resetting the boundaries of Jewish life and required, first and foremost, the establishment of a Jewish working class in Palestine. Consequently, Zionism became 'the only major migration movement with *a conscious ideology of downward social mobility*'.[26]

The tasks these parties took upon themselves at first extended beyond those generally ascribed to political parties. There was no government they immediately sought to dominate or seize, Palestinian Jewry lacked any overall organizational structure and the two parties were preoccupied with caring for the basic needs of their small memberships which were composed of immigrant workers, mostly single and under the age of 25. It was especially important to find employment for them, primarily on farms owned by the remnants of the First Aliyah. Here, they found themselves competing with Arab workers willing to accept much lower wages and who were therefore much preferred by Jewish farmers concerned for their margins of profit and worried by the political radicalism of the immigrants. A bitter struggle for 'Jewish labour' on farms owned by Jews was to ensue. Indeed, if a class of Jewish agricultural labourers was not entrenched in the country, and if the national needs of the Jewish people were going to be determined by the profit requirements of a small class of farm owners, how could the Zionist project survive?

The two parties were not the first to concern themselves with the labour question in Palestine. The BILU, as we have seen, were advocates of Jewish 'self-labour'. A short-lived *Agudat ha-Poalim* (Workers' Association) was formed in 1887, followed in the 1890s by a *Histadrut ha-Poalim* (Workers' Union) which survived until shortly after the turn of the century. In 1897 a printers' union was organized and broken in Jerusalem; the severely exploited workers had to face not only the wrath of the shop owners but also that of the rabbinate since most books being printed in Jerusalem at the time were religious in nature. The rabbis had vested interests both in the product itself and in quashing the threatening appearance of a secular workers' organization. Five years later another printers' union was formed and called a strike which led to a bitter three-week labour struggle. A solution was finally reached, via rabbinical arbitration, by which a ten-hour working day was conceded to the workers, and the union was disbanded.[27]

Membership of the two parties founded in 1905 was largely eastern European in origins, mostly immigrants of the 'Second Aliyah' (1904–14). During this decade there was mass emigration of Jews from Russia, with almost a million coming to the United States and between 20,000 and 30,000 to Palestine. Somewhat less than a third of the arrivals were youth and, according to some estimates, as many as 90 per cent of the immigrants didn't remain in the country. Those who stayed and laid the foundations of the Jewish state had been profoundly affected by the Russian upheaval of 1905 (together with the array of political ideologies – Marxist, populist, anarchist – current in rebellious Russia) and especially the pogroms that came in its wake. 'The eruption of political creativity in Palestine was . . . directly linked to the disruption of Jewish life in Russia in the years 1903–08'.[28] Some immigrants, such as David Ben-Gurion, who had been active in the Poale Zion in his native town of Plonsk, Poland, came because of prior ideological commitment. Others came out of despair. Berl Katznelson, the future spiritual mentor of the Labour movement and a native of Bobruisk, White Russia, later explained his choice to go to Palestine after several years of drifting from one leftist Jewish circle in Russia to another: 'I did not arrive at this decision on the basis of Zionist convictions, but out of a feeling of bitter humiliation and obstinacy'.[29]

Both Ben-Gurion and Katznelson came from homes versed in the *Haskalah*, a common characteristic of many of the future Labour leaders. Several decades after the Second Aliyah the Labour movement's archives surveyed 937 of its veterans and found that half the Second Aliyah derived from south-western Russia, and that they were almost entirely literate. Some 23 per cent had been to secondary schools, almost half had attended *heder* (the traditional Jewish elementary school) or yeshiva, and a small number had been to university. Some 45.14 per cent were fluent in Hebrew and 13.02 per cent were partially so. (Sexual differentiation was significant in this regard: only 30 per cent of the men knew no Hebrew, against 60 per cent of the women.) Most were not from major urban centres, some 55.17 per cent being children of merchants and 19.3 per cent of manufacturers or craftsmen. Some 67 per cent (75 per cent of men) over the age of 14 had been politically affiliated abroad, including some 61 per cent of Poale Zion members who had been members of that party in the diaspora. About 30 per cent identified themselves as socialists.[30]

The Second Aliyah immigrants were dismayed by the situation they found in Palestine, and especially disdained those First Aliyah veterans who had abandoned 'self-labour' to become farm owners exploiting cheap Arab labour. The new immigrants insisted – as the BILU had – that 'autoemancipation' was both a political and an economic phenomenon: the quest for Jewish political self-determination required 'self-labour' and this, in turn, led to the ideology of 'Jewish labour'. They demanded that Jewish farmers hire solely Jewish workers, in contrast to the path of the *colon*. Ben-Gurion told an American audience in 1915 that 'we are ... creating a positive content for self-definition (*hagdarah*) and [in Palestine] we have the *unlimited objective possibilities* for a normal national development'. In the Yishuv, the Jew could develop his character in a natural way 'without the contradiction between being a man and a Jew'. Hence, 'an internally autonomous life, based on economic independence, creates the real content in the Yishuv for national self-definition'.[31] In that same year he wrote in an article that 'There are many different ways to conquer a land. It can be seized by armed force, it can be possessed by political devices and diplomatic agreements. A land can be purchased by cash. All these methods of conquest have a single goal: domination in order to enslave and exploit.' He cited imperial ventures such as that of Britain in India as examples. However, he insisted:

Not we. We don't ask for the land of Israel to dominate its Arabs and we don't seek a market for Jewish goods from the diaspora [*golah*]. We are seeking a homeland in the land of Israel – we want to shed the bitterness of exile ... A homeland is not given or received as if it was a gift; it is not acquired by privileges or political contracts, and it is not purchased with gold or conquered by force; rather it is built by the sweat of the brow. A homeland is the historical creation and the collective enterprise of a nation [*am*], the fruit of its physical, spiritual and moral labour over generations ... The source of true rights to a land – like everything else – is not in political or legal authority, but in the rights of labour. The true, actual owners of the land are its workers.[32]

Ben-Gurion presents in this passage all the fundamental themes of the early Zionist Labour movement. The building of Jewish Palestine entailed the rebuilding of the Jews as a people and as individuals; the right to the land itself was based on a labour theory of value, rooted undoubtedly both in Marxist and Russian populist notions – it is the worker who creates value and who therefore ought to be the owner of that with which he mixes his labour.

The Palestinian Poale Zion was founded in November 1905 in Jaffa. Many of its members had participated in self-defence groups during pogroms in eastern Europe and many had been, as we noted, Poale Zion members in the diaspora; they sought to remain faithful to orthodoxies, particularly Borokhovist ones, that originated there. A 'Letter from the Land of Israel' addressed to the editors of the Russian Poale Zion's *Evreiskaia Proletarskia Khronika*, dated February 1906 (but published the following July), informed readers that the Palestinian party's goal was 'the creation of a Jewish state on socialist foundations by means of the class struggle' and that the party had some 60 members, 40 of them in Judea and 20 in the Galilee.[33] The Palestinian Poale Zion had a decidedly Marxist character and saw itself as the Zionist wing of the world revolutionary movement. A committee was created to formulate a platform and, after meeting secretly in the Arab town of Ramle, produced an orthodox Borokhovist document, the 'Ramle Platform', which declared that 'the history of mankind is the history of national and class war'.[34] The platform was revised for the first general Poale Zion party conference in Jaffa in early 1907. Following the Borokhovist prognosis, the party assumed Palestine would develop along capitalist lines and that its task was similar to that of other socialist movements, that is, class organization of the emerging proletariat in preparation for the inevitable class struggle – not class collabouration with bourgeois Zionists (although Poale Zion did send representatives to the Zionist Congress in the summer of 1907).

In effect this meant that Poale Zion was to follow a dual track: on the one hand it sought 'class entrenchment' (*'bitsur ha-maamad'*) of the Jewish proletariat in Palestine, and on the other it prepared for the class war. The programme proposed in Jaffa declared that the party 'aims to make the means of production public and to build a society on socialist foundations. The party sees the class struggle, whose nature is dependent on conditions of time and place, as the sole means to this end'. The party urged democratization of Jewish communal institutions, the formation of unions and 'political autonomy' [*autonomiyah medinit*] for the Jewish nation' in Palestine.[35] In its first years the party began sponsoring various political activities, including May Day celebrations. In Sejara it helped create Palestine's first socialist commune and it was instrumental in the creation of Ha-Shomer (the Guard), the first Jewish self-defence association in the country. Poale Zion involved itself in strike activities with a particular impact in the Rishon Lezion wineries. Furthermore, the party supported a renewed effort to unionize the printers which, though successful initially, was again undermined by 1909 by the shop owners and the rabbinate after several clashes and a rabbinical 'ban' of the Labour movement. The failure of this strike illustrated, among other things, the difficulties the party faced when trying to influence young Jewish workers of non-European background and from the Old Yishuv, who were dominant in the printing trades.[36] Poale Zion was aware of this problem, but unable to find a way to solve it.

The other Palestine Labour party, Ha-Poel ha-Tsair (the Young Worker), was formed in the settlement of Petah Tikvah just several weeks before Poale Zion and, like the latter, foresaw capitalist development as the course for Palestine. Like Poale Zion it sought democratization of Jewish institutions and rights for Jewish workers and women. The disagreements between the two parties were significant, however, and the source of intense rivalry; throughout 1907 Ha-Poel ha-Tsair's leading ideologue, Yosef Aharonovitch, engaged in a series of public debates with Poale Zion's Ben-Tsvi. A few years later Aharonovitch explained the differences between the two parties in these terms:

> One [Ha-Poel ha-Tsair] aspired to the renaissance of the Hebrew nation in the full sense of the word, and envisioned Hebrew Labour as the principal means and a necessary condition for this renaissance, and the second [Poale Zion] aspired to the renaissance of the Hebrew proletariat in order to enable it to be distinguished [*lehitbalet*] within the world proletariat, and conceived Zionism as a means to this goal. One group became workers because they were Zionists and one group became Zionists because they were proletarians.[37]

The gap between the parties began with the fact that Ha-Poel ha-Tsair was non-Marxist, shunned the very word socialism and, influenced by Russian populism, Tolstoyan ideas and Ussishkin's call for a new BILU, tended to emphasize and romanticize the Jewish return to the soil and to nature. It represented a more narrow nationalism than Poale Zion, did not view itself as part of international socialism but, to the contrary, solely as part of the Zionist movement. The self-conception of Ha-Poel ha-Tsair, which founded a publication with the same name, was as an indigenous Palestinian formation, rooted in Palestinian and not diaspora realities and ideas. It opposed strike actions and especially the Marxist notion of class struggle, so ardently advocated by Poale Zion. The latter considered Ha-Poel ha-Tsair to be utopians. However, to Ha-Poel ha-Tsair a Marxist version of class struggle was entirely incongruent to a largely feudal, agricultural country like Palestine, which lacked a significant bourgeoisie or a proletariat, not to mention Jews. In a statement of its goals, the journal *Ha-Poel ha-Tsair*, edited by Aharonovitch, declared that class struggle was a 'facile phrase'. Who, it asked, 'are these struggling classes within the Jewish people as a whole and among the Jews in the Land of Israel, in particular? To what extent can this class struggle contribute to the development of an undeveloped land and to the growth of a workers' party in it?'[38] The tasks before Jewish workers in Palestine, it insisted, were unique, and it attacked the belief that Palestine would develop according to 'predetermined laws'. At a 1922 party meeting Itshak Vilkansky stated that Ha-Poel ha-Tsair was oriented to the workers because of their national value, not because of working-class issues in and of themselves. In terms similar to those later used by Jabotinsky and the Zionist right against the Labour movement, he called Marxism 'alien' to Zionism, and insisted that it distracted the Jewish national movement from its true purposes.[39]

As opposed to class war, Ha-Poel ha-Tsair stressed the therapeutic value that physical labour had for Jews coming from a diaspora ghetto existence; it proclaimed 'the dignity of labour' and a 'religion of labour'. These notions were expounded by A. D. Gordon who, though not a party member, was the spiritual mentor, virtually a guru, for the young workers. A middle-aged, middle-class Russian Jew who came to Palestine at the age of 48 to become a labourer, Gordon preached to the youth around him that 'Work will heal us . . . If only we set up work itself as the ideal – rather, if only we bring into the open the ideal of labour, we shall be cured of the disease which attacked us. We shall then sew together the rents by which we were torn from nature. Labour is a lofty human ideal, an ideal of the future'.[40] This was an inspiring claim for youths painfully struggling to change themselves into workers in the difficult conditions of Palestine; it gave meaning to their daily battles. 'We are in need', Gordon told them, 'of fanatics in the cause of labour . . .'[41] Ha-Poel Ha-Tsair's goal was the 'conquest of labour' by the Jews who, in its vision, were to be 'pioneers' in their ancient homeland, creating a Jewish agricultural proletariat. The idea of '*halutsiyut*', self-sacrificing 'pioneering', became the ethos of the Second Aliyah, replacing Judaism's religious ethnic myth with a secularized struggle for redemption in which the *Haluts*, or pioneer, became the image of the new Jew, plough in one hand, rifle in the other, building a new national future instead of praying in the diaspora for a return to Zion.

Within several years of their founding, both parties found that the pressure of realities compelled a rethinking of their strategies and activities. Concurrently new ideas for Zionist settlement were moving more and more to the fore. The ZO leadership, having come increasingly into the hands of synthetic Zionists, was receptive to proposals advanced by the German Jewish sociologist Franz Oppenheimer for the creation of a system of co-operative agricultural settlements in Palestine based on profit-sharing and self-reliance. By such means, it was suggested, the Jews would be socio-economically normalized through the creation of a new foundation in Jewish life, a labouring class retrieving the land. 'Every nationality depends upon the rooting of a mass of humanity in the soil . . .', insisted Oppenheimer. 'If Zionism wishes to create a new nation, it must lay the foundation for a peasantry deeply planted in the soil'. This would be accomplished through co-operative villages which, concurrently, would be the basis for turning Palestine into a Jewish land:

We shall spread a net of farming colonies over the country we wish to win. When one wishes to spread a net, one first drives in stakes at the points between which it is desired to place the net. Then one extends between these stakes powerful ropes, and between the ropes strong cords are knotted, thus forming a coarse meshwork, which then may be made as fine as one pleases by working in smaller cords.[42]

Oppenheimer addressed the sixth Zionist Congress in 1903, but it was at the ninth Congress (1909) that the decision was made to implement his ideas. This was also strongly favoured by Arthur Ruppin, who had been directing the ZO's Palestine office since its founding the previous year.

By the time such schemes came to the forefront, Poale Zion had become increasingly discouraged by its inability to suit its theoretical programme of class struggle to the world in which it was living. As one historian put it, Poale Zion underwent an 'absorption' process into the reality of Palestine.[43] This absorption ocurred on the cultural level as well as on that of politics and economics. The language in which party literature was to be published had already been a source of vigorous dispute. Since Yiddish was the mother tongue of most of the immigrants and party members, Poale Zion decided to put out a Yiddish publication, *Der Onfang* (The Beginning), despite the vehement opposition of those, like Ben-Gurion, for whom Yiddish was the language of the Exile and for whom Hebrew alone could be the language of the new society being created. The undermining of diglossia and the establishment of the primacy of Hebrew reflected the national transformation – the creation of a 'new Jew' who was of a different cultural and sociological character from his diaspora forebears – that Labour Zionism was proposing. Only two issues of *Der Onfang* appeared. Just as Poale Zion expected its adherents to transform themselves into Palestinian workers, the language controversy – which was enacted in various guises in other sectors of the Yishuv as well – symbolized the process by which Poale Zion itself became a Palestinian rather than a diaspora party. By 1910 a Poale Zion weekly named *Ahdut*(Unity) was appearing in Hebrew with an editorial board composed of party leaders Ben-Gurion, Ben-Tsvi, Yaakov Zerubavel, Rahel Yanait and the novelist Y. H. Brenner. Within its first year it gained 350 subscribers.[44] Poale Zion changed, it could be said, from a diaspora Marxist Zionist party into a Palestinian socialist Zionist party.

The transformation of the party's practical politics was to have enormous significance, and was a manifestation of the ideological flexibility that came to characterize the Labour Zionist movement as a whole. Recalling her thoughts after the Poale Zion's conference in autumn 1908, Rahel Yanait, one of its leading activists (and later wife of Itshak Ben-Tsvi), wrote in her memoirs: 'We were moving far from the dogmas followed by the Poale Zion abroad. Our movement here was shaped by the new life, by the actual needs of the workers who were winning the Land back by the work of their hands.

The movement abroad must adjust itself to this reality'.[45] Where the actual needs of the workers seemed to be pointing was towards co-operative workers' settlements and the building of a labour, as opposed to a capitalist, economy – something much closer to Syrkin's than to Borokhov's ideas.

At a series of meetings in Europe in 1909, the various sections of the World Union of Poale Zion bitterly argued this point. Borokhov, then in central Europe, vigorously contested, on behalf of the Russian Poale Zion, the idea of co-operative settlements which in his view represented a type of utopian, as opposed to Marxist, socialism. These settlements, he tried to persuade his comrades, would be dependent on outside (bourgeois) control and would lead to an emphasis on agricultural as opposed to capitalist and industrial development. Thus the classic Marxist paradigm would be negated along with its concept of class organization and conflict. In its place would come co-operation with bourgeois elements in pursuit of settlement schemes. 'We have no need of settlement programs', he declared at the Russian Poale Zion Council meeting in Vienna in September 1909. 'This is not the task of a worker's party'. The task was to organize Jewish workers for the class struggle.[46]

Borokhov's position was rejected in December in Crakow at the meeting of the World Union of Poale Zion, which also decided to create 'Kapai', a 'Workers' Fund of Erets Israel', to serve as its own independent financial arm to aid Palestinian workers. Aharonovitch, reflecting the anti-Marxist and anti-class struggle stand of Ha-Poel ha-Tsair, criticized the establishment of Kapai out of the fear that it would function partly as a strike fund.[47] The forces ranged against Borokhov's approach indicated the evolution Poale Zion was undergoing. The Palestinians, led by Ben-Tsvi, a close friend and protégé of Borokhov, supported a new approach, and endorsed implementing the Oppenheimer plan in the Galilee. They were backed by the Americans, who now included Syrkin in their ranks (he had abandoned territorialism), and the Austrians, led by Shlomo Kaplansky. The Austrian Poale Zionists were strong advocates not only of the Oppenheimer plan but also of inter-class co-operation within the Zionist movement. Kaplansky's approach was to have an important impact on the evolution of what became known as the 'constructivist' strategy of Labour Zionism. Born in Bialastok, he lived in Vienna from 1903 to 1912 where he played a central role in organizing the Austrian Poale Zion. Influenced by Fichte and Lassalle, as well as by German Revisionist and Austrian socialist thinking, Kaplansky claimed not merely that there should be inter-class co-operation within the Zionist movement, *but that the working class ought to lead the movement* and pursue a general strategy of building economic institutions and co-operative settlements in Palestine that would be the harbingers of the future society.[48] This was, in fact, to become Poale Zion policy.

The changes in Poale Zion occurred concurrently with changes taking place in Ha-Poel ha-Tsair, which from the beginning had insisted on the specificity of Palestine. The 'conquest of labour' by Jews, it had discovered, was consistently undermined by the rivalry of Arab workers. Young Jewish workers were severely handicapped. At first they attempted to live on the lower wages that Arab workers were able to accept, and also to lower their own living standards. This, it quickly became clear, was impossible. Not only were the Arab labourers used to an entirely different standard of living, but they had important advantages, especially the fact that working in Jewish colonies was frequently a supplement to income from elsewhere, often from plots of land on which their families worked.[49] Jewish youth arriving with no pecuniary means of their own and even less agricultural experience could barely compete with them under these circumstances. Jewish farm and orchard owners found it economically worthwhile to discriminate against them and the Arab economy was entirely closed to Jewish agricultural workers. Despite bitter struggles on behalf of 'Jewish Labour' – the demand that only Jews be hired and that cheap Arab labour not be exploited on both the privately owned Jewish farms and orchards and on those owned and established by the ZO – by the Poale Zion and Ha-Poel ha-Tsair conferences of 1910, their leaders were despondent; it seemed that eastern European Jews might never become Palestinian farm workers. In fact, 1909 had become known as the year of the 'Great Despair'. The 'conquest of labour' was clearly being defeated, the labour groups felt isolated, and it was increasingly evident that the hope that private capital would lead the way in developing the country was ill founded.

Restlessness became particularly acute among the workers on the few 'national farms' established by the ZO and subsidized by the Jewish National Fund with the intention that they eventually be divided and sold to settlers after the land was prepared under the direction of agronomists. As Ruppin explained it, the agronomist-administrators not only lacked 'an understanding for the national aims of our colonization work and for the psychology of the revolutionary youth who had come from Russia' but were 'prone to treat the Jewish workers simply as wage-earners without encouraging them to share in the direction of the work, while the workers, on their side, placed particular emphasis on their development in that direction'.[50] On the Kinneret farm and elsewhere there were strikes and labour conflicts over the issues of Jewish labour and working conditions. Ruppin, by this time, had also concluded that parallel efforts at ZO-sponsored individual agricultural settlements were foredoomed because the ZO lacked the resources required to subvene them, and the aspiring farmers lacked both their own means and the preparation for such an endeavour.

In short, the ZO office and the Labour parties (whatever their ideological differences) found their perspectives and needs converging pragmatically on what became known as 'constructivism' ('revolutionary constructivism' in the future parlance of the left), a strategy of public development and initiative. Jewish Palestine would be built by employing 'national capital' (funds collected through the Zionist movement) to finance socio-economic institutions capable of organizing and settling significant numbers of immigrant workers. The initiative of private capital, which was modest to begin with and which was preoccupied with returns on individual investments rather than the entrenchment of the Jews as a whole in the country, was thereby relegated to a secondary status. The institutions backed by national capital tended to be those of the Labour movement which had an ideology of collective organization and action in the first place. Consequently, workers' settlements, such as the kibbutz, became strategically central in this effort, and this meant that collective farming, rather than the creation of a wage-earning agricultural proletariat, became the *halutsic* model.

That the young pioneers had come to political consciousness in Russia, where populists and radicals extolled the *obshchina*, the village commune, as the foundation of a future socialist and national life, undoubtedly gave this change its own attraction. Herzen, Chernyshevsky, Lavrov, Tolstoy and Kropotkin celebrated the peasantry; the last-named proposed that labour was a value in itself and that 'mutual aid' was a law of nature and the basis of ethical life. Even after Plekhanov converted from populism to Marxism he maintained a faith in the *obshchina*, and Marx and Engels, while anticipating the possible development of a Russian communism, queried whether this 'form of the primeval common ownership of land' might 'pass directly to the higher form of communist common ownership' in their preface to the 1882 Russian translation (by Plekhanov) of *The Communist Manifesto*.[51] Working together as members of an agricultural commune the young Zionists, through the pooling of their efforts and through developing a system of mutual aid and support, could accomplish as a group what had apparently not been possible for individuals. Self-labour in a co-operative framework would be established, whilst they, like Oppenheimer's stakes, implanted themselves in Palestine and thereby fulfilled the national aim of enlarging the Zionist presence there. The stakes for the net would be workers' settlements and workers' institutions.

From Ruppin's perspective, constructivism provided the means by which the energy – and the lives – of the young immigrants could be channelled into accomplishing the practical needs of the Zionist cause. He would be one of their staunchest champions in struggles with those in the ZO – mostly middle-class General Zionists – who mistrusted their radicalism, objected to subsidizing communes and institutions run by socialists, and even found the entire notion slightly mad. When Max Nordau, colleague of Herzl, and adamant political Zionist and foe of practical Zionism, was told by a young pioneer of the plans for collectives, he suggested that a psychiatrist was in order.[52]

For the labour parties, constructivism meant the possibility of identifying the interests of the emerging workers' movement and its institutions with the interests and needs of the Jewish people as a whole; for those with a Marxist bent, this allowed a Zionist reworking of the classic Marxist theme of a universal class. Importantly, the shift to constructivism helped lay the foundations for future co-operation between the two Labour parties and also with a third force on the left called the 'Non-Party Group'. Led by Berl Katznelson, David Remez, Itshak Tabenkin, and Shmuel Yavnieli among others, this group was particularly prominent in the formation of the Judaean and Galilean Agricultural Workers' Unions in 1911 and was insistent in criticizing the party competition as counter-productive, especially given the meagre ranks and resources of the Zionist workers. Katznelson and his colleagues became fervent proponents of Labour unity and of finding frameworks that transcended the existing divisions.

During the period of the Second Aliyah and the First World War, in addition to parties and agricultural unions, the nascent Labour movement built a network of mutual aid institutions. These ranged from health services ('Kupat Holim' – the Sick Fund) and a co-operative clearing-house for the products of workers' settlements ('Ha-Mashbir'), to labour exchanges, a mobile agricultural library, a clerical workers' union, self-defence organizations and assorted co-operative settlements and institutions. This process was both disrupted and hastened by the difficult conditions the war brought to Palestine. The need for such institutions intensified in the beleaguered Yishuv. Although Turkish policy tended to vary throughout the war, as it dragged on the military authorities found harsh measures against the Jews expedient at different times and the Yishuv suffered repression and expulsions along with economic deprivation. Poale Zion was especially embattled owing to its radical political character. This undermined illusions it held briefly about 'Ottomanizing' itself and becoming active in the empire's politics, an idea which Ben-Gurion had been vocal in advocating. The Zionists, as well as Arab nationalists, greeted the Young Turk revolution of 1908 with much hope. It quickly became clear, however, that the new Turkish government was at least as unsympathetic to the aspirations of both peoples as its predecessor. Poale Zion had sought contacts with other socialist groups in the empire and Ben-Gurion, Ben-Tsvi and Israel Shohat (the head of *Ha-Shomer*, the self-defence organization) left for Constantinople to study law in 1911–12. In retrospect, their misreading of what was happening in the Ottoman empire is striking; when the war broke out Ben-Gurion, having returned to Palestine, was among those who unsuccessfully proposed to the Turkish commander the creation of a Jewish battalion to help defend the country.[53] (The ulterior purpose of this suggestion was, of course, Zionist – its acceptance would have enabled the arming and military training of Jews in Palestine.)

Any illusions, however, were shattered by the end of 1914 when *Ahdut* was closed down and Ben-Gurion, Ben-Tsvi and Shohat were expelled from the country. The remaining Poale Zion leadership, headed by Yanait and A. Blumenfeld, found itself involved in the trying tasks of sustaining the Yishuv. During the war the party organization fell apart for all practical purposes and there was an internal dispute, as there was among their comrades abroad, over whether to remain neutral or support the allies. The situation changed dramatically in 1917 with the Turkish collapse, and the occupation of the country by Britain. On 2 November, 1917 a brief British policy statement known as the Balfour Declaration proclaimed that His Majesty's Government viewed 'with favor the establishment in Palestine of a national home for the Jewish people', and would 'facilitate the achievement of this object' by its 'best endeavors'.[54] In addition, the exiled Poale Zion leaders, many of whom had gone to America, now returned wearing the uniform of the Jewish Legion, a unit created within the British army to serve in the Middle East theatre, largely as a result of the efforts of Vladimir Jabotinsky.

While the new situation called for new Labour Zionist political formations, the strategy that would dominate the following decade had already begun to crystallize, as we have seen. What the years 1904–17 yielded was the practice and the theory of an independent Jewish workers' economy; by means of this, Labour would build its political power, and take the lead both in creative settlement endeavours and in absorbing newcomers into the country. This would give Labour the tools by which to set the political, economic and spiritual boundaries of a Jewish nation-and-state-in-the making. The fashioning of a self-sufficient '*am oved*' (working nation) was to be the revolution of modern Jewish life. It would create a way of life that was the antithesis of that of the diaspora. This entailed an ongoing dialectic of kernel and shell: the working class, and the world it created, was to be both means and end, the subject and object, of Zionism. Hence the Ben-Gurion statement, quoted at the beginning of this chapter, that there was to be a transformation 'from a working class to a working nation'.

By the 1920s, then a strategic perception was in place: since the working class was the centre of the new society, the 'national capital' of the Jewish people ought to be channelled first and foremost to aid its development and that of its institutions. Private capital, concerned as it necessarily was with returns on investment, could not be depended on to take the lead in building Jewish Palestine. For the left, this implied that socialist and co-operative structures would be built forthwith, and would be the chief tool, indeed the embodiment, of the Zionist project. In turn, this meant that, as Syrkin had hoped, the evils of capitalism might in some way be bypassed, and that Labour's project would be carried out in collabouration with the 'bourgeois' ZO which, of course, still controlled the finances of national capital. Class struggle was not banished from Labour's political vocabulary, but clearly, if a socialist institutional structure for Jewish Palestine as a whole was to be built, it was no longer fully applicable in any Marxist sense and would become a somewhat ambiguous component of Labour's ideology.

Herein was at once the final shift from Poale Zion's original Marxism (and especially Borokhovism) to a Zionization of Marx's universal class in the form of 'revolutionary constructivism'. A particular nation would be remade in the image of its own universal class. The road of this revolution was not that of overthrowing a capitalist regime – there was no such regime to overthrow – but one of socialist building. The organization of this revolution, the embodiment of the transformation from a working class to a working nation, would be crystallized in the Histadrut, wherein the Labour leaders sought to unify their ranks and centralize their power.

5
Labour's Road to Dominance I

It is not a question of what this or that proletarian, or even the
whole proletariat, at the moment *regards* as its aim. It is a question
of *what the proletariat is*, and what in accordance with this *being*,
it will historically be compelled to do.

Karl Marx[1]

I

The steps taken by Labour's leaders at the close of the First World War were
characteristic of the movement's future *modus operandi*: they sought to
combine their ranks and to centralize and organize their quest for power.
The idea of Labour unity in the Land of Israel, most forcefully championed
by Berl Katznelson, was to become an almost sacrosanct notion, and
perhaps, in the minds of its advocates, a psychological counter-principle to
the dispersed status of Jewry elsewhere. Belief in unity, however, did not
mean its immediate realization. The existing organizations would have to be
convinced to abolish themselves.

The impulse to movement unification had already emerged during the
Second Aliyah and was expressed particularly in the hopes of Katznelson's
non-party circle that the agricultural workers' unions formed in 1911 might
be a model for a more all-embracing organization. At the end of the First
World War a variety of factors came into play that made unity particularly
sensible and that impelled Labour leaders to innovation.[2] In a short
time-span in 1917 the Balfour Declaration was issued, the Bolshevik
revolution occurred, the British army occupied Palestine and the Ottoman
empire collapsed. These cataclysms created a new situation for the Zionists,
as well as for east European Jewry. A heady, messianic atmosphere was
engendered among many in Labour, especially those in Poale Zion and the
non-party group serving in the Jewish Legion together. History, it seemed,
had opened revolutionary new possibilities and the means to take advantage
of them needed to be established.

While still in Jewish Legion encampments in Egypt in the autumn of 1918, Poale Zion's Ben-Gurion and Ben-Tsvi met with 'non-party' leaders Katznelson, Tabenkin, Yavnieli and Remez to discuss building a new formation. In fact Ben-Gurion, who was at this point asserting himself as party leader, originally pursued unification talks with Katznelson in secret without fully consulting the party or Ben-Tsvi. His growing personal closeness to Katznelson corresponded to a distancing from the more ideologically rigid Ben-Tsvi, then Poale Zion's principal intellectual force.[3] Ben-Gurion wanted a broad workers' party that would integrate both political and economic activities. Such a framework, he hoped, would supplant and encompass what already existed, and could be an antidote to the failures caused by the past fragmentation. Katznelson wanted a wide-reaching, non-sectarian labour organization that would generate unity within the workers' ranks through the creation of a 'workers' community'.

In contrast, Ha-Poel ha-Tsair, whose pacifist leanings, support for non-identification during the war and fears of Turkish reprisals and of losing workers from the settlements had led to a largely negative view of participation in the Legion, urged more circumspection. Whereas many Poale Zion members and adherents of the non-party group had enthusiastically joined the Legion's ranks, A. D. Gordon had strongly opposed participation in it. This was, perhaps, the first time in Palestine that a segment of the Labour movement was adamantly against a project undertaken by Vladimir Jabotinsky, the Legion's main architect. (There was, however, a group within Ha-Poel ha-Tsair, which included Levi Shkolnik (later Eshkol), that opposed this party position.)

Ha-Poel ha-Tsair leaders, such as Aharonovitch and party secretary Yosef Sprinzak, warned against exaggerated messianic hopes and overestimation of the political options at hand. They reiterated that the essential task remained the difficult and labourious one of settlement-building.[4] As such, Ha-Poel ha-Tsair responded lukewarmly to unity initiatives. While receptive to the idea of some type of co-ordination, and while recognizing that in many practical activities the Labour groups were converging more and more, it believed its differences with the others, especially Poale Zion, were still too significant to allow full unification. Ben-Gurion unsuccessfully attempted to convince the leadership of Ha-Poel ha-Tsair that since all the Labour formations ultimately had the same goal, there were no current differences significant enough to preclude unification. Both he and Katznelson saw Ha-Poel ha-Tsair's resistance as a strictly organizational and not an ideological matter; the party, they felt, simply lacked the courage to disband. Ha-Poel ha-Tsair in fact did fear that the former Poale Zion would dominate any new structure. However, as Sprinzak insisted in lengthy discussions with his two counterparts, from his perspective ideological differences were essential; Ha-Poel ha-Tsair's firm opposition to class struggle and identifying with socialism were not questions of organization.[5] Its trepidations were undoubtedly reinforced when the committee established to facilitate unification accepted a classless society as one of the goals of the new formation – although without Ben-Gurion's supplementary demand that class struggle be programmatically included – and endorsed affiliations to the World Union of Poale Zion and the Socialist International.

Ha-Poel ha-Tsair's preference was for a federation of parties. Katznelson's non-party group was opposed to this idea and also, since it believed in principle that parties were divisive, to forming a new party. It suggested in their stead the creation of a 'workers' community', a quasi-syndicalist conception for which the agricultural unions served as a partial model. Poale Zion believed that a class party was essential to political struggle on behalf of the proletariat and for educating workers to their class interests; like European Social Democrats and the Bolsheviks, it saw the professional activities of unions as a separate sphere of activity, albeit one that the party, as the embodiment of socialist consciousness, ought to dominate.[6] A compromise was eventually reached whereby the new organization would not be called a party but would combine the functions of a party and a trade union. It would be called Ahdut ha-Avodah (the Unity of Labour), although it was only Poale Zion and the non-party group that unified in it, and Ha-Poel ha-Tsair decided to retain its independence.

In February 1919 57 delegates attended the 13th, and final, Palestine Poale Zion conference. Following three days of deliberation, which included a vigorous speech by Ben-Gurion insisting on the identity of the nation's and proletariat's interests and on the construction of a socialist society in Palestine by means of national capital, Poale Zion voted to dissolve and merge into a new organization.[7] Shortly thereafter a conference of agricultural workers was called in Petah Tikva to discuss the matter of labour unity; some 58 delegates were elected to it, of whom 28 were from the non-party group, 19 from Poale Zion and 11 from Ha-Poel ha-Tsair. With 48 votes for and 11 abstentions, the groundwork for Ahdut Ha-Avodah was established; it was formally founded several weeks later at a second congress, at which Ha-Poel ha-Tsair absented itself.

Although Ahdut ha-Avodah was a combination of party and trade union, political realities, and indeed its own three-tiered structure, increasingly impressed a party character on it. Its organizational units were economic, i.e. trade unions and collectives, but its central policy bodies were chosen by an annual national convention which was elected by the membership at large. The convention elected a Council, that was to meet three times a year, and a Central Committee to run daily operations. The latter rapidly became the centre of power, and this, in turn, guaranteed the predominance of the political aspects of the organization since the economic units had no direct representation on it.[8] Tabenkin claimed that Ahdut ha-Avodah was established as a 'non-party' organization in order to make it more politically effective, not because of an opposition to parties *per se*, and it was assumed that it would function as a party within the ZO.[9] In addition to its political and socio-economic endeavours, the party resolved in June 1920 to form a self-defence organization, the Haganah (Defence). (All members of Ahdut ha-Avodah were to join the Haganah, thus securing its 'popular' character as well as the party's control over military organization.)

In the first elections to the Asefat ha-Nivharim, in mid-1920, Labour gained 124 of the 314 delegates (70 for Ahdut ha-Avodah and 54 for Ha-Poel ha-Tsair). This demonstrated its emerging potential in the Yishuv. However, the Yishuv's direct influence in the ZO was modest and, consequently, the same was true for Labour. Ahdut ha-Avodah found itself in regular conflict with the Zionist Commission which represented the ZO in Palestine between 1918 and 1921 and which was accused of trying to block funds due to labour organizations. At the July 1920 Zionist Conference in London, Labour delegates unsuccessfully argued for a socialist settlement strategy in Palestine, emphasizing the theme of national capital and urging that all lands purchased by the Zionist movement remain the property of the Jewish National Fund. Labour's numerical strength at Zionist Congresses was small and it tended not to emphasize its activities there, focusing instead on Palestine itself. At the Zionist Congress in Carlsbad in 1921, the first in which major contending blocs were constituted, there were 306 General Zionists, 97 Religious Zionists and only 34 from Labour ranks. From Palestine Labour only Ha-Poel ha-Tsair participated in the coalition Executive that the Congress formed, Ahdut ha-Avodah being unwilling to enter a coalition with bourgeois parties. Ha-Poel ha-Tsair's Sprinzak became the first Labour representative on the Zionist Executive and was given charge of its Labour Department.

Between 1919 and 1923 the Third Aliyah came to Palestine bringing some 35,000 immigrants, many of them, like their Second Aliyah predecessors, youthful radicals and many of them fired by the events of 1917. However, the existing Labour organizations had great difficulty in attracting them. Indeed, a generation gap was to develop between the veterans of the Second Aliyah and the newcomers. Impatient for a rapid development of Palestine in the direction of socialism, and sympathetic to Bolshevik notions, many of them were also critical of Ahdut ha-Avodah's unification of party and trade union. The leadership of Ahdut ha-Avodah – among whom Ben-Gurion, Katznelson and Tabenkin were most prominent – concluded that their own organization (which was also having financial difficulties) could not adequately master the situation. Consequently, they began pressing for a new, even broader organizational framework for the Zionist Labour movement – one that would include within it all parties, be able to attract the newcomers under its umbrella and at the same time allow the Labour movement to be co-ordinated in its efforts to get funds from the ZO. In December 1920 in Haifa the Histadrut (the General Confederation of Jewish Labour in Palestine) was established as a united project of Ahdut ha-Avodah, Ha-Poel ha-Tsair and other, smaller, left parties. Some 4,433 workers voted for delegates to the founding conference in Haifa, with Ahdut ha-Avodah receiving 1,864 ballots and Ha-Poel ha-Tsair 1,324.

This was a critical step at a critical moment. It was through the Histadrut that the Labour movement's political and economic power was built and consolidated. Its success was partly due to its emphasis on the word 'general' in its full name. Membership was open to all workers, whatever their ideology. This 'house of labour' sought, by its own self-definition, to unite within it all who lived by their own labour and did not exploit the labour of others.[10] For Ahdut ha-Avodah, it represented the Jewish socialist state-in-genesis. At the founding conference Katznelson spoke of it politically as the Asefat ha-Nivharim of the workers.[11] Significantly Ha-Poel ha-Tsair was willing to co-operate with Ahdut ha-Avodah in establishing the Histadrut, despite serious differences in their respective views of its role and status. Ahdut ha-Avodah wanted a powerful, centralized authority for the workers' movement, while Ha-Poel ha-Tsair envisioned something much more limited in scope and ideological content: a de-centralized, non-political institution playing a functional and economic role. These differences became the source of continual debate particularly as the growing organizational strength of the Histadrut tended to eclipse the role of the parties. Ahdut ha-Avodah's Ben-Gurion became the Labour Federation's first Secretary-General – he remained in this position until 1935 – and acted forcefully to centralize the Histadrut's resources and power structure as a nascent workers' state within the state of Mandate Palestine. For a short period he championed the idea of turning the entire country into a single commune, something intolerable from the perspective of Ha-Poel ha-Tsair. While Ben-Gurion discarded this idea as inworkable, he retained the strong conviction that disciplined, collective action was the prerequisite for Zionism's success and once declared to the Ahdut ha-Avodah Central Committee, during a debate on the relative value of different types of settlements, that 'my communism was derived from my Zionism'.[12]

Ben-Gurion's efforts to fulfil his aspirations for the Histadrut were facilitated by the fact that Ahdut ha-Avodah gained an absolute majority of the delegates to the second Congress of the Histadrut in 1923 – which defined its structure and adapted its constitution. (130 delegates attended on the basis of elections encompassing 6,581 voters in 62 enterprises.[13]) The Histadrut incorporated into itself not only the existing trade unions (and Ahdut ha-Avodah's union functions) but also most of the other labour institutions. In addition it developed a vast array of new ones, including a network of Histadrut-owned economic enterprises. Within a short time-span there were a Workers' Bank (Bank ha-Poalim), new co-operatives, kibbutzim and workers' settlements, a Bureau of Public Works (which later became the Solel Boneh Histadrut construction company), an educational system, workers' kitchens, *Davar* (a daily newspaper) and assorted cultural institutions. The Haganah was also transferred to its auspices, despite the protests of Ha-Poel ha-Tsair which wanted to place it under the Vaad Leumi, and which increasingly found itself in the role of opposition party within the Histadrut.

The Histadrut developed as a vast enterprise of the workers' public, and it sought to point the way to a future socialist society. It represented, in the eyes of its leaders, the embodiment of the working class that was soon to be a working nation. Its structure thus encompassed three basic areas: (1) the economy of Histadrut enterprises, i.e. a socialist public economy-in-the-making; (2) trade unionism; (3) a miniature welfare state in the form of an array of social services ranging from health care to labour exchanges. The general framework of the workers' economy was the *Hevrat ha-Ovdim* (Workers' Society), the holding company for all Histadrut enterprises, to which all Histadrut members belonged as shareholders – theoretically, therefore, as collective owners. Ha-Poel ha-Tsair, not surprisingly, was fearful of the proposed *Hevrat ha-Ovdim*, and its qualms were not mitigated when Ahdut ha-Avodah leaders such as Tabenkin declared, 'A *Hevrat ha-Ovdim* that rules over everything – that is our slogan'.[14] In fact, the organizational principle underlying *Hevrat ha-Ovdim* was one of the keys to Labour's success and, as its leaders were acutely aware, one foundation of its growing political power. The Histadrut was able to link the public and personal spheres in Zionist politics and immigrant life. 'The fate of the individual – his condition, existence, future – became intertwined within the movement', Ben-Gurion declared after the Histadrut's first decade, adding that 'the great value of the Histadrut is the fruit of the organizational link established in Palestine between the essential needs of the workers' community and the historical needs of the workers' movement'.[15]

Each of its three sectors contributed to the aggregation of Histadrut power: a socio-economic base was created through the Histadrut-owned enterprises, the Histadrut exerted its influence in the private economy through its unions and the Histadrut provided the basic services required by both incoming immigrants and established settlers. Absorbing immigrants into the country was, of course, at the heart of the entire Zionist enterprise, and not only did the Histadrut construct a sophisticated apparatus by which to do so, it was acutely conscious of its integrative role for immigrant workers, most of whom came from non-proletarian backgrounds abroad. Evaluating its first ten years, one author wrote in *Davar* that the Histadrut aimed not just to make life better for workers, as did most unions abroad, but rather to create a 'working life'. He went on to represent the Histadrut as 'an organisation of the working class *in the making* as distinct from the Trade Union which is the classic form of organisation of a working class *in being*'.[16]

It was through this binding of constructivism and organization with ideological and spiritual assertion that Labour was able to define the boundaries of the Zionist effort; it gave immigrants means with which to cope with their existence in the new land and it gave purpose to their daily struggles. Concurrently, and not insignificantly, the Histadrut and its enterprises provided jobs for Labour activists, enabling the movement to have a core of partisans mobilized on an ongoing basis. As such, the very nature of the Labour project, as a co-operative organized endeavour, gave it an advantage over bourgeois competitors. Indeed, much of the first Ahdut ha-Avodah Council meeting after the founding of the Histadrut was a discussion of who would get what jobs in the new body. Most of the Histadrut's key leaders occupied positions in both the Histadrut and the party.[17] Thus in the Labour movement were united both the political and the economic, the spiritual and the material. The movement was imbued with the sense that it was both a means and an end; a new type of society was being created through its social experiments, and the needs of the Jewish nation were being accomplished at the same time.

II

'I am for Bolshevism', Ben-Gurion once declared.[18] The impact of Russian and Soviet political culture on Labour Zionist leaders, especially in the 1920s, is often noted in studies of their activities. It is reflected in the Histadrut's strong centripetal tendency in organization and in Ahdut ha-Avodah's orientation to collectivism, activism and centralism.[19] In this, perhaps his most radical, period Ben-Gurion was fascinated with and sympathetic to the Soviet experiment; more than anything else, he appears to have been attracted to the will-power and determination exhibited by the Bolsheviks in the face of adverse circumstances. He represented the Histadrut at the 1923 Moscow Agricultural Exposition and made numerous observations in his diaries about what he saw. He believed that the regime's negative view of Zionism was not derived from the Soviet system itself, and he was critical of attacks on the Bolsheviks by Russian Zionist émigrés; a collapse of the regime, he believed, would bring disaster for Russian Jews. However, Ben-Gurion also recognized that a change in Moscow's stand was very unlikely – though he didn't rule it out entirely. His estimate of the Comintern was considerably more negative, but his most bitter comments were directed at the Yevsektsia, the Jewish section of the Soviet Communist Party, which was famous for its anti-Zionism and hostility to Hebrew culture.[20] Above all, it was Lenin the master politician who made a profound impact on him:

> Indeed this man is great. He possesses the essential capacity of looking life straight in the face. He doesn't think in concepts or words, but

reflects on the fundamental facts of reality. His eye looks afar towards the forces that will dominate the future. However, before him he sees one direction, that which leads to his goal, and he turns neither left nor right, whilst he remains ready to use different routes as the situation demands. For he pursues one path – to his goal.[21]

Lenin, Ben-Gurion added (while travelling through the Greek islands en route home), was 'a man with a will of iron', a 'tactical genius', who knew when to regroup and when it was imperative to cast aside what seemed necessary the day before.[22]

The Russian influence on Labour Zionists was also reflected in the desire to build a socialist Palestine without an intermediate capitalist phase; they, like the Bolsheviks at an earlier stage, had given up the hope that the bourgeoisie would develop capitalism (respectively, in Palestine and Russia) as Marx's original paradigm posited, and therefore, like the Bolsheviks, they were attempting to create socialist structures in a country lacking those fruits of advanced capitalist development that Marx indicated as prerequisites for the new society. This aspiration was especially acute among Third Aliyah activists, in particular a group from Russia known as the Tseirei Zion Socialists, who originated in the left wing of Tseirei Zion ('Young Zion' – a diaspora youth movement with a constructivist, moderate socialist orientation linked to Ha-Poel ha-Tsair). Led by Menahem Elkind, the Tseirei Zion Socialists were committed to the Leninist organizational principle that party and trade union had to be separated. They were wooed by Ahdut ha-Avodah, and finally joined, but only after the Histadrut was established since this effectively forced Ahdut ha-Avodah, whose economic and trade union activities were transferred to the larger umbrella organization, to play a more strictly party role. With the founding of the Histadrut, Ahdut ha-Avodah in fact discussed self-dissolution, but eventually, after extensive debate, decided to continue as a political-educational entity. At the same time, a power struggle emerged between the Ahdut ha-Avodah veteran leaders (i.e. those who came with the Second Aliyah), who took over the key positions in the Histadrut, and Elkind's circle which was effectively denied them. The former Tseirei Zion Socialists, influenced perhaps by the utopianism and anti-bureaucratic posture of Lenin's *State and Revolution* (though hardly by what the Bolsheviks were actually doing), criticized the 'managerial' and bureaucratic nature of the Histadrut and were increasingly mistrusted by Ben-Gurion and Katznelson.[23]

Elkind and his associates, seeking the fastest path to socialism, became preoccupied with the 'Gdud ha-Avodah' (Labour Brigade), an attempt, according to its founders, at 'building the land by establishing a General Commune of Jewish Workers in Palestine'.[24] The Gdud, originally based in collectives in Ein Harod and Tel Yosef in the Jezreel Valley, was composed mostly of Third Aliyah immigrants, but it included some from the Second

Aliyah as well. Its commune was organized in battalions of labourers, eventually numbering some 700, who worked in various parts of the country, especially in road construction (the British administration had decided to build a road network throughout Palestine and contracted the work on it through the Labour parties and the Histadrut).[25] In the commune, a rigorously egalitarian life-style was created. The Gdud eventually split over the feasibility of establishing a centralized commune covering the whole country as opposed to a network of large, self-sufficient, autonomous collectives which would be model societies. The 'left' in the Gdud, led by Elkind, advocated the general commune principle and later became dominant in the Gdud's urban sector, and a 'right' led by Shlomo Lavi and Tabenkin, both Second Aliyah veterans who advocated the alternative path, dominated the agricultural sphere. The conflict initially took practical form in a dispute over whether Ein Harod was to be viewed as merely one element in the Gdud's general commune, in which case funds could be taken from the individual collective's treasury to aid the financially pressed national Gdud treasury. The right insisted that agricultural communes would survive only if they could do so on their own and, consequently, such a transfer of moneys would threaten the enterprise.

The Histadrut leaders and Ben-Gurion – though he himself had briefly advocated the idea of the Histadrut as a general commune – backed the right, partly because Elkind and his supporters were viewed as impractical, but also because they insisted that communes tied to a single treasury be the sole type of organization within the Histadrut. For all their centralist tendencies, Histadrut leaders like Ben-Gurion had concluded that a pluralism of organizational forms was needed within the Labour confederation. Furthermore, they feared the intentions of Elkind's group within the Gdud, especially since the Gdud's constitution stated that it would seek to 'guide' the Histadrut 'in the direction of Gdud ha-Avodah'.[26] The left in the Gdud became a left opposition within the Histadrut, but in the end, the Gdud itself was a short-lived experiment. The deep recession of the mid-1920s undermined the left, a small group within which, led by Elkind, returned to the USSR. There they made another attempt to build a commune, an effort that was eventually cut short by the government; Elkind and a number of his followers apparently perished in Stalin's purges.[27] The right, specifically Kibbutz Ein Harod, became the corner-stone of Ha-Kibbutz ha-Meuhad, one of the three major kibbutz movements founded in the late 1920s. (The kibbutz population rose dramatically from 700 in 1922 to 4,000 in 1927.)[28] When the Histadrut building firm Solel Boneh received various contracts from the Mandatory government for assorted public projects, Ein Harod was asked to assist. Groups were sent out but, unlike the Gdud ha-Avodah's projected national commune, they evolved into autonomous settlements in various parts of the country. Beginning as one kibbutz sending out temporary work 'battalions', a federation of large kibbutzim emerged.[29] Tabenkin became the charismatic leader of Ha-Kibbutz ha-Meuhad, and this movement took on a political role within the Labour movement far out of proportion to its actual numbers. Fifteen years after its founding in 1927, 10 out of the 52 members of the Histadrut Executive were from it, even though Ha-Kibbutz ha-Meuhad composed only 9.8 per cent of the Labour confederation's members. The kibbutzim had a structural advantage in political life: as collectives, they could allow some of their members to be fully or partly engaged in public life.

The concept of the Histadrut, as we have indicated, was a source of debate in Labour Zionist history from its inception. In the mid-1920s Ben-Gurion presented the Histadrut as an institution that superseded parties – something Ha-Poel ha-Tsair particularly opposed – and that constituted a kind of class democracy in and of itself. 'May the party platforms rest in peace', he declared in 1925, responding to Ha-Poel ha-Tsair critics who complained that he used the Histadrut to advance the interests and views of Ahdut ha-Avodah. 'It is our failure and shame that the Histadrut has not yet the force, strength, will, and ability to demolish the [party] platforms and uproot the party domains. The hour of the one, single, platform has not yet arrived'.[30] The Histadrut was, he insisted, a *general* institution of the workers and not a federation of parties. It was, of course, convenient for Ben-Gurion to make this argument considering the power his comrades in Ahdut ha-Avodah had in the Histadrut, and especially in its economic institutions. Yet one can also see in this argument the – very un-Leninist – suggestion that the Histadrut become what Ahdut ha-Avodah was originally intended to be: a combined party-union that represented unified labour. (The concentration of Ben-Gurion and many of his closest colleagues on Histadrut work had, in the meantime, led to a weakening of Ahdut ha-Avodah.) The role of parties, Ben-Gurion stated, ought to be restricted to the expression of world-views; it was the Histadrut that was responsible for the daily needs of the workers. 'The Histadrut was established as a kind of workers' state, the autonomous authority of the working class ... [its] leadership elected by the whole community ... The moral base of the Histadrut is not the equality of parties – but the equality of its members'.[31]

Following Katznelson's theme, Ben-Gurion often proposed at this time that party politics undermined Labour movement unity. In linking the proletariat's political and economic functions, his vision was totalistic: 'The working class and its mission cannot be separated, the subject and the predicate of the movement form one unit ...' The meanings of 'Petah Tikvah' (where Ahdut ha-Avodah was founded) and 'Haifa' (where the founding of the Histadrut ocurred) were different not in substance but in execution:

In Petah Tikvah the movement demanded the creation of a single vessel that would include both the subject of the movement and its predicate: a general framework inclusive and undivided in content. In Haifa and afterwards it was possible only to create the general framework. The party, which in practice preserves this unity within the Histadrut, was obliged to fill the vacuum in this framework.[33]

In other words, though his vision was totalistic, his politics was pragmatic. Ahdut ha-Avodah, he stated, saw in the Histadrut the tool by which to realize the mission of the Hebrew working class in Palestine, not an end in itself. Unity, however, *could not be imposed*. Since Histadrut power was preferable to party power, maintaining the Histadrut's flawed unity – i.e. a unity despite the parties in it – was therefore paramount. Consequently Ben-Gurion was resigned to the impossibility of returning to the old Ahdut ha-Avodah model. What he hoped for, however, was a united socialist Zionist party that would act within the Histadrut, the Yishuv, the Zionist movement, and within the Jewish world and the general socialist movements, on behalf of the Zionist workers' movement.[34] As we shall see in the next chapter, this would come about with the creation of Mapai in 1930 through the merger of Ahdut ha-Avodah and Ha-Poel ha-Tsair. It is important to note, however, that contrary to the Leninist model, and in spite of his totalizing organizational aspirations, Ben-Gurion and his colleagues accepted the principle of legitimate competition among Labour parties in Histadrut politics and elections.

III

The Histadrut's effectiveness is evident in the statistics: within two years of its founding, half the Jewish workers in Palestine were members, and by 1926 over 70 per cent.[35] Labour's strength was increasingly reflected in its status in Yishuv politics: in the 1920 elections to the Asefat ha-Nivharim, as we have seen, the Labour parties secured 131 out of the 314 delegates elected, in 1925 they obtained 84 out of 221 elected, and in 1931 Mapai gained 31 out of the 71 members elected, with three additional small Labour parties obtaining one representative each.[36] While Labour's strength never reached 50 per cent, it was able to become increasingly dominant in Palestine because it was much larger and so much better organized than any potential competitors.

The ideological predispositions of its leaders, particularly those from the Second Aliyah, placed a special emphasis on agriculture, something not incongruent with a Palestinian economy which was, at the beginning of the Mandate, two-thirds agricultural and about one-third composed of industrial and manufacturing enterprises of a limited nature. However, immigration patterns and economic developments shaped Histadrut endeavours, and as early as 1922 it began to organize urban workers more aggressively. The percentage of them in the Histadrut rose from 44.3 per cent in 1922 to 65.3 per cent in 1926; by that year some 60 per cent of Ahdut ha-Avodah's membership was urban. By 1927 the largest single group of Jewish workers, numbering about 10,000, was in Tel Aviv, a city which grew from 16,000 to 40,000 inhabitants between 1923 and 1926. These figures reflected the general direction of the Yishuv's composition which was 83.2 per cent urban and 16.8 per cent rural according by the 1931 census.[37] Practically and politically this meant that the Labour movement had to broaden itself generally and focus attention anew on questions pertaining to class organization of wage labourers in private (as opposed to Histadrut-owned) enterprises in the cities. This made class conflict a more potent issue again.

In urban settings the Histadrut created workers' councils which were responsible for local activities including both trade union branch organization and the distribution and management of employment through labour exchanges. The need for urban organization combined with the presence of the radicalized, class-conscious Third Aliyah immigrants to create an uneasy balance between constructivism and class action in Labour politics. In addition, the shift in weight to the cities and towns brought with it a corresponding growth in the power of the urban sectors in the Histadrut and in Ahdut ha-Avodah. Ha-Poel ha-Tsair, not surprisingly, became increasingly restless with these developments. At the 1926 Ha-Poel ha-Tsair conference one member stressed that *am oved*, not a socialist society, was the Labour Zionist goal.[38] Thus in Ha-Poel ha-Tsair there was a non-socialist notion of a 'working nation'.

Perhaps the most sophisticated argument against class conflict was made at that 1926 Ha-Poel ha-Tsair conference by a brilliant 27-year-old theoretician named Haim Arlosoroff. Born in the Ukraine in 1899, and the grandson of a prominent rabbi, Arlosoroff came from a family which moved to Germany following the 1905 pogroms. Educated at the University of Berlin, he studied with Werner Sombart, and wrote a thesis on Marx's theory of class war. Before Arlosoroff reached the age of 20 he authored an important theoretical pamphlet for Ha-Poel ha-Tsair expounding a concept of Jewish *Volkssozialismus* (People's Socialism) which, influenced by Russian populism, the utopian anarchist socialism of Gustav Landauer and the ideas of A. D. Gordon and Martin Buber, was opposed to Marxism and theories of socialism based on class struggle. He moved to Palestine in 1924 and quickly became one of the Labour movement's rising stars, and perhaps its most powerful mind. His 1926 speech on 'Class War in the Reality of the Land of Israel' merits extrapolation as one of the most important appraisals from within – and illustrations – of the problems Labour faced *qua* Labour movement at this time.

Vigorously rejecting the notion that all countries follow uniform developmental 'laws', Arlosoroff warned Labour Zionists that the question of class struggle depended on its suitability to the specific conditions of Palestine. After all, in contrast to Marx's theory, in the pre-revolutionary period in underdeveloped, agricultural, tsarist Russia, there were intense class conflicts and intensified class consciousness, while in the more advanced, capitalist, contemporary United States, the opposite appeared to be the case.[39] The two facts that Palestine was a British colony and a bi-national society, he argued, subverted the application of the principles of class struggle there. Marx's notion of class war assumed nationalism to be an epiphenomenon, and the state to be a tool of the bourgeoisie, but neither of these premises held in colonial lands. The 'state' in Palestine was the Mandatory authority, and rather than being a reflection of indigenous class forces and relations, its political character was due to the 'class forces of English society'.[40] In fact, in political matters the Palestinian Jewish bourgeoisie and Palestinian Jewish workers *did* face problems and have interests in common *vis-à-vis* the colonial administration. Arlosoroff – who, incidentally, constantly warned less astute Zionists that the emerging identity of Palestinian Arabs was as *Palestinian* Arabs, and not solely as members of a larger Arab nation – argued that in the country two peoples exist 'one of which is a majority [the Arabs] that negates the aspirations of the minority [the Jews] – and this fact completely blurs all class struggle in Palestine'.[41] In other words, the horizontal cleavages of class in Palestine were cross-cut and undercut by a vertical national cleavage.

In European countries like Britain and France, Arlosoroff went on, the proletariat had to struggle to have its most elementary rights and needs recognized. However, in Jewish Palestine, as a consequence of constructivism, the situation was reversed: the workers in town and on the farms were prized, perhaps more than anywhere else in the world. 'The organized workers' movement' in Palestine could not even be classified as 'proletarian', in his view, because the Histadrut represented the 'aristocracy of the settlement' and the worker was 'the leader of the Yishuv', at least in terms of political organization. Furthermore, the Yishuv was still in the process of self-creation; the Palestinian Jewish workers were constantly renewing their ranks by means of immigrants, most of whom came from non-proletarian backgrounds and were in the process of being transformed into workers; the Jewish economy was heavily dependent on imported capital; it had no normal cycle of production or division of national income within its cycle. These were characteristics of a society-in-the-making – a society entirely unsuited to Marxist theories of class warfare. This was even more the case since constructivist Zionism had created broad spheres of workers' control as well as cooperative enterprises all of which, in turn, influenced the structure of authority relations in the country's economy as a whole; in its treatment of employees, private enterprise had to pay special heed with collective workers' institutions existing next door.[42]

Turning Marxist categories against themselves, Arlosoroff asserted that there was a gap between class consciousness and class reality in Jewish Palestine that inverted accepted Marxist assumptions. Usually, socialists are faced with a working class whose consciousness is not yet adequate to its objective reality; the task, then, is to organize, agitate and educate to class consciousness. In the Yishuv, however, there was a working-class consciousness incommensurate with objective conditions:

> Marx, in his book *The Eighteenth Brumaire*, points to the fact that the peasants, who composed the majority of the population in France in the period of Napoleon III's war, were a crystallized class from the objective economic point of view, but lacked any recognition [*hakarah*] of this. They composed a class in itself, but not for itself. It is the opposite with us. The workers of the Land of Israel became a class in its own eyes before they developed into a class in itself. This abyss between reality and consciousness [*hakarah*] would have been impossible if our ideology had developed ii solely in the conditions of the reality of the Land of Israel. It was possible due to the import of ideas.[43]

In short, radicalized Jews were coming from the diaspora to Palestine with concepts of class struggle rooted in European conditions – those of fully developed societies and working classes – while the Yishuv's working class was yet in the making. Arlosoroff shrewdly reminded exponents of class struggle of Marx's insistence that the essential matter was not the consciousness of this or that proletarian, but the objective condition of the proletariat as a whole. This was the real reason why class struggle was inapplicable to Palestine, not simply the fact that it was a European idea. It was incongruent to the objective life situation of the working class there.

If class struggle was unsuited to the reality of the Land of Israel, the same did not follow for the socialist idea. Here Arlosoroff parted from many of his Ha-Poel ha-Tsair comrades who refused to identify themselves as socialists. Consistent with the rest of his argument, Arlosoroff forcefully asserted that the realization of socialism took on different guises, each dependent on the conditions of a country. For instance, the fact that England was the financial capital of the world made transferring the banks to public hands an essential part of the socialist programme there. Danish socialists, on the other hand, were deeply rooted in the agricultural sector and therefore raised the banner of rural co-operatives. There remained, however, a basic content to socialism, despite its various manifestations, and he presented it in these terms:

> In the future society no individual can remain the owner and master of the nation's property. Society will control the process of production and the division of its fruits. Productive powers will be directed in the first place to the fundamental needs of the workers, and only

afterwards to luxury needs . . . This public control cannot be realized unless there is organization in the national economy and an end to anarchy in the social regime. Only by organization can we arrive at a classless society.[44]

A socialism in the reality of Palestine would take on its own character, while still embodying the essential content of socialism everywhere, its social ideal.

In Arlosoroff's view, socialism in the Land of Israel would be closer to that of Denmark than to England or Germany, for he envisioned Palestine's future as agrarian. Herein was one of the fundamental problems with his entire argument, even though Labour Zionism was uniquely successful in establishing agricultural communes. Changes – such as the urbanization we have already mentioned – were already occurring while he spoke; the Histadrut could ignore them only at its own peril. The more an urban wage-earning proletariat emerged, the more class struggle would inevitably re-enter the picture. And with the Fourth Aliyah a plethora of new and urgent problems was thrust before the Histadrut, including an almost catastrophic economic crisis that threatened its very existence. The response to this crisis, as the next chapter shows, was political in character and entailed a fundamental reorientation as a consequence of which Labour would assert itself as the leader of the Jewish national movement.

6
Labour's Road to Dominance II

Establish facts and more facts – that is the cornerstone of political
strategy.

Ber Borokhov[1]

I

Between 1924 and 1928 the Fourth Aliyah, substantially from Poland and
middle class, came to Palestine. The arrival of these immigrants was due to a
combination of events in Poland and restrictions on immigration into the
United States. In Poland, the deflationary policies and increased taxation by
Wladislav Grabski's government squeezed the Polish commercial classes,
which were significantly Jewish, at a time of economic upturn in Palestine.
The result was the 'Grabski Aliyah', and with it an influx of private capital.
'The Polish prime minister, it was suggested, had done more for Jewish
Palestine than the World Zionist Organization'.[2] This led to a strengthening
of the private sector of the Yishuv economy, with capital invested especially
in building and land speculation.

The ZO and the Histadrut had been functioning together on the basis of
mutual interests, even if many of the bourgeois elements in the former
distrusted the latter. Both wanted immigrants to settle in Palestine, and the
Histadrut, more than any other institution, had been successfully accomplishing this task. This was especially the case during the Third Aliyah
with its young immigrant radicals who had little more than the clothes they
arrived in. On this basis, the Histadrut argued for, and received,
much-needed, and substantial ZO subsidies. (Substantial is, in this case, a
relative term because the ZO's resources were limited and it had chronic
financial problems in the 1920s.) Even though the Histadrut created the
'League for Labour Palestine' in 1923 to raise moneys for it abroad, it was
sufficiently dependent on ZO funds for their loss to have seriously disrupted
its enterprises. Since Labour's growing power rested partly rested on the
Histadrut's ability to settle and organize immigrants under its auspices, such
losses would have had important political ramifications as well.

The Histadrut had been primarily concerned with immigrants lacking means, and these made up about half the immigrants in the first 15 years of the Mandate. However, with the advent of the Fourth Aliyah, the population of middle-class immigrants rapidly came to equal that of the previously existing Yishuv; Labour's claim to be the key to Zionist settlement was thus open to question. Furthermore, if representatives of private capital took the lead in developing the country, it would become increasingly difficult for Labour to make its case for public development and the primacy of national capital invested through Histadrut projects. Zionist funds might be redirected to aid and reinforce private enterprises, and a capitalist infrastructure, rather than a Labour one, would come to dominate the Yishuv. Ironically, within the ranks of the Labour left there was one group that viewed this turn of events positively. The small 'Left Poale Zion', composed of those in Poale Zion opposed to the formation of Ahdut ha-Avodah and who were orthodox Borokhovists, saw the possibility – at last! – that capitalist development would occur in Palestine leading to the Marxist paradigm of class struggle as explicated by Borokhov's theory.

The situation changed dramatically, however, when the influx of capital and bourgeois immigrants was followed by general economic collapse in late 1925, partly engendered by a serious economic crisis in Poland consequent to the failure of monetary reform there and a precipitous drop in the *zloty*. The deflation affected Polish Jewry in general, and those who had gone to Palestine still had financial ties to and resources in Poland. The import of capital into Palestine halted abruptly and along with it the economic boom that it had generated. Jewish Palestine plunged from prosperity into economic chaos, with scores of bankruptcies, the collapse of the construction industry along with the Histadrut's Solel Boneh (which had serious problems preceding the crisis), large-scale unemployment (40 per cent of Tel Aviv wage-earners by 1927) and emigration.

The Mandatory authorities did little about the situation – Palestine law had virtually no labour provisions at this time – and the resources of the ZO, the Histadrut and municipal governments in Tel Aviv and elsewhere were inadequate to cope with the expanding crisis.[3] Ben-Gurion placed the blame on the aspirations of middle-class immigrants who wanted to transfer European life-styles to Palestine; they wanted, he complained, to continue their 'ways of making a living in the Golah and didn't understand that the Land of Israel was not Poland'.[4] Labour as a whole regarded the economic crisis as proof positive of the bankruptcy of bourgeois Zionism and strategies depending on private capital. Arlosoroff saw the situation as a result of the effort to pursue urban and industrial rather than agricultural development. From the political centre and right, however, came strong criticisms of Labour's responsibility for the situation.[5] The General Zionist Meir Dizengoff argued the reverse of Arlosoroff, claiming that Zionist policy had been too concerned with agriculture and not enough with urban development. Complaining of the 'zealous ideological hegemony of the workers' in Palestine, he asserted that Zionist policies and finances had been prejudiced to Labour's benefit and against private settlement:

> A weak stratum of capitalists in the very first stages of capitalist development faces a workers' movement which, in terms of organization and discipline, is comparable to advanced capitalist countries such as Germany and England. The capitalist is dependent on the workers. Wages are not determined by the needs of the labour market and supply and demand, but by the Histadrut'.[6]

In his report to the 15th Zionist Congress Dizengoff, who had resigned his position as director of the ZO's office of urban colonization because he considered the ZO insufficiently receptive to his complaints and suggestions, estimated that in the previous five years, out of 158 strikes, Jewish workers in Palestine were victorious in 107 of them, the employers in 24, and 27 had ended in compromise. He calculated that 5,381 workers had participated in the strikes with a total of some 80,000 working days lost.[7]

The Labour movement and the Histadrut found themselves in a precarious situation which soon seemed like a state of siege. Not only did Labour's constituents begin to lose faith in the Labour leaders, but at the 14th and 15th Zionist Congresses, respectively in late summers of 1925 and 1927, ZO policy priorities began shifting to urban rather than rural settlement needs, and to middle-class immigration. In early 1927 an angry Ben-Gurion suggested that Labour representatives quit the Zionist Executive to protest against its unemployment policies.[8] He was overruled by the Histadrut Executive, however, and at the Zionist Congress later that year Labour was ousted from the Zionist Executive. The ZO was, of course, dominated by bourgeois elements, significant numbers of whom – though by no means all – harboured deep suspicions of the Labour movement, and were critical of funding it from ZO resources; those not inclined to help the left in the first place were less prone to do so in very difficult circumstances. This was not, of course, a new issue. Earlier in the decade the American Zionists, led by Louis Brandeis, vigorously fought subsidization of Labour on the grounds that the ZO's investments should be in profitable enterprises. Weizmann and his European supporters, in this battle of 'Washington versus Pinsk', had argued the contrary case, that the colonization of Palestine by Jews was not the same thing as the colonization of America, could not be dependent on private capital and therefore required a centralized public effort on behalf of the Jewish people.[9] As early as his first visit to Palestine after the eighth Zionist Congress in 1907, Weizmann, though no socialist, championed the idea of Jewish labour as a necessary foundation for a Jewish state, singling out Poale Zion and Ha-Poel ha-Tsair for praise in a report he gave at the time to the Manchester Zionist Federation.[10]

It was Ruppin – also not a socialist – who was especially notable in defence of the Labour pioneers. He told the 15th Congress: 'The present struggle against the workers in Palestine is, in my view, no accidental phenomenon. I see in it the beginning of the conflict between *Halutsiyut* [pioneering] and *Baalbatiyut* [proprietorship], between the pioneering principle and the economic principle'.[11] In his view both 'mentalities' and the classes they represented had their places in the Zionist enterprise. However, he advised that the failure of the BILU and the First Aliyah was due to the triumph of 'Baalbatiyut' over pioneering. This victory undermined the drive required to face the challenges before Zionism, and he admonished his audience that 'on that day when the sole guiding principle of our work will have become the percentage of profit, our movement can be proclaimed as dead and no one will ever be able to resuscitate it'.[12] He conceded that the Histadrut's Solel Boneh had cost the ZO substantial sums, but there were 'middle class enterprises which have cost . . . twice as much'.[13] While Palestine would one day inevitably change from 'the pioneering to the economic stage', he none the less told the delegates that unlike in the diaspora, the Jews of Palestine dared not be concentrated in commerce. They had to be 'spread . . . in the right proportions through all the branches of a healthy national economy'.[14]

The Labour movement was shaken deeply when it became clear that an 'Experts' Report' commissioned by the ZO to examine the situation in Palestine – in preparation for Weizmann's planned extension of the Jewish Agency so as to involve prominent and moneyed diaspora Jews in the project of a Jewish national home – harshly chastised the Histadrut, its use of 'national capital', its settlement policies, the co-operative movement (it called for an end to the creation of kibbutzim) and generally lambasted the Labour parties and the Histadrut for 'doctrinaire theories'. It recommended instead that 'sound business principles' govern Zionist economics. The report sympathized with private capital and the principle that investments ought to get equitable returns, and proposed that labour disputes be solved by creating 'conciliation machinery', in other words, a system of arbitration, which it suggested ought to include the participation of representatives of both the workers and the employers.[15]

The report was immediately denounced by Labour. Shlomo Kaplansky told the Zionist General Council that it was a 'declaration of war' against the workers.[16] Although in the end the ZO decided to reject the report, it served to hasten a process already under way by which the Labour movement rethought its strategies and concluded that to ensure the very survival of its endeavour, let alone its ultimate success, the centrists in the ZO could no longer be depended on. Labour's strength in the Yishuv would not only have to be reinforced, it would now have to be translated into Labour hegemony over the ZO. Labour launched a vigorous political and ideological offensive.

Addressing the Histadrut Council in early 1929 Ben-Gurion stated: 'Our activity finds itself in a vicious circle: the decisive front of our movement is in Palestine, but the larger camp which fortifies it is in the *Golah*'. The 'logic of history' did not permit separating the project in Palestine from the backers abroad. Since the realization of Zionism required the transformation of a dispersed nation long detached from land and labour into a working nation in its homeland – 'the geographic political exchange is conditioned on the economic-social exchange' – Ben-Gurion called for a 'changing of the social guards' in Jewry. The 'owning class' had been leading the nation, determining its priorities and values in the diaspora, but 'Actualizing Zionism removes the national crown from the head of the propertied class and reveals its nakedness'.[17] Ben-Gurion allowed for the existence of a propertied class, but demanded that it no longer make the pretence of identifying *its* interests with those of the nation. Just as the transfer of national hegemony from the propertied class to the working class was *the* decisive factor in modern European history, so too was this the case in Palestine, Ben-Gurion declared, where, in contrast to the diaspora, the workers had their own political and economic base. Hence Ben-Gurion's famous claim: the Jewish working class's 'national goal' was to be transformed 'from a working class to a working nation'.[18]

This theme, resting on the assumption of a dialectical relation between the means (the workers) and the end (an independent, sovereign, working nation), was hammered in public by Labour between 1929 and 1933 – the four years in which its hegemony in the ZO was secured. General Zionism, Labour insisted, was responsible for Zionism's problems because of its very class nature. The success of Zionism – its ability to create a Jewish majority in Palestine – required the recognition of the contradictory roles of social classes in nation-building. The issue, Ben-Gurion told the Mapai Council in 1932, was neither whether 'capital should serve Zionism' or 'Zionism should serve capital', nor was it the conflict between the bourgeois as an individual and the worker as an individual. Rather it was a question of the 'masters' (*baalei ha-batim*) as a class whose world-view was rooted in the egoistic self-interest of the individual – which in practical terms meant the primacy of individuals pursuing private enterprises requiring profitable returns – as opposed to the class interests of the workers which 'coincide with the general interest' of the Jewish nation in Palestine.[19] The key to Zionism's success was not in private profit but in establishing a national public enterprise in order to create a normalized nation, in which Jews occupied all branches of the economy. This meant that national need, not personal gain, had to be the chief criterion of investment. Indeed, here was the essence of the debate over 'national' and 'private' capital. Even though Jewish private capital imports into Palestine during the Mandate were significantly higher than Jewish national capital imports, the latter could be directed to the needs of the Zionist enterprise as a whole – and it was more often than not the Labour movement's *halutsim*, with their ideology of self-sacrifice, who made the best use of it.[20]

The implication was obvious: the 'return' that Labour's *halutsiyut* sought on 'investment' was national entrenchment and re-creation, not individual financial remuneration. In fact, Ben-Gurion had basic economics on his side. Given the limits of Palestinian exports and the size of the Yishuv in comparison to the Arab population, developing a profit-making, self-sustaining home and foreign market was, at least at this time, a highly implausible goal. The Zionist enterprise could not succeed as a profit-making endeavour because basic economics demonstrated that it simply was not viable as one. Land had to be bought in Palestine, and this was often at exorbitant prices; relying on the cheapest available labour (Arabs) potentially threatened the entire Zionist enterprise; substantial investment had to go into creating defensible and sustainable conditions for the very existence of the Yishuv, irrespective of their strictly economic feasibility.[21] 'If all the capitalists in Palestine were Jews', declared Ben-Gurion, '. . . the country would be no more Jewish than it is now . . . If the workers in the country were Jews . . . it would be a Jewish country'.[22] Since the bourgeois General Zionists could not see beyond their limited, particularistic, class horizons, it was clear to the Labour leaders that the Zionist project could only go forth if the workers' movement – the movement of the universal class of the Jewish people – dominated the Jewish national movement, not only in the Yishuv but in the ZO. This accomplished, Labour would be able to direct where funds went in Palestine.

II

A struggle for political dominance required a reformulation and restructuring of Labour politics. It implied, in the minds of movement leaders, the need for Labour unity on the one hand and the need to reinvigorate party politics on the other. The Histadrut could not contest elections to the Zionist Congress, where the Executive and the policies of the ZO were determined. Both major Labour parties were overshadowed by the Histadrut, although Ha-Poel ha-Tsair had been determined to sustain its independent party life. Ahdut ha-Avodah, whose leaders were dominant in the Histadrut, had begun reviving itself as well.[23] In late 1927 the two parties again began discussions about a merger. It was clear that, given a flexible ideological framework, their programmatic commonalities and mutual constructivism outweighed their differences. The value of cooperative efforts was already evident in the form of the Histadrut. It was assumed that electoral gains would be consequent to unity as well.

In 1930 the two parties finally united to form a mass social democratic Labour party, Mapai (a Hebrew acronym for the Land of Israel Workers' Party). Although Ahdut ha-Avodah and Ha-Poel ha-Tsair had been working together, both had activists who criticized formal unification. Some Ha-Poel ha-Tsair members feared that internal democracy in the Histadrut would be jeopardized by the absence of a strong opposition party. Arlosoroff, to whom the political value of a united party was evident, continued to raise this issue after Mapai was established, and urged vigilant respect for the smaller, minority parties in the Histadrut. In addition he warned that as a consequence of the formation of a mass party, there would be changes in the character of the Labour movement. Bureaucratization and a distancing of leadership from the rank and file were virtually unavoidable, he warned. Some leading members of Ahdut ha-Avodah, including Tabenkin, Kaplansky and Ben-Tsvi, stood against unification because they thought it would dilute, if not undermine, class politics. In fact, when the Mapai programme was written, it was Ahdut ha-Avodah which conceded most on the issue of class.[24]

None the less, in the plebiscites held in July 1929 party members overwhelmingly endorsed unity. In Ahdut ha-Avodah 81.6 per cent voted in favour, and in Ha-Poel ha-Tsair 85 per cent. Ironically, the impact of unity on the electoral front does not seem to have been great. Labour parties had been making steady gains throughout the 1920s. In the elections to the 1921 Zionist Congress, the two parties (running separately) received 8 per cent of the delegates, whereas in 1929, as a united front, they received 26 per cent (63 per cent in Palestine). This, significantly, deprived the largest bloc, the General Zionists, of its majority and virtually ensured a Labour role in the coalition Executive again. In 1931, the first time the united party ran, Mapai received 29 per cent of the total (62 per cent in Palestine), which does not represent a dramatic change. In 1933 Mapai became the largest and dominant party in Zionism, garnering 44 per cent of the vote to the Zionist Congress of that year (71 per cent in Palestine), but there were a variety of factors besides unity at play. (We will turn to these in later chapters.)

A pattern similar to that in the ZO may be discerned in the other electoral arenas. In the 1925 elections to the Asefat ha-Nivharim, the combined total for the two Labour parties was 36.5 per cent, and Mapai in 1931 received 38 per cent. In the 1926 elections to the third Histadrut conference the combined total of the two parties was 79.2 per cent, and Mapai in the 1931 elections to the fourth conference received 81.6 per cent.[25] Since disagreements remained between the former parties, now blocs, within Mapai, the party's *modus operandi* was to seek the lowest common denominator among them, and a veto system in major decision-making developed in order to maintain party unity.[26] At the same time, the formation of Mapai inaugurated what Ben-Gurion called 'a dual-organizational regime: a general Histadrut and a united party'. It was the party, however, that was to become pivotal by straddling all three arenas – the ZO, the Asefat ha-Nivharim/Vaad Leumi and the Histadrut – and placing its own adherents in the key decision-making bodies of each (although never attaining a majority in any of them except in the Histadrut).

Students of Zionist and Israeli politics have long pointed to Mapai as an example of what Duverger's classic study of political parties called a 'dominant party': one which electorally outdistanced its rivals over an extended period of time, owed its strength to public opinion's belief in its dominance rather than to numerical majorities in elections – 'Domination is a question of influence rather than strength' – and whose 'doctrines, ideas, methods, [and] style' came to be identified with an epoch.[28] The lack of numerical majorities makes the spiritual or doctrinal aspect of dominance especially important, and this was particularly so in the Zionist case since consensus behind policy-makers was essential to a political movement lacking sovereignty but seeking to assert authority in a community.[29] Duverger defined a dominant doctrine in these terms: 'in every period some doctrine has provided the basic intellectual framework, the general organization of thought, with the result that even its adversaries have been able to criticize it or destroy it only by adopting its methods of reasoning'.[30]

This raises the questions Marx posed in his analysis of ideology, a concept he used in order to explain, among other things, how ruling classes, which are always minorities, succeed in securing acquiescence to their rule. 'The ruling ideas of each age', he declared with Engels in *The Communist Manifesto,* as in so many other places, 'have ever been the ideas of its ruling class'.[31] The link between dominance, class and party was especially important in the Mapai case. There was, however, this important difference: although Mapai never attained an electoral majority, it claimed to represent the working class, which it foresaw as the majority in the future Jewish state, not a minority ruling class. Antonio Gramsci elaborated on Marx in his concept of 'hegemony'. In his 'Notes on Italian History' he wrote:

> the supremacy of a social group manifests itself in two ways, as 'domination' and as 'intellectual and moral leadership'. A social group dominates antagonistic groups, which it tends to 'liquidate', or to subjugate even by armed force; it leads kindred and allied groups. A social group can, and indeed must, already exercise 'leadership' before winning governmental power (this indeed is one of the principal conditions for the winning of such power); it subsequently becomes dominant when it exercises power, but even if it holds it firmly in its grasp, it must continue to 'lead' as well.[32]

Duverger's 'dominance' parallels what Gramsci implies by 'intellectual and moral leadership' here, while Gramsci's 'domination' would parallel the use of coercive state powers which Mapai lacked until 1948. (Labour Zionism certainly never sought to 'liquidate' its foes in the manner described by Gramsci, though it was quite willing to use force when necessary and when threatened by antagonists who did the same, especially on the far right.)

Mapai clearly knew that it had to lead in order to establish its hegemony. According to Gramsci,

Undoubtedly the fact of hegemony presupposes that account be taken of the interests and tendencies of the groups over which hegemony is to be exercised, and that a certain compromise equilibrium should be formed – in other words, that the leading group should make sacrifices of an economic-corporate kind. But there is also no doubt that such sacrifices and such a compromise cannot touch the essential; for though hegemony is ethical-political, it must also be economic, must necessarily be based on the decisive function exercised by the leading group in the decisive nucleus of economic activity.[33]

In taking the leadership of the Jewish national movement, Mapai made the type of sacrifices described by Gramsci, while concurrently maintaining its control over key levers of economic power in Palestine and in the ZO. As early as 1926 Ben-Gurion, realizing that capitalists had been entrenched in the country, and a class society would be the result, concluded that one and the same process would not realize both socialism and Zionism.[34] Hegemony, for the Labour movement, now came to mean that it was going to play the role of major *partner* in national coalitions, and Labour's leaders, particularly Ben-Gurion and Katznelson, grasped that this entailed an 'economic corporate' sacrifice: Labour would no longer be able to function as if it were identical to the nation's interests. To do so would be to preclude coalition politics – and Labour saw its alternatives as either dominating coalitions or yielding leadership to others – which in the circumstances meant to the right wing headed by Vladimir Jabotinsky. In other words, Labour's strategic shift was reinforced by the fact that its rise was occasioned by a bitter battle with the far right; consequently, in order to vanquish the latter, Labour sought to head as broad a coalition as possible. This, in turn, implied a new relation with groups it had previously fought, together with acceptance of a 'compromise equilibrium' and an 'economic-corporate' sacrifice, in particular accepting the Histadrut as one pillar among others. Labour's leaders believed all this to be dictated by the pressing needs of the hour – and undoubtedly the new Labour politics brought political success. However, even though Labour frequently continued to employ its class rhetoric of the past, its operative assumptions, implicitly, had been very much transformed.

What this signified was the abandonment of the concept on which Labour power had been built in the first place: the identity of the interests of the working class and the nation. This was an important departure from the past and from a fundamental element of socialist politics. To see fully its implications, it is useful to view the emerging structure of the Yishuv not just from the class perspective but from that of 'segmented pluralism'. According to Lorwin's definition, segmented pluralism is a system in which 'cleavages have produced competing networks of schools, communications media, interest groups, leisure time associations, and political parties along

segmented lines of both religious and anti-religious nature'.³⁵ The notion of
segmented pluralism is derived from sociological analyses of 'verzuiling'
(literally, pillarization) in Holland: the development of coexisting *zuilen*
(pillars), bases on and in which strongly separated ideological or religious
groups create an array of institutions. Within them the social and political
lives of their adherents (both passive and active) take place. This form of
vertical socio-political segmentation can be contrasted with the horizontal
one of class, and assumes a neutral state apparatus above the pillars.

The Yishuv may be viewed as a system of segmented pluralism within a
system of segmented pluralism. In the first place the two major communities
– Jewish and Arab – had separate social systems and autonomous
institutions for virtually all aspects of life. This was legally and culturally
reinforced as an inheritance of the millet system. But there were pillars
within each of these pillars as well. In the Arab community there were
Islamic and Christian pillars, and the Yishuv was divided among Labour,
Religious (split between Zionists and non-Zionists), *Ezrahi* (after the
Ezrahim or 'Citizens', the General Zionist camp) and Oriental/Sefardi
pillars. Each had their own sets of institutions and organizations, some
more, and some less, developed. From this perspective it was Labour, with
an ideology projecting its horizontal base, that constructed the most
dynamic and organized pillar, one that was especially adept at integrating
newcomers within it and presenting itself as the bearer of the national
mission as a whole. Indeed, if the Histadrut was a workers' state-in-the-
making and the interests of the workers were those of the nation, the
inexorable conclusion must be that the Histadrut – the Labour pillar –
embodied the Zionist society of the future.

In this regard, the revolutionary constructivist politics of the Zionist
Labour movement bears comparison with the efforts of Austrian Social
Democracy, also in the 1920s, to establish its own 'public sphere' in 'Red
Vienna'. In Austrian politics, the three major political forces, represented by
the Christian Social party, the Socialists and the Pan-German nationalists,
each constituted a 'Lager' (camp), maintaining its own sub-culture and a
plethora of social, economic and political institutions. As an opposition
party lacking state power but maintaining a majority on the city council of
the capital city, the Austrian socialists pursued a programme of 'Institutionalism'. It was largely a policy of innovation in response to the
exigencies of the times, especially the fading of post-First World War hopes
for European revolution. In one sense it was a defensive strategy. However,
it was also based on the hope that Vienna would become a model of
'anticipatory socialism', at once a projection of the future society and a
political base for their party.³⁶ The Austrian socialists had their origins in
mid-nineteenth-century *Bildungsvereine* (cultural–educational societies), an
endeavour to use self-help and educational means, as well as consumer and
credit co-operatives, to further a proletariat hampered by government bans

on political organization. In the 1920s Red Vienna aimed 'to provide a sphere of proletarian socialization which extended the prewar ideal of Bildung to the new social institutions of the capital' and which would be a 'spiritual state within a state'.[37] While this effort had a pronounced cultural emphasis, and entailed extensive educational reforms, it also led to the establishment of an array of health facilities and, in a city with an acute and long-standing housing crisis, an ambitious housing programme with some 60,000 new apartments constructed in a decade. This was accomplished by taxing property, luxuries and luxury housing.[38] In short, assuming the interests of the working class to be those of the society as a whole, the socialists used the resources and means at their disposal in Vienna to pursue those interests at the expense of the upper classes – a logic resembling that employed by the Zionist Labour movement in its argument on behalf of national capital and the building of a Jewish public sector in Palestine, as opposed to relying on private capital. As we have already noted, Austrian Poale Zionists, like Kaplansky, were early advocates of a strategy by which the workers would lead Zionism to success via economic constructivism and co-operative settlements – their own 'anticipatory socialism'.[39] Likewise, both the Austrian socialists and the Labour Zionists placed great emphasis on party unity and sought, through the autonomous structures they built, to give birth to a 'new man'. Consequently, they both placed great emphasis on youth organization and education. Both also had military undergrounds, respectively the Haganah and the Republikanischer Schutzbund (Republican Defence League).

In short, Austrian Social Democracy and Zionist Labour developed, in the same decade, their own pillars, 'states' within states they did not control. Both movements deviated substantially – both in theory and practice – from traditional Marxist views of state. In the Austrian case, Otto Bauer, the party leader and political theoretician, was an advocate of a 'third way to socialism', one that was neither reformist in mould nor Bolshevik in organization. He was also, as we saw in the first chapter, distinguished as one of the few Marxists to have dealt seriously and substantially with the national question; concerned with 'the relation between the internal community and external power, which appears as the antagonism between nation and state', Bauer advocated a federal socialist state in which nationalities, defined on a personal rather than on a territorial basis, would be culturally autonomous.[40] His assumption, therefore, was that under socialism the state would not wither away, as Engels had posited, but rather that the conditions for healthy, progressive, national expression – as opposed to chauvinism – would be established. Similarly, he advocated, in his *Der Weg zum Sozialismus* of 1919, a type of Guild socialism in which enterprises would be governed not by capitalist stockholders but by an administrative council of representatives of the workers, the consumers and the socialist state (the latter to be the delegate of the 'national collectivity').[41]

In other words, as concerned the questions of socialism and nationalism, Bauer's operative assumption was that the state would take on a new form and therefore not be relegated, in Engels' words, to 'the Museum of Antiquities, by the side of the spinning wheel and the bronze axe'.[42] In *Der Weg zum Sozialismus*, written in the aftermath of the collapse of the Austro-Hungarian monarchy, Bauer posited the need for two revolutions. The first was political and had successfully established the democratic (First Austrian) Republic. However, this was 'only half the revolution' because, though political oppression had been destroyed, economic exploitation remained. 'The victory of democracy', he argued, 'inaugurates the struggle for socialism'.[43] That struggle entailed a slow, difficult process of revolutionary reforms, Red Vienna being an example. Thus Bauer distinguished the political and social aspects of socialist revolution, while assuming the continuation of the state.consequently, the Austrian state in which Bauer's party had in fact briefly participated as part of coalition governments between 1918 and 1920, and within which it then became an opposition force, had to be defined in terms other than those of traditional Marxism, for which the state was always class-dominated.

The state, Marx and Engels wrote in *The German Ideology*, 'is the form in which the individuals of a ruling class assert their common interests'.[44] *The Communist Manifesto* declared that 'The executive of the modern State is but a committee for managing the common affairs of the whole bourgeoisie'.[45] Bauer claimed that the Austrian revolution and the collapse of the monarchy had produced an equilibrium among the competing classes.[46] Austria's had not been 'an ordinary bourgeois Republic' or class state, but rather, 'the outcome of a compromise between the classes, a result of the balance of class power'.[47] No class could impose its will on the others. This explained socialist participation in coalition governments before 1920, and was also manifested, in the following decade, by socialist dominance in Vienna and other industrialized areas (e.g. lower Austria, Upper Styria), concurrent with conservative domination of the rural parts of the country. It also explained the strategy of the Social Democratic party after bourgeois control of the state apparatus had been established. The Austrian socialists, never obtaining a majority in parliamentary elections,[48] built and expanded their state within the state – assuming that in this pillar could be seen what, one day, the whole of Austria would look like – and thus in effect used the proletariat's extra-parliamentary strength as a counter to and restraint on the conservative classes. Thereby total bourgeois dominance was prevented, despite bourgeois control of the legislative and executive machinery.[49]

Ben-Gurion and the Labour Zionists were seeking to create a state within the context of Mandate Palestine – which, as Arlosoroff had pointed out, was controlled not by a local bourgeoisie but by a colonial power. The need to construct a community – indeed a working class – and institutions that would be the foundation and the infrastructure of a future state, in contrast to the goal of taking state power, differentiates the Labour Zionist endeavour from that of the Austrians. Labour Zionist success was premised on forming a working class out of immigrants, while the Austrians struggled within an existing society with a defined class structure; the Labour Zionists sought in Palestine to found a working class-in-itself, which already existed in Austria. Furthermore, the Labour Zionists saw their social and political revolutions – building a co-operative commonwealth in the form of a Jewish state – as concurrent, two sides of the same coin. And ideologically, the Austrians saw themselves within the Marxist tradition, while those Labour Zionist leaders who were once oriented to Marxism became increasingly less so.

Still, to the extent that Zionist constructivism created a structure that anticipated the future society, it represented an endeavour parallel to that of Red Vienna. However, while the violent destruction of Red Vienna in 1934 prevented it from universalizing itself throughout Austria, the Histadrut failed to do so in the Yishuv because the Labour leaders, in order to attain political dominance, decided to accept a principle which we will call hegemonic segmented pluralism: theirs would be but one – although the largest – of several pillars in the Yishuv.

As will be evident in ensuing chapters, Ben-Gurion's calculations paralleled Bauer in important regards: though Ben-Gurion had spoken of a 'changing of the social guards' in Zionism, and while Labour's power was continuously increasing in Palestine – the focal point of the Zionist endeavour – there was a balance of class forces and power in the Zionist movement as a whole. Its chief arena, the Zionist Congress, encompassed representatives of Palestine Jewry and the diaspora. This necessitated a compromise between the various class representatives. Thus Ben-Gurion came to argue at one and the same time that the interests of the Labour movement were those of the nation, but that members of the Zionist Executive – including those representing Jewry's universal class – had to recognize that all the parties were organic parts of the Zionist movement, and that while the Yishuv was central to all calculations, the Zionist Executive could not function solely with it in mind; and the Zionist Organization, which represented both the Yishuv and the diaspora, was the final authority in the movement.[50] Indeed, the fundamentals of the Labour Zionist analysis of the Jewish condition explained all this: in Palestine, the Jewish working nation – an organized Jewish working nation – was being created that did not – and could not – exist in the diaspora. This factor was inevitably reflected by the constellation of forces and balance of power in the Zionist movement as a whole. The Yishuv's bourgeoisie was, by and large, a petty bourgeoisie, which was composed of small businessmen, shopkeepers and artisans who were constantly in need of financial aid from the ZO in order to survive; most Zionists with more means at their disposal did not to come to Palestine.[51] As Yonathan Shapiro, following Marx, points out, a petty bourgeoisie tends in capitalism not to function as a class in itself, able to articulate its own interests, and therefore follows the lead of the dominant class (the big bourgeoisie in Marx's analysis of France in *The Eighteenth Brumaire of Louis Bonaparte*). In Palestine this meant inclining to Labour's leadership, a development reinforced by the fact that many of the most important bourgeois Zionist intellectual figures also did not move to Palestine.[52] The workers' movement was increasingly dominant in Palestine, but not in the diaspora. The consequence was coalition politics, consolidated progressively in the formation of the Zionist Executives of 1931, 1933 and 1935.

This evolution represented the first steps in the Labour movement's reification of Zionism. As long as the interests of the workers and the nation were presumed to be identical, the state and the nation in genesis were not, in the final analysis, things apart from the class community or from Labour's projection of a classless society. The means and the end were one; the subject of the Zionist movement, the working class-in-making, was ultimately its object, an independent working nation. However, as the Labour movement rose to dominance it became increasingly accepting of the other pillars – on the assumption, as we have said, that Labour's would always be the largest and cast its shadow on them. In so doing – in seeking a hegemonic segmented pluralism – Labour also accepted the principle that class, nation and state were separate, if not opposed, categories, things unto themselves above and beyond the project of Labour Israel – which henceforth became a particular, not a universalizing, endeavour. This split, one in which the working class loses its role as the subject–object of Zionist history, brought with it a pragmatic politics that in fact nourished Labour's rise to dominance and sustained it, but in the long run also carried within it the seeds of Labour's undoing. The universal project would become the state as a reified entity rather than as a means for the realization of the community of workers. This, in turn, was the foundation of the policy of *mamlakhtiyut* (statism) pursued by Ben-Gurion the prime minister in the 1950s, a policy which saw the state as the universal, and the workers' movement as a particular, category.

In short, a new path for defining the boundaries of Jewish autoemancipation was being marked, and Ben-Gurion took the first steps along it in the 1930s. Its full map was yet to be charted, and there were to be many twists and turns – and inconsistencies – on the way. In order to appreciate this transformation fully, we must turn to what distinguished the Labour movement from its right-wing foes, the Revisionists, and examine the terms of conflict between them, the course of debate and battle – in the ZO, in Palestine and over labour relations in the Yishuv – and how Labour's triumph was secured. From there, we shall turn to Labour in power – sovereign power.

7

Jabotinsky and the Challenge from the Right I

I remember how a student shot himself in my home town,
becoming unable to bear any more the struggle in his heart between
two opposing creeds – what they were I do not remember.

Vladimir Jabotinsky[1]

I

The emergence of the Zionist right, its character and its defeat in its first confrontation with the Labour movement were inextricably bound to its leadership by Vladimir Jabotinsky. The effect of Jabotinsky and his political mien, both on his own movement and on his opponents, is a dramatic illustration of the impact of personality on politics. He inspired almost blind adoration and awe in his supporters, and provoked intense fury from his foes. Virtually nobody was neutral about Vladimir Jabotinsky. If leadership entails the purposeful mobilization of political and psychological resources 'so as to arouse, engage, and satisfy the motives' of followers, it may certainly be seen in his career, although, ironically, in the final analysis he was as bad a politician as he was a formidable leader.[2]

Jabotinsky was a gifted, multilingual journalist and writer as well as a charismatic orator. He called himself a liberal, but had a defined, strong bent to sloganeering, demagogy and an authoritarian style – and style was all important to him. He seems to have been especially adept in tapping the sense of humiliation his followers felt as members of a much-disparaged people, compensating for their sense of deficiency with nationalist militancy. 'Beliefs relevant to national identity', writes Sidney Verba, '. . . may have heavy expressive loading in which the major satisfactions derive from the identification itself'. He goes on to define a 'highly expressive political style' as one which places 'heavy stress on the use of appropriate words to describe political acts, and the words might become more important than the acts to which they refer'.[3] As a political leader, Jabotinsky was not only effective with words and ritual but obsessed with them. He often mistook them for reality.

His politics of dramatic symbolism was, therefore, both his strength and his weakness, and in marked contrast to that of Labour's leaders, especially his chief antagonist, Ben-Gurion. For the latter, the expressive and the instrumental – like political and practical Zionism, and socialism and Zionism – were linked. Indeed, the first clash between the Zionist left and the Zionist right – a clash which created a Zionist/Israeli party system that lasted some four decades – can be discerned in the characteristics that differentiated Ben-Gurion and Jabotinsky as modern Jewish politicians, and as modern Jews. For the young Ben-Gurion, Hebrew and Zionism composed elements of a natural environment. His father, Avigdor Gruen, was a leader of Hibat Zion in a small town in Russian Poland, and his home was a regular meeting place for the local branch of the proto-Zionist group. In Plonsk, where the Jews formed a majority of the 8,000 inhabitants, Ben-Gurion learned Hebrew at his grandfather's knee beginning at the age of three. In fact, he later described this as his first childhood memory.[4] As mentioned earlier, according to his memoirs, the books that most affected Ben-Gurion as a youth were Mapu's *Love of Zion*, a historical romance set in ancient Palestine, Harriet Beecher Stowe's *Uncle Tom's Cabin*, which taught him, as he put it, to despise slavery and dependence, and Tolstoy's *Resurrection*, a story of degradation and rebirth through suffering.[5] One cannot help but see links to his future role; a romantic love of the Land of Israel, hatred of subjection, and the desire for redemption. 'When I was ten years old', he wrote, 'the word spread through town that the Messiah had come, that he was now to be found in Vienna, that he had a black beard, and that his name was Herzl'.[6]

Ben-Gurion joined Poale Zion in 1905, and in September 1906 immigrated to Palestine as a farm worker. The virtually mythic image of pioneering had such a hold on him that over half a century later, and decades after he had ceased to be one, the then prime minister Ben-Gurion, aged 62, told the newly born Jewish state's first census to register him as an 'agricultural labourer'.[7] While ever astute to Zionism's diplomatic and political needs, he was unshakeable in his belief that their success depended on practical accomplishments in Palestine, tedious and undramatic as they often were. Indeed, his response to the Balfour Declaration mixed joy with the observation that 'England is not returning Palestine to us, even in this moment of great victory . . . [It] is not in England's power to do so'.[8] While the political rights of the Jews had now been recognized by a great power, the primary task was to create a living reality to embody and thereby to secure them.

Culturally, the contrast between Ben-Gurion and Jabotinsky is, in some regards, reminiscent of that between Ahad Ha-am and Herzl. Jabotinsky grew up in Odessa, a commercial centre and port that was perhaps the most cosmopolitan of Russian cities. In it lived a vast diversity of ethnic and national groups. Whereas Ben-Gurion grew up in a Hibat Zion home in a small town with a Jewish majority, for Jabotinsky's schoolmates in an Odessa gymnasium 'the whole subject of Jews and Judaism just did not exist', as he put it.[9] He recalled no nationalist inclinations among the Jews in the class or interest in Hibat Zion. His father died when he was young, and his mother, while keeping some Jewish practices, was a devotee of German culture. Russian was the language of the home, and young Jabotinsky saw himself as a Russian, although he did study some Hebrew as a youth. He matured as a young intellectual, and had begun writing for the press when he went to Berne to study law, and where, among other things, he first read Marx. En route he saw the wretched conditions of life of Galician and Hungarian Jewry. It was in Berne, following a lecture by Nahman Syrkin and a debate on socialism and Zionism, that he declared himself a Zionist. Shortly thereafter he went to study in Rome for three years. He later remarked that 'If I ever had a spiritual fatherland, it was Italy more than Russia'.[10]

He was already interested in D'Annunzio; now he studied with some of the most prominent minds in Italy, including Labriola, Croce, Ferri and Pantaleoni. He left Rome believing in socialism, although he would soon reject it on behalf of liberalism. Most importantly, he left enraptured by the stories of Cavour, Mazzini and, more than anyone else, Garibaldi. Polish nationalism would also greatly influence him. He read Mickiewicz as a youth and later, in the 1920s, admired Jozef Pilsudski. The latter, like himself, travelled the road away from socialism to nationalism, and Jabotinsky compared the Polish leader to his own friend and collaborator in founding the Jewish Legion, Yosef Trumpeldor.[11] (This was a far-fetched analogy. Though Trumpeldor, who died defending a northern Galilean Jewish settlement shortly after the First World War, was Jabotinsky's comrade, he identified himself whole-heartedly with the Labour movement in Palestine.)

Back in Odessa, Jabotinsky, like so many of his generation, was shaken by the 1903 Kishinev pogrom, and threats of similar violence in his home town. He was a delegate to the sixth Zionist Congress where Herzl made an enormous impression on him, and in the tumult of revolution and pogroms in 1905–6 in Russia he made a dramatic entry on to the political stage as a champion of Jewish nationalism, and as a foe of class politics; in 1906, on the anniversary of the previous year's pogroms, he declared that the real problem was rooted in 'the objective pattern of impersonal forces', in particular the fact that the Jews were forever aliens where they were living. 'I have nothing to learn from pogroms suffered by our people; they can tell me nothing I did not know before . . . I love my people and Palestine: this is my creed, this is the business of my life . . .' He went on to proclaim that 'the Hebrew nation' was his 'Absolute God'.[12]

The transformation of Jewish political culture from a religious, politically quiescent to a secular, democratic and nationalist one is vividly illustrated by Jabotinsky's identification of the nation as his God; as Ahad Ha-am replaced one *mythomoteur* by another, so too did Jabotinsky, although what largely structured his was European nationalism – more accurately, his conception of European nationalism – rather than Jewish national culture. We can see this expressed dramatically in an article he wrote two decades later, a nationalist reflection on the Yiddish folk-song 'Affen Pripatchook' (By the Hearth). This song tells of a rebbe teaching children in a traditional Jewish school, where the 'Aleph-Bet' (the Hebrew ABCs) and religious texts were the chief subjects of study. Jabotinsky, who expresses his desire to be a choirmaster conducting the song as a 'great oratorio', suggests that the rebbe ought to reward the best Hebrew students with a flag. He adds: 'For this generation now growing before our own eyes and on whose shoulders will fall the responsibility for the greatest turning point in our history, the Aleph-Bet is very plain and simple: Young men, learn to shoot'.[13] What for Ahad Ha-am was the importance of Moses as embodiment of *Volksgeist*, for Jabotinsky was the importance of flag, parade and gun.

Jabotinsky's multi-faceted career placed especial emphasis on the projection of strength and the need for Jews to have military training. During the First World War he was the major architect of the Jewish Legion. 'We fear that our nation will be forgotten on the day of reckoning', he wrote with Trumpeldor in a letter addressed to Prime Minister Lloyd George. 'We ask for the Jew the privilege the Welshman and Scotsman enjoy – to fight for *their* country; to fight like the Welsh and the Scottish do – in regiments of their own, not scattered and nameless'.[14] Behind this was a Herzlian political strategy; the Ottomans, he was convinced, would lose the war and their empire would be dismembered. Jabotinsky hoped simultaneously to provide Jews with martial skills, while linking Zionist interests with those of the victorious allies, especially the countries with Middle Eastern interests, Britain and France.

The face of Jabotinsky's politics, and indeed the future political culture of his movement, had already taken form, however, before the First World War, and was perhaps best encapsulated in his 1912 article 'Reactionary' (*Mored or* in Hebrew, *Mrakobes* in Russian). In it the author asks how the contemporary world – in which many peoples, divided and enslaved as Italy once was, 'await their Garibaldi' – would respond to Garibaldis in its midst.[15] How would young radicals, yester-year's worshippers of the Italian nationalist, see him today? Doubtless, Jabotinsky wrote, the more radical, the less sympathetic they would be; leftists see such men as divisive, as obfuscators of class consciousness, and call Italian irredentists seeking Trento and Trieste reactionaries and chauvinists.

Jabotinsky dramatizes the legendary dialogue about Italian unity that young Garibaldi, then working on his father's ship, supposedly engaged in with a sailor-Carbonaro. The Carbonaro, Jabotinsky says, would not have told the youth that all men are brothers, but that the foreigners had to be chased from Italy; he would have sought to inspire the youth with 'the forbidden verses of Giusti'. Inspired, young Garibaldi would dedicate his life to the national cause. But update this story and what would happen, asked Jabotinsky. Giusti would be criticized for instigating Italians against Germans,[16] the Carbonaro would be accused of propagandizing and Garibaldi would be scorned for committing his life to a petty, chauvinistic, reactionary cause.

What *did* Garibaldi do? – asked Jabotinsky rhetorically:

> Did he remind his compatriots that Germans should be loved as one's brothers? To the contrary, every step and gesture he took stirred hatred of the foreigner anew in the Italian masses . . . To the contrary, he demanded unity of rich and poor in the name of love of the homeland; he demanded that they forget all conflicts and put aside [*lidhot*] all internal quarrels, until the nationalist ideal is realized.[17]

He was preoccupied not with democratizing Italian states but in compelling his generation to throw down the gauntlet for unified Italy. Consequently, Jabotinsky says to the left: I know you don't attack *Garibaldi* in these terms, 'But I ask you to read what is said and written about men who nowadays, and in today's conditions, dare to worship Garibaldi's gods. No epithet is spared them; they are declared humanity's haters, enemies of the brotherhood of man. They are reactionaries, foes of culture'.[18]

Expressed herein we can see all the fundamentals of Jabotinsky's future integralist nationalist programme, as well as the roots of his later conflicts with the Labour movement: for him the nation was primary and singular, while all other factors, such as wealth and poverty, or social class were of secondary importance at best. Such questions, in his view, ought not even to be raised until the national tasks are accomplished (although he did not indicate that they should then be raised either). By the 1920s he would counter the left's synthesis of socialism and Zionism with his own programme of 'monism' and 'pure', militant nationalism, unpolluted by foreign 'isms'. Recognizing that at stake was the definition of the future Jewish national political culture and the setting of its psychological and – importantly in his case – territorial boundaries, Jabotinsky compared his foes' synthesis of nationalism and socialism with *shaatnez*, a mixture of wool and linen prohibited in garments by Jewish tradition. Zionism, similarly, could hold but a single banner aloft because 'Having "two ideals" is as absurd as having "two Gods" '.[19]

In a letter to the New York monthly of Betar, his movement's youth organization, one can see his explicit preoccupation with redefining Jewish political culture. Jabotinsky made 'Hadar' (a Hebrew word not easily translated, but which means, basically, dignified pride) a central term in his vocabulary and an ideal for the next generation. In his mind it was a counter-image to the diaspora Jew. Hadar represented 'dignified beauty and harmony of manner, gesture, speech and attitude', apparently characteristics he thought lacking among dispersed Jewry. (In this, Jabotinsky seems to have accepted, to a certain extent, anti-Semitic caricatures of his own people.) Jabotinsky traced his inspiration for Hadar to Sokol, the Czech democratic nationalist youth movement. However, more often than not, his formulations of it tend to resemble Roman *virtu*. 'Pride' was 'not a mere word', but was also designated as a daily battle 'against the debasing influences of the squalor called ghetto, even a Fifth Avenue ghetto'.[20] In another letter, he summarized his view in a manner that starkly contradicted his own frequent espousals of liberalism and individualism:

> In things eternal, the highest expression of Monism is Monotheism. In things secular, the highest expression of the Jew's monism is 'Palestine a Jewish state on both sides of the Jordan'. Individuals and classes are nothing but instruments of the state-idea; their interests are subordinate, if necessary sacrificed, to the one and only interest of the great work of state-building.[21]

Jabotinsky often reduced matters to such simple formulae. This simplicity, however, was a reflection less of the man himself than of his estimate of the political motivations of men – which he believed to be, ultimately, simple. In an article of 1916 named 'Truth' he queried whether truth was something singular or plural. He reflected on a poem by an Irish nationalist executed after the Easter Rebellion; in the poem a leader who becomes a conquering king comes to contemplate the human soul, discovering in the end that all is ephemeral and relative. His troops, bored, promptly throw him out and replace him with someone 'who saw just what was before him, and who led them to salvation and glory'.[22] In contrast, in a 1934 essay entitled 'Leader' he expressed great discomfort with highly individualized politics, and the tendency of many leaders in his time to do all the thinking for their movements. But then, within the same article, he evaluates with admiration the father of political Zionism in these words: 'In the Russian language there is an expression more appropriate than the word "leader"; in past eras a beloved and honoured thinker was called "conqueror of thoughts" . . . That is what Herzl was: He conquered our thoughts. It was a fact not an office'.[23]

This view of Herzl as a leader – and apparently Jabotinsky's own ambitions – are characteristic of what one political scientist calls a transforming leader, one who seeks to exploit needs or demands among potential followers, who 'looks for potential motives' in them and develops 'a relationship of mutual stimulation and elevation'.[24] It also exemplifies an important aspect of Weber's definition of charismatic authority in that it rests on the followers' recognition, passive or active, of the leader's personal mission, rather than on jurisdictional authority: 'His power rests upon this purely factual recognition and springs from faithful devotion'.[25] Joseph Schechtman, one of Jabotinsky's closest aides, and later his biographer, described his relation to his followers in terms that bespeak more than hagiography: 'To the minds and hearts of many thousands of Jewish men and women, he was the incarnation of everything that was great and lofty and inspiring . . . Each of them felt that his or her personal life had been enriched and beautified by their even distant communion with Jabotinsky'.[26] Jabotinsky himself seems to have had faith in his own such powers. In a letter pleading for Avraham Stavski, a member of Betar who was sentenced to death for the June 1933 assassination of Haim Arlosoroff, Jabotinsky was able to declare, apparently without embarrassment, that 'Stavski belongs to Betar, a youth organisation of which I am the head; no Betari [member of Betar] would lie to me. I pledge my honour that S. is innocent'.[27]

Jabotinsky's radical nationalist politics were an expressive politics more than anything else; this too was both a strength and a fundamental flaw in his leadership and in his movement. On the one hand his strident demand for recognition and honour had potentially great appeal to a dislocated, degraded people victimized in a world of upheaval, nationalist exclusivism and anti-Semitism. As the status of Jewry radically deteriorated in the 1930s, this had a natural appeal. On the other hand it was a politics that placed its hope in obtaining recognition of the rights of the Jews by a preoccupied and, more often than not, hostile world. For Ben-Gurion, in contrast, the actual building of a strategic base – rather than making demands – was primary; Labour wanted to construct a foundation that made rejection of Zionist demands difficult when they were made. In his memoirs, Ben-Gurion recounts an exchange he had with Jabotinsky in London in October 1934, when the two conducted secret negotiations to defuse the tensions between their respective movements. Jabotinsky suggested that should the negotiations succeed, a 'grandiose project' ought to be implemented in celebration. The Labour leader agreed, suggesting a new Jewish settlement in Palestine as the ideal venture. Jabotinsky countered with one of his favourite projects, a world-wide petition campaign to pressure the British and other governments on behalf of Zionism. He told Ben-Gurion: 'You underestimate the value of a gesture [*demonstratsiyah*] and a slogan; the word, the formula possess enormous power'. Commenting on this, Ben-Gurion recorded that 'I felt that here we came to the fundamental conflict'.[28] For Ben-Gurion, the practical efforts at settlement and immigration were themselves *political* actions essential to Zionism, and not something secondary to diplomacy on the world stage.[29]

Herein is also a link between Jabotinsky's politics and the defeat of his movement by Labour. As a logical consequence of his 'monism' Jabotinsky and his followers focused on political affairs narrowly conceived, holding the flag aloft and demanding recognition of rights, something they later supplemented with a military underground, the Irgun Tsvai Leumi (the National Military Organization, or Etsel). What they did not build was their own socio-economic infrastructure. According to the official history of Jabotinsky's 'Revisionist' movement, 'of all the Palestine formations the Revisionist Party and its affiliates were the only ones who (with a few minor exceptions) possessed no settlements, no economic enterprises, or institutions of their own. This enabled them to preserve the integrity of their Zionist faith and their freedom of action'.[30] The Revisionists may have maintained 'the integrity' of their Zionism, but in a Yishuv in the process of *verzuiling*, this 'freedom of action' was in fact a disadvantage. Labour was busy building and strengthening its pillar and it was against this pillar that Revisionism would founder.

II

Jabotinsky's Revisionist party was born in 1925 and moulded around his presence. Its activities at first focused on the ZO, from whose Executive Jabotinsky had resigned two years earlier, bitterly accusing it of feebleness in responding to the vicissitudes of British policy. 'Revising' Zionism – hence the name 'Revisionists' – meant returning to the original principles of Herzlian political Zionism, which Jabotinsky believed had been corrupted. At first Weizmann was the foremost target of Revisionist ire. Jabotinsky sarcastically described him as the shallow, 'dean of the impressionistic school of Zionism'.[31] There was a certain irony in this since Weizmann, the great proponent of synthetic Zionism, owed his now dominant status in the ZO to his role as architect of the Balfour Declaration, the greatest single, political Zionist success until then. An Anglophile, Weizmann believed that great power support for Zionism was essential to its success, but like the Labour movement, he simultaneously emphasized practical efforts to build the Yishuv settlement by settlement, immigrant by immigrant. (Labour, on the other hand, did not share the firmness of Weizmann's faith in the British.)

Jabotinsky derided this as a 'little' Zionism, insisting that Britain could be pressured to play, by means of the Mandate, the role of a 'colonizing regime'. He and his followers maintained the centrality of political and legal guarantees which, together with international recognition, they emphasized as prerequisites for successful Zionist colonization, especially given the growing, and in Jabotinsky's view inevitable, hostility of the local (Arab) population. Jabotinsky summarized his point:

One must distinguish clearly and sharply between two methods of the Jewish renaissance movement: the political and the practical direct method.

The political is the most important. That is the eternal heritage left us by Herzl. His lore says that in order to create a Jewish state, one must first of all gain the official sanction of the governmental power concerned. Only then can a colonisation be a true colonisation; a process that leads towards a Jewish majority and a Jewish Government without political guarantees, this is simply impossible. What is possible without political guarantees is not 'colonisation', but only something that looks like colonisation – but in miniature, and is called 'colonial policy'. That is: immediate concrete undertakings, which are never able to give you the majority in the country – but they strengthen your positions, they spread your idea, and give it concrete form, in short they assist you towards the main thing – the political struggle for the political 'charter'.[32]

This implied an enormous faith in the conscience of the West and in imperial policy; Jabotinsky, too, was an Anglophile, and stated in a confidential memorandum to the Zionist Executive in 1922: 'I believe as firmly as ever that there is a real coincidence of interest between Zionism and the British in the Eastern Mediterranean . . . Furthermore, I believe that no British government will break the Balfour pledge'.[33] In addition, Jabotinsky occasionally portrayed the Zionist project as similar to the white man's burden. In a 1933 article he attacked communism for advocating revolt among 'the Eastern peoples' against European dominance: 'In its eyes this dominance is "imperialist" and exploitative; in my view European dominance makes them into civilised peoples'.[34]

Subsequently, as British–Zionist relations deteriorated and as it became increasingly evident that Whitehall was unlikely to fulfil its League of Nations Mandate to create a Jewish national home, Jabotinsky believed that the key political task for Zionists was the arousal of public opinion in Britain and elsewhere to pressure London. It was necessary, in his view, to educate Jews to oppose the British government while not opposing the British nation.[35] Revisionism, he declared, 'believes . . . in the all-powerfulness of moral pressure when applied to a good cause' and he urged his followers never to forget that 'England is ruled by its public opinion, not by its Ministers . . . a Minister's "no" is not yet a Nation's ultimate answer'.[36] It was with this in mind that he promoted the mass petition campaign to influence Britain. Beyond this, however, he had few concrete proposals and eventually became resigned to the fact that British policy had turned anti-Zionist.

In Palestine his party sought to extend, as much as possible, actual British responsibility for, and commitment to, the Yishuv. The Revisionists called, for example, for the re-creation of the Jewish Legion (which had been disbanded after the war) under British auspices and for placing the Yishuv's educational system under the Mandatory government (with the proviso that it provide a Jewish 'national' education). Labour, in contrast, wanted to build the Yishuv as an independent pillar, broadening Jewish autonomy, rather than British responsibility, as much as possible. Thus dependence on the Mandate would be minimized, Jewish self-control and self-reliance extended and the Mandate itself used as a shield to the degree that it could be. Similarly, Labour preferred an underground Yishuv-run military and Yishuv control of education rather than a legion under British command and having education in the hands of the Mandatory authorities.

Since the Revisionists, like Labour, wanted to reconstruct Jewish political–psychological boundaries in their own image, and since they sought the creation of what we might call a nationalist militant Jew for whom, as Jabotinsky put it, the nation was God, their nationalism was fervently integralist, and shunned any territorial compromises in Palestine. The Revisionists reified land. The programme Ben-Gurion came to champion was based on radically contrasting logic and premises: the partition of Palestine on the grounds that attaining a state with a Jewish majority in part of the country had priority over romantic territorial sentiments. Such sentiments were by no means absent in Labour ranks and Ben-Gurion faced strong opposition within Mapai. However, the party mainstream, pressed by its leader, eventually joined him in preferring to be a majority in a smaller Jewish state than to be a minority in a state encompassing the whole of historical Palestine. The Revisionists insisted also that Zionism proclaim its *endziel*, its final aim, loudly and clearly, and that that aim was a state with a Jewish majority within the boundaries of the ancient Hebrew kingdoms, encompassing both banks of the Jordan river. This would include Transjordan, which was given to Abdullah of the Hashimites at the 1921 Cairo conference. Jabotinsky derided all who would not speak forthrightly of Jewish statehood. Both Weizmann and the Labour movement regarded such proclamations as dangerous posturing. Jabotinsky's calls might appeal to frightened and degraded eastern European Jews, but they made no practical sense. The Zionists, Weizmann and Labour argued, were in a weak position to start with and such demonstrative declarations would accomplish nothing, and were politically reckless at a time when the Jews made up less than 20 per cent of the Palestinian population. While they were in fact more willing to make compromises than the Revisionists, as the latter often charged, what Weizmann and Labour preferred was a strategy epitomized by a suggestion Ramsay MacDonald made to the Histadrut Executive when he visited Palestine in the early 1920s: 'If you conceal the big cards at first and play the low ones, I am sure that you have hopes of winning the game'.[37] Weizmann himself put it in these words, expressing the same idea: 'Like a captain who does not want to jeopardise his vessel, we watch the ebb and flow in order to lie low at the ebb tide and to take advantage of the flood'.[38] Although Revisionists insinuated otherwise, Ben-Gurion's Zionism, from its inception, had Jewish statehood as its goal. Political circumspection led him to choose, on strategic grounds, when it was most beneficial to proclaim this as the aim of the national movement.[39]

Revisionist opposition to Weizmann's leadership naturally flowed into opposition to Labour, since Labour had a working relationship with Weizmann and preferred his hand to be strengthened rather than that of other General Zionists who were hostile to Labour; and Labour's own decision to dominate the ZO came just when the Revisionists were seeking to do the same. Ha-Poel ha-Tsair, which a decade earlier had been opposed to Jabotinsky's Jewish Legion project, was particularly pro-Weizmann and its ire was raised by Jabotinsky's attacks on him. Ahdut ha-Avodah's socialist militants could only become increasingly unsettled by a man who was bitterly critical of class politics. The General Zionists were poorly organized, and eventually divided between an 'A' and a 'B' faction – the former supporting and the latter (the stronger group) opposing Weizmann and collaboration with Labour. Jabotinsky's hostility to the left, which as we have seen predated the First World War, grew increasingly vociferous in the late 1920s as he competed with Labour. He used his considerable polemical talents to attack his foes and fought his battles through oratory and with the pen as much as by organization.

In 1925 Jabotinsky authored a clever, if patronizing, critique entitled 'The Left'. While recognizing the extent of its achievements and admitting that 'Hebrew Erets Israel is a land of workers', he declared that Labour was merely a socialist reinvention of Hibat Zion, a movement, in his view, superseded by Herzl's political Zionism. Socialism, by Jabotinsky's definition, meant nationalization of the means of production subsequent to class war. But the Palestinian co-operative settlements, he pointed out, were islands of the utopian socialism that Marx had so ridiculed; they weren't even self-sufficient. The workers, after all, relied on national capital to subsidize them and in effect this meant they were dependent on the other social strata (in the diaspora) whose contributions to the Zionist movement created that capital. This demonstrated that class collaboration, not class war, was paramount in the fulfilment of Zionism.[40] Jabotinsky claimed that the very notion of Jewish labour, so sanctified by the left, exposed the latter to be nationalist first, and socialist second. (Ironically, this was an argument often made by the anti-Zionist left in order to question Labour's internationalism.)

A broad political Zionist vision was the demand of the hour, insisted Jabotinsky, not a 'cult of the cow' in which, farm by farm, Zionism tried to make Palestine Jewish. However, despite his frequent protestations of 'class neutrality', of a 'monism' solely concerned with the nation as a whole and not one segment of it, Jabotinsky and his party – which was founded at the same time as the Fourth Aliyah middle-class immigration into Palestine – were clear as to who composed their prospective constituency. 'My dear man', Jabotinsky wrote to his colleague Schechtman on 4 July, 1925, 'don't delude yourself: though many workers are tempted to accept our programme, our true field of action is the *Mittelstand*'.[41] To counter Labour's claims on behalf of the proletariat, Jabotinsky proclaimed the future to be in the hands of 'We the "Bourgeoisie" ', as he entitled an article in 1927.[42] It was a title that revealed a great deal about his underlying social and political orientation.

As early as 1925 Jabotinsky accused the ZO of having been 'captured' by the left – it was an extremely premature accusation – and excessively preoccupied with subsidizing labour institutions, to the detriment of artisans in particular and private settlers in general.[43] Where Labour extolled the manual and agricultural worker, Jabotinsky extolled the shopkeeper and the historical role of Jews in commerce; materially and culturally, he declared, it was the merchant that carried progress forth.[44] Clearly, for all political and practical reasons, Jabotinsky and his backers were seeking to reset the Zionist agenda – and the political culture of Jewish nationalism – in direct opposition to Labour's emphasis on re-creating and 'normalizing' the socio-economic structure of Jewry, with the attendant stress on the role of the worker and national, as opposed to private, capital. And Jabotinsky had specific recommendations: reorient the ZO budget and priorities away from Labour institutions, kibbutzim and the Histadrut, and aid private settlers, the middle class and the artisans instead.[45]

Since Jabotinsky's Zionism assumed the primacy of the political, narrowly conceived, the Revisionists inevitably would seek to dominate that institution which conducted Zionist diplomacy, the ZO. Jabotinsky, in fact, was doubtful that this could be accomplished. However, he had to balance the need for unity within his own party – many of whose adherents opposed a break with the ZO and preferred to struggle within it – with his restless desire to pursue his own course, free from the restrictions of a larger organization, to whose rules and decisions he had to submit. More than this, his public and private statements make it appear that he was temperamentally incapable of playing the role of opposition leader within a democratic framework, in particular that of the Zionist Congress. In his utterances he expressed radical personal contempt for his opponents and, despite his proclaimed fidelity, alternately, to liberalism and to national and individual discipline, he displayed a manifest incapacity to abide by electoral defeat. According to Ben-Gurion, not long after the Revisionists broke from the ZO altogether to form, in 1935, a competing but quickly faltering New Zionist Organization (NZO), Jabotinsky approached him with a proposal to replace the ZO with a 'Jewish National Assembly'. Ben-Gurion asked Jabotinsky if he was willing to be subject to such an assembly if his list failed to gain a majority in elections, and Jabotinsky replied: 'I cannot be in a minority. I have nothing to do in the minority'.[46]

For Jabotinsky, there were two types of 'spiritual races', one which shrinks before difficult obstacles and one which is unyielding and returns to the fray fully, time and again.[47] He clearly saw Weizmann and the other ZO leaders in one category, and himself and his supporters in the other. A year after his party was formed he responded to criticisms that he was subverting the authority of the duly constituted leadership of the ZO by declaring that 'We consider it the duty of every true Zionist to participate in this hygienic work. Should we not purge ourselves of this "authority", the Zionist cause will soon be turned over to assimilationists, lose its spirit, sense and pathos . . .'[48] In a private letter in 1931 he wrote that he could not 'finish my days as "opposition" to a crowd of spiritual bastards which calls itself the ZO'.[49] One reason the ZO was vehemently opposed to Jabotinsky's plan in the 1930s for a petition campaign throughout Europe linked to calling a congress and creating a league of petitioners to pressure public opinion was the (probably justified) suspicion that he hoped to use this effort to undermine, and then to compete with, the ZO.[50]

A 'loyal opposition', one whose *modus operandi* is in harmony with a system's essential constitutional requirements, may be contrasted with an 'opposition of principle', whose behaviour reflects an aim of goal displacement incompatible with those requirements.[51] Jabotinsky and his party were frustrated in their role as loyal opposition, began to function as an opposition of principle and eventually left the ZO, seeking to replace it. However, in that process Jabotinsky was compelled to stage a putsch against the Executive of his own party which, in 1933, outnumbered him on the question of a split from the ZO. He simply announced publicly (in his 'Lodz Manifesto') that he, personally, was taking control of the party's institutions, re-creating the Executive, and then, cleverly outmanoeuvring his foes, declared that he *would* take part in the elections to the forthcoming Zionist Congress. This was followed by a plebiscite among party members confirming his move by a vote of 93.8 per cent to 6.2 per cent. The leader had the masses, but not his colleagues. As a close associate put it, 'He . . . railroaded the conflict onto a purely personal track: whom does the movement trust and prefer – Jabotinsky or his four colleagues [that he ousted from the Executive]?'[52] Those 'Democratic Revisionists' who found this behaviour intolerable remained as a loyal opposition within the ZO in the form of the 'Jewish State Party', led by Meir Grossman and Richard Lichtheim. In a pamphlet, this faction declared that it 'accepts the rule of the majority', and considered itself 'a constituent part' of the ZO, in which it would play the role of 'healthy opposition'.[53]

Before these events, however, in the late 1920s and in 1931, the possibility of Revisionist dominance in the ZO, in a coalition with the conservative General Zionists and the Religious Zionists, was a real possibility. The Revisionists were, besides Labour, the most dynamic force on the Zionist scene. Campaigning hard for a proclamation of Zionist *endziel*, Revisionist strength grew dramatically; while they received only 2 per cent and 4 per cent of the delegates to, respectively, the 1925 and 1927 Zionist Congresses, by 1929 the Revisionists were the third largest party and drew a quarter of the vote by 1931. This new potency was expressed both in the diaspora and in Palestine. Labour's Moshe Shertok, later to be the political secretary of the Jewish Agency, attributed the Revisionist surge in 1931 to 'skillful', but 'unscrupulous' 'exploitation' of 'the feelings of bitterness and impotent anger which have swayed the Jewish masses during the last two years'.[54] In Palestine this bitterness was partly the consequence of anti-Jewish rioting by Arabs in 1929, which was followed by a series of twists and turns in British policy that did not bode well for the Zionist project. In elections to the Asefat ha-Nivharim the Revisionists won 15 out of the 71 seats in 1931. Labour, which won 31 seats, saw this contest as primarily between itself and the Revisionists.[55] In Poland, perhaps the most important reservoir of the diaspora in the interwar years (after Stalin's Russia had been closed off), the Revisionists became especially strong, and doubled their vote to the Zionist Congresses between 1931 and 1933. As one historian has noted, 'Revisionism, with its great stress on integral Jewish nationalism, untrammelled by a socialist dimension, was well suited to gain adherents in a period of growing Polish nationalism and at a time when the various strategies of the General Zionists . . . revealed themselves to be bankrupt'.[56]

At the 15th and 16th Zionist Congresses (respectively, 1927 and 1929) Jabotinsky furiously, and unsuccessfully, fought Weizmann's plan to include wealthy and influential non-Zionists abroad in an extended Jewish Agency. Jabotinsky argued that it would make the Zionist Organization superfluous and destroy the Zionist Congress's character as a national assembly. By the 1931 Congress the conflict within the Zionist movement had dramatically intensified. The ZO leadership became increasingly alarmed by what it saw as Revisionist efforts to organize not just as a party but as an alternative to the ZO itself, and by the tendency of the Revisionists to act however they saw fit, irrespective of ZO policy. This led to a fierce struggle over the meaning of 'Zionist discipline'. The Revisionists, seeing the ZO as a creature of its foes, sought ways to pursue independent political activities, including diplomatic initiatives, aimed at various governments. The ZO saw in this an attempt to side-step policies determined by the Zionist movement as a whole through its elected representatives. In a period of increasing problems for Zionism and Jewry, the ZO's lack of sovereign status – its inability, as the nationalist organization of a diaspora people, to claim successfully, in Weber's phrase, 'the *monopoly of the legitimate use of force* within a given territory'[57] – was particularly evident. One could almost say that this problem illustrated the entire point of Zionism.

The ZO's effectiveness depended on its status as the recognized representative of the Jewish national movement. Its ability to function was clearly undermined if its constituents did not voluntarily submit to its decisions, and if, when disgruntled, they were at liberty to present themselves as the authentic voice of Zionism to whomsoever they pleased. Acquiescence to such a situation would have been suicidal. The ZO became increasingly alarmed by Revisionist behaviour, especially after the fourth World Revisionist Conference, meeting in Prague in August 1930, suspended its commitment, made two years earlier, to accept the Zionist Executive's political prerogatives. It was evident that direct collisions were unavoidable, both between the Revisionists and the Labour movement, and between the Revisionists and the ZO.

8
Jabotinsky and the Challenge from the Right II

No doubt the artist is the child of his time; but woe to him if he is
also its disciple . . .

Friedrich Schiller[1]

I

The 17th Zionist Congress took place in Basle in the summer of 1931. It
was there that left and right first faced each other with substantial
delegations, and the outcome, inevitably, was confrontation. The Revisionists came bidding for power and hoping to oust Weizmann. Jabotinsky,
several months earlier, indicated in private that his patience with the ZO
was worn out, declaring that '. . . unless this Congress satisfies my
Revisionist conscience, Revisionism must become independent and I, for
one, will no longer adhere to any organisation even theoretically subordinate to the ZO'.[2] Labour came both asserting itself and backing Weizmann.
Shortly after the Congress ended, Ben-Gurion wrote to his wife that of all
the congresses he had attended, 'I've never been to one as difficult, nerve
racking, and critical as this one'.[3]

   Polarization between left and right reflected the organizational weakness
of the centre, and also a general malaise in Zionism due to a series of
traumas it had sustained, beginning with the riots by Palestinian Arabs in
1929, which ended several years of relative quiescence in Jewish–Arab
affairs. 1929 was also a harbinger of what was to come in British–Zionist
relations, even though at this time severe tensions were only temporary, and
in the 1930s the Yishuv would make substantial progress. (Arab rebellion
and pressure eventually led to the effective repudiation of the Balfour
Declaration and an anti-Zionist policy on the part of the British government
by the outbreak of the Second World War). In the aftermath of 1929, the
General Zionists received much of the blame since they were dominant in
the ZO. It was Weizmann who suffered most since he was identified with a
pro-British policy and moderation towards the Arabs. The Shaw Commission,

dispatched by London to investigate the turmoil, issued a report which placed immediate blame for the bloodshed on the Arabs, but pointed to Jewish immigration into Palestine as the source of the problem. Then, in turn, came the Hope-Simpson Report and the Passfield White Paper, both of which challenged the feasibility of the Zionist project and especially large-scale Jewish settlement in Palestine. The White Paper reinterpreted the Balfour Declaration so as to emphasize British obligations to the Arabs at the expense of building the Jewish national home. (The Declaration stipulated that Britain would facilitate the national home, 'it being clearly understood that nothing shall be done which may prejudice the civil and religious rights of existing non-Jewish communities in Palestine'.[4]) While the 'MacDonald Letter' of 1931 nullified what Zionists found most offensive in the White Paper, the damage had been done in Zionist public opinion, and especially to Weizmann, even though he was responsible for the British prime minister's repudiation of the Passfield policy.

Weizmann's status was further compromised when, seeking to be conciliatory to the British and the Arabs, he told an interviewer in the midst of the 17th Congress: 'I have no sympathy or understanding for the demand for a Jewish majority [in Palestine]. A majority does not necessarily guarantee security . . . A majority is not required for the development of Jewish civilization and culture'. Making such claims, he went on, would lead the world to think erroneously that the Jews wanted to expel the Arabs. 'Why should we raise a demand which can only make a provocative impression?'[5] These remarks aroused the ire of the Congress delegates, including Mapai's. Labour's position was delicate; it found Weizmann's statement unacceptable, but also didn't want to see him undermined. In the end Weizmann was forced to step down as the ZO president, and was replaced by the Hebrew publicist and editor Nahum Sokolow.

The defeat of Weizmann, however, was not the victory of Jabotinsky. With much bluster, the Revisionist chief failed to get the Congress to adopt his resolution on the Zionist *endziel:* 'The aim of Zionism, which is expressed in the terms "Jewish State", "National Home", or "National Home secured by public law" [the last being the formulation of the Basle Programme – M.C.], is the creation of a Jewish majority on both sides of the Jordan'.[6] While Mapai and most of the other parties wanted a Jewish majority in Palestine as much as did the Revisionists, they found such a proclamation – even aside from the problem of its integralist formulation – politically ill-advised. Berl Katznelson compared Jabotinsky to someone shouting as loud as he could while walking through a forest filled with bears.[7] Some 13 years later, when Ben-Gurion advocated the public demand for statehood and struggled with opponents of it in the left wing of the Labour movement, he recalled why he adamantly opposed in 1931 what he later supported. At the 17th Congress, Ben-Gurion said, he was incredulous to discover that, in the aftermath of 1929, with Jewish immigration virtually at a standstill and no more than 170,000 Jews in Palestine, the Revisionists were preoccupied with making declarations about Zionism's *endziel*. This evidently struck him as a supreme example of preposterous political timing, combined with an irresponsible obsession with the expressive dimensions of politics.[8] In his speech to the Congress, Ben-Gurion ridiculed the 'easy Zionism' of the Revisionists for its reliance on slogans rather than concrete work, for a simplistic faith in the long-term efficacy of British protection of the Yishuv and for disregard of the Arabs on both banks of the Jordan.[9] Both Berl Locker and Haim Arlosoroff, from Mapai, made it clear that they thought a state was the means, not the end, of Zionism, the former declaring that the final goal was the liberation of the Jewish people, and Arlosoroff defining it as 'the creation in Palestine of conditions which would enable the Jewish people to determine its own destiny'.[10]

The Congress voted not to vote on Jabotinsky's proposal, and after his colleague Meir Grossman was shouted down, the frustrated Revisionist leader tore up his delegate card and walked out. Jabotinsky's failure was compounded by the fact that he saw himself as Weizmann's obvious successor. The new Executive that the Congress elected, whatever problems its members had with the former president's recent statement, basically accepted his Zionist strategy. The Revisionists were, at one point, very close to obtaining substantial political power, but then badly miscalculated – in a way which one is tempted to call characteristic. Emanuel Neumann, leader of the Zionist Organization of America, conducted negotiations on the formation of the Executive on behalf of most of the General Zionists, and in close contact with Mizrahi. These two factions, together with the Revisionists, could have dominated the Congress and stemmed the rise of Mapai. However, in his words,

> I found the Revisionists to be suffering from the consequences of their unexpected good fortune [Weizmann's collapse]. They were in sight of the 'Promised Land' – the capture of the Zionist leadership – which they hoped to achieve at one stroke, and they were laying down impossible conditions. Assuming that the Congress would now accept their proposal regarding the *Endziel*, they said they would consent to enter the Zionist Executive, provided they would be given fifty per cent of the seats on that body.[11]

This was unacceptable to Neumann – who, in fact, sympathized with the Revisionist demand on the *endziel* – and to others, but the Revisionists refused to compromise. Neumann feared that Mapai would never participate in the Zionist Executive on the basis of the Revisionist demands and felt strongly that the ZO would be damaged, perhaps irreparably, by a Labour exit on the heels of Weizmann's defeat. The result was the formation of a coalition with Mapai and without Weizmann or the Revisionists. Jabotinsky approached Neumann 'at the twelfth hour' seeking a compromise but by then the coalition agreement had been sealed.[12] 'As the leader of a party in opposition he [Jabotinsky] was not always sufficiently cautious in taking cover when attacking or in planning exactly where and how to carry out his plan', Meir Grossman later observed. 'He was himself so fascinated by the ideas he proclaimed that he was apt to forget the existence of obstacles and of many problems connected with the realisation of ideas which had to be taken into account'.[13] In a way, this summarizes Jabotinsky's failure as a politician in 1931, as well as in many other episodes.

Two out of the five elected to the new ZO Executive, Locker and Arlosoroff, were from Mapai, and the latter, known for his moderation on the Arab question, became the organization's political secretary. Yet Labour saw the Congress less as a triumph than as a blocking action. In Shertok's evaluation, the Congress 'brought no victories to the Labour movement or to Zionism as such. All that Labour can claim is that it helped to save Congress from committing disastrous blunders'. Labour, in his view, had underestimated the extent of the hostility to Weizmann and in backing him to the last moment almost pushed his General Zionist foes into an alliance with the Revisionists. Unhappy with the options before it, Mapai decided to prevent a centre–right coalition by forming one with the General Zionists and Mizrahi. Mapai was unable to establish 'an Executive all to its liking; but it brought about a coalition that turned its back definitively upon Revisionism'.[14]

II

Jabotinsky now found himself in an increasingly difficult situation. He pressed for a Revisionist break with the ZO, knowing full well how hazardous this path would be. Separatism was opposed strongly by some of his most respected colleagues like Richard Lichtheim and Grossman. On the other hand it was fervently advocated by his Palestinian supporters, whose most prominent figures tended to be the most extreme in his movement. To Lichtheim he wrote: 'I don't try to conceal from myself that this may prove the beginning of the end of my work and of me as a public man. But I cannot act otherwise than I am acting now. This congress was to me an ultimatum – change or sink – and I've got to go my own way'.[15] None the less, the issue of a split remained blurred for some time as the Revisionists tried to straddle the fence, now leaning more to independence, but still unresolved fully on a final break.

In late September 1931 the Revisionist Executive met in Calais and reached an internal compromise: the World Union of Revisionist Zionists would regard itself as independent, but concurrently it would not withdraw from the ZO. Individual members could, if they so chose, buy the Shekel (i.e. ZO membership and voting rights to Congress elections), but the Revisionist party's 'discipline' would have primacy over that of the ZO or any other organization. The Revisionist organization would feel free to pursue whatever diplomatic initiatives it saw fit and to launch the petition campaign Jabotinsky believed so important. Clearly, Jabotinsky thought that he now had a free hand – or at least a much freer hand – and just as clearly, and inevitably, the ZO saw this move as a direct challenge. The ZO had reiterated often that all Zionists had the right to form parties or organizations to represent their views and contest Congress elections; however, the ZO's policies, and decisions by its Executive, its congresses and its court, had to be considered binding on affiliates.

The 'Calais Compromise' manifestly violated this position, and the Zionist Executive issued a strongly worded statement in early December to the effect that its previous 'forbearance' had been 'misplaced' and 'abused' since 'Revisionist attacks against the Zionist Executive degenerated after the Seventeenth Congress into a struggle against the Zionist Organisation itself . . .' The recent Revisionist decision was perceived as 'far-reaching' and 'in complete disregard' of the ZO constitution in that Calais permitted the Revisionists to function as a sovereign body: 'It is to be free from the influence of the Zionist Organisation . . . but it claims the right to influence the decisions and the activities of the Zionist Organisation through members of the "World Union" [of Revisionist Zionists], who shall be at liberty to purchase the Shekel and to take part in Zionist Congresses'. The question of 'discipline' was the crucial one. The ZO, it was emphasized, was a democratic organization, its Executive was elected and it was impermissable for separate negotiations to occur between Zionist parties and governments without the consent and co-ordination of the ZO Executive. ZO membership entailed, 'Compliance with its rules and decisions, and it is incompatible with membership in an outside body requiring acceptance of a discipline which may conflict with and take precedence over the duty of allegiance to the ZO'. Finally the Executive warned that the ZO would have to 'combat with every means at its command the invasion of anarchy into the sphere of organisation and politics'.[16]

The following summer the fifth Revisionist World Conference endorsed Calais, asserted that the movement was no longer an 'integral part' of the ZO and went forth with the petition campaign.[17] The tension within the Revisionists, however, was still unresolved since individual Revisionists could still participate in the ZO. A meeting in Kattowitz the following spring was supposed to resolve the matter once and for all, and when it was unable to do so, Jabotinsky issued his 'Lodz Declaration', seized control of the organization personally, suspended his foes (some of whom then formed the Jewish State party) and committed himself to taking part in the next Zionist Congress – although it was clear that thereafter he would go his own way.

A constellation of circumstances complicated the situation still further. Both Labour and the Revisionists recognized that in Palestine itself the most formidable obstacle to Revisionist aspirations was Labour's pillar, the Histadrut, which had accrued a remarkable record of practical achievements there and was the forceful, organized proponent of a socialist vision in the country. Indeed, even if the right had gained control of the ZO, it would still have to face this formidable and hostile presence; since the Histadrut was a class institution by definition, it was as much Labour's bastion as it was anathema to the Revisionist programme. Bitter conflict over the organization of employment in Palestine became virtually unavoidable. In 1929 a new influx of immigrants began arriving in Palestine and among them were significant numbers of Revisionists and Betarim (members of Betar, the Revisionist youth movement). Jabotinsky's adherents refused to join the Histadrut and boycotted its labour exchanges on the grounds that job dispersal should not be under the auspices of a 'political' and class institution. This pleased some employers, but it also made for a very difficult situation for Betarim seeking work since the Histadrut exchanges dominated the organization of work recruitment.

The Mandatory authorities barred Jabotinsky's entry into Palestine after 1930, which was a considerable impediment to a movement so dependent on a charismatic leader.[18] At the same time, Palestinian Revisionism became perhaps the most radical and anti-Labour segment of the movement. In late 1930 it came under the dominance of its most extreme elements, and especially a group of former Labour adherents led by Abba Ahimeir, a fanatic and previously a Ha-Poel ha-Tsair member who was enamoured of Mussolini, wrote a newspaper column entitled 'From the Notebook of a Fascist' and whose followers formed *Brit ha-Biryonim* (the Union of Thugs). This shady group – which derived its name from an extremist sect at the time of the first Jewish revolt against Rome – not only espoused terror and assassination but denounced democracy and parliamentarism and advocated fascistic politics. They were especially vigorous – and vicious – in attacking 'Marxists', 'Leftists' and Labour's leaders in unabashed langauge. (In *Brit ha-Biryonim*'s publications Mapai's Haim Arlosoroff was, for instance, called 'Foreskinoff' and 'The Red Diplomat'[19]). Jabotinsky was often discomforted and angered by Ahimeir and his followers, particularly when they called on him to declare himself the 'Duce' of Palestine, and when their newspaper suggested that the Nazis had good ideas, apart from their anti-Semitism.[20] However, while Jabotinsky criticized Ahimeir's group (at times harshly), he would not reject it or dissociate himself from it.

An important element in the conflicts that soon unfolded was the fact that Palestine lacked labour legislation. Both the ZO and the Yishuv's representative institutions frequently called for enactment of social and labour laws – as well as a compulsory arbitration board and 'neutral' labour exchanges (i.e. employment offices including representatives of both the workers and the employers). At times the Vaad Leumi involved itself in solving labour disputes.[21] In 1925, as a result of ongoing labour conflicts, the Zionist Executive and the Vaad Leumi met with representatives of the employers and the Histadrut, and created a 'Commission of 15' under Arthur Ruppin in order 'to settle working conditions in the country as well as the relations between workers and employers'.[22] On the commission were five representatives from the employers and five from the workers, along with five from the Vaad Leumi and the Zionist Executive, and the secretary of the Labour Department of the Zionist Executive. This commission met several times and discussed hiring and firing practices, the role of labour exchanges, hours and wages, and participation of the employers in Kupat Holim (the Sick Fund – the Histadrut's Health Services).[23] However, in the end the commission accomplished little that was concrete; other efforts to establish a regime for labour relations were similarly inconclusive.

In the early 1930s Betar immigrants began strike-breaking and seeking to undermine the Histadrut on the grounds that, given its class nature and its dominance by Mapai, Histadrut efforts to establish closed shops were, virtually by definition, political acts, and that the labour exchanges were, in the final analysis, political weapons. The Histadrut was accused by both Revisionists and employers of establishing a dictatorship in the organization of work. It was evident that the concerns of the Revisionists were not solely economic and the finding of employment for their adherents. Their chief demands were the creation of 'neutral' labour exchanges (which would be under 'national' rather than Histadrut auspices, and which would be run by 'neutral' bureaucrats, with representatives of the workers and employers in an advisory capacity), and the establishment, under the auspices of the ZO or the Vaad Leumi, of a system of national compulsory arbitration of all labour disputes. Acceptance of such proposals would have weakened the Histadrut substantially as both a political and an economic force, and the Revisionists were acutely aware of this. Their demand was not for equal representation of employers and workers in the exchanges but 'national' control of them.

Labour, too, knew well the importance of the exchanges for its own power, but also saw them within the more general context of working-class needs. In a country totally lacking in legislation to protect labour, and in which there was constant immigration of Jewish workers who had to compete for work with cheaper local (Arab) labour, the organization and regulation of the labour market through labour exchanges were not only critical but, as one Labour advocate put it, 'an agent of collective bargaining', the tools by which immigrant workers, who shifted from locale to locale and from job to job frequently, could be in some way protected. Employers' complaints of 'dictatorship' by the Histadrut were dismissed on the grounds that the employers simply wanted to do what they accused the

Histadrut of doing: 'They wanted "freedom" to employ and dismiss, implying freedom to dictate their own terms of employment, in other words, freedom to exploit'. The Histadrut's reply, this author claimed – somewhat contradicting his own argument – was that 'this is not an issue of capital v. labour but, primarily, of chaos v. organisation'.[24]

The Histadrut was, in fact, willing to create joint exchanges with employers. In mid-1930 the Labour federation reached an agreement with the Magdiel Colony, later adopted in the villages of Raananah and Bnei Brak as well, in which a labour exchange was established which included representatives of the workers and the employers, together with an 'umpire' chosen by both sides. The agreement entailed provisions protecting local employment, forbidding work stoppages, and determining that all labour conflicts be brought to the exchange. Consequently, a Histadrut journalist wrote in response to Revisionist attacks that 'The theory of the "neutral exchange" is that there is something fundamentally pernicious about workers and employers arriving at a compromise of their own accord'. The Revisionist proposal for a separate national arbitration authority under the Zionist Executive or the Vaad Leumi, besides having 'a faint aroma reminiscent of the Fascist state theory', supposed that someone from the Zionist Executive was 'neutral' and would be able to grasp local problems adequately. In the end, such an arbitrator would be a 'helpless spectator' if agreements were violated. The ZO had no coercive powers and 'The Revisionists certainly know all this, their real aim not being to solve the wage labour problem, but to wreck the Labour Federation'.[25]

Ben-Gurion claimed that no arbitrator was 'neutral' or 'objective' because determining the relative value of an owner's profit margin and the workers' needs for remuneration was dependent on one's broader social and economic perspective.[26] In addition, the Histadrut was able to point out that it had previously worked out acceptable agreements on the division of labour and similar matters with other groups including the Artisans' Association and Ha-Poel ha-Mizrahi (The Mizrahi Worker – the Religious Zionist Workers' party). At least in principle, it was on the public record as willing to do the same with the Revisionists. The Histadrut leaders stressed the seriousness with which they had named their organization a *General* Confederation of Labour; they hoped to have all workers within its orbit.

A series of direct clashes, both verbal and physical, between Labour and the Revisionists rose in a crescendo in Palestine in 1932 and 1933 as Betar members were fairly successful in breaking strikes and placing the Histadrut on the defensive.[27] Employers who did not want to meet Histadrut wage demands or who were angered at the Histadrut's insistence on the principle of Jewish labour were encouraged. In Kfar Saba in 1930 planters collaborated with the Revisionists to bring in Betar workers to circumvent the labour exchanges. Ben-Gurion appealed to the Betar workers, assuring them that they had as much a right to work as other anyone else, but that it was only fair that they enter the local labour market the way other workers did, which meant through the labour exchange. The Revisionist workers refused and soon found themselves in physical confrontations and clashes with Histadrut workers and compelled to go to work under police escort.

The most explosive battle came in 1932 after the Jerusalem labour council called a strike against the Froumine biscuit factory. In localities around Palestine, Histadrut members elected labour councils which in turn directed, in conjunction with the national organization, the Histadrut's local activities, especially the labour exchanges. The strike was called when Froumine refused unionization, rejected the creation of a closed shop and declined to commit itself to hiring solely through the Histadrut labour exchange. When a woman worker who was not a Histadrut member insisted on working, and when Betar claimed, incorrectly, that she was one of their members, the strike snowballed into a Labour–Revisionist confrontation. After the strikers refused arbitration, Froumine began hiring Betar scabs, leading in the end to a defeat for the Histadrut, which was compelled to accept a settlement permitting scabs and strike-breakers to retain their jobs.[28] February 1933 saw a strike in the building industry in Petah Tikvah after contractors refused to recognize the union. Again Betar came in force to strike-break, with the backing of the contractors, local citrus-growers and segments of the Mizrahi and General Zionists.

The Revisionist press assaulted Labour without restraint and the latter replied in kind. Just before May Day 1933 Mapai posters appeared branding the Revisionists as 'the students of Hitler' on 'the Jewish street'.[29] From abroad Jabotinsky urged his followers on with incendiary articles. In one entitled 'Yes, Break Them', Jabotinsky, while admitting that workers needed organization, called for smashing the Histadrut's power in the name of the primacy of national over class interests. He called for a system of national compulsory arbitration, and expressed especial contempt for Histadrut involvement in organizing Arab workers. The thrust of his argument went as follows:

> Even a socialist understands that building a Hebrew country in our time is only possible in the framework of the present social regime. Without private capital, there is no possibility of building; and it is of the character of private capital that it goes where there is a hope of gaining profits. It may be that this characteristic of private capital is very bad, but it is a deeply rooted, organic characteristic which cannot be eradicated and it must be recognized unless one wants to postpone the building of the country and the realization of Zionism until the entire world is ruled by another social order.[30]

With sarcasm, he suggested that those interested in another social order stay in the diaspora and make a revolution there. However, if someone 'chooses to immigrate to Palestine, especially as a Zionist pioneer, it is obvious that he is no longer a "worker", or a "proletarian", but rather a volunteer' and volunteers go with the willingness to suffer for higher interests than material and personal ones; volunteers, therefore, had to rid themselves of 'sentimental compassion [*ha-rahamim ha-sentimentaliyim*]'.[31]

There was a transparently contradictory character to Jabotinsky's assertions: in the same breath he insisted on the rights of capital to profit while telling workers to sacrifice and forgo their sentimentalism. As enmity intensified and clashes mounted, Mapai conducted a vigorous internal debate on whether to respond to strike-breaking with controlled violence. Ben-Gurion at first took a radical posture – 'Whenever I hear an outcry against violence on moral grounds, I am unaffected, for all I see is class hypocrisy' – while Berl Katznelson argued against responding to the devil with his own tactics. He supported defusing the labour conflicts by accepting most of the Revisionist demands – the creation of a neutral labour exchange, resolving the Betar unemployment problem and establishing a system of national arbitration.[32] While Ben-Gurion himself eventually shifted to Katznelson's position, Mapai established 'activist' squads to strong-arm the Revisionists – which they did in a number of cases.

III

These tumultuous events occurred not only while Jabotinsky was in the process of splitting his own movement and reconsolidating it in preparation for an exit from the ZO, but also as the election campaign – Jabotinsky's last – for the 18th Zionist Congress, scheduled for summer 1933, was getting under way. The struggle between Labour and the Revisionists turned into a vitriolic electoral competition in the Yishuv which spilled over into the diaspora. Then, in June 1933, Arlosoroff was assassinated while taking an evening stroll with his wife on a Tel Aviv beach. The youthful rising star of the Labour movement, Arlosoroff was then the political secretary of the Jewish Agency, and had long been the target of Revisionist fury. He had been singled out recently because his efforts to get Jews out of Hitler's Germany included negotiating with the Nazis for a transfer of German Jewish properties to Palestine in the form of German products. For this he was accused of treacherously subverting efforts at an economic boycott of the anti-Semitic regime. Several Revisionists from *Brit ha-Biryonim* were charged with planning, inspiring and committing the murder. Among those arrested was Ahimeir, whose newspaper, *Hazit Ha-am*, declared, in reference to Arlosoroff on the day of the shooting, that 'Jews have always known how to deal with those who trade on the honor and beliefs of their people'.[33]

The horrified Mapai leadership was convinced that the accused were guilty. 'Arlosoroff represented moderation, caution, a balanced approach to world problems and, of course to our own', Golda Meir recalled some four decades later, 'and his tragic death seemed the inevitable consequence of the kind of anti-socialist rightwing militarism and violent chauvinism that was being advocated by the Revisionists'.[34] A controversial trial ensued a year later, with Jabotinsky and the Revisionists insisting that the accused were innocent and the victims of a Mapai 'blood libel'. (They were convicted and then freed owing to an absence of corroborating evidence.)[35] In the meantime Zionist public opinion recoiled and this undoubtedly helped Mapai to sweep the Congress elections. Mapai received 44 per cent of the vote (71 per cent in Palestine), up from 29 per cent in 1931, making it the major party in Zionism and essential to any coalition running the Executive. The Revisionists were resoundingly defeated, falling from 25 per cent in 1931 to 14 per cent. At the Congress itself they were isolated by Mapai whose *modus operandi* for future Zionist (and later Israeli) politics was now established, and can be summarized in one sentence in a letter Ben-Gurion sent after the Congress: 'I have always favoured a broad coalition – everyone apart from the Revisionists'.[36]

In fact, despite Mapai's success in quarantining the Revisionists – starting with their exclusion from the Congress presidium – it was unsuccessful in attaining a broad coalition. Such a coalition would have had to include both the Weizmannite General Zionists A, who were inclined to work with Labour but whom Ben-Gurion considered 'weak-willed', and the larger General Zionist B faction which, as Ben-Gurion accurately assumed, was ultimately hostile to Mapai.[37] Mapai was able to establish only a narrow coalition including General Zionists A. The new Executive of nine had four members from Mapai – a reluctant Ben-Gurion (who was concerned that his ZO work would interfere with his Histadrut responsibilities), Shertok (taking Arlosoroff's place as political secretary), Eliezer Kaplan and Berl Locker. Significantly, three of them were in Palestine where they would be able to dominate the increasingly central Palestine Zionist Executive. Sokolow was re-elected ZO president.

The Congress took several actions pertaining to the Revisionists. A resolution was passed barring ZO affiliates from negotiating with governments or the League of Nations except by permission of the Executive. It was declared that 'The adhesion of persons and bodies to the Zionist Organization presupposes that in all Zionist questions the duty of discipline in regard to the Zionist Organization must take precedence over the duty of discipline in regard to any other organization'.[38] The Congress voted to condemn strike-breaking and declared that 'The Congress regards the attempts to break up the camp of workers and to split its organisation as morally and economically detrimental . . .'[39] As to labour exchanges, the Congress resolved that 'the establishment of joint and harmoniously working labour bureaux by the employees and the employers on the basis of labour agreements' was 'a desirable means of solving the question of providing and equitably dividing labour among all in search of work'. The

Zionist Executive was entrusted with exploring, with employees and employers, the creation of 'a joint supreme labour authority'.[40] Before the Congress, at a meeting of the ZO General Council, a Commission of Inquiry was created at Mapai's request to examine violence in the Zionist movement, and at the Congress a resolution was passed establishing a commission to investigate 'allegations' that 'persons or groups of persons' within the ZO in Palestine used political violence.[41] This was clearly aimed at the Revisionists, and Katznelson declared that a file in his possession – part of which later mysteriously disappeared – demonstrated that within Revisionist ranks there were terrorists. It seems that the inquiry commission, which included some of the Zionist movement's most distinguished figures – Ussishkin, Leo Motzkin, Rabbi Meir Berlin (Bar-Ilan) – was appalled at some of the evidence, though they were not satisfied that a direct link between the terrorists (*Brit ha-Biryonim*) and the Revisionist movement as a whole was substantiated.

The Congress represented an important turning-point. The Revisionists were routed and Mapai was victorious, although in triumph it sought to leave doors open to cooperation with as many of its competitors – except the Revisionists – as possible. Mapai was now indisputably the leader of the national coalition; the Zionist centre and religious parties were moving towards working with it and recognizing its dominance which, in turn, was increasingly consolidated. The Revisionists became an increasingly isolated, sectarian force, as much by their own strategy and actions as by Mapai's efforts to delegitimize them. The Labour Zionist movement, in the meantime, could now dominate the priorities of the Zionist movement as a whole. However, as indicated above, and as will be shown at greater length in the next chapters, this entailed a final relinquishing of the politics that brought it to a position of hegemony in the first place; Labour's leadership was secured as it abandoned the identification of the interests of the working class with that of the nation.

9

Terms of Conflict

Two souls, alas, are dwelling in my breast,
And each would be severed from its brother.

Goethe's Faust¹

I

The Revisionists finally abandoned the ZO altogether after a dramatic last
attempt by Ben-Gurion and Jabotinsky to negotiate a compromise in the
autumn of 1934 in extensive – and at first secret – talks in London. It was an
unparalleled performance on the part of both of them. A series of
agreements was in fact reached, but Ben-Gurion's own Labour movement
voted them down following several months of furious debate. The London
episode is surprising both because of the concessions Ben-Gurion made in
order to maintain national unity – it amounted to a veritable *volte-face* –
and because of the genuine personal warmth and rapport that developed
between arch-enemies. Indeed, in a note Jabotinsky wrote to thank the
woman in whose house some of the discussions occurred he commented:
'Our mutual friendliness and cordiality is a surprise for both of us, and
when his [Ben-Gurion's] party learns how he broiled eggs on your gas-grille
for me to eat he'll be lynched'.[2] While Ben-Gurion was not hanged, a storm
of unprecedented proportions was unleashed within Labour ranks by this
turn of events.

The correspondence between the two men during the negotiations in
London and the ensuing controversy is revealing. Jabotinsky leaves the
impression that Ben-Gurion was presenting himself in a new way to his foe.
The Revisionist expressed excited delight because Ben-Gurion called him
'comrade' and 'friend', and indicated faith in the goodwill of his
counterpart. He doubted whether Ben-Gurion's sentiments were representative of Mapai as a whole, but 'the important thing' – which he found a
revelation – was what 'the brains [at] the top of the movement' thought.[3]
After Labour voted their accords down, cordiality remained a hallmark of

their letters; at the same time, they articulated vividly to each other what had separated the politics of their respective movements. Ben-Gurion's words are particularly striking because they sharply etch the world-view from which his practical politics were already deviating. Jabotinsky displayed all his characteristic eloquence.

On 30 March, 1935 Jabotinsky wrote to Ben-Gurion that despite the failure of their agreement, and despite the fact that they were likely soon to be embattled again, he held 'the man BG and his aim' in 'great esteem' as a consequence of London. His letter went on to capture, in a remarkable way, his general political perspective, together with all his criticisms of the Labour movement, and his belief in the politics of simplicity. The primal remained primary for Jabotinsky who averred that it is not multi-dimensional motivations that inspire human beings in politics. He is worth quoting at length:

> You told me that I exaggerate the influence of pure 'class consciousness' on the spirit of your Movement, and you showed me your articles, which indeed demonstrate that there is no 'Shaatnez' now in you. I asked then too: 'Are you sure that the bulk of your Movement is also like that?' and you answered 'Yes' with absolute conviction. In my heart of hearts I did not believe it (although I didn't expect that there would be a *majority* to turn down our agreement). I remembered from my youth the overpowering fascination of the Marxist doctrine, the chain of logic from which not a single link can be extracted except by violence. You and your generation, founders of the Zionist labour movement . . . fashioned a very delicate blend of that doctrine and Zionism; perhaps the two really merged in your minds, but it is a work of art which only artists can understand and cherish. New generations have now arisen who did not know your soul-searching and did not have any part in the quest for your truth. The delicate filibrations of logic that helped you weave two threads into one fabric – have been forgotten like Stradivarius's secret. There is in general, a new trend in the youth today, Jewish and Gentile: not to go too deeply into things. They incline rather to a direct, simple, primal, brutal 'yes' or 'no'. Of the two threads, they see the thicker, or the shinier one . . . To measure and re-measure the proportions of that merger, they call compromise or cowardice or worse.
>
> With what will you fight this brutality, with what balm? Will you try to teach them your art? I doubt whether this generation is capable of understanding it or even wishes to understand it. This generation is exceedingly 'monistic'. Perhaps this is not a compliment, but it is a fact.[4]

What is needed, Jabotinsky seemed to be saying, is that which stirs the heart, for just as the Irish poet (cited in the previous chapter) had said, followers cannot be otherwise moved.

Ben-Gurion wrote to Jabotinsky on 28 April, 1935, just a month after the accords were rejected by a Histadrut plebiscite. His adversary's warmth was fully reciprocated: 'Whatever comes, the London chapter will not be erased from my heart'. Should it be, he continued, that 'fate leads us to battle, know that among your "enemies" there is one who appreciates you and for whom your pain is his pain'. Ben-Gurion's hand would be 'stretched over the storms of battle'.[5] But then Ben-Gurion proceeded to refute Jabotinsky's claims of class neutrality – as if to refute Jabotinsky's comment that Ben-Gurion lacked *shaatnez*:

> You see class-ism [*maamadiyut*] in the workers' movement. I don't deny this class-ism. But why am I not allowed to see a class Zionism in the Zionism that claims to speak for the 'middle class'. Why am I not permitted to see class war in your war against the workers' movement? You find faults among the workers, I will be the last to ignore them. But I ask: are there no faults (I would say more damaging faults) within the owning class [*baalei ha-batim*]? Are these faults not linked to the class nature and class outlook of the owning class?[6]

Why is it, Ben-Gurion asked his interlocutor, that when the bourgeoisie has political dominion it is not considered class dominance, but when the workers do, the cry goes up for class neutrality? No Zionism, he continued, 'is possible without . . . "shaatnez". When you war against our "shaatnez" you don't war against "shaatnez" in general, but rather against a specific "shaatnez" you don't like. You too have "shaatnez". You undoubtedly believe it doesn't effect the purity of your Zionism. I believe you honestly believe this'.[7] However, the 'class-ism' (or class politics) and 'shaatnez' of Zionist socialism

> is not class-ism at all, but rather the negation of class-ism, the negation of class contradictions, the negation of class privilege; the necessary aspiration of the workers and all those for whom Zionism comes before class politics is to a united and free Jewish nation [*am*] with equal rights, within which there are no class differences and contradictions, but rather the economic and social equality proper to a free nation.[8]

On 2 May, 1935 Jabotinsky wrote to Ben-Gurion:

> I am sure that there *is* a type of Zionist who doesn't care about the social coloring of 'the state'. That is me. If I were assured that there was no road to a 'state' but through socialism, or even if this would hasten its creation in one generation, I'd be ready and able. Even more than that: if an Orthodox state in which I would be forced to eat gefilte fish morning after morning was what is necessary – I'd agree to it (if there is *no* other way). Even worse: a Yiddish state, which for me

would end the charm of the thing – if there is no other way, I agree to it. And I will leave a will to my children telling them to make a revolution. But I'll write on the envelope: 'To be opened five years after the Hebrew state is established'.[9]

Here, then, were the ideological differences between the Zionist left and the Zionist right expressed frankly by their respective leaders to each another: Jabotinsky claimed to be free of *shaatnez* and concerned with the state, pure and simple; Ben-Gurion replied that since no states or societies exist in the abstract, none can exist without *shaatnez*. Jabotinsky insisted on the primacy of the political, narrowly conceived, by making all socio-economic matters, as well as classes and individuals, secondary to politics. Ben-Gurion, on the contrary, insisted on a synthetic approach which, he insisted, alone corresponded to reality.

Behind this variance was something fundamental: disaccord between the two movements on the political culture each would have in its projected state; two contrary *mythomoteurs*, constitutive myths, were competing. For Labour, all things ultimately returned to the image of *am oved*, an independent working nation, able and willing to defend itself, but first and foremost concerned with construction and its own reconstruction; the nation was to be defined through its creative work. Its hero was the *haluts*, the pioneer working the soil, with a rifle over his or her shoulder, but that only out of necessity. The Revisionist hero, in contrast, was characterized by his rifle; his daily work was a matter of relatively little interest. Jabotinsky proposed a *mythomoteur* of a nation armed, a people defined through its discipline, army and flag. A full appreciation of what historically separated the left and the right, their politics and political culture, requires us to examine their terms of conflict in more detail. We begin with the assorted and often contradictory elements in Jabotinsky's *Weltanschauung*, since his intellectual prowess dominated the ideological formulations of his movement.

II

Jabotinsky's critique of the Zionist left was based, as we have seen, on his 'monism'. A striking aspect of the corpus of his speeches and articles is a corresponding tendency first to reify political categories, and then to deify the reifications. This is especially so with his concepts of nation and state, and is one source of the charge, frequently made, that he was a fascist. His concepts of nation and state were often at odds with the nineteenth-century liberalism and individualism that he simultaneously claimed to espouse. As his sometime colleague, sometime foe, Grossman noted in a perceptive obituary, he 'was full of contradictions and opposing extremes. There were many Jabotinskys, each different, often separated from the others by watertight walls'.[10]

Before the First World War Jabotinsky developed a theory of the racial foundations of nations in an essay on 'Race and Nationality'. In 1939 he felt compelled to append a note to a manuscript translation of it warning readers that it was written before the word race had acquired 'the accursed and sinister significance it conveys to the present generation'. He stated that 'one may be a firm adherent of all men's and all tribes' equality, yet firmly believe that "race" is a fundamental factor of all civilisation and all history: precisely in the same way as one need not be ashamed to admit the importance of sexual motives in poetry because there is lechery too'.[11] In the text itself, Jabotinsky ridiculed the notion of 'pure races'. He proposed that mixtures of elements of varied racial origin constituted the individuality of races; such mixtures, by their differing proportions, created a 'spectrum' or 'recipe' composing a given race. 'Some day', he supposed,

> science may achieve such refinement that it will become possible in a special analysis of the blood, or perhaps, the secretion of the glands, to establish the 'spectrum' or the 'recipe' of the various racial types, showing all the ingredients that go to making a typical Italian or an average Pole. I venture to forecast that most 'recipes' will be found to contain practically the same ingredients, only the proportions in which God and history have mixed them will prove different.[12]

Extending this, Jabotinsky claimed that all nationalities have 'distinct racial characteristics', that race determines mentality and that while he found attempts to define 'national psychology' hopeless, he did believe every nation to have a distinct racial psychology which 'permeates to a greater or lesser degree the personality of any average member of the group'.[13] Jabotinsky was a philosophical idealist; psyche 'or intellect or brain' was the primary factor in history and each race/nation creates its own civilization.[14] In an article of 1912 entitled 'Horoscope' he attributed Britain's ability to sustain its empire to the 'mystical essence' of 'national genius'.[15] He declared in 'Race and Nationality':

> The bedrock of all that is 'national' is race; I claim it even for such a cosmopolitanised province of corporate life as the structure of the State in whose framework, let it only be in remote fundamentals, the hallmark of racial likes and dislikes will always be traced. I maintain that even economy, despite all the levelling of tastes, prices, and methods inherent in modernity, still moves in every country, deep at bottom, on lines basically racial.[16]

An 'ideal type' of a nation, as posited by Jabotinsky, would be characterized by its 'racial spectrum', would inhabit 'from time immemorial' a specific territory without aliens in its midst, would have a unique language and religion (preferably 'a primaevally home-made one like that of the Buddhist Indians or of the Jews') and would embody an uninterrupted historical tradition dating to 'antiquity'.[17] Probably, he admitted freely, no such nation does or will exist. In the end, then, what we find in Jabotinsky's early essays, is a somewhat elastic psychological-racial determinism that he extends from nation to state.

At about this same time Jabotinsky published a lengthy essay on 'National Minority Rights', an offshoot of a thesis on 'State and Nation' that he wrote for a law diploma and which was clearly a by-product of his support of Jewish autonomy in the diaspora in 1905–6. Here, too, he saw race as the 'indelible essence' of nationality, but he also saw consciousness and declaration of ethnicity as sufficient criteria to establish legal membership in a nationality.[18] Thus objective and subjective factors were tenuously tied. While Jabotinsky clearly saw territorial concentration as the logical outcome of national identification, in multinational states he advocated a personal, not a territorial, definition of nationality. He endorsed the widest possible autonomy for national minorities, whom he thought should be united in 'personal constitutional' associations, having national and local cultural institutions.

As his later nationalism and etatism were at odds with his liberalism, so there is an intrinsic tension between Jabotinsky's acceptance of individual self-definition as the criterion for nationality membership and his theory of racial psychology. This tension between the collective and the individual is present in almost all aspects of his politics and it would seem that Jabotinsky himself was unaware of it. To take another example, he often expressed a strong sense of temporal displacement; he was, he said, a nineteenth-century liberal and advocate of limited government living in an era of personality cults and authoritarian figures, a time when peoples 'discover within them the God chosen leader with the stamp of Caesar imprinted on his forehead [*ha-manhig behir ha-el asher hotam shel kesar hakuk be-mitsho]*'[19]. Yet this same man was the object of a personality cult in his own movement and insisted that 'it is the highest achievement of a mass of free men if they can act together as one, in unison, with the absolute precision of a "machine" '.[20] Discipline, he declared, meant 'the mass is subordinate to one leader' who carries out the will of each as the conductor is empowered in an orchestra.[21]

This metaphor of the masses as a machine occurs frequently in Jabotinsky's speeches and writings. Indeed, he devoted an essay to the proposition that, horrible though war might be, militarism and military style should be neither unduly nor unfairly identified with it. An arch-assimilationist, he suggested, might well become, at least temporarily, a fervent Jewish nationalist if presented with a few hundred uniformed Jewish youth marching by. Each step should 'crash like thunder – "like a machine". There is nothing in the world that can impress us more than the ability of a mass to feel and to act at certain moments as one, with a single will, in uniform rhythm. For this is all the difference between a "mass" and a "rabble" [*erev-rav*] and a nation'.[22]

How might such images have been reconciled with espousal of individualism in Jabotinsky's own mind? To the extent that they were, and at the risk of repetition, the following passage helps to clarify his priorities, at least in Jewish affairs:

> What we Jews need, above all, is to learn moving in unison – stepping with one step, striking with one stroke. I know the value of individualism – it is a great asset too. But the highest rung of civilisation belongs to those who, though conscious and proud of their individuality, possess the power, at the moment of need, to conquer their own will, to fall in with the alignment of a nation, to act in their millions as though they were one single man or one single machine. A multitude incapable of unison, though each of its members be a genius, is called a mob; only the lore of unison makes of them a nation. This is what Herzl wanted to teach us when he created the [Zionist] Congress: a Big Parade . . . A day may come when much will depend on the question whether the Jewish people is able, at a sign given from one centre, to respond, all the world over, with one voice – like one man, 'like a machine'.[23]

Despite the qualifications – one acts in such unison 'at the moment of need' – there is here, as in so many of Jabotinsky's pronouncements, a radical subordination of the individual to the nation. Indeed, both nation and state appear in Jabotinsky's writings not as relations among human beings, but rather as things, as reified entities into which individuals as individuals seem to vanish. The nation, it would appear, is a machine whose elements are oiled by a racial psychology and armour-plated into the state. The state, as such, is not a means to an end, e.g. the reconstruction of a people, but becomes fetishized along with its symbols – flag, parade, uniform. Similarly, land was reified in his thought as it became an end rather than a means. Jabotinsky's Zionism, concerned as it was to be 'pure' nationalism, unpolluted by questions of class, was a monistic, integralist, *etatism*: 'In Zionism and in Palestine, you are but a puppet dangling from a wire and playing a prescribed part, and the hand that pulls the wire is called The State in Building'.[24]

Jabotinsky was acutely aware of who his chief foe was and of the rise of its spiritual dominance. Duverger, as we noted, wrote that a dominant doctrine compels its foes to argue in its own terms; this was the case with Jabotinsky who, though not primarily interested in such matters, wrote numerous articles in the 1920s and 1930s challenging Marxist and socialist socio-economic presumptions – he even, with tongue in cheek, went so far as to call himself a 'psycho-Marxist'.[25] In the midst of the world depression, when workers' movements around the world were struggling to assert themselves, Jabotinsky told his readers that at hand was not the crisis of capitalism, but rather 'the crisis of the proletariat'. Because of automation all workers would not be re-employed; the proletariat was becoming 'a socially unnecessary class', rather than the universal class of Marx (or the Labour Zionists). The 'cult of the proletariat', perhaps justifiable in the past, was entirely outmoded, along with the equation of the provider with the toiler, something he called 'an emotional conceit'.[26] Within half a century, he predicted at one point, automation would eliminate the working class altogether.[27]

Jabotinsky wrote that 'the whole of the world's proletariat, taken together throughout all the ages never did nor could exercise on the evolution of production an influence even remotely comparable to that of individual brains'.[28] Spirit, not muscle, was the key to production, and 'as an old-fashioned diehard Liberal I believe in Pantisocracy – I want all of us to rule the world in unison and without privileges. Yet *if* there should be privileges – then the power that rules, has ever ruled, should and will ever rule the world is the Brain of those few who've got it, not the millions of hammers and sickles – especially as they are so rapidly getting replaced by the switch . . .'[29] In a follow-up article he declared the exploitation of men immoral but that of machines 'the highest form of ethics'.[30] This is, of course, an instructive observation considering Jabotinsky's tendency to liken national solidarity to a machine, and his insistence on total subordination of the individual to 'the state in building'. More significantly, however, automation reflected, for Jabotinsky, a continuous process of rationalization of production which had an important consequence: the middle, commercial, and trading classes would be the classes of the future because the 'robot' cannot replace them, but could replace the proletarian. One cannot help but link these assertions with his racial–psychological theory of the nation and his championing of the role of commerce and that of the shopkeeper in Jewish history. It appears that, placed within the context of his general writings, Jabotinsky's Jewish nation is one in which the racial recipe produced a propensity to commerce, which, one must conclude, is the natural foundation of the future Jewish society. The fact of automation, Jabotinsky insisted, undermines class doctrine – by which he meant the class doctrine of the proletariat – and 'class egoism'. Besides, 'The word "proletariat" has long ceased to be a synonym for "underdog": on the contrary, compared with the other millions of *les pauvres diables* called artisans, or shopkeepers, or clerks, or intelligentsia, the industrial worker is a vastly privileged person. His wages are protected by law, when out of work he gets the dole'. Jabotinsky complained – obviously with the Histadrut in mind – that unions coerce membership, own banks, libraries, hospitals, and spend large sums on politics.[31] But, as always, the Revisionist leader insisted on his own class-neutrality: these arguments were aimed not at the proletariat or socialism, but only at 'class doctrine'. The needs of capitalist and worker ought to be subservient to state-building. 'We subordinate all human efforts, individual or collective, social, religious, etc., to the jealous primacy of the State idea . . .'[32] The goal of what he liked to call 'State–Zionism' was not to 'liquidate' class sentiments – something he admitted to be probably impossible – but to 'sterilise them while the state-building process was under way'.[33]

At the same time, Jabotinsky envisioned substantial social welfare legislation in his future state, echoing many of Herzl's ideas. The Bible, he asserted, provided the moral and humane precepts for a modern Jewish society. Here, as in his use of 'shaatnez', Jabotinsky harnessed religious symbols and secularized them for nationalistic – and clearly anti-socialist – purposes. In the Bible he sought a – purely Jewish – counter-authority to alien Marxism. The state, in Jabotinsky's view, should eliminate poverty and provide the basics of food, clothing, medicine, shelter and education. Beyond that, however, it ought to have no involvement in the structuring of social life, let alone the enforcement of equality. As long as the essentials were supplied,

> it is no concern of the state that Mr. X dwells in a palatial mansion and Mr. Y is grumbling why he too cannot occupy an equally luxurious palace. Who cares about that? Miss A is a famous beauty, while Miss B is not so blessed. Naturally that may be unpleasant for Miss A, perhaps it may even be tragic, but it is not one of the tragedies for which the State must provide relief. One may possess talent, another may lack it; one may be successful, another a failure. Innumerable 'tragedies' arise daily because of inequalities... but they are not our concern, as long as the peril of dying of starvation is removed.[34]

In this passage Jabotinsky presents a clearly liberal view of the state.

The Revisionist leader said he was equally opposed to strikes and to lock-outs, and he fervently espoused, as we have mentioned, a system of national compulsory arbitration in labour relations. All of this, too, was a natural extension of his 'monism', at the heart of which was his assertion of the primacy of the nation-state over all other elements. At the third World Revisionist Congress in Vienna in 1928 Jabotinsky submitted his arbitration plan; a judicial body would be created to fix 'in every single instant the limit up to which the wages of the workers and employees can be increased without disturbing the opportunity of making normal profits'.[35] Both classes, he claimed, needed each other, and there needed to be an 'equilibrium' in their respective strength.[36] A 'Supreme Institute of National Arbitration' would be established under the auspices of the ZO or the Asefat ha-Nivharim, based on a corporate conception of the economy:

We must first have an internal organisation of each important sector of the Jewish economy in the country: the grower of corn, the grower of vegetables, the grower of oranges, the textile industry, the furniture industry, and so on; the various branches of wholesale and retail trading, of export and import, the banks, the savings institutions, the intellectual professions and so forth.[37]

The employers and employees would each have a representative from their respective sector; the president and presidium of the Institute would be elected, perhaps by the Zionist Congress, and would stand 'above party'. The institute would have offices throughout the country, would examine all aspects of the economy, set minimum wages, create neutral labour exchanges and arbitrate both employer–employee conflicts and those between different branches of production. This would create 'a united Jewish economic front'. Boycotts of Jewish labour and all forms of class conflict would be considered a crime. Jabotinsky, finally, recognized that, since a sovereign Jewish state did not yet exist, the efficacy of the system he proposed would rest on social pressure and discipline.[38]

Again, while this corporatist proposal easily complements Jabotinsky's monistic view of the nation and his stress on discipline, it is clearly antithetical to nineteenth-century liberal concepts of economy and the limited role of the state. When one combines his 'monism', his hostility to the left, his 'racial psychology' of nationalism, his emphases on discipline, militarism and parades, and his radical subordination of the individual and class to the nation and the state (or state-in-building), the context in which he was accused – albeit at times indiscriminately – of 'fascist' leanings becomes clarified. A wide array of opponents likened him to the extreme right. Ben-Gurion was particularly prominent among the epithet-throwers, calling him 'Duce' repeatedly.[39] Unhappily for Jabotinsky, this was encouraged by Ahimeir – who saw 'Duce' as a compliment, and who, along with his supporters, was blatant in his sympathies with fascist ideas. Weizmann called Revisionism 'economically . . . nothing but Fascism'.[40] The prominent American Jewish rabbi Stephen Wise declared in a speech that 'the truth is that Revisionism is becoming a species of Fascism in Yiddish or in Hebrew' and accused it of assimilationism because it aped the worst aspects of Western civilization.[41]

In fact, Mussolini himself told the chief rabbi of Rome in 1935 that 'For Zionism to succeed you must have a Jewish state with a Jewish flag and a Jewish language. The man who really understands this is your Fascist, Jabotinsky'.[42] If one sets aside the connotations fascism has today and looks at Revisionist politics in the light of Italian fascist history, what stimulated such comparisons among Jabotinsky's foes becomes more evident. Italian fascism not only stressed integralist nationalism (the idea of Greater Italy), it fetishized state and empire, made Mussolini the object of a leadership cult, emphasized nation over class and banned strikes and lock-outs while supporting private enterprise and social welfare legislation. It created a corporate system for capital–labour collaboration under the aegis of the state, and established compulsory arbitration courts. Its political culture stressed militarism and uniformed parades.[43] The fascist 'Charter of Labour' of 1927 declared:

> The Italian Nation is an organism having ends, a life and means superior in power and duration to the single individuals or groups of individuals composing it. It is a moral, political, and economic unit which finds its integral realisation in the Fascist State.[44]

Although Jabotinsky preferred 'machine' to 'organism' – two images that are significantly different, given rigorous analysis – if one bears in mind Jabotinsky's racial–psychological theory, the similarities between his formulations and those of the fascists are striking. His statements on discipline, the individual and the state frequently sounded reminiscent to many of Mussolini's proclamations that 'The individual has no existence except insofar as he is part of the state and subordinate to its requirements'.[45]

The historical parallels are sufficient – if imprecise – to make the charge by the left that Revisionism resembled Italian fascism comprehensible in the atmosphere of the 1930s. After the First World War, as in the Zionist movement in the 1920s, the Italian Labour movement, in particular the CGL (*Confederazione generale del lavore* – the trade union of mainstream socialism), grew rapidly as did the socialists in parliament, whilst the mainstream bourgeois parties languished.[46] In the prelude to his seizure of power, Mussolini waged a fervent campaign against the socialist and Labour organizations in Italy; so, too, did the Revisionists in Palestine. Mussolini's supporters utilized, in the name of 'national' needs, their own labour organizations – the syndicates – to undermine the Labour movement; so, too, did the Revisionists who set up a 'National Histadrut' to compete with the Histadrut. Labour conflicts and the occupation of the factories in 1919 and 1920 in Italy were followed by a rapid growth of the previously weak fascists, with Mussolini championing economic progress through a structure of private enterprise and syndicalist collaboration. The neutralization of the Labour movement by such competition and also by violence were crucial to Mussolini's triumph.[47]

The analogies extend further. In Italy, the first *fascio* were supporters of Italian intervention in the First World War who, like Mussolini himself, left the Socialist Party.[48] Both Jabotinsky and the *Brit ha-Biryonim* began on the left. (In fact Jabotinsky, like Mussolini, first made his name as a journalist.) Giacomo Matteotti, the outspoken socialist opposition leader who challenged Mussolini's parliamentary 'elections' of 1924 – which occurred in an atmosphere of violence and intimidation – was murdered by fascist henchmen; those arrested for the murder of Arlosoroff, an outspoken foe of the Revisionists, in the tumultuous and violent period of the 18th Zionist Congress elections were from *Brit ha-Biryonim*, who had championed Mussolini.

Jabotinsky angrily denied the fascist accusation, denounced fascism and dictators, and insisted on his belief in liberal democracy, parliamentary government and freedom of speech and association. He was strident, fervent and vigorous in his anti-Nazi activities. In late 1938 Jabotinsky wrote to J. Bartlett, the editor of the London *News Chronicle*:

> Are you interested in the revival of Liberalism, the old-fashioned creed of the XIXth century? I feel its time is coming; I think in about 5 years it will have enthusiastic crowds of youth to back it, its catchwords will be repeated all the world over with the same hysteria as those of Communism used to be 5 years ago, those of Fascism to-day; only the effect will be deeper as Liberalism has roots in human nature which all barrack-room religions lack.
>
> If you are interested, and perhaps know of some budding initiative to act in this direction and to sponsor the launching of a militant or crusading Liberalism, I should like to help.
>
> I understand that some Jewish opponents of my brand of Zionism pretend to suspect me of being pro-Fascist. I am just the opposite: an instinctive hater of all kinds of Polisei-staat, utterly skeptical of the value of discipline and power and punishment etc. down to economic dirigee.
>
> It is hardly necessary to add that, speaking of Liberalism, I do not mean any British party but simply that philosophy which, shared by men of many parties in many countries, made the XIXth century great.[49]

Quite apart from the irony of a 1938 prophecy of enthusiastic crowds for liberalism five years hence – 'its time is coming' – it is difficult to reconcile this profession with the man we have witnessed championing discipline and the image of the masses as a machine, who complained that militarism had been given a bad name and who called for a corporate structure for labour relations. One must conclude that the contradiction between Jabotinsky's nationalism and liberalism is one of his most consistent features.

Such disparity, in point of fact, is not entirely absent from the history of liberalism or from that of Italian fascism. Many nineteenth-century liberals championed individual liberty while being blinded to brutalities suffered by individual members of the working classes in their own countries, let alone by 'natives' in lands victimized by imperial expansion. Numerous Italian liberals, fearful of the left, supported or acquiesced in Mussolini's rise to the premiership in 1922. The fascists promised to honour private property rights, so long as this promoted national development, and the fascist emphasis on the need for 'productivity' was found attractive by many economic liberals.[50] Mussolini, of course, insisted that he was neither of the right nor the left, claiming that in his proposed corporate system good fascists would act on behalf of both employers and the workers for the benefit of Italy; there would be labour peace and no nuisances like strikes or lock-outs.[51] De'Stefani, Mussolini's first fascist finance minister, was a believer in free trade and the liberalization of the Italian economy, which, at the time, the Duce supported, declaring it necessary to reduce the state's role in the economy.[52] While Mussolini was renowned for his contempt for liberalism – power, not ideas, was, of course, his passion – the term was not banished from fascist discourse. Giovanni Gentile, for instance, praised him, in 1925, for being in the true liberal tradition, and under Mussolini there were some fascists who proclaimed liberalism and fascism to be the same thing.[53] As late as the early 1930s Mussolini told foreign visitors that he favored a minimal role for the state in the economy (although his actions were not commensurate with such remarks).[54]

Hence Jabotinsky's denials of fascism do not diminish the parallels between some of his most cherished ideas – as well as his style – and those of the European extreme right; his refusals to accept defeat in Zionist Congress elections and his role as leader within his own movement do not lend credence to his liberalism either. Furthermore, his private correspondence, as well as some of his public utterances, demonstrated many ambiguities. For example, in a letter he declared that, 'Revisionism is not "Fascist". The only view it holds in common with Italian fascism is the negation of class war, the demand for arbitration as the only way to solve labour conflicts and the subordination of class interest to the interest of the nation'.[55] Here Jabotinsky denies fascism in one breath, while in the next he specifically admits commonality with its view of class. *But this was the central issue over which he was bitterly battling against his chief antagonists, the Labour movement.* Hence Labour's labelling of him as fascist was not simply name-calling. (In the same letter Jabotinsky insists, with some degree of embarrassment, that 'The brown shirts of Brit Trumpeldor [Betar] have been adopted in 1924, before anybody heard of the existence of Hitler's "troop". Brown was chosen as the colour of Palestine's soil. It is a dark chocolate brown, whereas Hitler's "brown" is practically yellow'.)[56]

In an article on 'Jews and Fascism' Jabotinsky claimed fascism to be inapplicable to Jewish life on practical grounds; all Jewish organizations were voluntary. This, of course, begged the question of its applicability in a Jewish state with coercive powers. 'As to the very old principle that the interests of a nation should supersede those of an individual, a family, or a "class" ', he added, '– to describe this idea as fascism is silly. This is every man's view, including ninety-five percent of all Socialists, probably all communists, if ever put to the test'.[57] Fascism only adds to this 'thoroughness of coercion' in social relations since it 'refuses to rely on workers' or employers' own patriotism: it simply commandeers all the workers and all the employees, treats them as battalions of the State, orders, forbids, and punishes'.[58] This, he reiterated, was impossible in Jewish life because 'compulsory arbitration' in Palestine would mean *voluntary* acceptance of arbitration. For fascists, he claimed, class war was forbidden, while for Zionists it was immoral. And, he noted, at least in Italy fascism was 'an ideology of racial equality'.[59]

Labour's attack on Jabotinsky and the Revisionists was multidimensional and ferocious. Katznelson accused Jabotinsky of distorting the legacy of Herzl's political Zionism and claimed that, contrary to Jabotinsky's insinuations, the Labour movement, and Ahdut ha-Avodah in particular, carried out a national (*amamit*) *political* Zionism through its settlement, labour, immigration, and cultural activities. All these were, he insisted, really political endeavors.[60] This assertion – which entirely bypassed Herzl's critique of practical Zionism – aimed to steal the thunder of Jabotinsky's claim to be Herzl's true heir. More importantly, Katznelson's remarks illustrated what the real chasm was between left and right: for the left, 'the labouring settlements, the national funds, the collective farms [are] not social oases or havens of moral satisfaction for a chosen few, but rather instruments and cells of the Jewish national economy'.[61] Labour's goal was political independence no less than Jabotinsky's, but the building of a national community in *Jewish* hands was the prerequisite, in its view, to independence. Otherwise, there was a great danger of unrealistic dependence on the British. Whereas Jabotinsky, with his broad cosmopolitan education, had faith in the moral character of Western civilization, Ben-Gurion, a Jew from a small town in Russian Poland, looked at the world differently: 'We do not share the faith of the Revisionists in the benevolence of an alien government'.[62] Political Zionism, Katznelson declared, 'in the true meaning of the ingathering of the exiles, mass immigration and political independence is the soul of our movement'.[63]

Ben-Gurion, perhaps more than any other Labour leader, tore aggressively at the Revisionist veneer. We are struggling for a state, he insisted, but not just any type of state; the true end is the re-creation and flowering anew of the Jewish people. Attacking bourgeois Zionism in general he told the Histadrut General Council in March 1928 that the realization of Zionism did not mean re-creating diaspora life in Palestine, but rather a 'deep historical transformation in Jewish life, a transformation not solely of geography', but in the people's entire social and economic structure. This – which was, as we have seen, a prominent Labour theme – was the direct opposite of Jabotinsky's embrace of shopkeeping. The working class, as such, was the 'principal subject' (*nose ha-ikari*) of the realization of Zionism.[64] In presenting the role of 'The Worker in Zionism', Ben-Gurion declared that 'In its essence, Zionism is a revolutionary movement. One can hardly imagine a more profound and fundamental revolution than that to which it aspires in the life of the Hebrew nation. It is not a question of a revolution against a political or economic regime, but a revolution in the mode of life of our people'.[65]

Directing himself to Jabotinsky's followers and the claim that Revisionism represented 'pure' political Zionism, Ben-Gurion stated before the Mapai Conference on 3 November, 1932:

> The social content of Zionism can be destructive, reactionary, steeped in slavery, exploitation, ugliness, and it can be positive, progressive, redemptive, liberating, representing social advance and moral beauty. A Zionism totally void of all social content, either good or bad, is a meaningless abstraction, lacking any living or concrete content. All talk of 'monistic' Zionism, in contrast to 'Shaatnez' is a fraud. The fascist Zionist who advocates blood, mud, and slavery, who wars on 'Marxists' and 'Leftists', the bourgeois Zionist who wants the rule of wealth and a class society, and the socialist Zionist who wants a free workers' society and a socialist land of Israel all have *Shaatnez* Zionism. The difference is in the result of the admixture.[66]

Socialism and Zionism, he went on, were not identical: one was a universal movement of workers of all nations, the other a movement of all classes within Jewry. This did not mean that their respective essences were contradictory. In contrast to Jabotinsky's unidirectional Zionism, Ben-Gurion declared that Labour Zionists stood in more than one circle, although 'when we stand in two circles it isn't a question of standing in two separate areas, one moment in one and the next in the other, but rather in what is common territory to both of them'. He continued:

> In reality we don't stand within two circles alone, but within many circles – as citizens of Palestine we stand in the circle of the Land of Israel, as Jews we stand in the circle of a nation that aspires to its homeland, as workers we stand in the circle of the working class, as sons of our generation we stand in the circle of modern history; our women comrades stand in the circle of the working women's movement in its struggle for liberation . . .[67]

In short, Labour's politics was not just *shaatnez* but multiple *shaatnez*; Labour's place was in a plethora of circles. Thus he rejected Jabotinsky's monism as a simplistic Zionism based on artificial and formalistic categories and slogans. The Revisionist leader's pretence to class neutrality was a smokescreen, both logically and in practice. Ben-Gurion's claims, whatever his own penchant for etatism and political centralism, rested on the refusal to see the state as an end in itself and as an abstraction; his image of many circles of Labour Zionism was one way of arguing that the type of state and society, the content within the form being built, could not be separated one from the other as Jabotinsky did by subordinating class and individual to state and nation.

Ben-Gurion accused his foes of 'class hatred' and of refusing to recognize that they were in reality fighting a class war on behalf of the bourgeoisie in the name of 'class neutrality'. To equate a strike and a lock-out, Ben-Gurion said, might seem fair play, but it obscures the discrepancy in power possessed by employers and individual workers; such an equation is really a defence of the capitalists.[68] Ben-Gurion denied that the Histadrut was unwilling to create 'mixed' labour exchanges; the problem was with Jabotinsky's argument for 'neutral' arbitrators. As we have seen, Ben-Gurion took a strong class-oriented position on this, insisting that determining an owner's profit margin in relation to the needs of workers was not an 'objective' determination but depended on an individual's broader concepts of society and economics.[69] Furthermore, since countries with arbitration systems employed coercive state power to enforce judgements, and since within Palestinian Jewry only the force of discipline and public opinion could be relied on, who were the Revisionists, of all groups, to champion such discipline in Zionist institutions and the Yishuv? They demanded discipline of the workers, but what of themselves?

III

Between the Zionist Congresses of 1933 and 1935, the conflict between the left and the right came to a climax and the Revisionists left the ZO. During this period Mapai and the ZO pressed the Revisionists with the few coercive means at their disposal. The Jewish Agency, as the officially recognized body working with the Mandatory authorities, controlled immigration permits and distributed them according to a party key to the constituents of the ZO. This was an obvious tool by which to pressure the right; if the Revisionists would not accept duly established authorities, those authorities could not be expected to treat them with equanimity. (The Revisionists were not alone in facing such pressures. Members of the Left Poale Zion also had problems in obtaining permits owing to their party's refusal to engage in 'class collaboration' within the ZO.)

Betar, accusing the Jewish Agency of discrimination, issued what became known as 'Order 60', instructing its members to circumvent the Agency and to seek work directly from employers in Palestine (who could, under certain provisions, make arrangements for those they were going to employ to enter the country). Publicly, Betar presented its actions as a protest against Mandatory immigration restrictions, but it was evident that the target was also ZO discipline and the Jewish Agency's authority. In the spring of 1934 Jewish Agency immigration offices received instructions to cease issuing permits to Betar as an organized group, and the Revisionists retaliated with boycotts of the Jewish National Fund, and the creation of their own 'Tel Hai Fund'.[70] They also sought to broaden their support within the Jewish public and pressed their 'petition' campaign (which, it was eventually claimed, obtained some 600,000 signatures).

It is particularly striking that during this period Mapai and the Revisionists pursued directly opposed strategies. Ben-Gurion and Labour – not without internal opposition – moved to change its path fundamentally; whereas class and national interests were formerly considered equivalent, Mapai, now presenting itself as the nation's leader, sought the broadest possible coalition politics and was willing to make considerable compromises in the process. This consolidated its strength and broadened its appeal. The timing of this change was politically fortuitous. Not only was there an upturn in the Palestinian economy, but a massive immigration from Europe – the Fifth Aliyah – began in the wake of the Nazi rise to power. Some 200,000 Jews poured into Palestine in the decade after Hitler became Germany's dictator, over 164,000 of them between 1933 and 1936. This immigration doubled the Yishuv's population by the time the Second World War broke out; in addition, its character was largely bourgeois and thus composed of individuals who were unlikely recruits to socialist Zionist ranks.[71] In contrast to the circumstances of the Fourth Aliyah, when Labour was busy constructing a separatist Histadrut economy (a pillar that eventually aimed to be all pillars) and when Labour faced a potentially catastrophic economic situation since it lacked substantial power in the ZO, Mapai was now the strongest force there and presented itself as the leader – but one willing to compromise – of a coalition. It was the biggest pillar, but not one seeking to encompass the whole of society. This did not mean that the Labour pillar, the Histadrut, declined; to the contrary, between 1933 and 1935 it increased its general membership 170 per cent.[72] However, since most of the new immigrant members had not come to Palestine out of ideological motivation, what they sought in the Histadrut was, first and foremost, the array of services it could provide in their new country. The Histadrut welcomed and was buttressed by them, but a gap between its original aspirations and the nature of its membership and role continued to grow, a gap reinforced by the changing political direction of the Labour movement.

While Mapai was busy legitimizing and nationalizing its role, that is, changing its orientation from a class to a national one, the Revisionists – the champions of national discipline and unity – pursued a path of separatism which played neatly into Mapai's efforts to delegitimate them. Whenever their views did not dominate, the Revisionists preferred to split or boycott. This can be seen as a consistent pattern throughout the 1930s: in a few short years, they decided to boycott the Vaad Leumi, to quit the Histadrut (and form their own 'National Histadrut') and to help create a faction within the Haganah that later became the Irgun; and after Jabotinsky split his own party, the Revisionists eventually left the ZO. All this occurred at a time of mounting pressure on the Jews in Europe and in Palestine, which discredited the Revisionist pretence to be the true party of national unity.

The Revisionists resolved to leave the ZO after the failure of the Ben-Gurion–Jabotinsky agreements. The two leaders – Ben-Gurion officially representing the Zionist Executive and Jabotinsky the Revisionist movement – reached three accords which sought to end the physical and verbal violence within the Zionist movement. In them, it appeared as if both right and left were accepting blame by the assertion that henceforth 'all parties undertake to refrain from means of party warfare which are outside the limits of political and ideological discussion and which are not in conformity with the moral principles of Zionism and civilized conduct'.[73] The Revisionists were to be reintegrated into the ZO and would suspend both 'Order 60' and the boycott of national fund-raising institutions; the ZO would suspend its restrictions on Betar's immigration rights; a working arrangement would regularize relations between the 60,000-member Histadrut and the 7,000-member 'National Histadrut', providing for a fair division of employment and a separate Revisionist labour exchange; Ben-Gurion also agreed that a minority of between 15 and 25 per cent (to be determined later) of the workers in an enterprise could overrule a strike vote and compel arbitration. However, if the arbitration failed, a strike would then be permissible.

As the news of the negotiations filtered into Palestine, Mapai leaders and activists became increasingly agitated, primarily about the agreement on labour relations. Berl Katznelson urgently cabled to the Histadrut Secretary-General to warn that his actions might destroy the Labour movement and his party, and that nothing should be settled before he returned to Palestine and consulted his comrades:

> The movement has been wounded and the danger is very great. What is the point of the miracle if the principal instrument of realization is broken. Continuation of negotiations pushes the public to anarchy and destructiveness. I have supported and continue to struggle for the labour agreement. I will not participate in ideological and political surrender to the enemy [*lo etstaref le-vitur raayoni u-medini la-oyev*]. No reconciliation with fascist-Zionism, with Calais, with adventurism. Don't commit yourself until your arrival. Come quickly, each moment is precious.[74]

Here Ben-Gurion was at a disadvantage; Jabotinsky was considerably more dominant in and able to impose his will on his movement than he was. Also, as Itshak Ben-Aharon, one of Ben-Gurion's chief party critics, put it, 'All that we, the opponents of the agreement, had to do was quote Ben-Gurion himself – and not what he had said ten years earlier, but statements on which the print was not yet dry'.[75]

Jabotinsky too faced resistance. The Palestinian Revisionists, especially the 'Maximalists' (mostly Ahimeir's supporters), and the leaders of the National Histadrut vigorously opposed the agreements. Some claimed that the fighting between right and left benefited the Revisionists because bourgeois circles turned to them as a shield against the socialists. Eliahu Ben-Horin warned that it was entirely unrealistic to expect the Revisionists to have 15 per cent of the workers in many enterprises.[76] None the less, Jabotinsky was able to secure ratification by the National Histadrut and also by the sixth World Revisionist Conference in Cracow in January 1935. At the latter meeting, one of his foes, a young leader of Polish Betar named Menahem Begin, angrily told him, 'You may have forgotten that Ben-Gurion once called you "Vladimir Hitler", but we have a better memory'. Jabotinsky responded that he also recalled Ben-Gurion's service in the Jewish Legion.[77]

Ben-Gurion may have officially represented the ZO in the discussions with Jabotinsky, but it was the endorsement of Mapai and the Labour movement, now dominant in the ZO, that he needed to make the accords a reality. Not only did Ben-Gurion lose the ensuing fight, but the struggle broadened fissures already emerging in Mapai – cracks that contributed to a split in the party almost a decade later. Within Mapai, Ben-Gurion's opponents were chiefly among the urban leaders (notably in Tel Aviv) and in kibbutz circles, especially the Ha-Kibbutz ha-Meuhad (United Kibbutz) federation led, significantly, by Itshak Tabenkin. Ben-Gurion's backers included Katznelson, and most of the Second Aliyah leaders (Tabenkin being an exception). He was also supported by the smaller kibbutz association, Hever ha-Kvutsot, the Gordonia youth movement and many of the former Ha-Poel ha-Tsair members.

This represented the emergence of several divisions in Mapai ranks, partly due to generational differences, but also rooted in contrasting views of the path Mapai was taking, and disagreements on the relation between nation and class. The Second Aliyah leaders, as a whole, inclined to the compromise, the Third Aliyah leaders and other younger activists opposed it. There was also considerable resentment because Ben-Gurion acted on his own without consulting the Mapai leadership (his excuse was that he negotiated for the Zionist Executive, not the Labour movement). Particularly striking is the extent to which the spectre of fascism was raised in the debate; repeatedly, the opponents of the agreement pointed to the process by which the right had triumphed over the left in the past decade-and-a-half in Europe, and especially in Austria and Italy. Ben-Aharon, admonishing that the agreements had provoked a crisis of confidence in Labour's leadership, reminded his movement that in a very brief period the worker had seen one of his leaders (Arlosoroff) murdered, a flood of strike-breaking and a concerted effort to break the Histadrut. All of this occurred while 'his working-class brothers' were being killed in Germany, Austria and Spain.[78]

The impact of the previous year's events in Austria apparently had particular salience. There, in February 1934, a socialist movement which, like the Histadrut, possessed an elaborate organizational, institutional, and cultural apparatus (especially in 'Red Vienna'), complete with its own army, the *Schutzbund*, had been smashed rapidly and violently. This happened after several years of wavering response to the advances of the right and Dolfuss's endeavour, at Mussolini's behest, to replace the Austrian Republic with a corporate state, complete with its own 'national' unions which sought to undermine and displace the Social Democratic and trade union movements. This was undoubtedly on the mind of Ben-Aharon, himself born in Austrian Bukovina, when he urged the Hebrew worker to demand that his leaders learn the proper lesson – the need 'to destroy Jewish fascism at its inception'.[79] Eliahu Golomb, an architect of the Haganah, warned that European precedents had to be born in mind, such as the short-lived agreement in the summer of 1921 between the fascists and socialists in Italy whose ostensible purpose was to defuse a tense and violent situation, but in the end hastened the alliance between the fascists and the bourgeoisie, thus helping the former in its quest for power.

Ben-Gurion's critics focused their wrath on the labour and arbitration proposals and on Ben-Gurion's willingness to permit a minority to bloc or stall strikes. These were likened to Mussolini's corporatism. Ziama Aharonovitz (later Zalman Aran) warned that employers would concentrate workers in order to sabotage strikes, and that a minority of workers would be able to dictate tactics to the majority. Besides, he insisted, the strike was a fundamental right of workers.[80] Tabenkin characterized the agreement as a surrender to the Revisionist concept of labour relations and worried aloud that it would be the first step to a coalition with the right in the Zionist movement. Echoing an argument Ben-Gurion had long used against Jabotinsky, Tabenkin questioned whether there was such a thing as a 'neutral' third party to put on an arbitration board.[81]

David Remez, who succeeded Ben-Gurion as the Secretary-General of the Histadrut in late 1935, not only embraced the agreements but stated his own willingness to be in a coalition with the right. Early in the debate, Ben-Gurion sought to persuade his colleagues that Revisionist strength had in fact peaked and that Labour's hegemony was secure.[82] It is doubtful that he actually believed this as his future actions demonstrated, and as illustrated by the telling comparison he made, when the accords were on the verge of being voted down, between his own behaviour and that of Lenin's when the Bolshevik leader agreed to Brest–Litovsk and enacted the Soviet New Economic Policy.[83] Both Brest–Litovsk and the NEP were adopted because of Bolshevik weakness, not strength. Furthermore, Ben-Gurion had expressed great fear that the divisions within the Jewish national movement were threatening the Zionist project itself as well as 'the instrument of statehood [*ha-makhshir ha-mamlakhti*] bequeathed to us by Dr. Herzl: a sovereign and united Zionist Organization'.[84]

Ben-Gurion derided the notion that acceptance of arbitration was equivalent to fascism, pointing out that several Zionist parties, none of which could be called fascist and including Ha-Poel ha-Tsair, had favoured the idea. Katznelson, originally a critic of Ben-Gurion's actions (although long an advocate of a labour arrangement with the Revisionists), supported his colleague with increasing vigour and accused his foes of being enmeshed in imported ideologies which were divorced from Palestinian realities. Strikes, he said, were not as important as establishing a just division of labour and finding work for workers. Just as Ben-Horin argued to the Revisionists that the terms Jabotinsky accepted were unrealistic given the meagre concentration of Revisionist workers, Katznelson stated that the likelihood of Revisionists anywhere having a sufficient number of workers to stop strike activity was extremely remote. Mapai, he insisted, had become the Zionist movement's leading party and this meant it had to be flexible.[85]

At the heart of opposition to the accords was the sense that something profound was changing in the relationship between nation, class and state, between means and ends, in Labour Zionist politics in general, and in Ben-Gurion's in particular. Ben-Aharon, perhaps more than anyone else, articulated what this change represented. He recalled that when Ben-Gurion returned to Palestine from the 18th Zionist Congress, he shocked some of his colleagues by declaring that 'We in the [ZO] Executive are emissaries of the entire nation and not only of a single class'.[86] Ben-Aharon then posed the fundamental question as to what endorsement of the London accords implied for Mapai's path:

> How is it that all these years we have been proclaiming the unity of the interests of the working class and the great majority of the nation, and now, when we receive the mantle of Zionist leadership, we establish opposing categories of class and nation? What is wrong with being emissaries of the working class in the [Zionist] Executive and directing the Executive from this point of view? Do we need, in addition to the historic standard of the working class in Palestine, yet another standard for the determination of our regime in Zionism, in the Yishuv, in the nation?[87]

The London accords posited a category of 'nation' as something whose interests were not identical to those of the working class. In short, Ben-Aharon accused Ben-Gurion of surrendering the Marxist-like content in the slogan 'from a working class to a working nation'. As Y. Shapiro has noted, when Ben-Gurion published a collection of articles and speeches in 1933 including the one from 1929 with the 'working class to a working nation' formula, the title he chose indicated the shift under way: *From a Class to a Nation*.[88] This implied that Labour was now the leader of, not identical to, the nation, and therefore it had to act accordingly. Hence Ben-Aharon, accurately, saw within the London accords something far beyond their immediate content: 'This conception says that only by concessions and a serious retreat from the socialist class concept is it possible to prolong the rule of the workers within Zionism and to win the hearts of the people'. Only he who abandoned the identity of class and national interests, an identity which was the heart and soul of the Zionist workers' movement, could sign such an agreement with the enemies of Labour, the enemies of the people, Ben-Aharon bitterly charged.[89]

While a majority in the Mapai Central Committee backed Ben-Gurion, it was decided that, given the fierceness of the controversy and the danger of a party split, it would be turned over to a party conference; the same concerns then led to the decision that a plebiscite of the entire Histadrut membership should resolve the matter. Here, however, Ben-Gurion faced not only Mapai adversaries but also strong antagonism from the other Labour and left organizations, in particular Ha-Shomer ha-Tsair and the Left Poale Zion. On 24 March, 1935 the Ben-Gurion–Jabotinsky agreement went down to defeat by a vote of 16,474 to 11,522. Immediately afterwards the Histadrut Executive invited the Revisionists' National Histadrut to work out an agreement to guarantee fair employment practices and to protect workers in the Zionist movement.[90] The Revisionists refused, although later various working arrangements were in fact established. The Mapai groups most prominent in defeating Ben-Gurion (Ha-Kibbutz ha-Meuhad and segments of the party's urban machine) eventually left the party in 1944 and renamed themselves Ahdut ha-Avodah, to indicate that Mapai's leaders had betrayed their own legacy; in turn, in 1948, this party would merge with other left Zionist opponents of the Mapai mainstream to form the Mapam (United Workers) party, which was a serious rival to Mapai in the early years of statehood.

Having suffered a severe personal and political setback, Ben-Gurion declared that Labour's rejection of the agreements was due not to principled opposition to an accord but to the specific terms he had negotiated.[91] Ben-Gurion was a man of enormous political resilience. He accepted his defeat and quickly moved to reconsolidate his own position as well as that of his party within the ZO so that in the future he would be able to take them both in the direction he wanted to chart. For Jabotinsky – who had doubted from the beginning that Labour would approve the accords – the plebiscite was the last straw; he would now seek to establish a new Zionist Organization.

10

Consolidations

The time we are living in is one of *power politics*. Moral values no longer have any force. The ears of the leaders are closed and all they can hear is the sound of canons. And the Jews of the Diaspora have no canons.

David Ben-Gurion[1]

I

Not only did the Histadrut membership vote down the Ben-Gurion-Jabotinsky pact in March 1935, but at the same time the ZO began taking additional measures to enforce Zionist discipline. The Executive's report, submitted to the Zionist Congress the following summer, declared that discipline was premised on the democratic nature of the ZO, and not 'the utter subordination of the individual will to the authority or dictatorship of a superior power such as is customary in the army or a school'. What the ZO claimed was the right to demand

> the subordination of the persons and bodies affiliated to it in regard to Zionist affairs to the collective will of the Organisation as expressed in its laws and decisions. Without such respect of its collective will, every social community would be doomed to decline or impotence. This applies particularly in the case of an organisation which, like ours, is not merely a debating society but has undertaken practical national aims that can be achieved only by joint systematic action.[2]

If the Revisionists found such requirements unacceptable in the past, they were deemed intolerable after the defeat of the London accords. Indeed, by the time this report was issued, the Revisionists had finally gone their own way. They announced secession in April, and a plebiscite in June ratified the decision.

Jabotinsky was firmly convinced that further wavering would undermine his party. He feared that the inability to obtain immigration certificates from the ZO, combined with months of 'holding fire' while seeking a compromise with it, would lead 'quite a number' of Betarim to quit a Revisionist movement perceived to be indecisive and unable to defend its own interests.[3] Such trepidations appear repeatedly in his correspondence: 'Our passivity during the last 9 months has been interpreted by our own rank and file as an admission of defeat, abandonment of the Petition idea, inability to provide certificates for our adherents etc. . . . The situation which I describe was fast nearing the verge of a final inner débâcle'.'[4] Approaches made in Palestine, Cracow and the United States to form a bloc with General Zionists B and Mizrahi did not succeed and Jabotinsky complained that the 'American Jewish middle class is . . . simply infatuated with "Labour ideals" '.[5]

Jabotinsky proposed a round-table conference of Zionist organizations in a final effort to avoid the break. The rejection of this suggestion, he explained in a long private letter evaluating the situation, would place the Revisionists in impossible circumstances in the ZO. At the next Zionist Congress they would constitute 'a helpless minority, against a tremendous Left majority, with Mizrahi and [General Zionists] B split and powerless'. Mere participation in the Congress would humiliate Revisionism in the eyes of its own followers after the events of the previous year. They would be compelled 'to swallow a series of resolutions aimed against us, the re-election of Weizmann in our presence etc.; and an ultimatum – either to pledge ourselves to blind obedience, or to leave the ZO'.[6] Jabotinsky bitterly reflected that the Jewish bourgeoisie had yielded the Zionist leadership to the left and he compared his circumstances to the struggles between the right and the left elsewhere: 'This fight is obviously too deep to be bridged over. It is the same as [is] going on all over the world: 'class war' adherents making a desperate bid for domination; in our Jewish case, owing to the peculiar cowardice of our bourgeoisie, they can do it with the financial help of that bourgeoisie'.[7]

The ZO turned down the round-table idea and it became evident to the Revisionists that even those they considered potential allies were against the petition campaign. Jabotinsky resolved to form a New Zionist Organization (NZO) which would openly challenge the prerogatives of the ZO and which, as a mass movement, would contrast with the 'notables' who, in his mind, ran the ZO.[8] Despite initial confidence, he was forced to reschedule the founding conference, planned originally for December 1935, to September, fearful that the Zionist Congress in August would steal his thunder.[9]

On the eve of the Zionist Congress, Jabotinsky declared in a letter to the (London) *Jewish Chronicle*:

> The [old] Zionist Organization is dominated by its Socialist Labour party; this party in its turn is dominated by its own 'Left Wing' – as shown . . . by the fate of the London agreement . . . Though bearing the signature of Mr. D. Ben-Gurion and supported by most of the old

guard leaders of Palestinian Socialism, it was voted down because it contained an admission of the principle that no strike should be proclaimed unless the employer refuses arbitration. Revisionism holds any form of 'class war' incompatible with the interests of the young economy whose unhampered growth is the only means of absorbing immigrants.[10]

In September 1935 delegates from 32 countries attended the 'Foundation Conference' of the 'New Zionist Organization'. The Revisionists had now gone full circle: from loyal opposition, to opposition of principle, to secession. In pursuing separatism they followed the same route they had taken in virtually all spheres of Jewish and Zionist politics. However, instead of a mass conversion to Revisionist ranks, the consequence was their increasing political ghettoization. At the same time, the Labour movement effectively exploited Revisionist tactics to its own advantage, and to delegitimate its right-wing foes. The accomplishment of this was facilitated by Mapai's own reorientation and moderation, and its pursuit of broad coalitions: Ben-Gurion's slogan was now 'Peace in the Yishuv'.

A month before the NZO met, the 19th Zionist Congress took place in Lucerne with a record attendance of 480 delegates and 1,500 guests.[11] Although the Revisionists had departed, the ZO claimed a substantial rise in Shekel-payers from 839,291 in 1933 to 1,216,030 in 1935.[12] Mapai, the largest party, came to the Congress with a defined goal: to consolidate its own status, and to complete the isolation of the Revisionists a month before their 'Foundation Congress'. This was achieved through the politics of national unity. Mapai sought to assemble within the ZO Executive a united front of all elements in Zionism, except, of course, the now absent Revisionists. It would, in fact, represent a balance of class forces within the Zionist movement as a whole. The aim was not just a broad Executive with Mapai at the head, but to demonstrate that it was the Revisionists who were breaking the solidarity of the Jewish people in an hour of distress. This crystallized the process by which Zionist politics became an exception to what has been called the 'minimum winning' rule of coalition formation, that is, the axiom that governing coalitions tend to be formed big enough to win, but no larger.[13] As a result of the consensus politics of the ZO – a politics dictated by its non-sovereign status, its consequent lack of coercive means and its self-image as representative of a people under siege – a pattern of seeking the *largest* possible coalition emerged. Participation in governing coalitions became, as such, the basis of inclusion in the 'national consensus' and a means of legitimation and delegitimation. The Revisionists were both victims and, by their separatism, a catalyst of this development.

Between 1933 and 1935 the opposition to the governing coalition in the ZO Executive was composed of the Revisionists, the General Zionists B, the Mizrahi and the Jewish State party. With the Revisionists gone, Ben-Gurion now sought to include all those remaining except the Jewish State party, which had 'all the disadvantages of the Revisionists, without the talents of Jabotinsky'.[14] A unity coalition was dictated not solely by the balance of forces and the battle with the Revisionists, but also by the general crisis faced by the Jewish world; Hitler was now in power, there were growing fears of war and in Palestine it was evident that relations with the British and the Arabs were only going to become more complicated.

There was, in addition, something more going on, something which is expressed in the following excerpt from a letter by Ben-Gurion:

> We are living in an era of implementation and ideology is not decisive. It's not important to me what a man thinks: what counts is what he does, what he has to and wants to do. I am familiar with all the dogmas and ideological systems in our party and other parties. But I discern in them one common factor which unites them all, whether they know it or not: and this is the life of work. Jewish Labour in Palestine: this is our Bible and our creed, the meaning of our Zionism and our socialism. That is what I tried to do in the Histadrut: to show that every working man is a brother and a comrade and that the union of all workers in a single Labour Federation must come before anything else.
>
> The Zionist movement is of course not the Labour Federation. But it also has a certain objective content and aim around which a united movement could be built . . . [During] an era of implementation the *way*, the *path* is all important.[15]

The means, in other words, had become paramount in Ben-Gurion's thinking about politics, and Mapai's actions at the Congress reflected this modification of its politics. The nation was no longer identified with class, and the nation was primary. For all of Ben-Gurion's fierce polemics with Jabotinsky, for all their epistolary arguments, it is difficult to imagine Jabotinsky disagreeing with the impulse – it was, we might say, a monistic impulse – implicit in Ben-Gurion's letter. There is a clear disdain for 'ideology' in it which one suspects Jabotinsky would have called a disdain for *shaatnez*, that is, for 'isms' affixed to Zionism.

At the Congress, Mapai took a conciliatory stance towards its past competitors and foes, pursuing protracted, difficult negotiations with them. For the General Zionist B group, concessions were made in labour relations, including acceptance of a plan to create a 'National Board of Conciliation and Arbitration' that could intervene in labour disputes by concurrence of both employers and workers. To the Religious Zionists of Mizrahi, who refused to join the 1933 coalition Executive when their insistence on Sabbath and other religious observances on land owned by the Jewish National Fund was rebuffed, Mapai offered to sponsor jointly a resolution confirming an earlier decision by the Zionist General Council in support of the 'obligation to rest on the Sabbath' and Jewish holidays in industrial and agricultural enterprises. When praised by Mizrahi for this move, Remez, on behalf of Labour, declared that 'the Labour Party knew how to esteem the common Zionist work of all sectors of the people based on relations of mutual respect between various parties without prejudice to anyone's freedom of conscience'.[16] Labour was but one pillar, albeit the largest.

Haim Weizmann was returned to the ZO presidency and Sokolow was accorded honorary presidency of the organization. Addressing the Congress, Weizmann reiterated his long-standing opposition to articulating a Zionist *endziel*: 'The issue of our ultimate aim has been touched upon by several speakers, and listening to them I realised the deep meaning of the commandment: *Thou shalt not take the name of the Lord in vain!*'[17] He spent much of his speech praising the accomplishments of the Labour movement and especially the Histadrut, which he characterized as a Palestinian 'synthesis' of the Haskalah and Marxism. (While chastising attacks on Marxism, he declared: 'I am no Marxist; I don't know whether I am a bourgeois, I am sure I am no capitalist'.)[18] Weizmann realized that his return to the helm of the Zionist movement was due to the consolidation of Mapai's strength there. At the same time it was clear that real power in the ZO lay not in the presidency but in the hands of the coalition Executive of seven, and especially its chairman – Ben-Gurion. (The Weizmann–Ben-Gurion relationship was to become increasingly tempestuous). The other six elected included two more from Mapai (Eliezer Kaplan and Moshe Shertok), two from Weizmann's General Zionists A (Selig Brodetsky and I. Gruenbaum) and one each from General Zionists B (F. Rottenstreich) and Mizrahi (Rabbi Y. L. Fishman). In addition, Louis Lipsky was to represent the United States, and Nahum Goldmann, designated as the Executive's representative to the League of Nations, was given voting privileges in matters pertaining to his responsibilities. The opposition to the Executive were Grossman's Jewish State party and the Marxist-oriented Ha-Shomer ha-Tsair which refused to enter a coalition with the Mizrahi and the General Zionists B.[19]

What was in effect a national unity Zionist Cabinet had been formed. Ben-Gurion's view of the matter was described at length in a letter that was personal but clearly meant for the eyes of posterity:

> Our party, the Labour faction, has reached the point towards which it was moving consciously or unconsciously, for years: we have become the basic force in Zionism. It depends on our leadership whether the Zionist Organisation will become a dynamic and effective representative body of the Jewish people, or whether it will become a miserable fiction, impotent and sterile.
>
> But our Labour movement is different from other workers' parties. The working class in other countries already has a state and a country

and an economy and a civilisation – and a class. Zionism, on the other hand, is not a State and it is not a government. We of the Labour wing cannot fight, as other workers do, for a working class economy. We are still fighting *to create something out of nothing*. Our historical aim in the Zionist movement is the building of the state, the creation of an economy, and a society, the foundations of a culture. None of these can come about without a general joint effort by all the constructive forces within the Jewish people.

It is a mistake to see the Zionists of other parties as enemies. There are indeed some people who hate us. But in every party there are young people who want to work in Palestine, who passionately want Zionism to succeed. The people who are workers in the Land of Israel were not workers in the Diaspora . . . And thousands of people in the Diaspora who are not workers now, will become labourers when they settle in Palestine. These people are our potential allies. We must explain this to them, not by waging a class war, but in a peaceful way, with love, patience, faith. It follows that we should seek a coalition for the sake of the whole of Jewry.[20]

Ben-Gurion here spells out the changes we have pointed to: the identification of working class and nation is gone, class war is rejected, building a workers' economy is a secondary concern. Clearly, short-term as well as long-range factors were making an impression on him. As Israel Kolatt perceptively points out, the vote on the London accords was the only time a general plebiscite of the workers (i.e. the Histadrut membership) was taken on a crucial issue, and the leader of the Labour movement found that the class whose interests he had identified as those of the nation had voted against what he determined were the national interests. In this regard, it is also noteworthy that in an address to the 19th Zionist Congress Ben-Gurion, having already altered his 'from a working class to a working nation' formulation to 'from a class to a nation', broadened his definition of 'national capital' to include private capital that employed Jewish labour. Throughout the Congress, Tabenkin vigorously fought Ben-Gurion on this and other issues bearing on the relation of class to nation.[21] In the eyes of the left in his own party, it was increasingly evident that Ben-Gurion's perspective had moved from that of class to that of nation, or, as Ben-Aharon had perceived in reference to the London accords, there was no longer an identity of nation and class. The Histadrut pillar was no longer the nation's pillar, but rather one of the nation's pillars; it was no longer the state in genesis but the tallest support structure of the struggle for statehood.

The same Ben-Gurion who just months before had branded Jabotinsky's *shaatnez* claims as fraudulent wrote after the Lucerne Zionist Congress of his desire to change the structure of the ZO in terms philosophically akin to those of Jabotinsky. When Herzl founded the ZO there were no parties and

'Everyone was just a *Zionist*', he observed. Now one had to join a party to be in the movement, 'But what happens to a Jew who doesn't want to join a specific party and who just wants to be an ordinary Zionist? At this moment he has no place in the Zionist framework'. While Ben-Gurion did not advocate abolishing the parties in the ZO any more than he did a decade earlier in the Histadrut, he wanted to see in each country 'a united Zionist organisation' including everyone 'whatever his political outlook'. This was because he believed that 'Zionism could become a *great national movement* which could attract *new masses of the Jewish people*. But they will be attracted by Zionism, not by parties'.[22]

The vision Ben-Gurion was projecting for the ZO went far beyond the recognition of a balance of class forces, which was implicit in his political strategy: it was, in fact, a type of General Zionism, albeit with profound respect and love for the worker and the value of labour. His priority, however, was now the 'ordinary Zionist' and not socialist synthesis. A decade earlier his frame of reference was workers in a class democracy in the Histadrut, as opposed to a federation of parties; now it was 'ordinary' Zionists within the nation. The Marxist-tinged identity of class and nation, so prominent in his earlier statements and arguments, had been replaced by a neutral notion of nation, which later became a neutral notion of state expressed, as we shall see, in his policies as prime minister of a sovereign state.

II

The first confrontation between the left and the right in Zionism was the product of two different strategies for resetting the boundaries of Jewish political culture and the socio-economic form and content of Jewish nationhood. It was a clash between rival versions of Zionist autoemancipation. One assumed that it was imperative to work from the bottom up, that is, it presumed that a substantive Jewish communal base with a certain character had to be built before ultimate political demands came to the fore. The other assumed political assurances to be prerequisites for substantive building. Ironically it was the Revisionists, the party that most fervently embraced national discipline, negated class and emphasized the efficacy of politics narrowly conceived, that ended up isolated from power; the NZO was never able to compete successfully with the ZO. Within a short period after its formation Jabotinsky was clearly disappointed and increasingly frustrated by its inability to challenge, let alone supplant, the 'old' ZO.

The Revisionist chief approached Weizmann and Ben-Gurion with the idea of establishing a 'joint provisional leadership' of the ZO and NZO in preparation for a 'Jewish National Assembly' to be elected on the basis of universal suffrage and which, in turn, he proposed would elect the leadership of the Jewish Agency.[23] This was a transparent attempt to recoup his losses. Organizationally and financially the NZO was so weak that by July 1936 – some ten months after it was founded with much fanfare – Jabotinsky invited 25 friends to a secret 'Beratung' in Carlsbad to decide on 'revival or disbandment'. He expressed the severity of the situation in these words:

> I have come to the conclusion that under the present conditions of working I can do nothing of any value. Our political possibilities are immense, but I cannot utilise them without a proper secretariat, without an English press organ, without agents and envoys. I refuse any longer to pretend that Betar is a school when I cannot give them teachers or literature. I do not want national workers in Palestine to go on fighting the red Histadrut and facing blows and hunger when I cannot even provide them with four walls to house their offices.[24]

However, in future years he characteristically remained insistent that 'I don't see myself in the role of loyal opposition to a Congress or Agency ruled by the Left . . .'[25]

The NZO did continue to function for a number of years. Poland was the foremost bastion of Revisionist strength. One of its more controversial moves was a strenuous effort to develop good relations with the anti-Semitic Polish government on the basis of what it considered a commonality of interests. Jabotinsky had previously negotiated with political forces considered abhorrent to most Jews. In 1919–20, while in retreat from the Red Army, the Ukrainian nationalist forces under Simon Petlyura had slaughtered tens of thousands of Jews. Petlyura, who was assassinated in 1926 by a young Jewish poet who had lost 15 members of his family in the pogroms, was detested by Jews for failing to do anything about the killings. In 1921 Jabotinsky reached an agreement with a representative of Petlyura's government-in-exile which was then preparing an army to invade the Ukraine. Jabotinsky's purpose was the establishment of a Jewish militia within the Ukrainian army to guard the Jewish communities. The invasion never occurred, and Jabotinsky, whose intention was hardly pernicious and who badly misjudged Jewish aversion to negotiations with Petlyura's forces barely a year after the massacres, was subjected to a barrage of angry criticism. In the late 1930s it was to the Polish government that Jabotinsky turned his diplomacy. He later justified this on the grounds that Polish anti-Semitism represented 'the anti-semitism of things', which he differentiated from 'the anti-semitism of men'. The latter was to be found especially in Germany. The former was an 'objective state of things which tends to ostracize the Jew almost independently of whether his neighbors like or dislike him'. It was rooted in the 'incompatibility between the normal evolution of [the] East–Central [European] economy and the Jews' foothold within that economy'. The 'anti-semitism of men' was 'a subjective repulsion, strong enough and permanent enough to become anything from a hobby to a religion', and thus had a 'fluctuating character'. Since it was 'of a somewhat elastic nature', it could at times be combated 'with a measure of success'.[26] On the basis of this rather strained argument, Jabotinsky reasoned that the Polish government and Zionism had objectively common interests in the mass evacuation of Jews to Palestine. The Polish government, seeking to improve its image in the West, was receptive to the idea, on the condition that Jewish rights in Poland itself would no longer be made an issue, something the Revisionists, but no other Zionists, were willing to concede.[27] The Revisionists continued this effort with the Polish government-in-exile after the Second World War began.

The NZO's general political effectiveness was modest and largely dependent on Jabotinsky's talents. His ability was particularly illustrated by the forceful presentation he made in 1937 to the Peel Commission which investigated the Palestine problem against the background of the Palestinian Arab rebellion which had begun the previous year:

> Oliver Twist came and asked for 'more'. He said 'more' because he did not know how to express it; what Oliver Twist really meant was this: 'Will you just give me that normal portion which is necessary for a boy of my age to live'. I assure you that you face here to-day, in the Jewish people with its demands, an Oliver Twist who has, unfortunately, no concessions to make. What can be the concessions? We have got to save millions, many *millions*.
>
> So when we hear the Arab claim confronted with the Jewish claim, I fully understand that any minority would prefer to be a majority, it is quite understandable that the Arabs of Palestine would also prefer Palestine to be the Arab State No. 4, No. 5, or No. 6 – that I quite understand; but when the Arab claim is confronted with our Jewish demand to be saved, it is like the claims of appetite versus the claims of starvation.[28]

The Peel Commission's Report, issued in July 1937, proposed the partition of Palestine into a small Jewish state (composed of the coastal plain from south of Jaffa to the Lebanese border, the Jezreel Valley and the Galilee), a much larger Arab state and a British enclave. The leadership of Palestine's Arabs immediately denounced this as a compromise with the Zionists. At the same time, the question of partition gave rise to another fierce debate within Zionism since Weizmann and Ben-Gurion, backed by the moderate wing of the Labour movement, endorsed it in principle while disapproving of the boundaries suggested by Peel. For Weizmann and Ben-Gurion, the essential thing was that the Peel Report recognized the principle of Jewish sovereignty. Since Ben-Gurion, as opposed to the Revisionists, saw the primary mission of the Zionist enterprise as the re-creation of an independent Jewish people, the retrieval or retention of historic lands within the boundaries of a Jewish state was a secondary matter. Both the far left and the Revisionist right inveighed vigorously against this position. For Jabotinsky such territorial compromise represented just one more concession of national rights by Weizmann and Ben-Gurion, and he hoped 'to use the Partition business for smashing the Weizmann–Mapai Agency'.[29]

In this, too, he was unsuccessful. At times Jabotinsky considered the possibility of a renewed effort to 'conquer the ZO', and as the situation of European Jewry radically deteriorated and World War threatened total catastrophe, he appealed for consultations with other Jewish leaders in order to establish a united front.[30] Jabotinsky originally thought a full-scale war between the major powers impossible, but once it had begun the implications for the Jews and his own movement were evident to him. 'The main feature of the new situation', he wrote on 22 September, 1939 after the Nazis invaded Poland (his strongest base), 'seems to be this: East-European Jewry which was the mainstay of all Zionism and particularly *our* Zionism, has been smashed'.[31] Within a year Jabotinsky himself was dead (he collapsed at a Betar camp in New York in midsummer 1940), thus depriving his leader-oriented movement of its charismatic central figure; after the war the Revisionists returned to the ZO. However, the Revisionist future was sustained not so much by its politicians as by its underground military arm, the Irgun, which, after statehood became the Herut party, headed by its commander, Menahem Begin, a former Betar leader from Warsaw. In contrast to Jabotinsky with his Herzlian diplomatic approach, Begin, as early as the third Betar World Congress, championed 'military Zionism', which, in his view, transcended the practical and political Zionisms of the past.[32]

Mapai, on the other hand, having followed a strategy resting on the construction of a substantial socio-economic base was largely able to define the Zionist project. Ironically, it built its pillar on a class basis, then translated the hegemony this enabled it to secure into national leadership, whereupon it accepted the principle of segmented pluralism. Labour's strategy for building a workers' economy in the 1920s, its linking of the long-term needs of the Labour Zionist movement to the short-term needs of immigrants for whom it had also provided a symbolic universe, a system of meanings with which to struggle in the difficult conditions of Palestine, had created the means both to build its own base and to defeat its foes. In short, Labour's strategy for state-building carried within it the spiritual and organizational means of its political hegemony. Once it had attained this, its self-conception changed and it played the role of dominant party as Duverger defines it. Mapai was never numerically a majority, but public opinion accepted its leadership role and came to identify it with the epoch.

This evolution proceded despite a serious rupture in Mapai. Developments both internal and external to the party produced a challenge from within that took the form of 'Siah B' (Faction B) which was composed of important urban elements within the party, especially its Tel Aviv machine, and Ha-Kibbutz ha-Meuhad as well. Together, they were the chief sectors within Mapai that had fought the London accords. In addition they opposed Ben-Gurion's acceptance of the partition of Palestine and his now overt desire to achieve statehood as soon as possible, even if this meant major territorial concessions. The arguments made by some on the left on this issue were similar to those of the right; they feared partition would lead to Zionist acceptance of a mini-state and the yielding of lands to which the Jews had deep historical ties. It was not only the radical camp of Tabenkin and Ben-Aharon that opposed Ben-Gurion, at least at first, on partition, but also some of his closest comrades such as Katznelson. He was supported by most of the former Ha-Poel ha-Tsair, including Sprinzak, Eliezer Kaplan, Pinhas Lubianiker (later Lavon) and Shmuel Dayan. Some of the former Ahdut ha-Avodah leadership, such as Shertok, Remez and Ben-Tsvi, backed him as well.[33] For Tabenkin, partition politics inevitably refocused socialist Zionism on etatism and the tools of a state, especially on the army, whereas his concern was the construction of a socialist commonwealth of kibbutzim. The Arab question was, in general, not central to Tabenkin's thinking, although he suggested a Jewish state was feasible only after the Jewish and Arab national movements had resolved their problems. Ben-Gurion's view was the exact opposite.[34]

Ben-Gurion reminded his socialist colleagues that the dispute with the Revisionists about Zionism's *endziel* was not over whether there should be a Jewish state, but over when it was politically intelligent to declare that goal. In addition, while he insisted that he was as attached to *Erets Israel* as any of his foes, there were broader, more urgent, questions that had to be considered. 'Outside Jewish history', he warned, '*Erets Israel* has no specific existence as a geographic and political unit'. The 'unity of the Land' was a 'spiritual fact' and spiritual facts ought not to be confused with political facts. And the fact was that the Zionist movement had two options before it, and only two options: continuation of the British Mandate over the whole of Palestine, or the establishment of a Jewish state in part of it.[35] For Ben-Gurion there was no question of which option to pursue. The events of 1936, the situation in Europe, the twists and turns of British policy, the failure to reach an agreement with the Palestinian Arabs (Ben-Gurion had extensive discussions with their leaders in the 1930s with little to show for it) and finally the Peel Commission's recommendations, led the Chairman of the Zionist Executive to the conclusion that statehood should – must – be pursued openly *now*.[36] Whereas he had previously stressed maximizing immigration into Palestine under the Mandate while seeking accord with the Arabs, he now advocated partition relentlessly; this meant statehood before mass immigration had come, and relinquishing part of *Erets Israel*.[37] A smaller state with its gates open to persecuted diaspora Jewry had priority over territorial sentiments. At the 20th Zionist Congress, in Zurich in late summer 1937, the question of partition was hotly debated as a consequence of the Peel proposals. The Zionist Executive was authorized by the Congress to hold discussions with the British government on partition proposals.

London soon repudiated partition as well as the very terms of the Mandate – the establishment of a Jewish national home. In 1939 Neville Chamberlain's government issued a White Paper which, in the midst of the Hitler era, not only restricted land sales to Jews, but limited Jewish immigration to 75,000 over the next half decade, and disallowed any more after that except by Arab sufferance. This only reinforced partition as an *idée fixe* in Ben-Gurion's mind, and at his behest an extraordinary conference of the Zionist movement in 1942 at the Biltmore Hotel in New York officially declared and demanded – for the first time – that a postwar world had to include a Jewish commonwealth in Palestine. What in the past had been a matter of verbal equivocation was now explicitly endorsed – the *endziel*.

The 'Biltmore Programme' was steadfastly opposed by the left wing of Mapai. It was preferable, argued Tabenkin and his supporters, to forgo immediate statehood if it came with partition; instead, the movement should redouble its efforts to expand the Yishuv through new settlements and new immigrants. The Mapai foes of partition found allies in the independent left-wing kibbutz movement, Ha-Shomer ha-Tsair. However, whereas Tabenkin's circle was composed of socialist integral nationalists, Ha-Shomer ha-Tsair was for socialist binationalism and attacked Biltmore because it failed to address the Arab question adequately. The two groups thus found common cause by reason of contrary logic and principles.[38]

Ben-Gurion's suspicions and animosity towards his left-wing critics steadily grew: in the 1930s they had crossed him on the London accords, and now were doing so on the issues of partition and immediate statehood. Furthermore, they were sympathetic to the Soviet Union, and Ben-Gurion and his supporters had become increasingly hostile to Moscow. Simultaneously, these conflicts expressed an intense internal struggle concerning the future nature of Mapai itself. Siah B and Ha-Kibbutz ha-Meuhad felt more and more that the party was becoming a reformist organization and losing its identity as a radical, socialist, class-oriented party. This was partly reflected in ongoing arguments about the Histadrut between Ben-Gurion, who accepted a more limited role for it, and Tabenkin, who wanted it expanded so that a co-operative economy would one day encompass the entire country. Exacerbating the tensions were Katznelson's unsuccessful attempts in the late 1930s to merge the two kibbutz movements affiliated to Mapai, Hever ha-Kvutsot and Tabenkin's Ha-Kibbutz ha-Meuhad, much to the chagrin of the latter.

While Tabenkin himself did not want to see Mapai split, events moved inexorably in that direction. In 1941 Siah B presented its own national list for the Mapai party conference.This step was followed by conflicts during and after the December 1941 election campaign for the fifth conference of the Histadrut. Mapai won some two-thirds of the votes (278 of 401 delegates), but the combined forces of the left, that is, Siah B within Mapai, the Socialist League (organized in 1936 on behalf of Ha-Shomer ha-Tsair and, at least in Ben-Gurion's view, now a potential threat to Mapai among urban workers) and the Left Poale Zion, controlled half the delegates. The Histadrut had been a primary focus of Siah B activities, and now both the power of the Histadrut and the power of the left within it became a special concern for Mapai, especially since before the balloting Ha-Kibbutz ha-Meuhad was promised a third of the Mapai seats in Histadrut institutions.

Siah B held its own convention shortly after the Histadrut conference.[39] As we have seen, Ben-Gurion's entire orientation to political organization, both in Mapai and in the Histadrut, was always based on centralism; now he and Katznelson found themselves confronted not only by factionalism within their party, but with the prospect that it might lose control of the giant Labour apparatus to the left. Mapai held its fifth party conference in the autumn of 1942 at Kfar Vitkin and voted to abolish all factions.[40] It was another two years, however, before a final break occurred. During that period Mapai's hold on the Histadrut, where it could not count on its own left wing, became increasingly tenuous. Ben-Gurion began taking measures to minimize the impact of a possibly disastrous split on his party. Such a fissure not only threatened Mapai in the Histadrut but would entail the loss of a significant number of party members, including an important cadre of younger activists who had been groomed for future leadership roles and who were tied to Ha-Kibbutz ha-Meuhad. Furthermore, a fracture meant losing much of Ha-Kibbutz ha-Meuhad itself, a good part of the Tel Aviv party machine and many of the key personnel in the Palmah (the elite strike force of the Haganah which was established in 1941 when Rommel was advancing across North Africa and which was based in kibbutzim of Ha-Kibbutz ha-Meuhad where its members worked part-time and trained part-time).

In point of fact, both Ben-Gurion and Katznelson had concluded that if Mapai was to function as they deemed it had to, a split was preferable to the status quo. The issue was forced in the winter and spring of 1944 as Siah B opposed Mapai in a Histadrut vote (concerning its delegation to a forthcoming meeting of the British Trades Union Congress) and Mapai's leaders moved to enforce the Kfar Vitkin discipline resolutions. Siah B decided to run its own lists in elections, scheduled for midsummer, of the Asefat ha-Nivharim and the Histadrut, and was duly expelled by the Mapai party conference of June 1944.[41] Retrieving the old party name, Siah Bet now called itself – ironically – Ha-Tnuah le-Ahdut ha-Avodah, the movement for Labour unity. The implication was clear, however: Mapai had betrayed its socialist Zionist legacy and that of the original Ahdut ha-Avodah.

Mapai was now a minority on the Histadrut Council as well as in the labour councils of Tel Aviv and Haifa. In response, it rapidly began an organizing campaign which culminated in a 'Zionist Socialist Conference' in late July 1944. It was, in fact, a remarkable effort. According to one estimate Mapai enrolled over 20,000 new members in only a few weeks.[42] The elections to the Asefat ha-Nivharim – which had been expanded from 71 to 171 members – were, not surprisingly, boycotted by the Revisionists and other segments of the right including General Zionists B. Of the 24 lists that participated, Mapai won 64 seats (37 per cent) as opposed to 21 for the *Hazit ha-Smol* (Left Front – the Socialist League and the Left Poale Zion) and 16 for Ahdut ha-Avodah.[43] The Histadrut elections occurred several days later with 90 per cent of those eligible voting (110,000 out of 120,000, up from 92,000 out of 105,000 in the previous election).[44] Mapai won 53 per cent of the delegates to Ahdut ha-Avodah's 19 per cent and the Socialist League's 20 per cent. Mapai had re-established its majority in the Histadrut and was no longer dependent on Siah B there. It also re-established its majorities on the Tel Aviv and Haifa labour councils.

These were impressive feats for the leadership of Mapai under Ben-Gurion and Katznelson (the latter died several days later of a brain haemorrhage).[45] A 3 per cent majority in the Histadrut was not, however, a great one, and Mapai would have to pay special attention to the needs of allies in Ha-Poel ha-Mizrahi (the religious workers) and the small workers' organization of the General Zionists.[46] At the next Histadrut convention four years later – after statehood had been established – the centre of attention remained the clash between Mapai and its left-wing opponents, now the United Workers' Party (Mapam). The latter, formed by the union of Ahdut ha-Avodah, the Socialist League/Ha-Shomer ha-Tsair and the Left Poale Zion, emerged as Israel's second largest party in the Jewish state's first parliamentary elections. Ben-Gurion remained a bitter, and increasingly contemptuous, antagonist of Mapam; he was an apostle of Labour unity, but unity had to be on his own terms. Just as the Revisionists were beyond the accepted perimeters of Zionist unity, so too was Siah B/Ahdut ha-Avodah beyond those of Mapai, although Ben-Gurion was willing to have Mapam as a coalition partner while this was out of the question with Jabotinsky's successors. However, Ben-Gurion would always seek to balance Mapam with religious and centrist forces.

The forms and modes of coexistence of parties defines a country's party system.[47] The first Zionist party system was effectively created in the 1930s and 1940s and survived, with some modifications, until the 1977 elections brought the Revisionists to power in Israel. Benjamin Akzin, writing in 1955, noted that parties 'occupy in Israel a place more prominent and exercise an influence more pervasive than in any other State, with the sole exception of some one-party states'.[48] The pre-state period saw the creation of a non-sovereign Zionist *Partienstaat* with defined characteristics. A multi-party system crystallized and operated within the framework of a 'legislature' (or legislatures – the Zionist Congress and the Asefat ha-Nivharim), elected by proportional representation. Coalition cabinets (in the Zionist Executive or the Vaad Leumi) were formed, and, finally, the far right (the Revisionists) and the far left (the Communists) were excluded, while Mapai was dominant. This, in turn, became the pattern of Israeli politics and the Israeli party system.

Part Three
Statehood

11
Mamlakhtiyut I:
Of Golden Calves and Messiahs

... the polis is prior in the order of nature to the family and the individual. The reason for this is that the whole is necessarily prior ... to the part.

Aristotle[1]

I

David Ben-Gurion profoundly doubted that the Jews were prepared for self-government. This was one source of *mamlakhtiyut*, the operative principle of his tenure as first prime minister of the independent state of Israel, that was established in 1948. *Mamlakhtiyut* may perhaps be rendered best as statism or etatism (*mamlakhti(t)* or statist/etatist in adjectival form). In the 1939 report on nationalism by the Study Group of the Royal Institute of International Affairs, *état* was defined as 'the sum of organisations and institutions by which the political aspects of life in common are made possible'.[2] This captures Ben-Gurion's use of *mamlakhtiyut*, but only in part because the Hebrew *mamlakhah* means kingdom. I shall therefore make general use of the Hebrew transliteration. The adjective *mamlakhti(t)* was an important feature of Ben-Gurion's political vocabulary from early in his career. He used it to emphasize the specifically political nature of the Zionist quest for Jewish self-determination. At the fifth conference of Ahdut ha-Avodah in 1926, he defined Zionism's goal as a 'Hebrew *mamlakhti* construction [*binyan mamlakhti ivri*]'. What the Jewish bourgeoisie lacked, he told the delegates, was precisely a *mamlakhti* sense of Jewish needs. In contrast, 'The class idea of the worker in Palestine is the *mamlakhti* idea [*raayon mamlakhti*] of political Zionism'.[3] In 1935 he referred to the ZO as the '*mamlakhti* instrument [*ha-makhshir ha-mamlakhti*]' created by Herzl.[4] With statehood, *mamlakhtiyut* became a mobilizing ideology and a concrete policy premised on the assertion of state primacy over those sectors and institutions in Israeli life, most of them originating in the pre-state system of segmented pluralism, that after 1948 were determined to be particularistic, and potentially detrimental to the unity of the state and the nation. In this chapter *mamlakhtiyut* will be examined primarily as an ideology, and in the following one it will be analysed in practice.

'Just as an independent state is the condition for the healthy existence of a nation', Ben-Gurion told the Mapai Council in 1951, so too was a nation's capacity for '*mamlakhtit* activity [*peulah mamlachtit*] a condition for the healthy existence of a state'.[5] It is noteworthy that he chose to build on *mamlakhah*, rather than *medinah*, the word adopted for 'the State of Israel'(*Medinat Israel*). The biblical Hebrew connotation of *medinah* was generally of a province, and indicated jurisdictional prerogatives; *din* means judgement. It did not, however, imply an independent sovereign state in the modern sense.[6] It was only at the 1942 Biltmore conference in New York that the Zionist movement specifically articulated Jewish statehood as its goal; as we have seen, for practical and political reasons preferred terms before then were Jewish 'homeland' or 'national home'. Two years after the New York meeting Ben-Gurion, then engaged in a vigorous debate with the Labour left which opposed immediate statehood if it meant the partition of Palestine, explained his use of *medinah* as a product of an internal party debate on the eve of Biltmore over whether to speak of a 'Jewish state' or a 'Jewish commonwealth'. (He transliterated 'state' and 'commonwealth' into the Hebrew.)

Ben-Gurion himself favoured 'commonwealth', although Hebrew lacked a precise rendering for it or an equivalent to *res publica* in Latin. (Ancient Israel was, of course a kingdom, a *mamlakhah*.) Ben-Gurion recounted:

> I checked every place where the word '*medinah*' appears in the Bible. It is found fifty times and each place means a province, not a state, a *gosodarstvo*, a *Staat*, or *état*. [In] the scroll of Esther, Ahasuerus had 127 *medinot*, provinces. In the Mishnah, the word *medinah* is sometimes the capital city and sometimes the opposite, that is, provincial towns. But nowhere is the word *medinah* in Hebrew necessarily state; but today we have no other word.[7]

The Biltmore Programme, whose goal was to proclaim the Zionist movement's postwar aims, urged that 'Palestine be established as a Jewish Commonwealth integrated in the structure of the new democratic world' that would follow the defeat of fascism.[8] 'Commonwealth' was chosen for the English version, said Ben-Gurion, for several reasons. On a practical level, it was viewed as appealing in the United States because an American president, Woodrow Wilson, who had been consulted in the drafting of the Balfour Declaration, stated in 1919 that its goal was the founding of a 'Jewish commonwealth'. Ben-Gurion also explained that 'commonwealth' denoted a 'state of freedom', something more than simply a state (*medinah*).

Furthermore, like the Hebrew *medinah*, 'state' in English does not have a fixed meaning; the United States was a state composed (then) of 48 'states'. 'In English', Ben-Gurion went on, 'the word state is not what our linguists think'.[9]

'Kingdom' (*mamlakhah*) implies something less precise, but also broader and more powerful than state (*medinah*). Certainly in Ben-Gurion's usage a political spirit was being invoked, something extending beyond the French word *état*, the German *Staat*, or Weber's formulation of a territory in which legitimate coercive force is monopolized. Ben-Gurion's intent was partly compensatory. Except in ancient Israel, the Jews had little experience with statecraft; he feared they lacked a political culture adequate to statehood. Just as he had shifted from class to state politics, as prime minister Ben-Gurion was preoccupied – occasional rhetoric notwithstanding – less with the old Labour Zionist concept of *am oved* (a working nation) than with what, before the Mapai National Council in 1951, he called '*am mamlakhti*' (a *mamlakhti* or statist nation).[10]

Ben-Gurion insisted that the Exodus from Egypt, the revelation at Mount Sinai, the conquest of the Land of Israel by Joshua and Israeli independence marked the essential determining events of Jewish history. Yet, because of cultural handicaps produced by centuries of persecution and the daunting tasks facing the young, besieged state, the Jews, in his view, faced conditions more difficult, and had less time in which to be transformed into an *am mamlakhti*, than had other peoples.[11] During his last political battle – an ill-considered, and frustrated challenge to his successors in Mapai's leadership two years after he stepped down as premier in 1963 – he told an interviewer that the Jews 'never understood *mamlakhtiyut* . . . Our people, most of our people, had lived under oppressors whom they hated, together with their states and governments. That does not produce *mamlakhtiyut*, a sense of public responsibility'.[12]

Neither his personal doubts, nor his life-long penchant for centralism, were the sole sources of *mamlakhtiyut*. It was an obvious product of the process we saw emerging in embryo in the 1930s, when Ben-Gurion and Mapai opted for a hegemonic segmented pluralism rather than a synthesis of national and class concepts. Presuming that nation and state stood above class naturally engendered a statist politics, although, as we shall see, that statist politics in turn diminished the pillars, especially Labour's, that it also originally assumed. While class rhetoric was not abandoned, its operational principles were replaced by statist ones.

This is illustrated by an especially symbolic debate in the spring of 1953. At this time the Israeli government was preparing to unify the country's educational system which, until then, was composed of politically affiliated and relatively autonomous Religious, Labour, and General educational sub-systems known as 'trends'. This was a change long advocated by both Ben-Gurion and the General Zionists, who were then partners in an uneasy coalition government. A furore arose over the permissibility of singing the Labour movement's anthem and flying red flags in the proposed state school system on May Day and the Histadrut's anniversary. The draft education law then under consideration made no mention of flags or anthems, but the General Zionists suddenly demanded that it specify that only the state flag and national anthem would be acceptable in state schools. This was an inopportune proposal from Mapai's perspective because of misgivings within the party over abolishing the Labour education system, which was then the largest and in which the red flag was flown and the anthem sung. Mapai's 150-member Central Committee met and overwhelmingly endorsed the right to fly the red flag and sing the Labour hymn twice annually (May Day and the Histadrut's anniversary) in schools where pupils were from predominantly working-class backgrounds, if so requested by their parents.[13] The Central Committee also resolved that its final position would be determined in a few months, thus leaving room for negotiations. The General Zionists rejected the Mapai position, and also the suggestion that the law make no mention of flags or hymns. Its four ministers resigned from the cabinet, and the smaller Progressive party, liberal allies of Mapai, threatened to do the same.

Ben-Gurion sided with the General Zionists. He insisted that forgoing the flag and anthem would not impair the Labour movement's special mission of making nation and class one, so that 'there would be a working people'.[14] The key to Ben-Gurion's position, however, is to be discerned from *when* he thought this mission would be fulfilled. In March 1949 he declared that only one stage of Jewish statehood had been achieved, hoping 'the day will come when a Socialist state will be built in Israel in our generation'.[15] Ben-Gurion frequently stressed that Israel was only in a first stage, but he made this point most often when he wanted to postpone specific questions of socialism. These, he made clear, were secondary beside the urgent matters of immigration, defence and 'building the land'. He therefore warned his party as well as his left critics that a regime of compromise was required.[16] His point, ironically, was akin to that made by Jabotinsky in a letter to Ben-Gurion that we have already quoted: 'I will leave a will to my children telling them to make a revolution. But I'll write on the envelope: "To be opened five years after the Hebrew state is established" '.[17] Jabotinsky wanted to postpone the 'social question' until half a decade after statehood; with the establishment of statehood, Ben-Gurion wanted to place socialism in abeyance. Having asserted in the 1920s and 1930s that Labour Zionism stood in many circles at once, in the 1950s Ben-Gurion was telling his nation that the 'Ingathering of the Exiles' was not just the complement but also the precondition of national and social liberation.[18]

Ben-Gurion derisively suggested to the Mapai Central Committee that insistence on the flag and anthem was a type of idolatry and an unnecessary means of asserting the party's credentials.[19] In the Knesset, ironically, he made his argument in terms of *shaatnez*, the ideological blending of Zionism and socialism that Jabotinsky had so opposed. Ben-Gurion reminded the assembled parliamentarians that he was 'no devotee of symbols and flags, nor do I value people who prostrate themselves before flags while exempting themselves from the duties which the flag merely symbolizes ... What matters is the quality of the flag, not the flag'.[20] Zionist Labour, he went on, 'has an uncompromising quarrel with the so-called "Monists" who say: you must choose between "people" and "class" '.[21] He insisted that there was no need to apologize for carrying both national and class standards at once: the banner of the nation represented the whole of Jewry, and that of the Labour movement represented its eventual transformation into a working nation, a merger of class and people. Instead of attacking the right's national monism – the historical foe against whom he had formulated this argument originally – he turned it against class monism on the left.

However, having reaffirmed the Zionist socialist synthesis, he then pursued an argument whose logic opposed the categories of nation and class to each other, and posited the nation-state as a thing standing above class. While Labour carries two flags, 'to the extent that the flag symbolizes ideological content, the flags are not mixed'. Only the national flag – which 'symbolizes the integrity and the unity of the nation' – would therefore fly over state institutions, including schools, and Zionist Congresses. Even if *all* pupils in a school belonged to Mapai families, he declared, only the state flag should fly. Unification of the schools meant that they would belong to the whole nation and not just to part of it.[22] Later that summer the Knesset voted to establish a unified school system, and in November 1953 the Mapai Council nullified the earlier Central Committee decision by a vote of 108 to 25, with 22 abstentions. The General Zionists were again in the government.[23]

Ben-Gurion's position assumed that the interests of the working class were *particular* interests, and that it was in the state that the universality of the nation was to be located. Labour was but one pillar, albeit rightfully the largest, in the Jewish state. The Ben-Gurion who, three decades before, insisted that the Hebrew working class was 'the principle subject [*ha-nose ha-ikari*] of the realization of Zionism' now believed that 'The State has ... become the principle and driving force in the achievement of Zionist aims'.[24] Where the working class was once both the subject and object of the Zionist enterprise, the bearer and location of its revolution, and the face of its future, this identity was now sundered and the role of the working class had been assumed by the state.

Ben-Gurion's use of *shaatnez* in the Knesset debate is striking if we recall his defence of *shaatnez* against Jabotinsky on the grounds that Labour Zionists stood in many circles – Zionist, socialist, national, international, etc. His formulations now identified social justice as espoused by the biblical Prophets – something specifically Jewish, though expressing universal values – as the element he synthesized with Zionism. His synthesis was, therefore, not really *shaatnez*, at least not in the sense used by Jabotinsky, who himself had argued that the social values of the Jewish state ought to be derived from the Bible rather than from 'foreign' sources such as Marxism.[25] That the young Ben-Gurion was a socialist whose Zionist formulations were influenced, consciously or unconsciously, by certain Marxist concepts is evident in his speeches, writings and strategies; just as apparent – indeed, more so – is the extent to which he had completely left behind that symbolic universe by the 1950s, although without entirely abandoning its phraseology (particularly when political expedience demanded otherwise). In a 1968 interview he dated abandonment of the title 'socialist' to the the Second World War years.[26] Ben-Gurion, as we have seen, once declared that his communism derived from his Zionism; the implication was that communism was a means for his Zionism. When Ben-Gurion described Lenin in the 1920s, what he particularly admired in the Bolshevik leader was his ability to discard what had seemed essential only the day before. Ben-Gurion's trajectory from the 1930s to the 1950s followed a similar principle, although it was socialism that he discarded while retaining statism and centralism, both of which, it should be noted, were features of Russian political culture and that of Western Social Democracy. More specifically, what replaced socialism was *mamlakhtiyut* mixed with a foggy national messianism which he claimed espoused universalistic values.

Messianism always influenced Ben-Gurion's *Weltanschauung*, dating back to his earliest years in Plonsk when many of his neighbours believed that the Messiah had arrived in Vienna in the bearded person of Theodor Herzl. It is likely that his original attraction to socialism was rooted in Jewish messianism. After the birth of Israel he was wont to proclaim that 'We live in the days of the Messiah', although adding that the Messiah had not yet actually arrived because the ingathering of the exiled Jewish people into Israel was not yet complete.[27] The 'Jewish vision of redemption', as Ben-Gurion saw it, was premised on the 'ingathering of the exiles' who, in their own land, could be a 'chosen people' and a 'light unto the nations'.[28] (At times, however, he qualified the use of some of these terms by noting that each people 'to some extent, is a chosen people in its own eyes at any rate'.[29])

'Chosenness' and messianism were, for Ben-Gurion, secular and symbolic, not religious, notions. In this, his formulations – though not always consistent – were akin to those of Ahad Ha-am in replacing religious ethnic myths by national cultural ones. 'I am convinced', he once told an interviewer, 'that . . . the Jews were the "choosing" people rather than the "chosen", that it is they who chose God rather than the reverse'. This chosenness consisted in fidelity to the 'ideal of moral perfection' and a 'perfect people', as articulated by the Prophets.[30] According to Ben-Gurion, it was the task of the Jews, along with their own redemption, to preach a *universal* Prophetic message of peace, justice and brotherhood. Echoing Hess and Mazzini, he insisted that 'the redemption of one nation is inconceivable without the redemption of all humanity and all humanity will not be redeemed if one of its members is not redeemed'.[31] We can also see Ben-Gurion's secularization of religious myth in his profound, and often stated, admiration of Spinoza. This Jewish philosopher, who was excommunicated, was described by Ben-Gurion as someone who 'broke away entirely from any attachment to formal religious custom and tradition and analysed biblical narrative' with 'a penetrating critical mind. It is true that he proffered some harsh and unjust remarks concerning the sages of Israel, yet he remained a proud and believing Jew until the end of his days'.[32]

Messianism is an important, though varied, component of Jewish history which seems to flourish in taxing times. It entails a fundamental reorientation of attitudes to temporality by radically counterposing the present and Messianic era, and focusing on the final event, something accompanied by disruption and catastrophe – the 'birthpangs of the Messiah'.[33] In Pharasaic and Rabbinic Judaism 'restorative ethnic–national and historical elements' such as the rebuilding of the Jerusalem Temple and the 'Ingathering of the Exiles' became essential parts of Jewish messianism, as one authority notes.[34] For most of its history it 'retained its national, social, and historical basis whatever the universalist, cosmic, or inner and spiritual meanings accompanying it'.[35]

Ben-Gurion may thus be placed within the Jewish messianic tradition, at least to the extent that he projected national and universal – though secular – redemption after a century of Jewish catastrophe. Furthermore, as we shall see, while messianic *mamlakhtiyut* spoke of broad visions, in policy it engendered not just identification with the state but a narrow focus on its mechanisms. As Shlomo Avineri once observed, messianism in power 'turns from a yearning for new moral horizons into a defense of the power structure'.[36] The foremost historian of Jewish messianism, Gershom Scholem, has argued that it engenders a life of hope but also of deferment, and consequently represents 'the real anti-existentialist idea'. As such, 'Jewish so-called *Existenz* possesses a tension that never finds its true release'.[37] We can discern something like this in Ben-Gurion's concurrent proclamations of messianic times and deferment of social and national redemption until the ingathering of the exiles was completed. Scholem also argued that the messianic life of deferment makes the accomplishments of the as-yet-unredeemed seem inconcrete.[38] This was certainly not the case with Ben-Gurion who was the most practical of politicians; indeed Scholem noted that the messianism that came with Zionism – 'the modern Jewish readiness for irrevocable action in the concrete realm' – was 'a readiness which no longer allows itself to be fed on hopes'.[39] Ben-Gurion's political decisions were brutally of the here and now, and, ironically this was one key to his political prescience. An important collection of his speeches and articles was entitled *Vision and Path* (*Hazon va-derekh*), and the extent to which Ben-Gurion spoke of vision was often the extent to which he was actually fixated on the path.

There was a profoundly anti-existential strain in Ben-Gurion because despite messianism's stress on the future, he saw the creation of Israel as the resolution of the fundamental crisis of identity that had faced the Jews as a people and as individuals. He reiterated endlessly that the diaspora Jew was a divided being, living in the milieu of the Jews and concurrently in that of a hostile external world on which he was dependent but in which he could never be at home. There was a rending 'between the Jew and the Man' which was only 'healed' in Israel where the Jews were 'subject to a Jewish state framework' moulded and determined by they themselves, and in which 'Everything is a hundred per cent Jewish and a hundred per cent human'. Israel gave birth to 'the new Jew and the new man', a being 'rooted in the soil of his homeland, confident in himself and master of his fate', an integrated, whole being equally at home with his 'distant Biblical characteristics' and as a citizen of the contemporary world community.[40]

In short, the new Jew knew who he was, was no longer riddled with diaspora *Angst* and could get on with his life as any normal member of a normal nation. Here, in fact, was the great tension within Ben-Gurion and much of Labour Zionism. On the one hand Ben-Gurion called on Israel to be a light unto the nations, a perfect exemplary people, while on the other he wanted it to be a normal nation, one like all others. This contradiction rests in the very notion of an *am mamlakhti* as bearer of messianic vision. In the end, the younger generation of Mapai that Ben-Gurion tutored was composed, as we shall see, of technocrats; the mechanism, the path, not the vision, was their frame of reference. Broad visions are rooted in *Angst* and existential crisis, and this is precisely what Ben-Gurion thought he was banishing from Jewish existence. Eight years after independence, he declared with satisfaction: 'There is no need to prove to the generation growing up in Israel the necessity for a Jewish State. It wants to know how to build the state, to maintain it, to strengthen it, develop it, to mould its character'.[41] Indeed, Ben-Gurion's messianism reinforced such claims; proclaiming peace and justice as messianic goals defers, if not denudes, their practical reality. If the old questions of socialism were no longer of interest, as Ben-Gurion averred, and if fundamental Jewish existential questions were resolved, then managing the new means that the Jews had in their hands, the state, becomes the all-consuming concern and 'peace and justice' become projections of the future with little immediate concrete content.

In the plethora of Ben-Gurion's messianic utterances there is a continuity with Labour Zionism's aspiration to synthesize a particularism (nationalism) with a universalism (socialism). However, there was a very strong particularism in Ben-Gurion's messianic universalism, and this was in his pronounced inclination to counterpose Jewish messianism with what he derided as 'foreign' elements entering Zionism. Here again, he is reminiscent of Jabotinsky's attacks on the left in the 1930s. However, this was also an extension of that attitude in Mapai – articulated especially in the pre-state period by Berl Katznelson – which radically emphasized the specificity of Zionist socialism and its Palestinian/Israeli context, sometimes with more, sometimes with less, justification.

We saw this expressed as early as the Second Aliyah, when Labour Zionists questioned whether or not Palestine could be forced into the mould of Borokhov's theory. In later decades the Mapai leadership not only warned against imposing European concepts on Palestinian conditions, but more and more tended to negate current and historical influences on them by European socialism, as if to say that Zionist Labour had developed entirely out of the Jewish Prophetic tradition and had little to learn from elsewhere. Ben-Gurion declared in 1950 that Zionism did not need political formulae 'borrowed from other nations' since they could not express its 'inner truth'. He explained that 'Ours is a Messianic movement, and that is the most suitable word, for it is a specifically Jewish expression which is very apt. Ours is a movement which seeks the redemption of the nation together with the redemption of the world'.[42] This was more than a matter of 'inner truth'. In an important speech to the Histadrut's eighth convention in March 1956, the premier declared that Israel's socio-economic structure was 'singular and cannot be forced into sociological definitions that grew out of a totally different reality'.[43] There is, of course, a basic truth in this since all societies have their singularity; however, if Ben-Gurion's comment is taken to its ultimate conclusion no comparative sociology is possible at all. Undoubtedly, Ben-Gurion's sense of Jewish chosenness informed his claims, although here too he was not consistent in expressing such singularity. At times, he stated that Israel had something to learn from British, Scandinavian and Burmese socialists.[44] Also, his particularist inclinations did not prevent him from – very publicly – studying and admiring Greek and Indian philosophy. But like Jabotinsky before him, Ben-Gurion's emphasis on Jewish specificity was a tool in his own battles with the parties on his left.

II

In the first elections to Israel's 120-seat parliament, the Knesset, 87 per cent of eligible voters cast ballots, and Mapai, winning 46 seats, emerged as the largest party, thus retaining its dominant role. Second to it, with 19 seats, was its socialist competitor, Mapam. The next years saw a continuous duel between these two major forces in the Labour movement. Their contestation was exacerbated by the fact that with Mapai's 46 and Mapam's 19 seats, a left majority government could have been established, but

Ben-Gurion preferred a broader coalition including centrist and religious parties. The latter would balance Mapam and vice versa, or so his logic went. The two socialist parties failed to reach an agreement to secure Mapam's participation, and it went into the opposition. There was a personal element in the Mapai–Mapam conflict since Mapam included the former Ahdut ha-Avodah, Ha-Shomer ha-Tsair, and the Left Poale Zion – those groups which thwarted the Ben-Gurion–Jabotinsky agreement, opposed Ben-Gurion on the Biltmore Programme and the partition of Palestine, and who themselves were embittered by Ben-Gurion's disbandment of the left-dominated Palmah during in 1948.

More significantly, the division between Mapai and Mapam reflected different approaches to socialism, class and, consequently, foreign and domestic policies. Israel originally followed a neutralist foreign policy, refusing to align with the West (from whom economic aid was needed) or the East (from whom the arms that won the 1948 war were obtained). In addition, the USA and the USSR both had large Jewish communities. Mapai's 1949 programme declared:

> Our socialist conception, our belief in the absolute necessity of international peace, makes it imperative for us to keep out of any big power alignment . . . It would be folly, for many reasons, to join one of the two major blocs competing for world supremacy. It would be sheer lack of responsibility in relation to the needs and hopes of the Jewish people.[45]

Ideologically, however, Mapai leaned to European Social Democracy and was hostile to Soviet communism. By 1951 Ben-Gurion was moving decisively towards the Western camp, reinforced by the Soviet turn to the Arab world. Mapam was pro-Soviet, though this was much more so in Ha-Shomer ha-Tsair (its largest element) than in the Ahdut ha-Avodah wing, whose leadership thought Leninism inapplicable to Israel, and who defended Tito against mainstream Mapam attacks on Yugoslavia which echoed Moscow.[46] All these factors contributed to a 1951 split from Ha-Kibbutz ha-Meuhad (a Mapai faction formed a new kibbutz movement) and then a 1954 split in Mapam itself, leading to the reconstitution of Ahdut ha-Avodah as a party based on Ha-Kibbutz ha-Meuhad.

Ben-Gurion's advocacy of *mamlakhtiyut* rather than class politics inevitably engendered conflicts with the left over domestic and economic policy (especially controls on capital), and the Histadrut's role and direction. With *mamlakhtiyut* came an emphasis on the state and its institutions, especially the army, as the primary embodiments of *halutsiyut* (pioneering), rather than the Labour movement. The term had a military significance in its biblical origin, where the first to volunteer for battle are called *halutsim* (pioneers).[47] While the kibbutz was viewed, at least originally, as *the* great embodiment of *halutsiyut*, the word retained its military connotation in its modern usage, although for Labour's mythical *haluts* (pioneer), who ploughed the ancient homeland with one hand while carrying a rifle in the other, the weapon was a necessary evil. Military metaphors are found frequently employed in socialist literature, including Marx's writings and especially those of Engels and the Bolsheviks. The proletariat was, after all, struggling to conquer power in a class war. The two aspects of the *haluts* – farmer and soldier – represented to Labour Zionists a dual response to the 'abnormality' of the economic structure of the Jews of the diaspora, and to their defencelessness there in the face of pogroms. Members of the Second Aliyah were veterans of Jewish self-defence groups in Russia, and in the Labour Zionist symbolic universe *haganah*, defence, had a very prominent place. The life of Yosef Trumpeldor, a one-armed veteran of the Russo-Japanese War and champion of communal settlement who died defending the upper Galilee colony of Tel Hai against Arab marauders in 1919, took on heroic and mythical proportions in Labour Zionist political culture. (Since Trumpeldor helped Jabotinsky to found the Jewish Legion, the Revisionists also mythologized him, although celebrating his military exploits and ignoring his commitments to the Labour movement.) In addition the myth of Masada, the fortress whose defenders committed mass suicide rather than surrender during the first Jewish revolt against Rome, and that of Bar-Kokhba, leader of the second Jewish revolt against Rome, were prominent in Zionist education. After the Arab rebellion of 1936–9, the need to augment the Yishuv's defence capacity was imperative, and its youth anxiously joined the Haganah's expanding ranks. This, combined with the Second World War and the ensuing struggle for Israeli statehood, further accented the military aspect of *halutsiyut*. Within the Labour movement, its most outstanding embodiment was undoubtedly the Palmah, the elite Haganah troops who spent part of their time working on kibbutzim and part of it in military training, until disbanded by Ben-Gurion, who feared its dominance by the left, in 1948. Ben-Gurion, in contrast to the parties on his left in the Zionist movement, was comfortable with the downgrading of the socialist, and increased emphasis on the military, aspect of *halutsiyut*, processes he sought to advance after statehood was established.

'What is *halutsiyut*?', Ben-Gurion asked on one occasion, providing this definition:

It is recognition of a historic mission and offering oneself in its service without conditions or flinching from any difficulty or danger. Pioneering is the moral ability and the spiritual need to live each day according to the dictates of one's conscience and the demands of the mission. Pioneering is what man demands of himself. It is the personal realization of destiny and values, the values of truth, justice and love of one's fellow. It is the will and ability to perform deeds of creation ex nihilo.[48]

There was nothing intrinsically socialist in such a definition.The kibbutz, more than any other Labour institution, had been identified with *halutsiyut* in the pre-state period, and even though Ben-Gurion briefly, and with intentional symbolism, retired to the Negev desert kibbutz of Sde Boker in 1953, he frequently charged the kibbutz movements with 'elitism'. Where Borokhov, before the First World War, criticized communal settlements from a Marxist perspective, fearing they would turn into islands of utopian socialism in a capitalist sea, Ben-Gurion accused the kibbutz movements of becoming a socialist aristocracy detached from the needs of the state. In the early 1950s he quarrelled with the kibbutz movements over their role in absorbing Jewish immigrants from Arab lands. The premier wanted the collective farms to employ them as hired labour while the kibbutzim, seeing wage labour as a form of exploitation and fearful that this would undermine their socialist character, opposed the idea. Ben-Gurion accused them of failing the national community, and publicly insisted more and more that communal settlements were not the only form of pioneering. He pointed instead to the army as the nation's chief pioneer, apart from the state itself.

Not all of Mapai saw itself in the same terms as did Ben-Gurion. However, most of the Mapai leaders such as Pinhas Lavon, Levi Eshkol, or Golda Meyerson (Meir), who later fought either Ben-Gurion's statism or that of his disciples Moshe Dayan and Shimon Peres, played important roles in carrying it out in the early and mid-1950s. However, one newspaper reported during the 'Flag and Anthem' furore, there was significant unease within Mapai rank and file that Mapai's socialism 'was being forsaken in the din of state-making'.[49] By the 1951 elections, the Mapai platform had substantially modified its accent on class, and was accepting of the private economy, alongside that of the Histadrut and the government. The discontent of the left opposition (Mapam and Ahdut ha-Avodah) with Ben-Gurion was rooted in his emphasis on state over class, and his corresponding tendency to empty the idea of pioneering of socialist content. We can see this vividly exemplified in the language of a minor incident in late 1954 and early 1955. Anticipating forthcoming elections and seeking to take advantage of the recent split between Mapam and Ahdut ha-Avodah, Ben-Gurion proposed the creation of a 'Pioneer Front' headed by Prime Minister Sharett. To this end he sought meetings with Ahdut ha-Avodah, Mapam and Ha-Poel ha-Mizrahi (Religious Workers), as well as with the General Zionists and the Progressives. The goals of the 'Pioneer Front', as Ben-Gurion articulated them, were settlement of wastelands, furthering economic independence and productivity, and national unity.[50] This effort, not surprisingly, ended in public recriminations, with Ben-Gurion attacking

Mapam and Ha-Shomer ha-Tsair for sectarianism, and the left accusing Ben-Gurion of wanting a 'Pioneer Front instead of a Workers' Government'. An editorial in Ahdut ha-Avodah's organ, *La-merhav*, mocked Mapai's ability to sit in a coalition with the anti-socialist General Zionists: 'A pioneer front is one thing, and a coalition with the bourgeois parties quite another'. A true 'Pioneer Front' meant 'the hegemony of the workers in the national leadership'. Ben-Gurion was accused of obfuscating concepts like *halutsiyut*, and *La-merhav* declared that 'A Pioneer Front cannot include the pioneers of Lilienblum Street [the site of the black money market in Tel Aviv]'.[51] (As if to confirm the critique of his foes the prime minister, several years later, referred to the government he then headed as a 'pioneering government' as opposed to a 'labour government'.[52])

An additional aspect of the dispute over 'pioneering' is reflected in Ben-Gurion's occasional subtle tendency to play down the centrality of the Second – his own – Aliyah, long hailed as the foundation of socialist Zionism. The 50th anniversary celebration of the Second Aliyah in Petah Tikvah led to a controversy over its character and heritage. While Ben-Gurion declared Mapai to be its heir and stressed that this historic period was marked, first and foremost, by its dedication to the idea of Jewish labour, he concurrently declared that the Second Aliyah immigrants could not take all the credit for this principle.[53] The same tendency may be discerned in Ben-Gurion's treatment of pioneering in the article he authored on the First Aliyah for the 1962–3 *Israel Government Yearbook* and in his *Israel – A Personal History*, which contains pages on the First Aliyah, and only a few paragraphs on the Second Aliyah.[54] Also, in celebrating Zionist history, Ben-Gurion had a tendency to extol Herzl and Pinsker rather than the Labour movement's founding fathers. At the 23rd Zionist Congress, the first in the sovereign Jewish state, it was not the writings of Hess, Syrkin, Gordon, or Borokhov to which he turned first and foremost, but rather to Pinsker's Autoemancipation ('the outstanding classical pamphlet of all Zionist literature which has never been matched, either before its time or since, for its powerful and concise expressiveness and its acute and profound analysis of any prospect for Jewry in the Dispersion').[55]

In a derisive attack on Mapam's allegiance to 'the forces of tomorrow' (i.e. Moscow), and on the General Zionists – who, he sniggered, believed that 'man serves capital' and that the state should be a tool to this end – the prime minister insisted that Israel was *neither* socialist nor capitalist. After all, over half of its workers were employed by the (Histadrut) co-operative sector of the economy or by the national or municipal economies, leaving only a minority as traditional wage labourers.[56] He thus implicitly assumed that the state stood above a balance of class forces. The question, as he posed it to his foes, was: 'in whom shall we believe? For whom shall we work? And the workers of Israel need to choose: the Kremlin or Jerusalem? And the entire nation living in Zion must choose: The Golden Calf or the

Messiah?'[57] These were favoured metaphors that he employed, along with likening Mapam to the 'Hellenizers' that the ancient Maccabees fought. His point was clear: Mapam's ultimate allegiance was to things foreign. In a typical retort, Mapam's Yaakov Hazan, at his party's second conference in 1951, chastised Ben-Gurion's 'submission to the West', declaring the real choice to be not between the Kremlin and Jerusalem but between Wall Street and Jerusalem. To Ben-Gurion's *mamlakhti* Messianism, he insisted that 'The self-reliant worker is the Messiah'.[58] In other words, the universal class remained the midwife of a redeemed world, not the state.

At least it was the theoretical midwife; in practical politics Mapam tended to find a moustachioed incarnation of the Messiah in the Kremlin, an incarnation, it should be noted, whose etatism was estimably more vigorous and rigid than that of the Mapai leader. Mapam's position was considerably undermined and the party traumatized by the anti-Semitic outbursts of the Kremlin and in eastern Europe in the early 1950s. Ben-Gurion had long departed from his 1920s enthusiasm for the USSR, and for all his centralist proclivities and insistence on united, collective action, by the 1940s had denounced Soviet totalitarianism publicly and asserted the importance of the individual for the Labour Zionist movement.[59] He unceasingly proclaimed that Israeli socialism could learn from Moscow only what *not* to do.[60] Similarly Mapai, in 1949, declared that it 'rejects the notion that the individual human being should be made a subservient helpless tool of an all-powerful state'.[61]

This did not mean Ben-Gurion and Mapai had sympathies for concepts of *laissez-faire*; quite to the contrary. Ben-Gurion was a statist, but of his own, peculiar, democratic – if not particularly tolerant – kind. He told the new state's Constituent Assembly that Israel's government had to be 'positive and dynamic. It must initiate, control, encourage, plan, direct and push forward in every sphere of economic, cultural, and social life'.[62] He was thus able to pursue a fervent politics of *mamlakhtiyut* while at the same time speak of the USSR as 'One of the great revolutions of our days' which had 'degenerated and become distorted as a result of placing all the emphasis on the domination of the Government machine over both the means of production and the producer, and instituting a tyranny of the few over the many'.[63]

It was not only the term 'socialist' that Ben-Gurion had cast off by the 1950s. Annoyed by the failure of diaspora Zionists, particularly in the West, to immigrate to Israel, he declared that he was no longer a Zionist. In an important presentation of his views, an article entitled 'Terms and Values', Ben-Gurion opined that the reality of the world had so changed since the time in which they were written that there was little to be learned any longer from either the socialist or Zionist classics of the nineteenth and early twentieth centuries. Nobody, he expounded, could still seriously accept Marx's claim that all history was that of class struggle, especially given the contemporary sagas of African and Asian struggles for *national* liberation. Just as significantly, most socialist programmes were delineated in a European context while 'We are building a society and an economy from the beginning . . .'[64]

As a political strategist, Ben-Gurion had an outstanding sense of time; with two exceptions – his agreement with Jabotinsky in 1934 and the Lavon affair of the 1960s – the decisions he (sometimes) imposed on his movement derived from a remarkable prescience in political calculus. In ideology, however, his categories of time became quite ductile, a phenomenon frequently manifested in nationalist and messianic thinking. In Jewish – and other – messianisms time is especially important because of the radical contraposition of eras before and after redemption. Ben-Gurion had a fixation about the future and antiquity at the same time as he was rejecting the more immediate Jewish past (the history of the diaspora); concurrently he was focused sharply on action in the present. We have noted his claim that there were four major events in Jewish history. All of them, except Israeli independence in 1948, were in antiquity. Ben-Gurion endlessly stressed the biblical heritage of the Jews and negated the 1,900 years between the fall of the Second Temple and the Zionist effort at resettling the Land of Israel. From his earliest years in Palestine, Ben-Gurion described the Hebrew worker there as a being *entirely* different from his diaspora counterpart, so apart in nature, origin, role and aspirations as to incarnate a completely re-created Jew. However, as Zeev Tzahor aptly points out, Ben-Gurion made such declarations within a decade of his arrival in Palestine, even though he and his comrades were, in fact mostly from eastern Europe and had spent very little time in Palestine playing the role of this new being.[65] (And with little success, we might add.)

Having averred that Israeli society was being made from its beginning and that early Zionism and socialism were relevant only to a vanished reality, Ben-Gurion, in 'Terms and Values', passionately, and unabashedly, advocated that the 'original sources' and the 'Book of Books' be the mediators of contemporary thought and reality. Although the actual world of the Bible – as opposed to that of biblical sites throughout Israel – was considerably more removed from the mid-twentieth century than Marx or Herzl, he believed that

> The stories of our forefathers 4,000 years ago; the acts and life of Abraham; the wanderings of Israel in the desert after the Exodus from Egypt; the wars of Joshua and the judges that followed him; the lives and doings of Saul, David and Solomon; the deeds of Uziyahu, King of Judah, and Yeruboam II, King of Israel, all of these have more actuality [*yoter aktualiyut*], are closer, more edifying and meaningful for the younger generation maturing and living in the Land of Israel than all the speeches and debates of the Basle Congresses.[66]

This went beyond symbolism; Ahad Ha-am's notion that it was what

Moses embodied rather than his historicity that really mattered was vehemently criticized by Ben-Gurion on the (rather naive) grounds that a figment of the imagination could not 'be turned into an educative force of the nation'.[67] Given these sentiments it is hardly surprising that he promoted a national preoccupation with archaeology and Bible studies. (He was especially taken with the story of Joshua's conquest of Caanan.) These, in turn, reinforced Jewish attachment and claims to the land. There were Bible study groups in the prime minister's residence that were given much publicity.[68]

In all of this we see the expression of a *mythomoteur*, at the heart of which there are two structures of thought whose distinctiveness, one from the other, was often blurred: *am mamlakhti* and messianic statism. Taken as a whole, they represent the reification of the Labour Zionist symbolic universe because in Ben-Gurion's terms and actions – as well as those of his protégés – the question of whether the state was the kernel or the shell of the Zionist endeavour became increasingly obscure, and the state and its institutions became increasingly fetishized, even though he often insisted on the opposite point:

> I do not accept the view that the State and Zionist movement can exist separately. A Zionism which is not whole heartedly bound up with the State is no Zionism. At the same time, a Jewish State which fails to realise that it is only the main instrument, that it represents no more than the first step in national redemption ... has no chance of survival. The State and Zionism are one and the same thing. For we must realise that the State to which the Zionist Movement and the Jewish people looked forward does not yet exist.[69]

Or again:

> This State is the only one in the world which is not an end in itself, but serves as a means – a central and principal means – for the fulfilment of Zionism: the Ingathering of the Exiles and their coalescence into a free nation in an independent State.[70]

In these formulae he defines the state as a means of Zionism and the complete 'ingathering' as the end. However, he also identifies Zionism with the state so there seems to be at least a rhetorical confusion as to whether the state is a means or an end. What is evident is his view that the state, rather than the Labour movement, was now 'the embodiment of the *halutsic* movement and its highest, sovereign expression'.[71] This remark can either mean that the state expresses the *halutsiyut* of the Labour movement (the Histadrut, the kibbutz, etc.), or that the state itself was now the embodiment of *halutsiyut*. Clearly, the latter was the case for Ben-Gurion. It was the obvious conclusion from our previous analyses of Ben-Gurion's trajectory away from a class–nation synthesis. The acceptance of hegemonic segmented pluralism assumed the state and the nation to be things-unto-themselves above classes, and we have seen that Ben-Gurion averred that the state of Israel was neither socialist nor capitalist.

Furthermore, he told a 1951 gathering of the World Union of Zionist Socialist Parties that 'In order to unite the majority of the nation, in order to stand firm in the face of any emergency, political, economic, of military (and we must expect all these to transpire), we must establish an alliance between working class and middle class circles, a course of action on which we have recently embarked.'[72] Ben-Gurion often pointed out that the class (the working class, that is) and the nation were not *yet* one and the same, indicating that while theoretically they would eventually be so, present action could not be predicated on such equivalence. Implicitly, present action had to assume a class balance. This was the framework and ideological rationalization by which *am mamlakhti* as opposed to *am oved* could be his fundamental concern. In one of his most important statements of *mamlakhtiyut*, his March 1956 speech on 'The Histadrut in the State', to the Histadrut's eighth Conference, he not only rejected any application of a Marxist definition of the proletariat to the Israeli working class but he declared that 'In the days of the Second and the Third Aliyot the member was tied to the Histadrut by ideals and vision. Now there is primarily a tie of interest. In fact there is no necessary contradiction between a tie of vision [*zikat hazon*] and one of interest, that is, *if the interest is general*' (my emphasis – M.C.).[73] His not-so-hidden assumption was that the working class's interests and its institutions could no longer be seen as general. For many Histadrut members, he went on, their interests in the Labour organization were private, i.e. what it could give them in terms of services. The working class's vision, unity and pioneering spirit had faded, and a particularism had asserted itself instead. Consequently, 'In the state there exists a more efficient and comprehensive tool than the Histadrut. It is up to us to draw the proper conclusions from these two facts'. The conclusions were that the state's institutions, not the working class's, were universal, and that 'The Histadrut is neither the state's rival or competitor, but rather its faithful aid and loyal supporter'.[74]

Mamlakhtiyut inevitably engendered a focus on the tools of statehood and organization. This, in turn, accorded special status to those within them, particularly as the state was identified as the embodiment of pioneering. The Israeli political sociologist Yonathan Shapira has provided an insightful analysis of the development of the Israeli bureaucracy. As early as the 1920s, and in the next decades, a significant migration took place within the Yishuv from the rural labour settlements to the cities. Many of these migrants, though adherents of Labour parties whose ideologies championed physical work on the land, became the civil servants of the Jewish community, staffing the Jewish Agency/Zionist Organization (later the government) apparatus, as well as those of the Histadrut and the party organizations. Of the professional unions, the Clerical Union grew most rapidly, becoming the biggest in the Histadrut after the Histadrut's first decade. In 1929, 9 per cent of Histadrut members were from the Clerical Union, in 1945 they composed 11.5 per cent, and in 1955 they were 15.3 per cent. In the first three years of Israeli statehood, while the Histadrut membership as a whole doubled as a result of the mass immigration, the Clerical Union tripled. Those in this expanding union tended not to be the new immigrants but rather former Labour pioneers who, having begun their lives in Palestine as ideologically committed manual workers, now preferred to find another, higher status in the cities.[75] In the pre-state period clericals had relatively good living standards but low prestige because they lived in a society extolling *halutsiyut* and canonizing physical labour in communal rural settlements. Still, their ranks swelled, and in the early years of independence much more rapidly than other countries on a level of development comparable to Israel.[76] For those who worked in the government, and for those discomforted by the living conditions and radical egalitarianism of the communes, *mamlakhtiyut* was an ideal compensatory ideology – indeed, it almost made them *halutsim*. Consequently, there was a certain converging of interests between Ben-Gurion, *mamlakhtiyut*, and the bureaucracy which all served to reinforce *mamlakhtiyut*.

The military, as we have seen, had a special role as 'pioneer' in Ben-Gurion's programme. As an arm of the state, it was to play a critical role in unifying the nation and integrating immigrants into it. The army, Ben-Gurion told its High Command in 1950, had become 'the creative force of the nation's pioneers, the cultural instrument for the assimilation of the returnees.' He insisted that 'The insipid prattle of the critics of the military that by its very nature it is an instrument which breeds stupidity, careerism, idleness, arrogance, etc. – Let that not disturb us. The nature and character of the army, as of other institutions, depends on the content which we put into them . . .'[77] In some ways Ben-Gurion's assertions were reminiscent of those of Jabotinsky essay 'On Militarism', which complained that military life had unfairly been given a bad name. Practically speaking, Ben-Gurion was accomplishing two things at once: he invested an especially important tool of the sovereign state with potential moral value, thus reinforcing *mamlakhtiyut*, while simultaneously building the image and self-image of that institution on which Israelis were dependent for their very survival.

Along with his statist and messianic vocabulary, science and technology were key words in Ben-Gurion's language. He was obsessed by science. If his messianism was secular, his veneration for science and his faith in its capacities were virtually religious. At times this turned into a naïve positivism, reminiscent of early twentieth-century social democrats: 'There is no limit to the capacity of man to penetrate the secrets of Nature and the universe'.[78] He told a 1960 'Conference on Science in the Advancement of New States' that the two great revolutions of the day were to be found in the national struggles for independence throughout the world and in the new developments in science which would enable the conquest of nature for the sake of human progress.[79]

Ben-Gurion's attitude to science was tied to his admiration for Spinoza. This esteem, like that of Moses Hess, arose because of Spinoza's refusal to oppose matter to spirit. Ben-Gurion saw in Spinoza the first Jewish philosopher who was at home in the world of science.[80] He took great pride in the role Jews played in modern science, something he thought intrinsically linked to the spirit of Judaism – so much so that he offered Albert Einstein the presidency of Israel after Weizmann's death in 1952. Just as Hess criticized Christianity for dualism, that is, for contraposing the City of God to that of man, and failing to grasp Judaism's insistence on making *this* world holy, Ben-Gurion contended that 'The Jewish genius, from the days of the prophets until Einstein, has never recognized the dualism of matter and spirit . . . Jewish intuition, both religious and scientific, has always stressed the unity of the universe and existence'.[81] Like the Bible, modern science did not accept a duality of matter and spirit, according to the premier. This drive towards wholeness manifested by Ben-Gurion's attitude to spirit and matter parallels his statism, and his desire to 'heal' the diaspora Jew by giving this being, defined for centuries through religion, a material basis – a homeland – on which to re-create his spirit. Concurrently, Ben-Gurion insisted that scientific accomplishments were increasingly 'the estate of all peoples' and that this was perhaps 'the most universal spiritual triumph of our era'.[82]

Little effort is required to find Ben-Gurion's discourses on science self-contradictory. In one speech he managed to assert 'the all-embracing unity of existence, the one-ness of mind and matter', 'the supremacy of spirit' over matter, and that science 'by its very essence stands beyond good and evil' but that it 'in isolation . . . cannot suffice; it needs *moral* force to direct it'.[83] If there is a unity of the spiritual and the material, then science is hardly beyond good and evil. Of course Ben-Gurion was a political leader with an enormous intellectual hunger, not a philosopher. Certainly, there is something remarkable about a premier who devoted substantial energy to correspondence with physicists, as Ben-Gurion did. Nonetheless, his statements on science and the supremacy of spirit should be seen politically as well, and in a very practical and material way. Israel, a country small in geography, demography and resources, was trying to absorb masses of immigrants while engaged in an ongoing war with an Arab world many times its size. Quality had to triumph over quantity if it was to survive, and science, in Ben-Gurion's mind, was one essential key to the edge the Jewish state required.

III

The politics of *mamlakhtiyut* had a defined trajectory and pointed a direction for the Labour movement. Inappropriate though it may be to judge Ben-Gurion as a philosopher, he must be considered as a political tutor. This is not only because he sought to mould a culture and a political culture, but because he actively nurtured the 'Tseirim' (younger generation) of Mapai to take up where he, the aging leader, would be leaving off. Importantly, this was a generation integrated into a symbolic universe significantly different from that of the older Mapai 'Veterans'. For Ben-Gurion's protégés, the state and the army were the *halutsic* tools *par excellence*; the state, the nation and science were their universal conceptual categories. They were Mapai members, but the Labour movement *qua* Labour movement was, for them, a secondary concern; it was the state's helper at best. The careers of *mamlakhtiyut*'s children were fashioned primarily in state (especially the civilian defence) and military estab-lishments, rather than through the party or the Histadrut. They saw themselves as 'bitsuistim' ('activists', or 'doers'), and looked askance at the socialist language of their elders. They acted on Ben-Gurion's anti-existential assumptions; Shimon Peres, who with Moshe Dayan came to symbolize the *Tseirim*, echoed the prime minister when he told a meeting of Young Mapai in 1960 that the problem of his generation was 'not to know what we want to be, but what we want to do'.[84] If *mamlakhtiyut* represented the reification of Labour Zionism, messianic *mamlakhtiyut* took reified form in the outlook of a generation of technocrats preoccupied with questions of doing, not being. While some of their number, like Dayan and Peres, were enormously capable individuals, they represented Israeli counterparts to the ideologists of 'the end of ideology' in the West. Thus Peres insisted that Mapai, a party long self-defined as socialist and committed to equality, could not be classified as left, right, or centre.[85] Again, Ben-Gurion's collection of speeches and articles may have been called *Vision and Path*, but his disciples were focused on the path.

The emergence of the *Tseirim* must be traced to the 1944 Mapai split. The exit of Siah B and most of Ha-Kibbutz ha-Meuhad left Mapai with a dearth of younger leaders as well as an organizational lacuna because its Tel Aviv party machine had been dominated by the party's left wing. The apparatus was rebuilt by what became known as Siah Gimmel (Faction C), organized by a fiercely pro-Ben-Gurion group of Mapai faithful led by Shraga and Devora Netser, Golda Meyerson (Meir) and Mordekhai Namir (later Histadrut Secretary-General). This, in turn, became the 'Gush' (Bloc) which, from its Tel Aviv base, served as the bedrock of the Mapai national machinery. It dominated the party's internal nominations and appointments processes which, as Peter Y. Medding has analysed in detail, were traditionally done through committee and co-optation. In the post-1948 era, the Gush's organizational prowess and loyalty enabled Ben-Gurion to preoccupy himself with the security and the mechanisms of the state.[86]

The *Tseirim*, most of whom were in their late twenties and thirties in the early 1950s, originated partly in the discontent of young party members who felt their political advance thwarted by the all-too-well oiled party machine run by an older generation. In 1949 a Party Youth Club was formed. It held regular meetings, ostensibly for social and cultural purposes, but also to discuss the state and the party. The club had a limited impact and was later followed by a 'Hug ha-Tseirim' (Youth Circle). Like its predecessor it lacked ongoing organization, but did include in its ranks young Mapai members of increasing prominence in the government and the Histadrut, though not within the party organization itself. In early 1951 one of them, Avraham Ofer, organized a convention of about 1,000 of the *Tseirim* to advocate 'revitalization' and democratization of Mapai. They called for party primaries and the replacement of the country's electoral system of proportional representation with a constituency system (an idea strongly advocated by Ben-Gurion). One participant was Moshe Dayan, who made critical comments about the *modus operandi* of the party's old guard and chastised them for ignoring the rank and file.[87]

The need to usher a new generation into the party was partly a function of the loss to Ahdut ha-Avodah of some of the best of Mapai's younger leaders including Yigal Allon, Israel Galili, and Itshak Ben-Aharon. Still, a pronounced generation gap between the *Tseirim* and the Veterans who ran daily party affairs and the Histadrut became rapidly evident. Until the late 1950s this was contained: all Mapai camps were devoted to Ben-Gurion, both the man and the charismatic vote-getter, and all were preoccupied with state-building and carrying out *mamlakhtiyut*. In the meantime Dayan was in the army, becoming a national hero as a result of his role as military chief of staff during the 1956 war, and Peres was a very successful and well-regarded Director-General of the defence ministry.

Tseirim cultivated by Ben-Gurion increasingly took prominent political roles by the mid-1950s. It was the entrance of Dayan and Peres into active politics that crystallized Mapai's internal conflicts. The two of them brashly articulated a *mamlakhti* world-view and programme which the Mapai Veterans, even the most Ben-Gurionist among them like Golda Meir, found more and more disconcerting and threatening. Ideological resentment was, however, secondary. As Medding notes, there were very few important Mapai leaders 'not committed to *mamlakhtiyut*, and all that implied'.[88] The conflict between the *Tseirim* and the Veterans took on generational, institutional and personal characteristics. The Mapai Old Guard, led by Finance Minister Levi Eshkol, Foreign Minister Meir and Education Minister Zalman Aran, resented the fact that the *Tseirim* sidestepped the party apparatus in their political advance by means of Ben-Gurion's patronage. The 1958 elections for Mapai's ninth Conference and local party branch councils were marked by vigorous rivalry between the *Tseirim* and the Veterans, and it was primarily due to Ben-Gurion's efforts throughout 1958 that his protégés secured safe places in the Mapai list to the fourth Knesset elections in 1959. *Mamlakhtiyut* stressed the importance of the institutional roles – in the state and the army – of the *Tseirim*, while downgrading those of the Veterans. The Gush was increasingly unsettled, torn between loyalty to Ben-Gurion and hostility to the *Tseirim*.

The *Tseirim* were vocal and determined in their attacks on the party, and especially on the Histadrut. In the name of *mamlakhtiyut*, they asserted the primacy of the state, and the particularism of the Labour movement. Dayan chastised the Histadrut as a vested interest and the *Tseirim* called for the nationalization of important functions and institutions of the Labour movement.[89] Many of these demands historically had been identified with the right and centre of the political spectrum, so it is not surprising that the 'Younger Generation' of the General Zionist party publicly invited Dayan to be its leader.[90] Both Dayan and Peres were, in fact, echoing Ben-Gurion's themes, and 'the Old Man' made his support of them very evident. Dayan attacked the symbolic universe of Labour Zionism, belittling 'pioneering' focused on co-operative settlements, and declaring that pioneering was less a matter of *what* one did than *how* one did it. The state had to be a 'pioneering state'.[91] He defined 'pioneering' as 'a way of life incorporating two elements: activity in the service of the nation and the state, and a difficult life involving self-sacrifice'.[92]

The emphasis in Dayan's formulations was on means, not ends. Not only was he openly critical of the Labour movement but he felt no need to legitimize his statements via references to its symbols and values apart from pioneering – which he, like Ben-Gurion, emptied of socialist content, and expropriated for a statist world-view. In his frequent attacks on the Histadrut he accused its trade union policies of encouraging inefficiency, and called for a stern wage freeze policy. This led Pinhas Lavon, then Histadrut Secretary-General and a bitter personal and political antagonist of Dayan and Peres, to comment that the former chief of staff sounded like a General Zionist. Dayan, in a famous retort to the Histadrut leadership, declared: 'The people who crawled with their rifles among the rocks of Israel for the past twenty years know as much of their country's needs as those who have spent their time sitting on the fifth floor of the Headquarters'.[93] (The reference was to the offices of the Histadrut Secretary-General.) Here Dayan, in a tactic he frequently employed, held up his role as a military hero in a besieged country to privilege his experiences over those of critics, who had been preoccupied with the Labour movement and the state's economy. This was rhetorically effective, if demagogic as military talents hardly prove proficiency in economics.

Interspersed with his attacks on the Labour establishment, Peres, even more than Dayan, articulated a technocratic *mamlakhti* outlook. Implicit in his politics was an ideology of the end of ideology. The questions socialists debated were of minor interest to him because in his eyes the essential task was not projecting long-term or ultimate goals but managing the new means of politics the Jewish people had in its hands – the state. He went so far as to declare that Israel was a classless society, thus implying that issues like class and community – traditionally pressing for socialists – were no longer the relevant ones.[94] 'The world', he declaimed, 'has evolved beyond the social patterns that fashioned the generation of early Zionists, and Israel entering the second decade of her political existence must look beyond the romantic ideas of her founding fathers'. More significantly, Peres declared:

The last generation was a generation of aspirations; the new generation must take up planning. The previous generation had dreams and visions, the present one will have to realize concrete tasks. Though there is no contradiction between vision and concrete tasks, there is a difference in emphasis . . . Action is required, the writers and ideologists will come later.[95]

In other words, questions of ends were not the order of the day, the practical needs of the state was. The Mapai Veterans resented Peres's insinuations, especially since they saw the Zionist Labour movement as the most practical of socialist endeavours, one whose concrete accomplishments built the foundations on which Peres stood when he called for 'pragmatism'. While the Veterans saw their vision and concrete tasks as inseparable aspects of the same venture, Peres, as he put it, had a different emphasis. The shell, not the kernel, was his central preoccupation.

This is particularly well illustrated by an article Peres wrote in 1960 advocating electoral reform. In it he argued that liberty and democracy had to be regarded as ends, and not means that could be sacrificed for equality. Equality, however, was defined as a means, one 'to strengthen the citizen's independence of those in power and to fortify the democratic system so as to free it of discrimination'.[96] Rather than a democratic socialist dialectic between democracy and equality, by which *both* are means *and* ends, Peres raised the essential mechanism of a free society, democratic state structures, to the level of end, while making egalitarianism a means to the end. At times he used logic reminiscent of that Jabotinsky used against Mapai in the 1930s. 'In a desert', Peres explained, 'the guiding principle is not that of justly dividing the "pie", but of growing the grain needed to bake bread'.[97] Whereas the Zionist socialists once argued that, for them, growing and dividing were two aspects of the same project – because the type of society and state were as essential as building them – the Revisionist chief had argued that questions of equality and just division were distracting, secondary matters, and that a monistic focus was required, a focus solely on growing the grain, or, non-metaphorically, building the state. Once the shell was safely secured, the kernel could then – and only then – seriously be contemplated.

Peres asserted that the major issues previously debated by the Labour movement – statehood, movement unity, education, ties to Moscow and the West – were essentially resolved. Israel was becoming a less homogenous, more complex country, and therefore many of the older institutions – and by implication what they symbolized – were outdated. At times, Peres seemed to be referring not only to the Histadrut but to political parties. He expressed great contempt for party politics and divisions: 'For our youth . . . the contrast between the real unity in the ranks of the army and the divisions and dissension of civilian life is heightened by the obsolescence of the forms which those divisions continue to assume'.[98] Although he insisted the following year (in the above-mentioned article) that democracy was an end in itself, here, in contrast to most modern theories which assume party conflict to be essential to the health of a democratic state, unity of the state as expressed through the army, not the quarrelling of diverse political groups, is what Peres found most healthy and natural.

Peres's numerous articles in this period, which appeared both in the Hebrew press and in the English language *Jerusalem Post*, tried to reconcile *mamlakhtiyut* with customary Labour Zionist categories much more than did Dayan's public pronouncements. However, the many contradictions within Peres's brief tracts further illustrate the tension between the technocratic and reified thinking engendered by *mamlakhtiyut* and the traditional assumptions of Zionist socialism. For example, Peres, partly echoing Eduard Bernstein, once characterized Mapai as a 'movement' with 'a direction but no final goal. The direction is the sum total of its human make-up, dedicated to serving the worker in the State until the State becomes entirely a working nation'.[99] Peres first says that Mapai has no goal, but then defines goal as a 'state' which is entirely a 'working nation'. Furthermore, after saying this he adds that 'It is no secret that in a democratic regime the middle class plays a growing part. It is generally these unaffiliated classes who form the deciding factor . . .' Consequently, a democratic workers' party must 'find a compromise which will not be destructive of its essential purpose'.[100] Clearly, if the essential purpose of the workers' party is a 'working nation', the issue cannot be the compromise that Peres suggests, if, as he himself argues, the middle class is and will be continuously growing. (Also, it is hardly self-evident or historically accurate to say that in most democratic societies the 'middle classes' are 'unaffiliated classes', especially when they are in conflict with the needs of working classes.) Of course, none of this can be reconciled with Peres's assertions that Israel was a classless society.

The trajectory of this politics is manifested as well by the internal tensions within Rafi (acronym for the 'Israel Workers' List'), the slate Ben-Gurion formed to contest the 1965 elections, having resigned from the premiership two years earlier. Both Peres, and a more hesitant Dayan, followed him in this futile attempt to challenge the Old Man's successors in Mapai. (Ben-Gurion's chief motive, the Lavon affair, will be discussed in the next chapter.) There was an ongoing debate in Rafi to determine its character. Was it to be a Histadrut-oriented list loyal to Ben-Gurion or a centrist political force whose ideological posture would place it between Mapai and the right-wing parties? Peres, Rafi's Secretary-General, was the chief advocate of the latter course. He sought to bring non-Labour circles into Rafi and to fashion its programme so that it would reflect the favoured issues of the *Tseirim*, i.e. nation and state over socialism and class, electoral reform, and the importance of science and technology. Peres 'kept pressing to the right and talked about our need for "liberation from Marxist nostalgia" ', as Yosef Almogi, a Rafi foe of Peres, put it.[101]

Peres saw Rafi as a type of 'cultural revolution' which, in contrast to Mapai, was concerned with youth, industry, 'the scientificization of the state' and internal party democracy.[102] His views, almost a quarter of a century later, substantially reflected the same foci and concerns. Articles Peres wrote on 'The New Socialism' in 1982, when he was leader of the Labour party opposition to a right-wing government, pointed to Japan as the best contemporary example of the power of science and technology, declaring that although it was not socialist, Japan's system had many aspects of socialism as he conceived it. The most pressing issues, as Peres presented them, were science, technology and efficiency rather than community – in other words, questions of means rather than ends.[103]

In a 1983 interview he made the same point in virtually the same language he had used in the late 1950s: the essential issue for Israeli socialism was how to 'bake the cake', not how to divide it.[104] *Mamlakhtiyut*, in Peres's view, was something as inevitable as it was desirable: indeed, it 'saved' the Labour movement.[105] Before Israeli independence, he argued, there was no contradiction between party and state. Mapai was then a Labour party and the Histadrut was 'the draft of a state'. The Histadrut could no longer be so after statehood was established, but had to be subordinate to the state; likewise, in a democracy, a state and a party could not be regarded as equivalent. 'The ideology that leads to the creation of a state', he insisted, 'cannot remain after the state is created'.[106]

In all of this Peres, like Dayan, was a true child of Ben-Gurion's *mamlakhtiyut*, especially in the questions he did not pose. For instance, if socialist Zionist constructivism proposed to build a certain type of society, *why* was its ideology valid before, but not after, statehood, especially if state and society were *still* in genesis, as Ben-Gurion, Peres and Dayan often reiterated (especially in response to criticisms from the left)? How far the politics of *mamlakhtiyut*, with its accent on the anachronistic character of socialist ideas, was from Labour Zionism's earlier animating spirit can be seen by contrasting Ben-Gurion's rejection of the socialist label, and Peres's comment on the irrelevance of pre-state ideology, with Mapai's 1949 programme, which states the conviction that 'Socialism must not be left to a distant future . . . it must be integrated with the foundations of the nascent Jewish society in this country . . .'[107]

In a sense, the attacks on 'ideology' and Marxism on behalf of *mamlakhtiyut* brought Labour Zionism back to one of its starting points. It was, of course, within a long Labour Zionist tradition to insist on the specificity of the problems of *Erets Israel*; during the Second Aliyah, such a claim was essential to the assertion of 'constructivism' against Borokhovism, which was criticized for imposing European categories on Palestinian realities. Borokhov, it may be recalled, argued that the Jews had to first be 'normalized' politically and economically before the class struggle could lead to socialism. Syrkin and Katznelson, on the other hand, envisioned realizing socialism and Zionism at one and the same time. In that sense, the new Zionist society in Palestine would not be 'normal'. When Ben-Gurion or Peres in the 1950s and later asserted that the national priority was baking the cake (i.e. building the state) rather than dividing it, this implied that questions of socialism and equality had to be – and ought to be – postponed until a 'normal' state had been created for the Jews. This was Borokhov's position – the class struggle would come after normalization – rather than Syrkin's, although Ben-Gurion and Peres were anything but Borokhovists. What is essential is this: they rejected the radical potential of the working class *at the same time* as they were effectively discarding the key concept of revolutionary constructivism, that is, the simultaneous building of a socialist society and a Jewish state. Many twentieth-century socialists have questioned the capacity of the workers to fulfil the socialist vision and to be a universal class, especially given the great differences between the evolution of capitalism as imagined by Marx and the actual development of late capitalism. Whether the unique circumstances of Labour Zionism and 'revolutionary constructivism' could have realized a classless society in its own way can now only be a matter for historical conjecture. What Ben-Gurion, Peres and those of like mind ultimately opted for, however, was a type of statist normalization rather than the creation of a revolutionary society. It might be said that in consolidating statehood, the Zionist revolutionary impulse gave way to an impulse with which it had always coexisted dialectically, but in great discomfort – the Zionist impulse to Jewish normalization. This inevitably meant the splitting of *hazon* from *derekh*, and *mamlakhtiyut* substituted for their previous unity.

Since the pre-1948 Histadrut, 'the draft of a state', sought to create a co-operative economy and had legitimate democratic elections, a socialist strategy, it would seem, ought to have aimed at extending this model over the entire society. The politics of *mamlakhtiyut*, on the other hand, sought to confine it as one pillar supporting the state. The distinction is crucial, for the former projects socialist community in the form of *am oved* (a working nation), a concept which was once the essence of the pre-state Labour movement ideology, an ideology which assumed a dialectic between the kernel and the shell of the Jewish national enterprise, while the latter rests on the vision of *am mamlakhti* (a *mamlakhti* nation) in which the kernel and shell are on the one hand separate and reified, while on the other they are blurred. One can see this illustrated in comments Ben-Gurion made to a March 1949 meeting he held in his home with various Israeli intellectuals. 'The formation of our national character', he stated, 'its spiritual and moral character, cannot be carried out by the government, although the government is not completely alien to spiritual matters'. He added that the government's main concern was necessarily economic and political, i.e. defence, immigration, housing, labour regulations, taxes. While political and economic tasks determined Israel's immediate fate, the historic task of the Jewish state was not to be discerned in 'its economy or its politics, but rather in its spirit'. The true measure of the state would be 'its moral character and its human values'.[108] In short, the state's moral character, its spirit, is here made the essential question by Ben-Gurion, while at the same time he implies that all the fundamental issues of politics and economics – that which actually shapes human relations – are apart from such spiritual matters.

For Ben-Gurion and his protégés, the state was exalted over the Labour movement that created it; concurrently the Labour movement's claim to be creating a model society was expropriated by them for the state and statism. Hence the profession by Ben-Gurion and his supporters that their goal was a state of Israel that would be a 'light unto the nations'. Those social experiments which aspired to be the foundation of a different type of modern society – the Histadrut, the kibbutz – were given secondary status behind the state and the army. This was the essence of *mamlakhtiyut* in policy, and is the subject of the next chapter.

12
Mamlakhtiyut II:
From *Am Oved* to *Am Mamlakhti*

. . . the key function of a Prime Minister is the fixing of priorities.

David Ben-Gurion[1]

All reification is a forgetting.

Max Horkheimer and Theodor Adorno[2]

I

War, massive immigration, especially of Middle Eastern Jews, and the dominance of Ben-Gurion and Mapai were the key factors shaping the formative years of the Jewish state. Hopes for peace after the 1948–9 conflict proved to be chimerical, and the rise of Nasser's aggressive Pan-Arabism, continual border tensions and the 1956 Sinai Campaign combined to make basic security the urgent item on the Israeli agenda. This was reflected in the centrality of the Israel Defence Forces (IDF) in Israeli society, and Ben-Gurion's dual role as prime minister and defence minister. With the burdens imposed by defence and the absorption of immigrants, the new country's economy faced enormous difficulties; Israel's first years were marked by a severe government austerity programme.

The *raison d'être* of Zionism was provision of a home for a persecuted people. Memories of the British blockade of Palestine during and after the Hitler era were still vivid when, in July 1950, the legislature of the sovereign Jewish state passed the 'Law of Return', giving to all Jews the right to settle in Israel. Within the first half year of statehood, 100,000 immigrants came into the country. In its first four years Israel's population doubled. Between 1948 and 1964 the Jewish population rose 211 per cent from 649,777 to 2,115,6000. (Approximately 68 per cent was due to the immigratory processes, and 32 per cent to natural increase.[3]) In practical terms the government was entirely unprepared to cope with the situation. In addition, the immigrants changed the demographic character of the population substantially. Whereas almost 90 per cent of Jewish immigrants during the Mandate period were from Europe, in Israel's first decade-and-a-half a majority (54.6 per cent) were from Asia, Africa and the Middle East.[4] The Yishuv's population, on the eve of statehood, was 78 per cent from eastern European or Western background, while just over a half was a decade later. This transformation was a function of modern Jewish history. The vast majority of Jewry lived in eastern and western Europe when the Zionism of Pinsker, Herzl and Syrkin was formulated. The people they expected to compose the primary human reservoir for a Jewish state were slaughtered by Hitler, and their remnants who came to Palestine/Israel did so in the years immediately after the war and the declaration of Israeli statehood. The Israeli government, anxious to increase the country's Jewish population, was at once encouraged and overwhelmed by the massive influx of Middle Eastern Jews. Coming from non-Western, traditionalist and religious backgrounds, these new Israelis were remote from the environment that nurtured Israel's leaders, dominant party and ideology. Absorbing them was one of the fundamental challenges before Mapai, both for the state's future and its own. By the 1980s Israel's Jewish populations were 55 per cent of Middle Eastern derivation.

In coping with this situation, Ben-Gurion and Mapai faced no serious threats from the far right. The story was more complex with the General Zionist party, chief heir to anti-Labour General Zionism. Although they did poorly in the first Knesset elections (1949), winning only seven seats (5 per cent of the vote), the General Zionists ran strongly – and Mapai poorly – in the 1950 municipal elections. This was a function of the 'Tsena', the period of austerity in which Mapai tried to cope equitably with the country's economic difficulties. As an avowedly bourgeois party and champions of capitalism, the General Zionists had an alternative economic programme to Mapai's stringent controls and rationing. When early national elections were held in 1951 after a crisis in Ben-Gurion's coalition over educational policy, the General Zionists gained dramatically, winning 20 seats and becoming the second largest party. From 1952 to 1955 the General Zionists were in the governing coalition with Mapai. They then began losing ground to Herut, the extreme rightist party that was the heir to the Revisionists and the Irgun. However, Herut, headed by Begin, had its own problems deriving from its delegitimated status in Zionist politics.

In the 1949 elections Herut, championing integral nationalism, achieved very modest success – 14 seats (11.5 per cent). In the 1951 elections Revisionist fortunes declined further. After an exhausting war, a party obsessed with conquering biblical territories was unappealing to the vast majority of Israelis, especially since Herut lacked any serious economic programme in a time of economic problems. Herut's share of the vote fell precipitously to a meagre 6.7 per cent of the total vote (eight seats). A number of leading party figures, including Begin himself, took leaves of absence from politics. Begin returned, however, hoping to use the question of Israeli negotiations for German reparations to revitalize his party. He castigated the government for its willingness to accept 'blood money'. Ben-Gurion, insisting that the funds were desperately needed for economic survival, retorted that through reparations at least some of the Jewish property stolen by the Nazis would be retrieved, thus depriving at least some of the surviving plunderers of their spoils.

Begin's effort backfired and Herut's public image of irresponsibility was reinforced by his incendiary behaviour, both outside and inside the Knesset. (It led to his temporary suspension from the legislature.) The army was forced to employ tear gas to break up a violent demonstration he addressed preceding the parliamentary debate. Dozens were injured in the streets and Begin in his speech warned 'that maniac who is now Prime Minister' that if reparations were accepted, 'anything is allowed'. Handed a piece of paper, he told his agitated audience, 'I have not come here to influence you but the note which has just been handed to me states that the police have grenades which contain tear gas made in Germany – the same gas which was used to kill your fathers and mothers'.[5] Later, during the Knesset debate – with tear gas entering the hall through windows broken in the riot – Ben-Gurion remained taciturn while Begin, in a display of public hysteria, denounced him as a 'hooligan', adding that 'some things are worse than death. We are willing to leave our families and die . . . people went to the barricades for lesser things . . . I know we will be dragged to concentration camps . . . We will die together'.[6]

Begin violated all norms of loyal parliamentary opposition, and his foes took full advantage of it. The evening after the riot the prime minister made an urgent radio broadcast to the nation warning that 'Yesterday the hand of evil was raised against the sovereignty of the Knesset and the first steps in the destruction of democracy in Israel were taken'. He proceeded to quote threats by Begin from the latter's party newspaper. Apparently referring back to the 1948 'Altalena affair' (in which the Israeli army sank an Irgun ship that violated government commands) Begin had declared: 'When you fired on us with your canon I gave the order "No". Today I give the order "Yes". This will be a war of life or death'. Ben-Gurion made it clear that the state would take whatever actions necessary to protect itself and its democracy.[7] The implication was obvious: the creator(s) of the state would secure it against the blatantly menacing behaviour of the extreme right. By his bombast, Begin handily enabled Ben-Gurion and Mapai to reinforce their identification with the state while Herut displayed the undemocratic, undisciplined posture that had long been associated with the Revisionists. Although Herut gained some ground in the 1955 elections, it would have to pursue a long detour to legitimate itself as a plausible party of government acceptable to the public. In the meantime, it became the party of *ressentiment*, ostracized and mocked by the dominant party whose leader, the premier, made a habit of telling the public that any coalition partner was acceptable to him except Begin and the communists.

The isolation of the Revisionists was reinforced by *mamlakhtiyut*. We have seen that inherent in Revisionist 'monism', in the political culture and symbolic universe that the far right projected for a Jewish state, was a reified Zionism which fetishized the state, its tools and especially the military. *Mamlakhtiyut* did something similar, except that it was articulated by the man who actually read the proclamation of statehood, along with his party, in a significantly less crude and more moderate form. This made it all the more difficult for Begin and the right to compete with Ben-Gurion and Labour, *at least in the short run*. However, with continuous war, and with waves of immigrants alien to the world of European Social Democracy being absorbed into a political culture stressing the primacy of the state and the secondary place of the Labour movement, *mamlakhtiyut*, in the long run, played into the hands of the right. To see how this happened, we must examine some of the key policy components of *mamlakhtiyut*.

II

In defence policy, *mamlakhtiyut* had two principle manifestations that can be distinguished analytically, but which were, in significant regards, inseparable. The first was tied directly to security needs and was an necessity: the unification of the Yishuv's three undergrounds into a single army with a single command. The second was the political, cultural and educational role Ben-Gurion assigned to the army in Israeli society.

Simple survival dictated the creation of a *tsava mamlakhti* (a *mamlakhti* army) in 1948 since Israeli independence in that year brought with it invasions by several Arab armies. Each of the pre-state Zionist forces had distinct political orientations. The most important was the mainstream Haganah, which was obedient to the duly constituted Jewish communal authorities, opposed terrorism by Jews as well as by Arabs and educated its troops to 'self-restraint' and 'the purity of arms'. By 1947 it had approximately 45,000 troops, 3,100 of whom belonged to its elite force, the Palmah. The Revisionist Irgun, under Begin's command, had some 2,000–2,500 troops and was infamous for some of its actions. The smaller Stern Group, with only a few hundred members, was even more extreme. The origins and nature of these organizations were an essential aspect of the events of 1948.

The Haganah was established by Ahdut Ha-Avodah in 1920. It was intended to supersede *Ha-Shomer* (the 'Guard' organization created by Second Aliyah pioneers) and was envisioned as a Jewish-controlled self-defence underground, to be under the dominance of the party and its goals. In this it contrasted with Jabotinsky's call for the re-establishment of a Jewish Legion on the the First World War model, that is, under British auspices. After the formation of the Histadrut, the Haganah was transferred to its charge. The Haganah National Command that was established in the 1930s included representatives from both the Histadrut and the bourgeois camps. A process of nationalization of a Labour movement institution was taking place. This was part of Ben-Gurion's 'class to nation' strategy, and also served to increase the isolation of the Revisionists – who split from the Haganah to found the Irgun – because it made the Haganah a joint project of the left and the moderate centre-right. By the end of the decade the Haganah came under the authority of the Jewish Agency, now dominated by Mapai. The years 1936–9 were especially important in this entire process because the Arab rebellion during this time led to intense efforts to professionalize and expand the Haganah, as well as to centralize its command structure (through the formation a General Staff in 1939). However, as Yoram Peri has shown, while the Haganah was formally under the Jewish national institutions as a whole, it was under the effective control of Mapai.[8] After statehood 'systematic party activity' continued in the military via a secret Serviceman's Department in the Mapai Central Office. (The latter was abolished after its discovery led to a major controversy during the 1969 elections.)[9]

With independence, the Haganah became the backbone of the IDF. Since no state can permit a multiplicity of armed forces within its boundaries, least of all when enemies are invading it, the unification of the Haganah, the Irgun and the Stern Group into one state-controlled force was an urgent priority. Accordingly, Israel's Provisional Government issued an ordinance on 26 May, 1948 establishing the IDF and prohibiting all other armed units within its jurisdiction. The Irgun represented the major problem in this process of consolidation, first because it was a Revisionist armed force, and also because relations between it and the Haganah during the last years of the Mandate varied from tense to hostile. None the less, agreements were reached whereby both the Irgun and the Sternists would disband and join the IDF as separate units under their own commanders (except their Jerusalem units which retained independence at first since the city was not yet legally part of Israel). Mistrust was, however, very deep and a confrontation took place in the third week of June when the Irgun sought to land arms and troops in a ship called the 'Altalena' (one of Jabotinsky's pen-names). After manoeuvres and unsuccessful negotiations, Ben-Gurion ordered the seizure of the ship. Shooting broke out and the Altalena was sunk by a Palmah unit. There was an immediate danger of civil war which was averted when Begin ordered his troops to yield. This effectively ended the history of the Irgun. Ben-Gurion strongly defended the action – 'To burn this ship was the most loyal service we could render the Yishuv' – on the grounds that a state, not to mention one at war, could have only one military; he also expressed fears of an attempted Irgun *coup d'état*.[10] The Irgun's actions, he told the Provisional State Council, represented an attempt 'to wound the unity and the sovereignty of the State'. No state

could 'countenance private citizens or organizations . . . importing on . . .
personal account even the tiniest armory, much less the wholesale
consignment of rifles and machine-guns that the Irgun tried to land'.[11] The
Irgun units in the IDF were disbanded, their troops redistributed and, in
September, after the Stern Group assassinated UN mediator Count Folke
Bernadotte, the Irgun's Jerusalem units were disbanded and the remains of
the Stern Group repressed by Ben-Gurion's government. The right had been
militarily disarmed.

The situation with the left was more complex. Until the end of the Second
World War Ben-Gurion's actual policy-making role in the Haganah was
limited. His expertise was considered to be political, and while he was kept
informed as chairman of the Zionist Executive, he was resentful of his lack
of full access.[12] At the 1946 Zionist Congress long-standing differences
between Ben-Gurion and Weizmann came to a head with the ousting of
Weizmann from the ZO presidency. Ben-Gurion's personal authority was
thereby strengthened, and at this time he took on a newly created
'portfolio', that of 'Defence', in the Zionist Executive. He was convinced
that war with the Arab world would come and that he, as political leader,
had to take charge of security. He then moved to consolidate his authority
in this sphere. Most of the Haganah senior officers were members of the
Ahdut ha-Avodah (Mapam after January 1948). Ben-Gurion saw in Ahdut
ha-Avodah one of his most serious political rivals, and it did not suit him to
have the military so identified with the left. This was complicated by the
prestige of the Palmah, whose ranks had their own leftist *élan* and were the
best trained in the Haganah. Founded in 1941, the Palmah was dominated
by, and largely based in, the communes of Ha-Kibbutz ha-Meuhad. Its
commander from 1945 to 1948 was Yigal Allon, and like him, most of its
senior officers were from Ahdut ha-Avodah and Ha-Kibbutz ha-Meuhad, as
were some 40 per cent of their troops.

Besides political complexion, what sharply differentiated the Irgun and
Stern Group from the Palmah was the fact that it was integrated into the
Haganah and unquestionably subordinate to its command (and later that of
the IDF). It did not constitute a separate army, but rather an elite and
thoroughly loyal element, albeit with a leftist orientation, within the
military. None the less, throughout 1948 Ben-Gurion sought to undermine
the influence of the left in the Haganah/IDF Command, an effort which
culminated in the dissolution of the Palmah. If Ben-Gurion had fears of
armed resistance from the left, this was proved entirely misplaced because
the Palmah, though incensed by Ben-Gurion's moves, dutifully followed
orders and dissolved itself. In this process and afterwards, however, there
were continual recriminations and strife due to Ben-Gurion's plans to
reorganize the military's structure. Furthermore, with little subtlety and
often with total disregard for merit, he replaced Mapam officers in key
positions with Mapai loyalists and non-partisan professional officers who

served in the British army during the Second World War. This continued after statehood, and Ben-Gurion, in the end, successfully secured his own hegemony in military matters.[13] He did this under the banner of *mamlakhtiyut*, which in this case was presented as the need to have a professional military force subordinate to the state and not to political groups. In fact it meant checking the influence of the left and the right. Thus the principle of a neutral military was subverted, in effect, not in the name of the party but in the name of *mamlakhtiyut* – which assumed that Ben-Gurion and Mapai were identified with the state.

Perhaps nothing concerned Ben-Gurion the prime minister more than the IDF and its place in Israeli society. On the one hand this was a matter of the state's serious security needs. On the other it was a question of *mamlakhtiyut* and the country's political culture. A country led by social democrats that finds itself in continuous war is necessarily going to be preoccupied with the role of the military in its daily life. As we have seen, Ben-Gurion portrayed the state and especially the IDF as embodiments of *halutsiyut*. The IDF, Mapai's leaders hoped, would be a different type of military, a model, moral army and, significantly, a key mediator between the individual and the state and society: 'Our army must serve as a school of civic good-comradship and fraternity, a bridge between different Jewries and different generations. It is, and must remain, a unique army, because it will be, as it was, the instrument of a unique enterprise of pioneering and statebuilding. . .'[14] Ben-Gurion accented the educational role of the army and saw in it the chief means by which new immigrants would be absorbed into Israel. After all, as a consequence of the Arab–Israeli conflict all youth were drafted for national service, and after their release males were liable for annual reserve duty for an additional 30 years. The army touched the life of all Israelis. It was thus natural that Ben-Gurion's chief protégés, Dayan and Peres, built their careers through the defence establishment, the former as a soldier, the latter as an administrator. However, as Ben-Gurion was extolling the role of the IDF as national integrator, educator and social mediator, there came a concurrent downgrading of the role of the Labour movement in these tasks in the name of *mamlakhtiyut*. In other words, *mamlakhtiyut* posited that the moulder of Israeli culture and political culture, the key socializer and social mediator, would be state and not class institutions. The state was a thing unto itself. There would be the state and there would be the citizen. We see this – and its consequences – clearly in the debates concerning Israeli education.

III

The creation, re-creation, and at times invention, of a nation inevitably requires efforts at cultural integration and the consolidation of peoplehood, particularly through the media of language and land. In Zionism these factors were especially salient because the Jews, whose culture traditionally placed great emphasis on learning, were engaged in a return to their ancestral homeland concurrent with the vernacular revival of the Hebrew language. Since Zionism represented a recharting of Jewish political culture, and since intense competition among ideologies and parties characterized most of its history, education was inevitably a matter of considerable importance both before and after statehood. As one scholar recently noted, 'The broad issues of how much schooling will be given to a population and who in that population will receive what kinds of education are issues generally settled by political bodies outside the school system'.[15] Such factors were at play in the politics of Zionist and Israeli education, shaped as well by the segmented pluralist nature of the Yishuv and the place of coalitions in running its Executive bodies.

Before the advent of the British Mandate, Palestine had no Jewish education system *per se*. The traditionalist schools and yeshivas of the Old Yishuv were narrowly focused on religion and tied to particular segments of the community, usually according to origin; in general they shunned the use of Hebrew, the 'holy tongue', as a language of instruction. Various philanthropic organizations from abroad, such as the Paris-based Alliance Israélite Universelle and Baron Maurice de Hirsch's Jewish Colonization Association, also sponsored schools. Eliezer Ben-Yehudah established, and the Hibat Zion fostered, some Hebrew schools in the late nineteenth century. The questions of education and culture were bitterly argued at the early Zionist Congresses as exemplified by the clashes between Herzl, Ahad Ha-am's supporters in the Democratic Faction and the Mizrahi. Ahad Ha-am, as we saw, called for pluralism in Zionist education at the second conference of Russian Zionists in Minsk in 1902. The Second Aliyah and the ZO's turn to synthetic Zionism towards the end of the century's first decade inevitably led to more of a focus on practical activities in Palestine, including education.

The development of Hebrew language schools was stimulated by a fierce 'language conflict' in 1913, provoked by the effort of the non-Zionist *Hilfsverein der deutschen Juden* (German Jewish Aid Society) to found a German-language technical high school in Haifa.[16] This infuriated the Hebrew Teachers' Union which, from its founding in 1903, had viewed its role as national and ideological more than pedagogical. Just as Hebrew gained ascendancy over Yiddish in the Poale Zion, so it gained ascendancy in the Yishuv as a whole over other languages, except in the non-Zionist ultra-orthodox communities. The 'language conflict' led to direct ZO funding of Hebrew schools. In the meantime, Mizrahi began to develop its own nationalist-religious educational system before the First World War, and by 1920 it had 25 schools with 2,000 pupils. It also agitated against Zionist funding of schools which lacked what it deemed proper respect for religious tradition and fought to keep the ZO out of the area of educational policy. The 10th Zionist Congress voted to encourage Hebrew schools reflecting the multiplicity of currents within Zionism, and the 11th Zionist Congress voted to found a Hebrew University in Jerusalem.[17] In the two years preceding the war, a dozen ZO schools were established with some 1,064 students in them; by 1920 there were 272 educational institutions with 12,830 students attending.[18]

In the period between the end of the First World War and the birth of Israeli statehood the Yishuv population increased tenfold, and the educational system expanded with it. Article 15 of the Mandate, building on the millet tradition, affirmed the right of each community in Palestine 'to maintain its own schools for the education of its members in its own language, while conforming to such educational requirements of a general nature as the Administration shall impose'.[19] At a 1920 London conference the ZO, which by then subsidized almost 90 per cent of the Yishuv's educational budget, planned the organization of the Hebrew school system, allowing for the autonomy of the Mizrahi schools. The system thus had two 'trends', a 'General' (or 'secular') one and a religious (Mizrahi) one. To this a third, Labour, trend was added in 1923, under the charge of the Histadrut. In the 1930s the non-Zionist orthodox party Agudah Israel established a fourth trend which functioned apart from the Yishuv system.

In 1929 the 16th Zionist Congress resolved to centralize further the administration of Jewish education in Palestine, and in 1933 it was decided to transfer authority from the ZO to the Yishuv (specifically to the Vaad Leumi).[20] The Revisionists, true to Jabotinsky's strategic view, opposed this move because they wanted to extend British obligations to the Yishuv. As they originally advocated a Jewish Legion rather than an underground Haganah, they wanted the Mandatory authorities to take on responsibility in education. They argued, with considerable justification, that while Palestinian Jewry carried the main burden of taxation in the country, the subsidization of its schools by the government was a pittance.[21] Labour, more cognizant and mistrustful of potential variations in British policy, championed the transfer of the system to the Vaad Leumi, viewing this as one more essential area in which the Yishuv could gain autonomy. Katznelson insisted before the Asefat ha-Nivharim that the community serviced by the schools ought to control them.[22]

Already in the 1920s complaints were heard about the partisan nature of the different trends. The General Zionists and the Revisionists regularly advocated abolishing the trends and establishing a unified, 'objective', educational system. The religious Zionists, for whom only religious education was acceptable, opposed this. As for the left, one observer noted not long after Israeli independence that 'the question of indoctrination is not evaded by the spokesmen of the Labour schools. They contend that objective teaching is a contradiction *in adjecto*'.[23] Shortly after Mapai was formed in 1930, it sought to impress its influence on the Teachers' Union which had links with the General Zionists and a difficult relationship with the Histadrut. Ben-Gurion declared that 'we now want to build a party that will carry all political, educational, and cultural activity for the entire public'.[24] This clearly implied that whatever role the teachers played, it would be under Mapai dominance.

The transfer of educational authority to the Vaad Leumi included maintenance of the trends (which remained until 1953). In the year before the transfer, the General trend was the largest, both in the number of students attending (14,444) and in number of schools (138). Mizrahi had 6,663 pupils and 54 schools and the Labour trend had 2,804 pupils and 80 schools.[25] Administration had three components: a Board of Directors, to handle budget and administration, an Education Committee for pedagogic questions and to ensure a minimum curriculum for all three trends, and an Education Department to carry out policy. The trends were equally represented on the different boards and each, within this framework, had enormous autonomy including its own supervisory board to determine the structure and course of study along with the hiring of principals, teachers and inspectors.[26]

The General trend, run by General Zionists, sought, in the words of a memorandum submitted by the Vaad Leumi to a British Inquiry Commission, 'to give its pupils a National Zionist education combined with the progressive ideals of humanity'.[27] The schools were co-educational and not tied to any specific social theory, although along with national education the special role of the *haluts* in the Zionist effort was emphasized. While the General trend was secular, Bible was taught and religion was treated positively (the emphasis tended to vary from school to school). Its curriculum devoted 9–11 hours a week to Jewish subjects, and stressed Hebrew language and literature, Zionism, and knowledge of Palestine.[28]

In contrast to the General trend, both the religious and the Labour trends tended to supplement the basic curriculum considerably, and both had longer school hours. 'The difference of method is particularly apparent as between the Orthodox and general schools', stated the 1927 Report of the Zionist Executive. 'In the former the children are trained to observe religious traditions by teachers who are themselves Orthodox. From the 5th class onwards, 8 to 10 hours weekly are devoted to religious subjects, especially the Talmud . . .'[29] Those who taught both religious and secular subjects were orthodox in the religious schools; boys and girls were separated. The curriculum, over half of which was dedicated to specifically Jewish and Hebraic subjects, sought to inculcate religious beliefs and practice into the students. The schools stressed Bible and prayer, which were presented in a fundamentalist manner, making 'as few concessions as possible to the influence of contemporary life' and totally ignoring modern educational theories or techniques.[30] The Agudah system was even more remote from modern eduction, and lacked the national element in the Mizrahi schools.

Since the Labour movement was generally preoccupied with social experimentation, it is hardly surprising that its trend, under the charge of the Histadrut Education Centre, was the most innovative. M. A. Beigel, who in 1923 founded 'Beit ha-Hinukh', the first Labour school (and model for future ones), stated: 'It is our aim to educate children for the creation of a unified Hebraic labor society which will realize in Palestine the ideals of justice, equality, brotherly love, and peace'.[31] The schools sought to utilize progressive pedagogical theories. The motto of Beigel's Beit ha-Hinukh was 'Labour and Learn'. It stressed the dignity and value of physical labour, individual development and the idea of 'children's community'. 'Pioneering' was emphasized, along with social responsibility and 'mutual aid'.[32] A non-coercive environment was sought in which the teacher was to be more of a counsellor than a traditional authority figure. Student communal democracy and government were stressed as well. The activities of Labour Zionist youth movements were integrated into the school system. The entire approach was premised on the view that traditional education was part of a socio-economic system rejected by Zionist socialism.[33]

In its early years the Labour system had serious economic problems, and its teachers voluntarily accepted salaries equal to those of other Histadrut employees – which meant less than most other teachers – so that funds could be utilized to open new classes and hire additional teachers.[34] In the curriculum, social studies, history and natural sciences were more prominent than in the other trends, and current events were discussed within the framework of Labour ideology. In significant contrast to the other trends, Labour incorporated vocational training, as well as shop, handicraft and gardening classes. The Bible was taught from a critical, historical, or literary perspective, and utilized to enhance the attachment of the students to the Land of Israel. A specialized kibbutz education system developed within the trend in order to emphasize the collectivist values and life-style of the agricultural communes. In them, as one observer remarked, the children were taught to 'habituate themselves to ways of living in a community where the very words "mine" and "thine" became foreign'.[35]

In the school year 1947–8 about half the students in the Yishuv attended General schools, and about a quarter were each, respectively, in Mizrahi and Labour schools. In the period of mass immigration between 1948 and 1952, the student population tripled and the educational system found itself in the most taxing of circumstances, taking in almost a thousand new students a week.[36] By the 1952–3 school year, after which the Knesset voted to abolish the trends, the percentages had changed dramatically with the Labour trend becoming the largest with 43.4 per cent of the student population, compared with 27.1 in the General, 19.1 in the Mizrahi and 2.1 in the Agudah trends.[37] The politics of education in this period was critical for the future political culture of the Jewish state.

With statehood, a ministerial committee on education was established under David Remez, the transport minister in the provisional government and former Histadrut Secretary-General. In September 1949 the first compulsory education law in the Middle East was enacted by the Knesset. By the 1951–2 school year all children aged 5–13 would be provided free education in one of the trends, which were all maintained. The three major trends were guaranteed their autonomy, but placed under a Ministry of Education. In addition, 'non-official but recognized schools' were permitted, which included the Agudah's and various Christian and Moslem schools, among others. The personnel of the Ministry of Education tended to be civil servants carried over from the pre-state period.[38] Those who criticized the government for retaining the trends were warned by the newly appointed minister of education, Mapai's Zalman Shazar, that the combined parliamentary strength of the Labour parties sufficed to establish a unified state system composed solely of Histadrut schools.[39] None the less, it was well known that important Mapai figures, including Ben-Gurion himself, opposed continuation of the trends and favoured a unified system.

Within half a year an acrimonious public debate began, leading, among other things, to Shazar's resignation and his replacement by Remez. The issue was education of incoming immigrants, especially Yemenite Jews. As the education reporter of one newspaper noted, Israel's leaders were 'jockeying for position in order to get a hold on the electorate of the day-after-tomorrow'.[40] The various trends competed for students in the immigrant transit camps, resulting in friction between Mapai and the religious parties who were partners in the governing coalition. In the meantime, the right and centrist opposition sought to exploit the situation to press the case for ending the trends. The debate was triggered by February 1950 disturbances in two Yemenite transit camps. The religious parties accused the government, the minister of education and the camp superintendents of coercing religious children into secular schools. They insisted that since the Yemenites were a traditionalist community, only the religious educational trend should educate them.

Nahum Levin, the Education Ministry official responsible for the camps (and a Mapai member), retorted that Yemenite Jews were as 'foreign' to the eastern European orthodoxy of the religious parties as to the other trends. Levin, however, was opposed to having any trends in the camps and favoured, along with Ben-Gurion and the right-wing and centrist parties, a unified *mamlakhti* educational system in the camps and the entire country. Only 'the magic of the state' and the 'language of the state' could represent a unifying force for the whole nation, and prevent a future *Kulturkampf*. The 'bridge of the state is the only bridge . . . which can turn the Yemenites into citizens of the state'.[41] In this, he expressed the essence of the *mamlakhti* world-view. At the same time orthodox elements were accused by Police

Minister Bekhor Shitrit and others of instigating riots in the camps.[42] Some fanatics handed out leaflets telling immigrants, 'The evil instructors and clerks are forcing you to turn your children, of holy seed, over to the Devil, who will train them to abandon the ways of the righteous and become part of the unclean life in Israel'.[43]

The immediate crisis subsided when a compromise amendment to the education law was passed ending the trend system in the camps, and ensuring religious education for the Yemenites and both secular and religious options in the other camps. Parents would decide which education their children received. Since religious education had been available to all who wanted it in the first place, evidently the real issue for the religious parties was the success of the Labour schools among new immigrants, and the fear of the orthodox that they would lose their monopoly over religious education because the Labour trend was establishing its own religious subdivision. By February 1951 the governing coalition, which was increasingly unstable for a variety of reasons, fell following the parliamentary defeat of a government programme on immigrant education. Early elections were called and education played a prominent role in the campaign.

The parties most supportive of the trend system were weakened in the polling, and some of those advocating unification gained. Mapam dropped from 14.7 per cent of the vote and 19 seats to 12.5 per cent of the vote and 15 seats. The party was also weakened by internal strife, leading eventually to a halving of its parliamentary strength subsequent to three splits in the following four years. The united Religious Front which ran in the 1949 elections broke up as the Zionist elements (Mizrahi and Ha-Poel ha-Mizrahi) quarrelled with the non-Zionist Agudah parties. In contrast, the General Zionist party made an impressive gain of 11 per cent, giving it 16.2 per cent in comparison with its 5.2 per cent in 1949. Mapai gained 1.6 per cent, and maintained its status as the dominant party.

Faced with exorbitant demands by the General Zionists, Ben-Gurion formed a narrow coalition with the religious parties. This was possible because of an agreement that certain controversial issues, in particular unifying the educational system, would be avoided temporarily. By late 1952, however, the coalition was in crisis; Agudah withdrew in a dispute over plans to draft orthodox women for non-military national service and Ha-Poel ha-Mizrahi withdrew because of yet another argument over education. The General Zionists along with the liberal–centrist Progressive Party, both advocates of *mamlakhti* education, joined the coalition at this point. The coalition agreement specifically called for abolishing the trends, and the General Zionists were given the chairmanship of the Knesset Education and Culture Committee. Ben-Gurion's hand was now considerably strengthened on the educational question, aided as well by the presence of Ben-Zion Dinur (Dinaburg), a historian and particularly forceful advocate of *mamlakhti* education, who became education minister in 1951 following the death of Remez.

Unifying education now became a chief priority. It was vigorously opposed by the left, in particular by Mapam, but also by some within Mapai too. Giving up the Labour education system meant relinquishing a key means of socializing future generations, and precisely at a time of large-scale immigration. Foes of unified education admitted that the rapid expansion of the Labour trend after 1949 brought with it serious problems, including a shortage of teachers trained and committed to Labour values. However, there was a general shortage of teachers in the country, and from the perspective of the left, dealing with this was a matter of reorienting priorities. Furthermore, to secure support of the religious parties Ben-Gurion was willing to retain two trends within the proposed state system, a General secular trend and a religious one which would have substantial autonomy. Thus it appeared that only the socialist education system would vanish and that state, rather than class, institutions would be the mediators between future generations of Israeli children and the world.

Mapai's 1951 election platform had specifically called for a unified education system, despite objections from the Education Department of the Histadrut. In January 1952 the Cabinet appointed a committee to develop a plan for state education in the elementary schools, and soon thereafter the Education Ministry set up a committee with representatives from the trends to outline a basic curriculum for state education. On 12 August, 1953 the trend system was abolished with the passage in the Knesset of the 'State Education Law'. This was with the endorsement of both Mapai and the Histadrut Executive (and after the intervening Flag and Anthem debate).

Under the Education Ministry, the Histadrut and General Zionist schools were merged into a General state system, and Mizrahi's schools became a Religious state system. (The kibbutz schools were allowed a special autonomy within the General trend). The law allowed for non-official but recognized educational institutions, and this was the status awarded to the Agudah's schools. The second paragraph of the law, defining the goals of the two state trends, gave them a national and quasi-Labour orientation:

> The object of State education is to base elementary education in the State on the values of Jewish culture and the achievements of science, on love of the homeland and loyalty to the State and the Jewish people, on practice in agricultural work and handicraft, on *halutsic* (pioneer) training, and on striving for a society built on freedom, equality, tolerance, mutual assistance, and love of mankind.[44]

It was determined that up to 25 per cent of the curriculum of a given school could be supplemented according to the ideological bent of the parents of the children attending. However, paragraph 19 of the law specifically stated that 'A teacher or any other employee at an educational institution, shall not conduct propaganda for a party or other political organisations among the pupils of an educational institution'.[45] In the school year beginning September 1954 a unified curriculum was in place, and in the following school year the General state schools encompassed 69.4 per cent of Israeli children, the Religious state schools 23.9 per cent, and non-official, but recognized, schools 6.7 per cent.[46]

Ben-Gurion presented his case for state education in a variety of ways, partly depending on his audience. Three months before the bill's passage, he told the Mapai Central Committee that the issue at stake was 'When do we appear as a nation and when do we appear as a class?'[47] He criticized the left's opposition to abolishing the Histadrut trend, but he did so in the language of Labour Zionism's fight with Revisionism. Ben-Gurion rejected the notion that the category of nation had to exclude that of class and vice versa. He emphasized that the originality of the Labour movement was embodied in its special mission of transforming 'the class into a nation', and remaking the nation in the working class's image. He reasserted that the interests of the workers were those of the nation – even though his original question 'When do we appear as a nation and when do we appear as a class?', assumed their non-equivalence.[48]

He told his comrades that the purpose of state education was to transform class education into national education; in other words, state education would embody the principles of Labour education and pioneering. In this sense, for Ben-Gurion the nationalization of education paralleled the nationalization of the Haganah, which became the backbone of the IDF.[49] However, the premier also informed his party that the nation was not yet prepared for the nationalization of May Day. The red flag, he declared, may symbolize the future of the nation and that of free humanity, but there would be no red flag over an army base for the same reason there had to be a state education system: the army and education were part of the *national* framework, and not that of the working class alone.[50]

Ben-Gurion's presentation rested on the assertion of the theoretical identity of working-class and national interests on the one hand, and their temporal non-identity on the other. *Am oved*, he stipulated, would only be a reality when there was a possibility of a classless world and the complete ingathering of the Jewish exiles. One could almost characterize this as an argument against socialism in one country, but for the fact that Ben-Gurion's preoccupation was no longer socialism. Consequently, for all his messianism, the key to his actions and goals are to be discerned in his comment, aimed at advocates of class education, that, 'Either there is a state or there is not a state. And there is a state only when there is a single state for all the Jewish people, and not only part of the Jewish people'.[51] Only one conclusion can be drawn from this remark: Israel was not a class state and the state was, and ought to be, a neutral structure standing above class. In other words, *am mamlakhti*, not *am oved*, was the real political agenda, and this assumed that Labour Israel was one of several pillars within the state of Israel, even if theoretically, in an unspecified future, they ought to be one and the same. In the meantime, Labour's success, according to Ben-Gurion, was determined by its ability to nationalize itself, that is, to transfer Labour's institutions to the more general framework of the state so that 'we are emissaries of the nation and not only class emissaries'.[52]

In early July 1953 Ben-Gurion had a meeting with a conference of Mapai-affiliated educators in Tel Aviv and declared to them that state education would express Labour's values. Unified education, he insisted, was third in importance for the nation, ranking only behind the establishment of the state itself and the IDF. The state created a new reality and it was outdated romanticism to seek to retain the Labour trend. The premier provoked resentment by stating that the Labour trend was a 'fiction', and that the trends in fact meant party rule over the souls of children. He denounced 'partisan education'.[53]

Such a denunciation – which he had made, forcefully and repeatedly, for years – completely contradicted his claim that the state system would embody Labour values. And it assumed that statist education would not be a type of rule over the souls of children. As Ben-Aharon, Ben-Gurion's long-time critic, later observed, the Mapai leader was too much of a realist to believe that several sentences extolling pioneering and justice in the text of the law would sustain socialist education. Ben-Gurion 'dismantled the workers' educational system because he no longer saw any reason to perpetuate it'.[54] If the state was the pioneer, and if it was above class, then clearly the primary goal of education was education to the state and to the nation, not to class, which, in any event, he repeatedly declaimed as 'partisan'. And again, all of this was tied to Ben-Gurion's doubts about the capacity of the Jews for self-government. He explained:

> The law calls for fostering loyalty to the state. In every other state, this is something that is self-evident and expected; but not with us. For 2,000 years we did not cultivate a *mamlakhti* feeling [*regesh mamlakhti*], and the mere proclamation of the state does not grant a sense of statehood [*thushah mamlakhtit*] to a people. This is a quality that demands nurturing in Israel more than in any other new country because ours is not merely the state of its inhabitants, but of thousands and tens of thousands who are still scattered across the globe, and the supreme mission of the state is the ingathering of the exiles.[55]

The goals of *mamlakhti* education are revealed especially in the arguments Dinur, Ben-Gurion's education minister and a key architect of the law, made on its behalf. State education, he propounded to the Knesset, meant not only ending 'partisan' schooling but giving the state 'total, indivisible and incontestable' responsibility in this field. Education was 'a deliberate, planned and organized activity to methodically influence the development of the generation as it grows up'.[56] Israel, Dinur stressed, faced a problem of political demography. A significant proportion of its pre-1948 population had come to the country with great motivation and spirit. The post-state immigrants, however, were of a different character, and the state alone could adequately absorb them. The individual, he stated, had to be one with the state: 'The state won't be able to preserve its independence for long . . . if the state doesn't live in the hearts of each and every one of its citizens, if each and every one doesn't view the state as a fundamental part of his personal existence'.[57] In contrast to the unifying power of the state, the trend system was 'an ideological civil war organized by the state'. Thus it was 'incumbent upon the state to educate its citizenry to fully and completely identify with the state, each individual with the state, its future and its survival'. Indeed, 'each and every single cell of the state' must educate, and among the goals of such education is 'the feeling that the state is the home of the individual'.[58] Dinur had always believed that education had to foster an intense national identification with the land itself. 'The primary objective of education in Israel', he declared in a speech the previous year, 'must be to train the younger generation to penetrate into the secrets of the Land'.[59]

Consequently, for Dinur the school was 'the first, fundamental tool of the state'.[60] He praised what the trends had accomplished, but argued that each of them represented a level in the history of Jewish culture and that now, with the existence of the state, their existence contradicted a higher unity. In other words, nation-state represented a level superior to class (or religion), and it was also the bearer of universality. Dinur's argument implied what we might call a state formalism that was characteristic of classical liberal thought. The state was not a class state – working or otherwise – for him, and just as the army was one mediator between the individual, regarded not as a member of a class, but strictly and abstractly as an individual member of a nation, so too ought education to be. Here we see the logical conclusion of *mamlakhtiyut* as well as characteristic reified thinking. Ironically, however, the departure is not just from socialist and class politics, but also from the premises of the segmented pluralism that helped to engender *mamlakhtiyut* in the first place, for ultimately the state is now viewed as a thing unto itself, and the pillars – Labour, religious, or otherwise – no longer have the same essential places in the society. There is simply the abstract national citizen and the state. We can see ramifications in two areas of educational policy: the question of equality between Western and Oriental Jewish communities in Israeli education in the 1950s and 1960s, and the 'Jewish Consciousness' programme of the Ministry of Education which began in the late 1950s.

Even before the massive post-state immigration of Oriental Jews, research, especially in Jerusalem, had shown significant problems of educational disadvantage among Oriental Jews in Palestine when compared with Western Jews there.[61] Studies by the Szold Institute presented by Moshe Smilansky to Dinur in 1953 demonstrated further that Oriental students were significantly behind their Western counterparts. Dinur's educational programme, however, was premised on 'formal equality', as Elad Peled has shown.[62] Just as each citizen had equality before the law, so all students were equal before the 1949 and 1953 State Education Laws. Consequently there would be 'equality of educational inputs' (i.e. educational means and methods) for all students, regardless of ethnic or social background, on the assumption that this would 'automatically produce equal results and academic progress'.[63]

Dinur assumed that since during the Yishuv period equality of educational inputs worked for European Jewish immigrants, this would be the case for the newcomers from the Middle East and North Africa. 'There must obviously be a single curriculum for all students', said the education minister. 'We do not wish to establish two kinds of schools in Israel . . . All Jewish children through out the country share this curriculum. And this must be our ambition: the achievement of intellectual and cultural equality for all Jewish children'.[64] Hence Dinur's vision of *mamlakhti* education regarded students as undifferentiated citizens, each formally equal before the educational laws, each to receive undifferentiated treatment whatever their actual differences. This combination of *mamlakhtiyut* with a liberal concept of abstract individual equality contrasts directly with what, at least theoretically, one would expect from a socialist approach to educational disadvantage. The latter would assume the need for compensatory programmes, at least on the basis of class – though not necessarily ethnic – differentiations.[65]

Dinur stepped down in 1955 and was replaced by Zalman Aran, a leading Mapai figure who was a particularly dedicated education minister. By the late 1950s new studies revealed the failure of Dinur's approach. Of great impact was a 1957 report by Arye Simon demonstrating that the Oriental immigrant children in primary schools were substantially below minimum standards. Smilansky, now an aide to Aran, reported on the increasing gap between Ashkenazi and Sefardi students in secondary schools, and urged programmes of preferential treatment so that 'real' instead of 'formal' equality would be established.[66] Aran championed this principle, and educational disadvantage among the children of Oriental immigrants became a chief preoccupation of his tenure. He pressed for the development of compensatory programmes and, later, for changes in Israeli textbooks and curricula which tended to focus on the Western and Ashkenazi Jewish heritage. Unlike many of his Mapai colleagues, Aran understood from the late 1940s that the traumas undergone by Oriental Jews in their absorption process into the country were producing simmering resentments towards the Labour movement whose policies tended to be paternalistic, and assumed that as they became loyal to the state the new Israelis would become loyal to Mapai.

In July 1959 there were riots in Wadi Salib, an immigrant slum district in

Haifa, following the shooting of an inebriated Moroccan Jew while being arrested. Demonstrations by a 'Union of North African Immigrants' complained that North Africans were discriminated against in Israeli society, and politically exploited by the major parties. The issue of Oriental Jewry was now forcefully placed before the public eye, but the government's attempts to address it were at best modest. In education, Aran lacked the political strength in his party and in the government to initiate the reforms he thought necessary.[67] He resigned in 1960, partly in frustration over the fact that apart from public utterances and a substantial budget allocation, education was rarely an issue of priority in the top levels of government.[68]

Abba Eban, who succeeded Aran, followed his predecessor in championing compensatory programmes. Upon entering the ministry Eban found the Simon Report on his desk and viewed it as 'horrifying'. He brought it to a Cabinet meeting where,

> my colleagues, and especially Ben-Gurion, were fascinated and surprised. It was unusual to hear a report on education at the Cabinet table, which usually occupied itself most of the time with international and security problems. Ministers were shocked by evidence that a hard core of misery, resentment, bitterness, and ultimate social revolt was deeply in our society and yet had been so remote from the horizon of ministers and high officials . . . I told the Cabinet that there was no room for 'equal' educational treatment of all segments of the population, since the point of departure was not equal.[69]

An inter-ministerial committee was formed and Eban promoted the creation of several programmes and special schools to start dealing with the problem. Aran again became education minister in 1962, but now, as a result of changes in internal Mapai politics, he was in a much stronger position in the party (a position which was reinforced when Levi Eshkol became prime minister in 1963). Aran now pressed hard for major structural reforms in elementary and secondary education in order to encourage ethnic integration and a narrowing of the gap between Oriental and Western Jews. These were eventually approved, though Aran, as one observer put it, virtually had to 'bludgeon' it past an unsympathetic Mapai and a hostile Teachers' Union. The implementation of the reforms was, however, a slow process, especially after Aran left office in 1970.[70]

Another important aspect of Aran's tenure was the 'Jewish Consciousness' programme formulated in the mid-1950s during his first period in office. In response to what was viewed as a decline in attachment of young Israelis to Jewish tradition and diaspora Jewry, the programme was designed to intensify the study of Jewish culture, history and especially tradition in the state secular schools. The goal, theoretically, was not to encourage religious practice but rather to deepen the commitment of the students to Judaism. This paralleled Ben-Gurion's non-religious emphasis on the centrality of the Bible in Israel's culture.[71]

Mapai and most of the centre and right parties supported this initiative. The left opposed it as a coercive encroachment of religion into the secular schools. The religious parties opposed the programme, but because it did not seek to inculcate religious practice based on a fundamentalist approach to Scripture and tradition. There were also 'Canaanite' criticisms from intellectuals who envisioned statehood as a radical break from the Jewish past, and thought that for Israel to be a 'normal' nation-state it had to disengage from world Jewry which ought either to move to Israel or be split off from it.[72]

Aran's strenuous efforts on behalf of compensatory education were the antithesis of the formalism of Dinur's *mamlakhti* approach; similarly, one of the premises behind the 'Jewish Consciousness' programme – the need to reinforce the ties of Israelis to world Jewry – was also a non-*mamlakhti* concept. In both cases the state of Israel – the means – was not reified and regarded as the end unto itself, and broader questions of cultural, social and inter-human relations became the key to policy. None the less, and despite Aran's personal socialist commitments, the long-term impact of relinquishing Labour's educational system, and thus forfeiting a crucial means of reproducing its own symbolic universe, was enormous. By 1948 the Labour movement had succeeded impressively in imprinting Labour Zionism on the emerging society, and in education it was considerably more advanced than the centrist or right-wing parties.[73] In the period immediately after statehood, the Labour trend had, in the words of one authority on Israeli politics, 'achieved outstanding success in the settlements of the new immigrants'.[74] However, with the abolition of the trends, the Ministry of Education issued new texts to enhance the unification of the curriculum, diluted the political orientations of school staffs by transferring principals and teachers, reorganized the teachers' colleges and sent children of new immigrants to newly established schools.[75]

Consequently, proclaiming Labour values in the text of the 1953 Education Law was one thing, actually transforming the state system into a *de facto* Labour one was another – even if Ben-Gurion had truly intended this. The Israeli educational system became a *mamlakhti* one, with a secular sector whose focus was on the state and the nation, and a religious one. In this context, it is noteworthy that 'Jewish consciousness', not 'socialist' or 'Labour consciousness', became the preoccupation. Two Israeli scholars, viewing Labour Zionism as a 'civil religion', have summarized the result succinctly:

> The unified educational system caused a radical transformation in the status of Zionist-Socialist education that had long range consequences for the Labour Zionist community of believers. Unlike religious

education, preserved by the religious camp's maintanence of its own school system and much of its autonomy as a division in the Ministry of Education, Zionist-Socialist education simply disappeared. The new national educational system became a vehicle for the transmission of statist symbols and values.[76]

In effect, General or Religious – but not socialist – Zionist education remained the options of Israeli students. A decade after the State Education Law went into effect, Ahdut ha-Avodah's Yigal Allon complained that 'Not only did the "general trend" *not* acquire a pioneering content, but the new joint "general" and "labor" trend, which forms the basis of the State system, has even *less* pioneering content than the "general trend" itself had before the establishment of the State'.[77]

We have seen that Ben-Gurion often declared that apart from the founding of the state and the IDF, education was the key priority in Israel. Along with the General Zionists, he was the strongest proponent of state education. Mapai always expected that it would control the Ministry of Education, and Ben-Gurion once remarked that he would rather turn the Finance Ministry over to the National Religious party (founded in 1956 through the merger of Ha-Poel ha-Mizrahi and Mizrahi) than the Education Ministry.[78] However, as Shimshoni notes, 'From the point of view of political control, the General Zionists . . . lost out; but from that of ideology, the system became "general". The expected transfer of Labor values and symbols to the state system did not come to pass . . .'[79] And in 1977 when Labour lost the elections for the first time and the National Religious party joined a right-wing governing coalition, it obtained the much-coveted Education Ministry, thus giving it control of both the secular and religious systems.

Mamlakhtiyut succeeded in defence: one army was created and the right lost its independent military force while the left lost its military status. And just as the nationalization of the Haganah meant that the IDF would be a state and not a Labour army, the nationalization of the Labour education system and its merger with the General trend produced a statist, not a socialist or Labour education system. *Mamlakhtiyut* did not entirely succeed in education because Ben-Gurion accepted the existence of two educational trends in order to guarantee the coalition participation of the Religious Zionists. However, it was the Histadrut system that vanished, and *mamlakhti* education in the secular system focused on the state, not on class. Ben-Gurion had, after all, made it clear that in his view the state and the nation were the generalized categories of Israeli life, not class; these became the categories of Israeli political culture and socialization.

Since the future of a political movement is dependent on its ability to reproduce itself, Mapai, through its education policies, took important steps in undermining its own ability to do so. At the same time, it continued to function as if it would always be the dominant party in the country. The combination of these two factors was significantly determinant of the fate of the Labour movement.

IV

State primacy was not controversial in all areas. An Israeli state legal structure supplanted the pre-1948 system of Mandatory courts (and informal courts within the Jewish community, which was often loathe to utilize the Mandatory authorities). However, following the precedent of the Mandate, a millet-like system was retained for personal affairs. This allowed for religious control in areas such as marriage and divorce through Jewish, Moslem and Christian courts which were created for these purposes and which existed side by side with the general state judiciary.[80] Civil service regulations were enacted to standardize bureaucratic recruitment, although the parties in the governing coalitions used their ministries to place their own supporters as much as possible. The Jewish Agency/ZO, having lost their functions as quasi-governing institutions with the establishment of a formal state apparatus, took on the more restricted roles of encouraging and absorbing immigration into Israel, as well as facilitating ties between Israel and the diaspora.

However, *mamlakhtiyut* necessarily raised questions of the status of both Mapai and especially the Histadrut. With the nationalization of education, the Histadrut no longer had the crucial role of teacher, and therefore lost an important means by which to assert the Histadrut vision of society. It still had enormous power by virtue of its vast economic enterprises, trade unions and social welfare network. At the same time, it had become less and less of a dynamic, innovative social body, and more and more of an ossified Labour bureaucracy. The Histadrut did use its strength to minimize social stratification and, officially, the Mapai-dominated government took a similar posture. In 1955 Minister of Labour Golda Meyerson (Meir) declared in traditional socialist fashion that 'the large majority of Israel's citizens are working people and we will therefore never permit the creation of a thin strata who lives in comfort, while at the same time the majority have not a minimum'.[81] However, government policy, aimed at rapid economic growth, increasingly allowed for broader stratification.

Unfortunately for Mapai, significant parts of the working population would eventually regard the Labour bureaucracy as the society's privileged strata. Furthermore, the Histadrut acceded while Mapai leaders who spoke socialist rhetoric allowed a restricted capitalism to develop, propelled by a large influx of desperately needed foreign investment capital, particularly in the form of loans from foreign governments and banks, private funds through the sale of Israel Bonds, Jewish contributions from abroad and

German reparations. Also, while Mapai-dominated governments pursued economic programmes that especially favoured the Histadrut and national quarters of the economy, there was no attempt at nationalizations of the private sector and wage policy shifted from what was called 'family gradation', that is, based on principles of need, to one based on professionalism and less socialist or egalitarian criteria.[82] A joke later had it that Israel became the first example of the peaceful transition from socialism to capitalism. Faced with the tasks of housing and finding employment for masses of immigrants, the premier insisted that attracting foreign capital was essential for the development of the economy. He insisted simultaneously on the principle of full employment, but told the Knesset that 'the right to work entails an obligation and we recognize equally the right to a fair profit for the promoter and capitalist, who help develop the country and absorb immigration'.[83] The man who once declared that his communism derived from his Zionism, now seemed to be saying that his Zionism dictated (at least a limited) acceptance of capitalist principles.

The pressures of Israel's early years, along with *mamlakhtiyut*, engendered a fundamental reorientation of the Histadrut's role. By definition, statehood and *mamlakhtiyut* meant that its former self-conception as the Jewish-socialist state-in-genesis was a thing of the past. We have already mentioned Ben-Gurion's articulation of this at the 1956 Histadrut conference. There he argued that Israel was neither socialist nor capitalist, and that the workers were in the Histadrut for practical reasons, not a vision of the future. The working class and its institutions, according to the Histadrut's first Secretary-General, were now particularlist in orientation, and the state was the comprehensive tool, the universal structure. Therefore, 'The Histadrut is neither the state's rival nor competitor, but its faithful aid and loyal supporter'. And while *denying* that this meant an etatism or total nationalization, he claimed that 'Every service benefiting the entire public should be under state control'.[84]

Until the late 1950s and early 1960s, when the clash between the Mapai veterans and the *Tseirim* crystallized along with the Lavon affair, the Mapai party leadership, the government and the Histadrut carried out *mamlakhtiyut* under Ben-Gurion's direction; criticisms, by and large, came from the left-wing opposition parties. Mekorot, the Histadrut Water Company, founded in 1936, was nationalized without much criticism. When the government, with the support of the Histadrut majority, decided to nationalize the labour exchanges, opposition came mostly from the left. In this case, however, the symbolic irony was great. As we have seen, the Zionist right bitterly opposed Histadrut control of the labour exchanges in the 1930s and the Labour movement, under Ben-Gurion's leadership, defended them as an intrinsic aspect of the organization and protection of workers, especially of new immigrant workers. In the late 1930s, after the conflicts culminating in the failed Ben-Gurion–Jabotinsky agreements, a working arrangement was established between the Histadrut, the Jewish Agency, and most of the Yishuv – excluding the Revisionists – for fair management of the labour exchanges and the use of a party key to distribute both staff positions in them and work allocation through them (the Labour movement received 60 per cent). Here, as in so many other areas, Mapai's strategy was one of coalition that assured its own dominance. Since Zionism was an immigration movement, political power was intimately tied to those who provided work and other necessities for new arrivals. All the parties knew this. Thus in the 1950s as in the 1930s, the exchanges were of a practical political value. In fact, all immigrants were given temporary membership in the Histadrut, which also enabled them to use its extensive health care system, the *Kupat Holim* (Sick Fund).

The circumstances were propitious in the 1950s for nationalizing the exchanges. The coalition agreement following the 1955 elections guaranteed that work would be distributed in a non-prejudicial manner, and the Progressive party made nationalizing the exchanges a requirement for its participation in the government. (Even Mapam advocated nationalizing them when it briefly controlled the Labour Ministry during the provisional government in 1948–9. The ministry was thereafter in Mapai hands.) Following a brief retirement in late 1953 during which he was replaced as premier by Sharett, Ben-Gurion returned first as defence minister and then as prime minister in 1955. Giora Yosephtal, one of the *Tseirim*, became Mapai Secretary-General in 1956, and championed *mamlakhtiyut* as well. Finally the Secretary-General of the Histadrut itself, Pinhas Lavon, presented the nationalization proposal that was endorsed by the Mapai Central Committee, again with little opposition. The plan called for a State Labour Exchange which would have charge of all issues pertaining to the workforce and employment under the governance of a council composed of an equal number of representatives of the employers (including Histadrut firms) and the employees. It would be chaired by a Labour Ministry representative.[85] Arguing against objections by Ahdut ha-Avodah in the Histadrut Council, Lavon pointed out that in the State Exchange, which was to replace 'partisan' ones, the administration would be appointed by the labour minister, obviously implying that since this minister would be a Mapai member, the Exchange would still in effect be controlled by Labour.[86] In 1958 the Knesset passed the State Employment Service Law and the following year the Histadrut no longer had labour exchanges.

If nationalization of the labour exchanges represented a successful and relatively smooth transition for the policies of *mamlakhtiyut*, its price was the failure of the attempt to transfer another major Histadrut function – health care – to the state. The failure had broad and narrow political contexts tied to one of the great ironies of Israeli public policy. In most countries it is the left wing of the political spectrum that champions the establishment of state health services, while in Israel its major proponents have been the centre-right parties, the General Zionists and Herut. In addition, nationalized health was championed in the late 1950s by the *Tseirim*, especially Dayan and Peres.

The Israeli health system is based on voluntary insurance through (mostly) non-profit health services. The most important of these is the Histadrut's Kupat Holim which covers 75 per cent of the population and is partly subsidized by the state.[87] Membership in the Histadrut includes enrolment in Kupat Holim and access to its array of clinics, hospitals, laboratories, rest homes and other facilities which extend beyond the major population centres to the more remote parts of the country. Since 1937 membership in Kupat Holim has been restricted to Histadrut constituents, and a large proportion of Histadrut dues (about 40 per cent in the 1950s) go to funding it. Clearly, Kupat Holim was a major attraction for joining the Labour confederation, and its loss would weaken the Histadrut in membership, financial and political terms.

This was well understood by the right-wing parties as well as by Dayan and Peres, many of whose foes were entrenched in the Histadrut. Supporters of Histadrut retention of Kupat Holim saw it as one aspect of building an autonomous Labour sector of society. The health services were seen, in Yigal Allon's words, as 'a most admirable example of mutual aid'.[88] In contrast, one critic sympathetic to Dayan and Peres argued that Histadrut ownership of Kupat Holim exemplified some of the worst aspects of Israeli politics, institutions and parties – and especially those of the Labour movement. It was, Shabtai Tevet complained, a system of 'Control by Illness' in which immigrants pouring into the country, by automatically receiving three months of Kupat Holim insurance paid for by the (Mapai-dominated) Jewish Agency, were subtly recruited into and made dependent on the Labour movement. After that time, knowing no other address, they naturally joined the (Mapai-dominated) Histadrut in order to continue receiving its health and other services. This reinforced the unhealthy tendency of Israeli parties to develop constituencies dependent on them, rather than being parties dependent on their constituencies.[89] Apparently even foreign visitors, such as the Director-General of the Norwegian Health Services in 1960, saw the Israeli system as an efficient means of (partial) control of immigrants. Some Israeli critics openly insisted that state subsidies for the Histadrut's Kupat Holim were in effect a political subsidy, particularly of Mapai, because of Kupat Holim's role in maintaining the Histadrut's strength and Mapai's control of the Histadrut. It would be better, it was suggested, to used state funds to establish a *mamlakhti* health system.[90]

Both Mapai and the Histadrut recognized the potentially deleterious impact of nationalization of health services on the Histadrut. Ben-Gurion acceded to Histadrut retention of Kupat Holim as a partial trade-off for nationalization of the Labour Exchange. There was another calculation, however: nationalizing the health services was a much more costly proposition than its proponents realized. It was estimated that such a step, together with remunerating the Histadrut for the lost of its extensive facilities and properties, would have cost the government its development budget for the next decade. Furthermore, it would have necessitated a substantial tax increase in an already heavily taxed country, not only for compensation but just to maintain the system.[91]

The debate over Kupat Holim was also one element of a bitter, explosive battle that racked Mapai and became a *cause célèbre* in 1960, eventually leading to the decline of Ben-Gurion and his exit from office as well as from the party he had led since its founding. The Lavon affair – or simply *Ha-parashah* ('The Affair') as it was known – also served to galvanize the anti-*mamlakhtiyut* forces in Mapai.

Pinhas Lavon had long been regarded as an exceptionally talented rising star in the Labour movement. His allies saw him as a likely prime minister in a post-Ben-Gurion Israel; his foes, while recognizing his intelligence, questioned his character. He had been an ideological leader of Gordonia, a Labour Zionist youth movement, played an important role in building the Hever ha-Kvutsot kibbutz movement, became a Knesset member and Histadrut Secretary-General in 1949 and, relinquishing the latter, minister of agriculture and then minister without portfolio for Ben-Gurion. In 1953–4, during the period of Ben-Gurion's retirement to Kibbutz Sdeh Boker, Lavon became minister of defence under Sharett, with whom he had tense relations. Much of the Mapai establishment, including Meyerson, Eshkol and Aran, opposed his appointment. A dove who rapidly became a hawk as defence minister, Lavon also had exceptionally bad relations with his ministry's Director-General, Shimon Peres, and the IDF Chief of Staff, Moshe Dayan.

During Lavon's brief tenure, Israeli agents, and several Egyptian Jews recruited by them, were arrested in Cairo for seeking to complicate American and Western relations with Egypt through acts of sabotage. This operation had evidently been a response to a variety of developments, among them Nasser's belligerence. *Who* conceived it, however, became a source of controversy within the government. (Israeli censorship prevented publication of the details and the public was kept in the dark for another six years.) Lavon vigorously denied that he gave the order, but an investigatory committee appointed by an angry Sharett could not determine responsibility. Unable to clear his name, Lavon was compelled to resign and was reappointed Secretary-General of the Histadrut. No public explanation was given.

Lavon took an activist role in the Histadrut, asserting its socialist heritage on the one hand while reshaping it to the needs of *mamlakhtiyut* on the other.[92] Lavon championed more direct representation of workers on management boards of Histadrut enterprises, and pursued reorganization plans for Hevrat ha-Ovdim. He told the eighth Mapai Conference in May 1958 that there was no reason for state–Histadrut rivalry and that the Histadrut had to adapt to the new post-statehood situation. Lavon characterized the Histadrut's acceptance of the nationalization of the school system (which occurred while he was still in the Cabinet) as representative of the Labour movement's commitment to national, and not narrow class interests.[93]

Lavon was head of the Histadrut at a time when Dayan and Peres were, on behalf of *mamlakhtiyut*, regularly submitting it and the entire Labour establishment to verbal assault. He responded forcefully. Their personal animosities, and mounting clashes between the *Tseirim* and the Mapai Veterans who, along with the Gush-controlled Mapai party machine, were increasingly wary of Ben-Gurion's protégés and their political styles, complicated the picture further. In 1958 Meir, Aran and Lavon went so far as to tell Ben-Gurion that they feared a coup attempt by Dayan.[94] The emerging crisis had an important structural dimension. The *Tseirim* were neither based in nor dependent on the party/Histadrut apparatus. Their past and present positions in the state (especially the military) gave them an independent status and foundation from which to champion *mamlakhtiyut* against the ossified traditional socialism of the Mapai Veterans. The latter were further angered by the entry of Dayan and Peres into the Knesset in 1959 on the Mapai list under the premier's patronage. In a security conscious country the youthful 'activists', Dayan and Peres, were identified with the defence establishment while the Veterans were veterans, an *old* guard who, in the public mind, were best known for their socio-economic achievements. The Veterans felt that the future of Mapai and its character were fundamentally jeopardized by the young 'statists'.

These factors linked the interests of the Veterans – led by Eshkol, Meir, Aran and Pinhas Sapir – to those of Lavon, despite their previous misgivings about him. In addition, the Veterans and the Gush found themselves increasingly unable to reconcile personal loyalty to Ben-Gurion with mounting anger at his protégés. Lavon and the Veterans did not find themselves in a direct clash with 'the Old Man' himself until mid-1960 when the Lavon affair burst on to the public stage when the Histadrut Secretary-General demanded public exoneration from Ben-Gurion for the 'security mishap', following revelations that perjury had been committed in the original investigation. Ben-Gurion insisted that this was not his prerogative. A furious public entanglement ensued over the proper procedure by which to pursue the matter. It was exacerbated by appearances by Lavon before the Knesset Foreign Affairs and defence Committee which were leaked to the press. In them he not only presented his side of the 'mishap', but insinuated that Dayan and Peres, though not involved in the affair, exploited it against him for their own unsavoury purposes. Ben-Gurion steadfastly refused to exonerate Lavon – apparently he strongly suspected that he did give the order – and would not accept the unanimous conclusions of a Cabinet committee that Lavon was innocent. Ben-Gurion insisted that only a formal judicial inquiry could deal with the matter.

The Affair also served to bring into the open a simmering ideological dispute within Mapai, focusing on *mamlakhtiyut.* Before the Affair had been reopened in the public eye, in a speech to a plenum of the Histadrut Executive in the spring of 1960, Lavon found it necessary to respond to an assertion by Ben-Gurion that the Histadrut, like any other organization, had to bow to state needs. Lavon averred that the Histadrut was *not* a partisan institution like any other within the state, and that it was in a partnership with the state. He had recently also served notice that the Histadrut would transfer no more of its functions to the state. During the summer of 1960 attacks by the *Tseirim,* particularly Peres, against the Histadrut and Kupat Holim intensified. The Histadrut leadership was particularly defensive about proposals to establish compulsory arbitration in labour disputes in the aftermath of a particularly difficult labour conflict with the teachers. Ironically Ben-Gurion, who had once been the most vigorous foe of compulsory arbitration when advocated by Jabotinsky on the grounds that there could be no 'neutral' arbitration panels, proposed a system of binding arbitration under state auspices by which the wage demands of workers would be evaluated by a 'neutral' panel of 'experts', presided over by a judge.[95]

Attacking *mamlakhtiyut,* the *Tseirim* and especially Peres, Zeev Haring, the Histadrut's organization chief, warned of the dangers of etatism, declaring that it was for the good of the state – which was 'not an end in itself' – that etatism had to be fought. The state, he warned, 'is only an instrument to promote human and social interests' and the workers – whose representative was the Histadrut – made up the majority of the population. Was it conceivable that the state's interests could be contrary to those of the vast majority? 'Will the sick really be better cared for by *mamlakhtiyut?*', he chided Peres in response to his calls for nationalizing Kupat Holim.[96] Lavon entered the ideological foray more forcefully in late autumn 1960 after beginning his campaign for rehabilitation and the deterioration of his formerly proper relations with the premier. At a press conference on the Histadrut's 40th anniversary he warned of 'the spread of the dangerous philosophy of "etatism" among certain circles in the state'. Contrasting etatism to the voluntarism that historically characterized the Labour movement, he warned that etatism assumed that the state should replace the free activities of voluntary bodies. This, he argued, threatened the principle that national politics ought to represent an amalgam of state and voluntaristic activities. Mapai's Secretary-General, Yosef Almogi, a Ben-Gurion loyalist with a long personal history in the Histadrut, countered: 'We are in no danger of a surplus of state orientation, but of a lack of volunteering spirit. So long as the Party remains responsible for the

Government and the Histadrut, neither are endangered by etatism'.[97] Almogi's rebuke skirted the problems raised by Lavon and his colleagues: etatism, they suggested, brought with it a de-emphasis on volunteering virtually by definition, and represented a fundamental reorientation of Labour movement priorities.

Lavon's comments reflected a general critique of *mamlakhtiyut* by Mapai intellectuals close to him such as Natan Rotenstreich, a Hebrew University philosophy professor and party activist who was later the moving force in 'Min ha-Yesod' (From the Foundation). This group, which by 1962 was publishing a journal of the same name, sought to be a movement for ideological reform and renewal in Mapai, as well as support for Lavon in his struggle within the party. While it was not a homogenous group, its adherents generally criticized Mapai for having become a creature of its own apparatus, and losing sight of its own ideological premises as a consequence of an exaggerated 'pragmatism'. Min ha-Yesod, and especially Rotenstreich, made a socialist pluralist argument against *mamlakhtiyut*'s totalism; the emphasis on the state and its tools, it was asserted, undermined the vision of Israel as a pluralistic society. The idea of 'statist pioneering' was a contradiction in terms: pioneering represented voluntary self-sacrifice and initiative, not state-organized activity. There was, they warned, a danger of making the state a deified abstraction, and consequently the social innovation long characteristic of Labour would be lost as it ossified in state and bureaucratic structures. A pluralism of social life and debate were prerequisite to a healthy Israel, and this could not be achieved – in fact, was threatened by – *mamlakhtiyut*.[98]

In a significant sense, these criticisms were a socialist reinvention of the critique Ha-Poel ha-Tsair made of Poale Zion and the original Ahdut ha-Avodah.[99] As Ha-Poel ha-Tsair once criticized its fellow Labour parties for subsuming their politics under principles of class and centralized organization, so Lavon, Rotenstreich and their supporters criticized *mamlakhtiyut* for subsuming everything within the state, thus jeopardizing pluralism and the voluntaristic socialism of the Labour movement. With this critique, *mamlakhtiyut* came full circle. Its origins, as we have seen, were in the divorce between class and national politics, in the abandonment of the hyphen in Zionist-socialism. We dated this to the 1930s, and the acceptance by Labour as its operative political principle of hegemonic segmented pluralism, with its assumption of state and nation as categories and things above class. The abandonment of a class orientation remained the hallmark of the left's (Mapam and Ahdut ha-Avodah) criticism of Mapai and *mamlakhtiyut*, which we could call the socialist class critique of it. With statehood, *mamlakhtiyut* in practice entailed the assertion of state primacy and the dimunition of the Labour movement and, at least theoretically, other pillars within the state. The socialist pluralist critique argued that the state *qua* state was in danger of becoming the all-consuming category of

Israeli political culture – indeed, culture – and the only point of reference in its symbolic universe. Ironically, the necessary condition of *mamlakhtiyut* – the acceptance of segmented pluralism rather than a radical class politics – was threatened by *mamlakhtiyut* itself.

V

The Mapai leadership found Ben-Gurion's persistence in demanding a formal judicial inquiry into the Lavon Affair increasingly unsettling. Fearful of a party rupture, they wanted to close the Affair as quickly as possible, and were disappointed when the ministerial committee's report did not accomplish this. If the Mapai leadership was disconcerted by Ben-Gurion, its anger at Lavon also grew continually, fuelled by his apparent disregard for the party in his campaign, beginning with his appearance at the Knesset committee. Lavon's December press conference attacking etatism, combined with a decision not to invite Ben-Gurion to address the Histadrut's 40th anniversary celebration, led to an unprecedented step: Lavon became the first leading Mapai figure to be publicly censured by the party Central Committee.

Ben-Gurion made it clear that Mapai had to chose between him and Lavon, and he resigned on 31 January, 1961. Some of the Mapai Veterans and the Gush now found themselves on the same side as the *Tseirim*; losing Ben-Gurion would be much more of a débâcle for the disarrayed party than losing Lavon. Within a week the Mapai Central Committee ousted Lavon from his position at the Histadrut by a vote of 159 to 96 with 5 abstentions. Among the negative votes were Sharett, Meir, Aran and Sapir. Rotenstreich, organizing the nucleus of Min ha-Yesod, brought together some of the country's leading intellectuals and academics, who were appalled at the treatment of Lavon, to criticize Ben-Gurion's posture and the Mapai decision. Clearly there was significant support for Lavon, but the decision was final and Ben-Gurion withdrew his resignation. That Lavon's dismissal, organized by Finance Minister Eshkol in the hopes of closing the Affair, was done in summary fashion further damaged Ben-Gurion's image. As the public perception that Ben-Gurion was conducting a vendetta increased, so his authority waned. Also, while the party had backed him, the episode none the less undermined his relations with the Veterans, and also government stability as Mapam and Ahdut ha-Avodah refused to serve in a coalition under him. Mapai was forced to call new elections in which it lost 10 per cent of its vote. A new coalition was formed with some difficulty, but Ben-Gurion remained prime minister only until June 1963 when, exhausted and discouraged by his loss of authority, he resigned for the last time and was replaced by Eshkol.

The exit of the Founding Father left his protégés facing a Mapai controlled by the Veterans, in particular the 'Troika' of Meir, Aran and Sapir. For a period, Dayan and Peres retained their respective positions (agriculture minister and deputy defence minister), but were under increasing pressure as the Veterans sought to reassert Mapai's socialist identity and to reinforce themselves against the *Tseirim*. At Mapai's ninth Conference in 1963 Eshkol, Aran and others called for revivifying socialist ideas among the workers, and going beyond the welfare state to a socialist Israel in the following decade.[100] The conflict between theirs and the *mamlakhti* approach was illustrated publicly when, following Eshkol's lead, Reuven Barkatt, now the Mapai Secretary-General, told the delegates that Mapai had to reassert its belief in social equality and Dayan, in turn, urged economic development at the expense of equality. Dayan stressed the importance of technology – which, he insisted, was 'not a matter of ideology' – and branded Eshkol's reaffirmation of traditional Labour ideology and institutions as obsolete.[101]

Mapai's internal peace was but a fragile phenomenon and by 1965 the party split. Ben-Gurion conducted a furious campaign against Eshkol when, backed by the Troika and the Gush, the premier sought to restore a semblance of party unity by repairing ties with Lavon's supporters in Min ha-Yesod. Ben-Gurion, appearing to be a man obsessed, mobilized his backers. Dayan and Peres at this time found their status in Mapai increasingly untenable. Both were alarmed by efforts to create an electoral alignment – originally supported by Ben-Gurion and championed by Ben-Aharon – between Mapai and Ahdut ha-Avodah. The two parties had been working harmoniously in the Cabinet and two decades after the Siah B split their differences had narrowed, now that the Mapai leaders were reasserting their socialism and Ahdut ha-Avodah had distanced itself from the pro-Soviet Mapam position of the early 1950s. For Dayan and Peres, Ahdut ha-Avodah was especially threatening because in its ranks was an alternative young leadership, epitomized by former Palmah commander Yigal Allon, that was socialist in orientation, 'activist' on defence policy and identified with military heroism.

The tenth Mapai Conference in 1965 was a bitter affair in which Ben-Gurion again demanded a judicial investigation of Lavon and attacked the party leadership. Eshkol, Meir and a dying Moshe Sharett furiously assailed Ben-Gurion for yet again disrupting Mapai with his fixation on Lavon. 'How could Churchillian greatness', a Ben-Gurion critic wondered aloud, 'suddenly appear in the guise of provincial pettiness, vindictiveness and rancor?'[102] Ben-Gurion's supporters were defeated in their proposal to have Mapai endorse a judicial inquiry. They did, however, receive a substantial 40 per cent of the vote. At the same conference Mapai voted for alignment with Ahdut ha-Avodah. That summer Ben-Gurion decided to contest the forthcoming elections on his own 'Israel Workers' List' (Rafi). He took with him those who felt that Mapai was being 'de-Ben-Gurionized', including Peres (who became Rafi Secretary-General and hoped to turn it into a centrist *mamlakhti* force), and later a more reticent Dayan.

Rafi did poorly in the 1965 elections (7.9 per cent of the vote). In 1968 it merged with Mapai and Ahdut ha-Avodah to form the Israel Labour party which Dayan and Peres joined. Ben-Gurion refused and formed his own 'State List' to champion *mamlakhtiyut*. Four years after he died in 1973 this Rafi remnant entered the Israeli government as part of the Likud, the right-wing alignment that brought Jabotinsky's heir, Menahem Begin, to the premiership. Labour, now led by Peres, faced the difficult task of adapting to a role it had never played in the sovereign Jewish state – and which it had not played since it entered the Zionist Executive coalition of 1931 – that of opposition party. Dayan promptly left Labour and became Begin's foreign minister.

Conclusion:
The Zionist Hedgehog and
the Zionist Fox

The state is an abstraction; the people alone is concrete.

Karl Marx[1]

The achievements of the Labour Zionist movement were possible because in the process by which Jewish national boundaries were redrawn it successfully built an organizational apparatus, and fostered a political culture, that corresponded to its own political and socio-economic strategy – revolutionary constructivism. In the long term, however, Labour not only failed to reproduce its own dominance, it pursued policies that helped to subvert it. This began long before the Labour party's actual defeat in 1977 and is reflected both in election results and in various studies of Israeli political attitudes and political culture carried out in the last decade.

As early as the 1959 elections, a trend to the right among younger voters was discernible. By the end of the following decade evidence showed a definite turn, and revealed that those who supported the parties of the left were increasingly from the older generation.[2] In the 1969 national elections the Labour Alignment (a common electoral front of the Labour party, led by Prime Minister Golda Meir, and Mapam) was significantly backed by voters who saw themselves to the right of the left; less than half of those who cast ballots for the Alignment identified themselves as politically on the left or the moderate left.[3] The picture becomes more complex when the evolution of Israeli political attitudes between 1962 and 1981 is considered. This period marked the transformation of the Jewish state from a dominant party system, in which the leadership role of Labour was taken for granted, into a competitive party system in which it struggled with the right-wing Likud bloc for power. One study of these two decades concluded that 'although the country . . . moved to the right politically, the distribution of attitudes on important matters . . . remained basically constant'. Identification with the political right quadrupled from 8 per cent (1962) to 16 per cent (1969) to 23 per cent (1973) to 28 per cent (1977) to 32 per cent (1981), while identification with the left and the moderate left showed the reverse tendency, descending from 31 per cent (1962) to 25 per cent (1969) to 22 per cent (1973) to 18 per cent (1977) to 17 per cent (1981).[4] In the 1970s these trends manifested themselves in Labour's decline both in Knesset and, significantly though less substantially, in Histadrut elections.[5] At the same time, while 54 per cent of the Israeli population in 1962 thought the country's economy ought to be socialist or more socialist, compared with 26 per cent that thought it should be capitalist or more capitalist, in 1977, the year of the right's first electoral victory, 56 per cent of the population thought the economy should be socialist or more socialist, and 29 per cent thought it should be capitalist or more capitalist. In 1981, 60 per cent thought it should be socialist or more socialist and 35 per cent thought it should be capitalist or more capitalist.[6] It seems that some of the values of a social democratic nationalism had taken root, but concurrently a transmutation in the terms of political discourse had occurred, indicating, in turn, that a transmutation in the relative weight of political values and identities was also taking place. The label 'right-wing' no longer had pariah status; in addition, the extent to which Labour lost ground to the right among working class constituencies (especially of Oriental origin) was striking, particularly considering Labour's ideological history.[7] Collectivism, as an element or impulse within Israeli nationalism, would eventually be channelled towards right-wing populism rather than towards socialism in some significant segments of the Israeli population.

An analysis of Israeli political culture based on survey data collected in 1973 emphasized that a cleavage had emerged between the ruling Labour party and its world-view, and attitudes within the public at large. 'Left', it noted, had been associated generally in Israel with socialist and egalitarian policies, while 'right' denoted an 'activist', and a forceful foreign policy stance. The latter, it should be added, was very salient given the influence of ongoing war on the public mood. However, the study concluded that the 'left' was no longer associated with 'equality' in the public mind, while the 'association of leftism with socialism and rightism with activism' did, by and large, hold. Therefore, although the Labour party in fact had, through its policies, been in tandem with

the changing orientations of the public by being less adamant on the issue of equality . . . and by allowing marked income differentials to develop in Israel; and while the dominant party no longer appears to be the champions of the 'labourers' in their 'class struggle' against 'capitalists', it has consistently perpetuated a socialist-oriented policy by fostering the public sector of the economy as over the private one and by maintaining tight government control of the economy as a whole . . .

... In summary it seems that a discrepancy has been developing between the official ideology of the dominant party and some socio-economic patterns devised by it.[8]

An apparently contradictory picture forms of a population that consistently favoured socialism or more socialism, identified socialism with the left, but no longer identified equality with the left and defined itself to be increasingly of the right. Clearly there had not been a displacement of collectivist values by bourgeois, that is, radically individualist, ones. However, a right-wing nationalist populism espoused by Herut could – and would – feed on such a situation. It is also worth noting that in 1980–1, at a time when the state's economy was in a precarious condition while there were, none the less, rising living standards for many individuals as a result of election-oriented governmental economic policies, a survey found that concern with economic efficiency and recovery substantially outweighed those of both social equality and personal economic improvement. The image of the Israel worker, who received much blame for economic problems from those in the survey, was particularly negative, as was that of the Histadrut. Initiatives from and stimulation of the private sector in order to deal with economic problems was the preference of respondents, although not to the exclusion of action and expansion in the public sector.[9] All these studies indicate substantial distance in public opinion from the political culture of Labour Zionism, with its lionization of the worker and emphases on egalitarianism and public initiative. The distance between Labour's historical vision of Zion and the reality, as well as the perception of it by citizens, of the Jewish state, seemed far indeed.

In indicating how Labour's own evolution helped establish the preconditions for this situation, I have focused on the internal dynamics of a process which occurred within a broader context. Mapai's political rise began with its decision to dominate the national agenda of Zionism; its decline corresponded with the long, but ultimately successful, effort of the Revisionists to break out of their sectarian political ghetto. Among the essential factors that facilitated a political atmosphere increasingly receptive to the nationalist right was the omnipresent pressure of the Arab–Israeli conflict. It is difficult to understate the impact on Israeli society of the threat posed to it in May 1967, the aftermath of the Six Day War in early June (which placed Israel in occupation of a substantial Arab population), the regeneration of Palestinian Arab nationalism, continuous terrorist attacks by Palestinian organizations against Israeli civilians and the trauma of Israeli defeats and casualties in the initial stages of the 1973 war. All these exacerbated Jewish fears and sense of isolation. They encouraged, and then reinforced, the re-emergence of militant Jewish nationalism, both of religious and secular varieties. The political salience of these developments is reflected in the concurrent rise in identification with the right and the maintenance of socialist attitudes towards the economy that we cited above. 'Activism' and toughness in the face of Arab hostility were increasingly identified with the right, even though Labour did not lack for hawks in its leadership, particularly in the Rafi and Ahdut ha-Avodah factions of the Labour party. The dovish elements in Labour were consistently outflanked, and their inability to assert themselves in fact fortified the trend to the right.

Israel's rapid demographic changes and growth as a consequence of the immigrations of the 1950s inevitably planted some of the seeds of political transformation. The Oriental immigrants were more religiously traditional than the Labour movement and never experienced the turn-of-the-century upheavals and revolts that created secular socialist nationalism in eastern Europe; also, they had not participated in the 'heroic era' during which Labour led the struggle for statehood. They arrived in an Israel which on the one hand was being shaped by Ben-Gurion's *mamlakhtiyut*, messianism and personal charisma, and on the other was dominated by a secular Labour movement that increasingly took on the form of an ossified, paternalistic elite. The immigrants were faced not with a vibrant, revolutionary and innovative Labour movement seeking to integrate them into its symbolic universe, but with an apparatus which, through its extensive system of patronage, sought to secure their political loyalties. Inevitably this produced resentments and political reorientation, especially as a younger, more educated generation of Oriental Jews grew up and sought to make its way in a Jewish state whose rulers were not a capitalist class but a Labour bureaucracy composed mostly of eastern European or Western Jews. The decline of Ben-Gurion, and his eventual exit, also injured Mapai among the Oriental Jews. Indeed, as early as 2 February, 1961 it was noted in the daily *Ha-arets* that the exit of the charismatic leader would injure the Labour movement because the new immigrants tended to identify Ben-Gurion with Mapai.[10]

Increasingly, many Oriental Jews saw themselves as an unfairly excluded part of Israeli society, and Begin's party, then pursuing the difficult task of legitimizing itself in a dominant party system, saw and presented itself as the same. Whereas Jabotinsky, in the 1920s and 1930s, pursued a policy of separatism, now his heirs followed a strategy of inclusion. To the dismay of the Labour parties, Herut decided in 1963 to form a faction in the Histadrut after three decades of non-participation in the Labour confederation.[11] In 1965 it formed 'Gahal', an alignment with the Liberal party, to contest Knesset elections. The Liberals were heirs to the anti-Labour General Zionists who had twice served in the Cabinet. Herut could thus appear more as a part of the political mainstream. Despite Begin's penchant for posturing and rhetoric, Herut slowly established itself as a more credible loyal opposition.

It was fortuitous for the right that this occurred when the Mapai leadership, despite Eshkol's reassertion of his party's socialist heritage, sought to calm the political atmosphere after the upheavals of the Lavon affair. Even while Ben-Gurion was still premier, in July 1962, some Mapai figures, both from the older and younger generations, aired the possibility of Herut as a coalition partner.[12] As prime minister, Eshkol officially requested the reinterment of Jabotinsky in Jerusalem, something Ben-Gurion had refused to do.[13] In June 1966 Eshkol and important Cabinet ministers, along with the Histadrut Secretary-General and the head of the ZO/Jewish Agency, symbolically attended Herut's eighth convention. The premier told the delegates that the government in a democracy represented the entire nation, and that his presence at his opposition's conclave was intended as one step in making Israeli public life more civil.[14] Mapai and Herut slowly began treating each other more as political rivals than as outright enemies. By the winter of 1967 Ben-Gurion, still furious at Mapai's leaders because of Lavon, was declaring that Rafi was not purely a Labour party because 'the people of Israel takes precedence', and expressed his willingness to have Herut in the cabinet if he again became prime minister.[15]

The wall excluding the Revisionists from the 'national consensus', built in the 1930s, was finally breached following one of the most tense periods in Israel's short history. In May 1967 three Arab armies, led by Nasser's Egypt, mobilized on the borders of the Jewish state and publicly, and explicitly, threatened its extinction. Gahal was brought into the national unity government formed on the eve of the Six Day War. Under enormous political pressures Eshkol relinquished the defence portfolio, which he, like Ben-Gurion before him, had held together with the premiership. Significantly, he was compelled to yield it to the hero of the 1956 war, Moshe Dayan. The latter was active leader of Ben-Gurion's Rafi, and had agreed with Begin that their respective parties would not enter a national unity coalition without the other.[16] Menahem Begin became a minister without portfolio and was thus given a new legitimacy.

In the Six Day War Israel defeated Egypt, Jordan and Syria, and occupied territories of each. In the aftermath Herut, now a party of government, sought to portray itself as a responsible participant in national decision-making and to project itself as the 'watchdog' of national security in a government dominated by a Labour leadership prone to territorial compromise in exchange for (what Herut deemed to be) the chimera of real peace with the Arabs. In its hostility and refusal to negotiate with the Jewish state, the Arab world was the unwitting ally of the Israeli right wing. Oddly enough, another ally was to be found in the Ahdut ha-Avodah faction of the Labour party. Ahdut ha-Avodah's origins, as earlier chapters showed, were in especially left and class-oriented elements in the Labour movement. Based on Ha-Kibbutz ha-Meuhad, its historical leadership, most prominently Tabenkin, was among the most forceful foes of Ben-Gurion, and the most radical critics of rapprochement, let alone co-operation, with the Revisionists (dating back to the Ben-Gurion–Jabotinsky agreement). After statehood,

Ahdut ha-Avodah opposed *mamlakhtiyut* from a Marxist-oriented class perspective, and vigorously attacked Rafi, which it saw as the embodiment of the politics of *mamlakhtiyut*. In the 1940s, Tabenkin's circle fought the Biltmore Programme and Ben-Gurion's willingness to partition Palestine. Instead, it championed a Jewish commonwealth of kibbutzim in the entire Land of Israel as a matter of ideological imperative; its priority was possession of the whole country and the creation of a collective society there rather than immediate statehood. The insistence of Ahdut ha-Avodah on the territorial integrity of the land re-emerged with the victory of 1967, and Ha-Kibbutz ha-Meuhad, a vanguard in the pre-state settlement efforts, became an aggressive advocate of settling the territories taken in the Six Day War. It tended, therefore, to a left-wing hawkishness, though with some notable exceptions such as Ben-Aharon. Fixated on territory in the post-1967 period, Tabenkin and his followers saw the formation of the Labour party, through Ahdut ha-Avodah's merger with Mapai and Rafi, as one way to restrain Mapai's relative moderation on territorial issues. Rafi's leaders, Dayan and Peres, doubted Arab readiness to come to terms with Israel, and consequently held hawkish positions for pragmatic – as opposed to Ahdut ha-Avodah's more ideological – reasons. None the less, for Ahdut ha-Avodah, Rafi now became an acceptable, indeed valuable, ally against withdrawal.[17] (Ben-Gurion, on the other hand, feared the consequences of Israeli annexation of areas with large Arab populations and counselled concessions and moderation on territorial questions.) Similarly, Tabenkin's group championed the continuation of the national unity government for the sake of territory. Those who once opposed any co-operation with Revisionists and General Zionists for class reasons now wanted them in the government for territorial ones. 'Comrades, national unity is no disgrace', Tabenkin declared to the Central Committee of the Labour party on 7 May, 1970.[18] He told the Secretariat of Ha-Kibbutz ha-Meuhad on 30 July, 1970 (shortly before the end of the 'War of Attrition', a bloody and protracted artillery and aerial duel between Israeli and Egyptian forces across the Suez Canal): 'We are struggling for our existence as always . . . A single Jewish front is needed, Mapam and the Revisionists'.[19] Ironically, Ahdut ha-Avodah and Tabenkin, who had been especially vehement in attacking Ben-Gurion's *mamlakhtiyut* on the grounds that it fetishized the state, now fetishized land; rather than reifying the state, they reified territory. The Revisionists continued to reify both.

The blow dealt to Israel by the Egyptian–Syrian surprise attack of October 1973 seriously damaged the Labour party's public image. Gahal, which left the national unity government in the summer of 1970 in opposition to the cease-fire conditions that ended the War of Attrition and which formed, with other rightist groups, the Likud electoral bloc in August 1973, could not be held culpable by the public for Israel's considerable losses. Soon after the Yom Kippur War, the last of the Labour movement's founders, Golda Meir, stepped down as premier, and Labour's younger generation came to power, with Itshak Rabin, formerly IDF chief of staff and ambassador to Washington, as prime minister and Peres as defence minister. This inaugurated the final period of the decline of Labour dominance; the mid-1970s were marked by intense personal rivalry between Rabin and Peres, a series of scandals, a split in the Labour party (creating the short-lived 'Democratic Movement for Change') and finally its defeat in the Knesset elections of 1977.

The débâcle of 1977 represented more than an electoral set-back for a Labour party; it symbolized the corrosion of its project of a Jewish Labour civilization. It was not simply a dominant party in a narrow sense that fell in 1977; 'Labour' in its revolutionary constructivist incarnation was much more than a party or an apparatus. It would be more accurate to speak of the historical undoing of a dominant movement which, instead of evolving and developing its agenda of ideological and practical innovation, devolved into a dominant party. Had Labour not suffered a split (in the form of the 'Democratic Movement for Change'), it might well have won the elections of 1977. However, defeat would have come sooner or later. The first third of this book examined why, at the heart of Zionist politics, there was not only an attempt to face a volatile historical situation but a refashioning of Jewish political culture by means of national politics. This redrawing of Jewish national boundaries represented the first turn in the internal development of Zionist politics, and established the circumstances in which the Labour Zionist endeavour was born. The second turn was dominated by the struggle between left and right to shape the emerging Jewish society and its political culture, and ended with Labour victorious. However, through *mamlakhtiyut* Labour disarmed itself, and it was therefore unable to confront a plethora of changing factors and conditions in such a way as to reproduce its own hegemony. Fundamental to this was the reification of Labour Zionism, a process in which, especially after the achievement of independence, the state, instead of being a (necessary) means in dialectical interplay with the end of a certain type of society, increasingly became, as an operative principle, an end unto itself. One long-term consequence was the eventual emergence of a technocratically oriented Labour leadership primarily focused on the instrumentalities of statehood; the value system Labour Zionism based itself on became, for them, recited formulae which they viewed as hopelessly outdated at best, uninteresting at worst. There has been no serious ideological reform movement within Labour since Min ha-Yesod, and even Labour's defeat in the 1977 election led to little serious soul-searching or reconsideration. All of this may be seen as an outcome of the reified thinking of *mamlakhtiyut*. Ben-Gurion, it should be recalled, believed the fundamental existential problems of the Jews resolved with statehood; the younger generation, he said, wanted to know what to do, rather than be preoccupied with what to be, and his protégés echoed him. He made these claims as his socialist politics was eclipsed by his messianism. His messianic proclamations, however, were one thing; his operative – etatist – politics were another. There was a disjuncture between Zion and state.

What did this imply for Labour Zionism? Since he claimed that the state embodied the universal, Hegel called the bureaucracy – the civil servants of the state – the universal class. It had 'the universal as the end of its essential activity'.[20] Marx, in turn, posited the proletariat as the universal class because its suffering represented human suffering in general, and consequently its liberation would mean human liberation, through a revolutionary process which would overthrow the dominant, ruling, particularistic interests. Labour Zionism faced no entrenched Jewish ruling class in Palestine comparable to Western capitalism, and its 'revolutionary constructivism' posited the coincidence of working-class and general national interests. In what I have called the Zionization of the notion of the universal class, Labour envisioned the emerging Jewish proletariat as the universal class of a particular nation. It would be the agent which, in liberating the nation, would remake it in its own image in the form of a classless Jewish society built by means of the Histadrut and co-operative settlements in the Land of Israel. This meant that the national community would become the class community, or rather, since what was projected was *am oved*, a working nation, it would be a classless national society. However, when Labour, beginning in the 1930s, pursued a politics of hegemonic segmented pluralism, rather than one predicated on an identity of class and national interests, it assumed that the Labour society being constructed was only one, though the largest, of the pillars in the Jewish state. It is striking, in this regard, that while the 1920s was a decade of remarkable social creativity and experimentation by the Labour movement, in the 1930s such innovation virtually vanished.[21] State and nation came to be regarded as categories above class, and this transition matured in *mamlakhtiyut*. State or nation-state, not class or a class-nation synthesis, became the operative universal category, and this was manifested in both Ben-Gurion's arguments for *mamlakhtiyut* and in the policies of *mamlakhtiyut*. In a sense this was a reversion to Hegel's position: as Hegel spoke of the state as the universal and the bureaucracy as the class embodying it, Ben-Gurion asserted the primacy of state orientations and institutions over those of class, and proposed statist *halutsiyut* as the supersession of its class-oriented pre-state version.[22]

Here it is instructive to return to the comparison between Austrian socialism and the Zionist Labour movement. Unlike orthodox Marxists who envisioned the abolition of states and nations with the advent of a classless society, both Austrian and Zionist socialists assumed that both would be essential parts of the political future. Before the First World War, the Austrians argued for an Austria that would be a federation of nations within a state apparatus; after their brief participation in the government of the First Republic just after the war, they sought, through the construction of Red Vienna, to build their own pillar of anticipatory socialism, which they hoped would one day extend to all of Austria. Labour Zionism, a national and socialist movement, was concerned to establish a state, and through its Labour state-within-a-state – the Histadrut – it constructed its own anticipatory socialism. In a critical study of the Austrian case one scholar has argued that it was precisely because of the socialist failure to gain state power that Austrian anticipatory socialism ('institutionalism'), with its emphasis on the quest for spiritual/cultural dominance, did not succeed and was quickly, and brutally, destroyed by the right in 1934.[23] The great irony of Labour Zionism is that it both built and dominated a state, was able to do so as a result of its own 'institutionalism', but once in power it expropriated from itself and for the state, spiritually and materially, much of the means which brought it to power. Instead of pursuing a socialist strategy by which state power would be used to *expand* the autonomous public sphere of the working class, Mapai narrowed it. Instead of expropriating a bourgeoisie as socialists, at least theoretically, aim to do, Ben-Gurion and Mapai nationalized key Labour movement institutions and then increasingly emptied them of socialist content, while at the same time raising the banner of the state. Thus the Labour movement inevitably disarmed itself, and under the enormous pressures of war and immigration helped to plant the seeds for a political culture much more suitable to its historical foes.[24]

Mamlakhtiyut was not fully successful, as the retention of Kupat Holim by the Histadrut demonstrates. However, the *mythomoteur* of *am mamlakhti* displaced that of *am oved*, even if the vocabulary associated with the latter did not vanish, and the vast majority of Israelis remained wage labourers.[25] As the symbolic universe of *mamlakhtiyut* arose in its firmament, Labour yielded one essential means of political socialization – its schools. In addition, as the army and the unified *mamlakhti* education system became the essential means of political socialization, the place of the Labour movement's youth movements also declined, as did the status of the kibbutz as the embodiment of *halutsiyut* and the good society.

Mamlakhtiyut, as noted earlier, signalled the Israeli version of the 'end of ideology'. It took hold at the same time that the 'end of ideology' was proclaimed by various social scientists in the West, especially the United States.[26] 'The End of Ideology' was, as many of its critics noted, an ideology in itself, one of technocracy and the status quo. 'Ideology' – which more often than not was a code word for socialist ideas – had 'ended' because all major problems, it was believed, could be solved within the existing systems, thus permitting everyone and everything to be happily and acceptably integrated. The assumption was that the proper manipulation of instrumentalities, of means, was the issue of the day, not 'ideological' questions about ultimate political and socio-economic ends. Means and ends were divorced in political discourse. Ben-Gurion's – like any – messianism was at least theoretically preoccupied with ultimate ends, but in awaiting the Messianic age the expositor of this messianism became operatively focused on the means; we can see this in Ben-Gurion's stress on the state, its instrumentalities and science, and his disdain for 'outmoded' socialist concepts, all of which were relegated to the realm of ideology. Thus by the time Labour was defeated in 1977, it is not surprising that it had long mistaken its control of the mechanisms of power for its own hegemony in Israeli society.

The transformation of Mapai/Labour partly parallels what Otto Kirch-heimer, in the 1960s, pointed to as the development of 'catch-all parties' in Europe. Like their European socialist counterparts, the Zionist Labour parties originally played an integrative role for their adherents, while forcefully projecting a future society that would be brought about by collective struggle. However, Mapai/Labour later relinquished 'the intellec-tual and moral *encadrement* of the masses' and 'all-embracing concerns', exchanging 'effectiveness in depth for a wider audience and more immediate electoral success'. It sought to maintain working-class support while spreading its electoral net wider and transformed itself more and more from a 'class-mass' into a 'catch-all' party. If intellectual and moral *encadrement* of the masses is discarded, 'de-ideologization' is almost a necessary counterpart and ideology is transformed 'from partnership in a clearly visible goal structure into one of many sufficient but by no means motivational forces operative in the voters' choice'.[27] At the same time, Mapai/Labour depended on the Labour movement's control of and patronage powers within extensive segments of social and economic life – through the government and the Histadrut – to bolster loyalty to the party, although precisely these factors encouraged resentment, especially within the Oriental Jewish working class. The post-statehood division between *hazon va-derekh*, between vision and path, certainly helped to sustain Labour in power for a good number of years. However, self-de-ideologization, and the corresponding assumption that as a consequence of the (apparent) stability of Israel's political culture the opposition could never emerge victorious, eventually helped to undo the dominant party.

The final irony, revealed in the third turn of Zionist political history, was that, just as America experienced an explosion of ideological constestation in the decade (the 1960s) after the 'end of ideology' was proclaimed, the technocratic Labourites were defeated by a party headed by an ideologue, Menahem Begin. In the 1977 elections Begin's ideological posturing was not especially salient as he was confined to a hospital for a good part of the campaign (a factor that may have aided the right at the time). However, it was as an ideologue, as a man who projected *a strong sense of direction* – a

formidable asset in a country in siege, as Labour itself once recognized –
that Begin kept his parliamentary opponents at bay; his government was
anything but efficient. It is sometimes suggested that *mamlakhtiyut* was the
opposite of the integral, land-oriented 'neo-Zionism' of the Begin era.
However, if our analyses have been correct, this cannot be simply asserted.
In the first place, Jabotinsky, Begin and the Revisionists were historically
both integral nationalists and etatists at one and the same time; after all,
they opposed partitioning the Land of Israel in order to incorporate all of it
within the state. Second, and most importantly, *mamlakhtiyut* functioned
historically not as the foe of integral nationalism, but as a midwife of its rise
by promoting a formalistic, yet particularist, etatism and engendering a
depletion of the Labour movement's concrete socialist content and
universalist vision. Thereby a void was created that was filled after the events
of 1967 with 'neo-Zionism' and helped produce Labour's undoing in 1977.

Labour, uncomprehending of its own defeat, had long since ceased
serious debate of its basic principles and strategies. Internal struggles were
primarily matters of ambitions and personalities, particularly those of
Itshak Rabin and Shimon Peres. John Stuart Mill, in a different context,
argued that without vigorous contestation a political doctrine, *even if
entirely true*, becomes inefficacious, a little-understood prejudice whose
meaning is 'in danger of being lost, or enfeebled, and deprived of its vital
effect on the character'.[28] The Israeli counterpart of the end of ideology
brought something similar to Labour Zionism. Consequently, the circumstances Labour found itself in with Begin's victory were reminiscent of those
of the protagonist of Amos Oz's story 'The Way of the Wind'. It was
hanging upside-down, unable to communicate with its own heritage. And
when Labour returned to power in 1984, after seven years in opposition, it
projected no more of a socio-political vision to the Israeli public than it had
when it was defeated. Indeed, in its 1984 electoral campaign Labour chose
to stress its superior competence rather than fundamental differences with
its right-wing foes; Labour sought its political rehabilitation through a
return to power, rather than by re-creating the conditions for its power.
Thus there was no great irony in its return to government as part of a unity
coalition with the Likud (in which Labour was, certainly, the more
competent component).

In a much-renowned essay on Tolstoy and Maistre, Isaiah Berlin quoted
the Greek poet Archilochus's remark that 'The fox knows many things, but
the hedgehog knows one big thing'.[29] Labour Zionism's original achievement rested on its ability to be both the Zionist fox and the Zionist
hedgehog at once; it projected and sought a big thing while concurrently
devoting itself to the many smaller, though essential, tasks required by
nation, state, class and community-building. Although Ben-Gurion would
surely have insisted on its opposite intent, what *mamlakhtiyut* engendered
was a narrow focus on those smaller tasks – the quotidian use and defence

of the instrumentalities of state – and cynicism regarding actualization of the big thing, a unified social and national vision. The opening chapter suggested that a 'nation', may be metaphorically conceived as something like Freud's psyche, or as a historical entity composed of differently conditioned, and changing, realities, cultural impulses and mechanisms. How Israeli Labour chooses to shape and to harness – to direct – those impulses, and how it regards and defines those mechanisms, will determine whether it will, unlike Gideon Shenhav, land on its feet again; this, in turn, will determine its own future and character, as well as that of the Zionist revolution as a whole.

Notes

Preface: The Vision of Zion and the Realities of Statehood

1 David Ben-Gurion, 'A new Jew arises in Israel', *Jerusalem Post*, 16 May, 1958, p. 5.
2 'Peres: living in a dangerous era', *Jerusalem Post*, 30 August, 1960, p. 1.
3 Eccles. 11:5. All biblical citations in Hebrew and in English are from *The Holy Scriptures According to the Masoretic Text* (Philadelphia, Pa: Jewish Publication Society of America, 1955).
4 See translator's note to 'The way of the wind', in Amos Oz, *Where the Jackals Howl and other Stories*, tr. Nicholas de Lange (New York: Bantam Books, 1982), p. 41.
5 All quotes from 'The way of the wind' are ibid.
6 Shmarya Levin, *The Arena* (New York: Harcourt, Brace, 1932), p. 213.
7 See especially chapter 2 in Jonathan Frankel, *Prophecy and Politics: Socialism, Nationalism, and the Russian Jews, 1862–1917* (Cambridge and New York: Cambridge University Press, 1981).
8 I use 'symbolic universe' in Berger and Luckmann's sense, as 'bodies of theoretical tradition that integrate different provinces of meaning and encompass the institutional order in a symbolic totality.' Peter L. Berger and Thomas Luckmann, *The Social Construction of Reality* (Harmondsworth: Penguin Books, 1972), p. 113.
9 Sidney Verba, 'Comparative political culture', in Lucien W. Pye and Sidney Verba (eds), *Political Culture and Political Development* (Princeton, NJ: Princeton University Press, 1965), pp. 555–6.
10 See Karl Marx, *Capital*, vol. 1 (Moscow: Progress Publishers, 1965), p. 72.
11 Georg Lukács, *History and Class Consciousness* (Cambridge, Mass.: MIT Press, 1972), p. 83.
12 Ibid., p. 89.
13 The concept is discussed at more length in chapter 6 and is derived from Val R. Lorwin, 'Segmented pluralism', *Comparative Politics*, January 1971.
14 On the problems of precise rendering of *mamlakhtiyut* into English, see chapter 11.
15 Lucien Goldmann, *Sciences humaines et philosophie* (Paris: Editions Gonthier, 1966), p. 48.
16 See, for examples, Walter Laqueur, *A History of Zionism* (New York: Holt, Rinehart & Winston, 1972); David Vital's two volumes, *The Origins of Zionism* (Oxford: Oxford University Press, 1975) and *Zionism: The Formative Years* (Oxford: Oxford University Press, 1982); Yosef Gorni, *Ha-sheelah ha-aravit ve-ha-beayah ha-yehudit* (The Arab Question and the Jewish Problem) (Tel Aviv: Am Oved-Ofakim, 1985) (forthcoming in English as *Zionism and the Arabs 1882–1948* (Oxford: Oxford University Press); Shabtai Teveth, *Ben-Gurion and the Palestinian Arabs* (Oxford: Oxford University Press, 1985); Elkanah Margalit, *Ha-Shomer ha-Tsair – Me-adat nearim le-marxism mahpkhani*

1913–1936 (Ha-Shomer ha-Tsair – From Youth Community to Revolutionary Marxism 1913–1936) (Tel Aviv: Tel Aviv University and Ha-Kibbutz ha-Meuhad, 1971); Zalman Abramov, *Perpetual Dilemma: Jewish Religion in the Jewish State* (New York and New Jersey: Union of American Hebrew Congregations and Fairleigh Dickinson University, 1976). The books on Israeli foreign policy and the Arab–Israeli conflict are legion.

17 The course on Ben-Gurion, based in part on a dissertation, subsequently took book form and specifically referred to the reification of Zionism, although without, in my view, fully appreciating the full implications of such an observation. See Avraham Avi-hai, *Ben-Gurion: State-Builder* (Jerusalem and New York: Israel Universities Press and John Wiley, 1974), p. 278.

18 See, for examples, my 'Ben-Gurion and statebuilding' (a review of Avi-hai's book), *Jewish Frontier*, March 1975; 'The Jewish question becomes the Zionist question', *Response*, Summer/Fall 1976; 'Introduction' to 'Symposium on negating the diaspora', *Jewish Frontier*, December 1979; 'The end of Zionist ideology?', *Sh'ma*, 15 April, 1983.

19 See Goldmann, *Sciences humaines et philosophie*, p. 45.

Chapter 1 Nations

1 'L'oubli, et je dirai même l'erreur historique, sont un facteur essentiel de la création d'une nation . . .' Ernest Renan, 'Qu'est-ce que une nation?', *Oeuvres complètes*, vol. 1 (Paris: Calmann-Lévy, 1947), p. 891.

2 *Nationalism: A Report by a Study Group of Members of the Royal Institute of International Affairs* (London: Frank Cass, 1963 (originally Oxford: Oxford University Press, 1939)), p. 163. E. H. Carr chaired the group.

3 Karl Marx, 'On the Jewish question', in Karl Marx, *Early Writings*, ed. and tr. T. B. Bottomore (New York: McGraw-Hill, 1964), p. 36.

4 John A. Armstrong, *Nations before Nationalism* (Chapel Hill, NC: University of North Carolina Press, 1982)p. 6.

5 Hugh Seton-Watson, *Nations and States* (Boulder, Colo: Westview Press, 1977), p. 5.

6 Leonard Tivey, 'Introduction' to L. Tivey (ed.), *The Nation-State* (Oxford: Martin Robertson, 1971), p. 4.

7 Guido Zernatto, 'Nation: the history of a word', *Review of Politics*, 6 (1944), p. 252.

8 Quoted in Hans Julius Wolff, *Roman Law* (Norman, Okla: University of Oklahoma Press, 1976), pp. 82–3.

9 Johan Huizinga, 'Patriotism and nationalism in European history', in *Men and Ideas: History, the Middle Ages, the Renaissance* (Princeton, NJ: Princeton University Press, 1984), pp. 106–7.

10 Ibid., p. 114.

11 Zernatto, 'Nation', p. 354.

12 Ibid., pp. 356–61.

13 See Seton-Watson, *Nations and States*, p. 8, and Elie Kedourie, *Nationalism* (London: Hutchinson University Library, 1971), p. 13.

14 G. de Bertier de Sauvigny, 'Liberalism, nationalism, and socialism: the birth of three words', *Review of Politics*, April 1970, p. 50.

15 Quoted in ibid., p. 155, my translation. 'A l'instant où les hommes se réunirent en nations . . . ils cessèrent de se reconnaître sous un nom commun. Le *Nationalisme*, ou l'amour national, prit la place de l'amour général.'

16 Ibid., p. 157.

17 Ibid., p. 156.

18 J. G. Herder, *J. G. Herder on Social and Political Culture* (Cambridge: Cambridge University Press, 1969), pp. 165, 284.

19   Isaiah Berlin, 'Herder and the Enlightenment', in *Vico and Herder* (London: Chatto & Windus, 1976), pp. 158, 181.

20   Herder, *Social and Political Culture*, p. 310.

21   Huizinga, 'Patriotism and nationalism', pp. 100–1.

22   de Sauvigny, 'Liberalism, nationalism, and socialism', p. 151.

23   Baron de Montesquieu, *The Spirit of the Laws*, vol. 2 (New York: Hafner Press, 1975) p. 102.

24   Abbé Emmanuel Joseph Sieyès, *Qu'est-ce que le Tiers état?* Edition critique avec une introduction et des notes par Robert Zappperi (Geneva: Librairie Droz, 1970), p. 119.

25   Ibid., pp. 121–6.

26   Ibid., p. 126.

27   Ibid., p. 180.

28   Ibid., pp. 188–9, 184.

29   Tom Nairn, 'The modern Janus', *New Left Review*, November–December 1975, p. 18.

30   L. B. Namier, 'Nationality and liberty', *Avenues of History* (London: Hamish Hamilton, 1952), pp. 21–2.

31   Anthony D. Smith, *Theories of Nationalism* (New York: Holmes & Meier, 1983), p. 16.

32   Johann Gottlieb Fichte, *Addresses to the German Nation* (New York and Evanston, Ill.: Harper Torchbooks, 1968), pp. 171, 191.

33   Namier, 'Nationality and liberty', pp. 21–2.

34   Moses Hess, *Rom und Jerusalem* (henceforth *RJ*), in *Ausgewählte Schriften*, ed. Horst Lademacher (Cologne: Joseph Melzer Verlag, 1962), p. 223.

35   John Emerich Edward Dalberg-Acton, 'Nationality', in his *The History of Freedom and Other Essays* (London: Macmillan, 1907), pp. 270–1.

36   Ibid., p. 273.

37   Acton, 'The history of freedom in antiquity', in ibid., p. 3.

38   John Stuart Mill, *Considerations on Representative Government* (Indianapolis, Ind.: Bobbs-Merrill, 1975), p. 230.'

39   Namier, 'Nationality and liberty', p. 230.

40   Karl Marx, *Grundrisse* (Harmondsworth: Penguin Books, 1973), pp. 84–5.

41   Acton, 'The history of freedom in antiquity', p. 3.

42   Giuseppe Mazzini, 'Dei doveri dell'uomo' (henceforth 'Doveri'), in *Scritti editi ed inediti di Giuseppe Mazzini*, vol. LXIX (Imola: Cooperativa Tipografico-Editrice Paolo Galeati, 1935), p. 59. In English see Joseph Mazzini, 'The duties of man' (Henceforth 'Duties'), in *The Duties of Man and Other Essays* (London and New York: Dent and Dutton, 1910), p. 51.

43   Mazzini, 'Doveri', p. 17; 'Duties', p. 15.

44   Ibid.

45   'La Patria è una communione di liberi e d'equali affratellati in concordia di lavori verso un unico fine . . . La Patria non è un *aggregato*, e una *associazione*', in 'Doveri', p. 66; 'Duties', pp. 56–7.

46   'La Patria sacra in oggi, sparirà forse un giorno, quando ogni uomo rifletterà nella propria coscienza la legge morale dell'Umanità', 'Doveri', p. 72; 'Duties', p. 61.

47   de Sauvigny, 'Liberalism, nationalism, and socialism', p. 160.

48   Mazzini, 'Doveri', p. 46; 'Duties', p. 40.

49   Mazzini, 'Doveri', p. 60; 'Duties', p. 52.

50   Mazzini, 'To the Italians', in *Duties,* p. 244.

51   The city on Mount Moriah is Jerusalem. Hess, *RJ*, p. 223. My own reading of Hess is indebted to Shlomo Avineri's work, and especially his richly suggestive 'Socialism and Judaism in Moses Hess's *The Holy History of Mankind*,' *Review of Politics,* April 1983. This article is incorporated into his full-length study of Hess which appeared after my own chapter was completed. See Shlomo Avineri, *Moses Hess: Prophet of Communism and Zionism* (New York: New York University Press, 1985). On Hess, also see Isaiah Berlin,

'The life and opinions of Moses Hess', in *Against the Current: Essays on the History of Ideas* (New York: Viking Press, 1980) and Jonathan Frankel's chapter on him in *Prophecy and Politics: Socialism, Nationalism, and the Russian Jews, 1862–1917* (Cambridge and New York: Cambridge University Press, 1981).
52 Hess, *RJ*, p. 241.
53 Quoted in Frankel, *Prophecy and Politics*, p. 21.
54 Hess, *RJ*, p. 240.
55 Avineri, 'Socialism and Judaism', p. 235.
56 Moses Hess, 'The young philosophers', in L. P. Stepelevich (ed.), *The Young Hegelians: An Anthology* (Cambridge: Cambridge University Press, 1983), p. 361.
57 Avineri, 'Socialism and Judaism', p. 239.
58 Ibid., pp. 250–2.
59 *RJ*, p. 232.
60 *RJ*, note II, p. 422.
61 *RJ*, p. 232.
62 *RJ*, p. 264.
63 In the late 1850s, however, Mazzini was willing to accept unification in the form of a constitutional monarchy under Victor Emmanuel.
64 See Mazzini, 'To the Italian working class', in *Duties*, and ch. 11 of 'Doveri.'
65 Kedourie, *Nationalism*, p. 9.
66 Hans Kohn, *The Idea of Nationalism* (New York: Macmillan, 1944), p. 4.
67 Karl W. Deutsch, *Nationalism and Its Alternatives* (New York: Knopf, 1969), p. 19.
68 John Plamenatz, 'Two types of nationalism', in Eugene Kamenka (ed.), *Nationalism* (London: Edward Arnold, 1976), pp. 23–4.
69 Otto Bauer, 'The concept of the "nation" ', in T. Bottomore and P. Goode (eds.), *Austro-Marxism* (Oxford: Clarendon Press, 1978), p. 107.
70 Seton-Watson, *Nations and States*, p. 1.
71 Deutsch, *Nationalism and Its Alternatives*, p. 10
72 Ibid., pp. 14–15.
73 Rosa Luxemburg, 'The national question and autonomy', in *The National Question: Selected Writings* (New York and London: Monthly Review Press, 1976), p. 138.
74 V. I. Lenin, 'The right of nations to self-determination', in *Selected Works*, vol. 1 (Moscow: Progress Publishers, 1970), p. 601.
75 Nairn, 'The modern Janus', p. 12.
76 Karl Renner, 'The development of the national idea', in *Austro-Marxism*, ed. T. Bottomore and P. Goode (Oxford: Clarendon Press, 1978), p. 118.
77 Bauer, 'The concept of the "nation" ', p. 104.
78 Ibid., p. 103.
79 Ber Borochov [Borokhov], 'The national question and the class struggle', in Ber Borochov, *Class Struggle and the Jewish Nation: Selected Essays in Marxist Zionism*, ed. with an introduction by Mitchell Cohen (New Brunswick, NJ: Transaction Books, 1984), p. 57.
80 Benedict Anderson, *Imagined Communities: Reflections on the Origins and Spread of Nationalism* (London: Verso Editions, 1983), p. 14. This short volume is undoubtedly one of the most perceptive recent studies on nationalism.
81 Huizinga, 'Patriotism and nationalism', p. 100.
82 Anderson, *Imagined Communities*, pp. 15–17.
83 Otto Jesperson, *Growth and Structure of the English Language* (Chicago: University of Chicago Press, 1982 (1905)), p. 16.
84 Seton-Watson, *Nations and States*, pp. 25–9.
85 Ibid., pp. 42–8.
86 The ensuing discussion closely follows Seton-Watson, *Nations and States*, pp. 77–87.
87 See Nicholas Riasanovsky, *Nicholas I and Official Nationality in Russia 1825–1855* (Berkeley, Calif.: University of California Press, 1959), particularly ch. 3.

88 John A. Armstrong, 'Mobilized and proletarian diasporas', *American Political Science Review*, June 1976, p. 400.
89 Seton-Watson, *Nations and States*, p. 87.
90 See Emiliana Pasca Noether, *Seeds of Italian Nationalism 1700–1815* (New York: Columbia University Press, 1951).
91 Georg Lukács, *The Historical Novel* (Harmondsworth: Penguin Books, 1981), p. 15.
92 Ibid., pp. 20–2.
93 Anderson, *Imagined Communities*, pp. 20–3.
94 Jürgen Habermas, 'Toward a reconstruction of historical materialism', in *Communication and the Evolution of Society* (Boston, Mass.: Beacon Press, 1979).
95 Thomas Carlyle, 'On heroes and hero-worship', in *Selected Writings* (Harmondsworth: Penguin, 1980), p. 244.
96 See Anderson, *Imagined Communities*, ch. 3, which in turn makes extensive use of Lucien Febvre and Henri-Jean Martin, *The Coming of the Book* (London: New Left Books, 1976).
97 Ibid., p. 73.
98 D. J. Enright, *Academic Year* (Oxford and New York: Oxford University Press, 1985), p. 101.
99 Anderson, p. 77.

Chapter 2   Historical Crucible

1 Leo Pinsker, 'Autoemancipation', in *Roads to Freedom: Writings and Addresses* (New York: Scopus Publishing, 1944), p. 88.
2 See John A. Armstrong, 'Mobilized and proletarian diasporas', *American Political Science Review*, June 1976; John A. Armstrong, *Nations before Nationalism* (Chapel Hill, NC: University of North Carolina Press, 1982), pp. 207–11; Hugh Seton-Watson, *Nations and States* (Boulder, Colo: Westview Press, 1977), ch. 10.
3 See Bernard Lewis, 'Semites and anti-Semites', in his *Islam in History* (New York: The Library Press, 1973) for a particularly valuable analysis of the political uses and abuses of these terms.
4 Jacob Katz, *From Prejudice to Destruction: Anti-Semitism 1700–1933* (Cambridge, Mass.: Harvard University Press, 1980), p. 260.
5 Gen. 12:2; Num. 23:9.
6 'Judaism', *Encylopaedia Judaica*, vol. 10 (Jerusalem: Keter, 1972), pp. 383–4; 'Jew', in ibid., pp. 21–2.
7 Gen. 11:6.
8 Gen. 10:5.
9 C. Umhau Wolf, 'Terminology of Israel's tribal organization', *Journal of Biblical Literature*, 65 (1946), p. 45.
10 Gen. 27:29; Isa. 43:9.
11 Exod. 7:16 and 19:5–6.
12 See Avraham Even-Shoshan, *Ha-milon he-hadash* (The New Dictionary) (Jerusalem: Kiryat Sefer, 1972).
13 See Gen. 15:14; Exod. 21:8; Isa. 42:6.
14 Max Weinreich, *History of the Yiddish Language* (Chicago and London: University of Chicago Press, 1980), p. 193.
15 Salo W. Baron, *The Jewish Community*, vol. 1 (Philadelphia, Pa: The Jewish Publication Society of America, 1942), p. 53.
16 Ibid., p. 73.
17 Ibid., pp. 86–7.
18 Ibid., pp. 141–7.

19 Salo W. Baron, *Modern Nationalism and Religion* (New York and London: Harper & Row, 1947), p. 215.
20 Jacob Katz, *Out of the Ghetto: The Social Background of Jewish Emancipation 1770–1870* (New York: Schocken Books, 1978), pp. 1–2.
21 Jacob Katz, *Tradition and Crisis: Jewish Society at the End of the Middle Ages* (New York: Schocken Books, 1971), p. 44.
22 Immanuel Kant, 'An answer to the question: "What is Enlightenment?" ', in H. Reiss (ed.), *Kant's Political Writings* (Cambridge: Cambridge University Press, 1971), p. 54.
23 Gotthold Ephraim Lessing, *Nathan the Wise* (New York: Ungar, 1980), p. 118.
24 Max Horkheimer and Theodor Adorno, *Dialectic of Enlightenment* (New York: Seabury Press, 1972), p. 7.
25 This goes to the root of the problems some on the left have had with the Jewish question and Zionism. By uncritically accepting what is essentially a product of the capitalist era, i.e. the compartmentalization of what it means to be a Jew, they make Judaism strictly into a religion, and thereby, through thoroughly ahistorical premises, deny Jewish peoplehood or nationality.
26 It was precisely the problem of this dual bind that Ben-Gurion, in his notion of 'the new Jew' and 'the new man' mentioned in the preface, hoped Zionism would resolve.
27 See Hugh Seton-Watson, *Nations and States* (Boulder, Colo: Westview Press, 1977), p. 284.
28 Armstrong, 'Mobilized and proletarian diasporas', pp. 393–4 and 405–6.
29 Ibid., p. 394.
30 Armstrong, *Nations before Nationalism*, pp. 7–9 and 293. He derives this term from Ramon d'Abadal i de Vinyals, 'A propos du legs Visigothique en Espagne', in *Settimare di Studio del Centro Italiano di Studi sull'Alt, Medioevo*, 2 (1958), pp. 541–85.
31 Armstrong, 'Mobilized and proletarian diasporas', p. 395.
32 Ibid.
33 Ber Borochov, 'On questions of Zionist theory', in *Class Struggle and the Jewish Nation: Selected Essays in Marxist Zionism*, ed. with an introduction by Mitchell Cohen (New Brunswick, NJ: Transaction Books, 1984), p. 38.
34 Quoted in Arthur Hertzberg, *The French Enlightenment and the Jews* (New York: Schocken Books, 1968), p. 360.
35 Simon Dubnow, *History of the Jews,* vol. 5 (New York and London: Thomas Yoseloff, 1973), p. 143.
36 Katz, *Tradition and Crisis*, p. 3.
37 Gershom Scholem, 'The neutralization of the messianic element in early Hasidism', in *The Messianic Idea in Judaism and Other Essays on Jewish Spirituality* (New York: Schocken Books, 1971), p. 202. This was one of the issues in an ongoing dispute between Scholem and, among others, Martin Buber on the nature and development of Hasidism. The classic study of Sabbatai Sevi is Scholem's *Sabbatai Sevi: The Mystical Messiah* (Princeton, NJ: Princeton University Press, 1973).
38 Steve J. Zipperstein, 'Haskalah, cultural change, and nineteenth century Russian Jewry', *Journal of Jewish Studies*, Fall 1983, p. 193.
39 Louis Greenberg, *The Jews in Russia: The Struggle for Emancipation*, vol. 1 (New York: Schocken Books, 1976), p. 27.
40 I have used a somewhat broad definition of diglossia. C. A. Ferguson, whose work has been especially influential in examining this phenomenon, defined it as follows: 'DIGLOSSIA *is a relatively stable language situation in which, in addition to the primary dialects of the language (which may include standard or regional standards), there is a very divergent, highly codified (often grammatically more complex) superimposed variety, the vehicle of a large and respected body of literature, either of an earlier period or in another speech community, which is learned largely by formal education and is used for most written and formal spoken purposes but is not used by any sector of the community*

for ordinary conversation.' C. A. Ferguson, 'Diglossia', in Paolo Giglioli (ed.), *Language and Social Context* (New York: Penguin Books, 1982), p. 245.

41 On the relation between language, nationalism and notions of ethnocultural identity, see Joshua A. Fishman, *Language and Nationalism* (Rowley, Mass.: Newbury House Publications, 1972), pp. 43–6.

42 Chaim Rabin, 'Language revival: colloquialism or pluralism?',*Jewish Frontier*, September 1958, pp. 11–12. My discussion here is also particularly indebted to Rabin's 'The national idea and the revival of Hebrew', *Studies in Zionism*, Spring 1983.

43 This is pointed out in David Patterson, 'Revival of literature and revival of language', in Eisig Silberschlag (ed.), *Eliezer Ben Yehuda: A Symposium* (henceforth *EBY*) (Oxford: Oxford Centre for Postgraduate Hebrew Studies, 1981), p. 20.

44 See ibid., pp. 19–22.

45 David Ben-Gurion, *Zikhronot* (Memoirs), vol. 1 (Tel Aviv: Am Oved, 1976), p. 10.

46 Eliezer Ben-Yehudah, 'A weighty question', in *EBY*, pp. 2–3.

47 Eliezer Ben-Yehudah, 'A letter of Ben-Yehudah', in Arthur Hertzberg, (ed.), *The Zionist Idea* (New York: Atheneum, 1969), p. 161.

48 Ibid., p. 164.

49 Quoted in Jonathan Frankel, *Prophecy and Politics: Socialism, Nationalism, and the Russian Jews, 1862–1917* (Cambridge and New York: Cambridge University Press, 1981), p. 98. My discussion of 1880s is indebted to Frankel's invaluable analysis.

50 Shmarya Levin, *Youth in Revolt* (New York: Harcourt, Brace, 1930), p. 24.

51 Ibid., p. 9.

52 Chaim Chissin [Haim Hissin], *A Palestine Diary: Memoirs of a Bilu Pioneer 1882–1887* (New York: Herzl Press, 1976), p. 31.

53 Chaim [Haim] Weizmann, *Trial and Error: The Autobiography of Chaim Weizmann* (New York: Schocken Books, 1966), p. 17.

54 Frankel, *Prophecy and Politics*, pp. 50–1.

55 Shmarya Levin, *The Arena* (New York: Harcourt, Brace, 1932), p. 6.

56 Frankel, *Prophecy and Politics*, pp. 50–1.

57 Levin, *The Arena*, p. 3.

58 Joseph LaPalombara and Myron Weiner, 'The origins and development of political parties', in LaPalombara and Weiner (eds.), *Political Parties and Political Development* (Princeton, NJ: Princeton University Press, 1966), pp. 3–4.

59 Pinsker, 'Autoemancipation', p. 75.

60 Ibid., p. 77.

61 Ibid., pp. 83–4.

62 Ibid., p. 94.

63 Pinsker, Letter to A. L. Levanda, 26 October, 1883, in *Roads*, pp. 107–8.

64 Pinsker, 'Opening address to the Kattowitz conference', 6 November, 1884, in *Roads*, pp. 107–8.

65 Ibid., p. 108.

66 Chissin, *A Palestine Diary*, p. 33. On the BILU also see, Shulamit Laskov, 'The Biluim: reality and legend (with selected documents)', *Zionism*, Spring 1981; David Vital, *The Origins of Zionism* (Oxford: Oxford University Press, 1975); David Ben-Gurion, 'First ones', *Israel Government Yearbook 5723* (1962–3) 'Jerusalem, 1963'.

67 Chissin, *A Palestine Diary*, p. 103.

68 Ibid., p. 146.

Chapter 3 Kernel and Shell

1 Ahad Ha-am, 'Sacred and profane', *Selected Essays of Ahad Ha-am* (New York: Atheneum, 1962), p. 41.

2 Theodor Herzl, Entry of 3 September, 1897, *The Complete Diaries of Theodor Herzl*, vol. 2 (New York and London: Herzl Press and Thomas Yoseloff, 1960), p. 581.
3 Ahad Ha-am, 'The first Zionist Congress', in Ahad Ha-am, *Ten Essays on Zionism and Judaism* (London: Routeledge, 1922), p. 30.
4 Ben Halpern, *The Idea of the Jewish State*, 2nd edn (Cambridge, Masso., London: Harvard University Press, 1969), p. 25.
5 Ahad Ha-am, 'Reminiscences', in Ahad Ha-am, *Essays, Letters, Memoirs* (Oxford: East and West Library, 1946), p. 333.
6 Ahad Ha-am, 'The wrong way', in *Ten Essays*, p. 1.
7 Ahad Ha-am, 'Moses', in *Nationalism and the Jewish Ethic: Basic Writings of Ahad Ha-am* (New York: Schocken Books, 1962), pp. 208–9.
8 Ahad Ha-am, 'The first Zionist Congress', in *Ten Essays*, p. 31.
9 Ahad Ha-am, 'Slavery in freedom', in *Nationalism and the Jewish Ethic*, pp. 64–5.
10 Herzl, Entry of 5 July, 1895, *Complete Diaries*, vol. 1, p. 196.
11 Herzl, Entry dated 'Around Pentacost, 1895', *Complete Diaries*, vol. 1, p. 7.
12 Quoted in Alex Bein, *Theodore Herzl* (New York: Atheneum, 1970), pp. 115–16.
13 Herzl, Entry of 6 July, 1895, *Complete Diaries*, vol. 1, p. 196.
14 Max Weber, 'Politics as a vocation', in H. H. Gerth and C. Wright Mills (eds.), *From Max Weber* (New York: Oxford University Press, 1946), p. 84.
15 Herzl, Letter to Zaduc Kahn, 16 September, 1896, in *Complete Diaries*, vol 2, p. 467.
16 Herzl, Entry of 2 May, 1901, *Complete Diaries*, vol. 3, p. 1089.
17 Ahad Ha-am, 'The Wrong Way', in *Ten Essays*, p. 8.
18 Herzl, Entry of 23 February, 1896, *Complete Diaries*, vol. 1, p. 306.
19 Ahad Ha-am, 'The Jewish question and the Jewish state', in *Nationalism and the Jewish Ethic*, pp. 79–80.
20 Ibid.
21 Ahad Ha-am, 'Positive and negative', in *Selected Essays of Ahad Ha-am*, p. 66.
22 Theodor Herzl, *The Jewish State* (New York: Herzl Press, 1970), p. 51.
23 Theodor Herzl, 'Practical and political Zionists', in Theodor Herzl, *Zionist Writings: Essays and Addresses*, vol. 2 (1898–1904) (New York: Herzl Press, 1975), p. 131.
24 Herzl, Entry of 28 June, 1895, *Complete Diaries*, vol. 1, p. 191.
25 Herzl, *The Jewish State*, pp. 50–1.
26 David Vital, *Zionism: The Formative Years* (Oxford: Oxford University Press, 1982), p. 3.
27 David Vital, *The Origins of Zionism* (Oxford: Oxford University Press, 1975), p. 358.
28 Herzl, Entry of 10 July, 1895, *Complete Diaries*, vol. 1, p. 198.
29 Nachman [Nahman] Syrkin, 'Beginnings of socialist Zionism', in Marie Syrkin, *Nachman Syrkin, Socialist Zionist: A Biographical Memoir with Selected Essays* (New York: Herzl Press, 1960), p. 239.
30 'The Basle Declaration', in J. C. Hurwitz (ed.), *The Middle East and North Africa in World Politics: A Documentary Record*, vol. 1: 1535–1914 (New Haven, Con., and London: Yale University Press, 1975), p. 466.
31 Vital, *Origins*, p. 365.
32 See Maurice Duverger, *Political Parties* (London: Methuen, 1964), especially the introduction.
33 Quoted in Jehuda Reinharz, *Chaim Weizmann: The Making of a Zionist Leader* (Oxford: Oxford University Press, 1985), p. 91. This, the first volume of Weizmann's official biography, provides an exceptionally useful analysis of the Democratic Faction's role in early Zionist politics.
34 Ibid., p. 195.
35 'On the functions of the Congress' in *The Letters and Papers of Chaim Weizmann*, vol. 1, series B, Papers, August 1898–1931 (New Brunswick, NJ, and Jerusalem: Transaction Books and Israel Universities Press, 1983), p. 12.

36 See Reinharz, *Chaim Weizmann*, p. 88.
37 Giovanni Sartori, *Parties and Party Systems*, vol. 1. (Cambridge: Cambridge University Press, 1976), p. 16.
38 See Gerhard Loewenberg and Samuel C. Patterson, *Comparing Legislatures* (Boston, Mass., and Toronto: Little, Brown, 1979), p. 7.
39 Duverger, *Political Parties*, p. xxx.
40 Ibid., pp. xxxiv–xxxvi.
41 See Moshe Burstein, *Self-Government of the Jews in Palestine since 1900* (Tel Aviv: Ha-Poel ha-Tsair, 1934), pp. 69–70.
42 See 'Jewish Community Regulations, 1927', *Official Gazette of the Government of Palestine* (Jerusalem), no. 202, 1 January, 1928, pp. 10–14.
43 'The Mandate for Palestine, 22 July 1922', in J. C. Hurwitz (ed.), *The Middle East and North Africa in World Politics: A Documentary Record*, vol. 2: 1914–45. (New Haven, Conn., and London: Yale University Press, 1979), p. 306.
44 See the section marked 'Confidential' in *The Development of the Jewish National Home in Palestine: Memorandum submitted to His Majesty's Government by the Jewish Agency for Palestine, 1930* (London: Jewish Agency, 1930), p. 76.
45 For instance, Yonathan Shapiro makes numerous comparisons with Russia and the Soviet Union in *The Formative Years of the Israeli Labour Party: The Organization of Power 1919–1930* (London and Beverly Hills, Calif.: Sage Publications, 1976).
46 Of course, the Americans were nurtured in a political culture very different from Russia's as well.
47 Loewenberg and Patterson, *Comparing Legislatures*, p. 14.
48 Ibid., p. 295.
49 'The complementary tasks of political and practical Zionism', in *The Letters and Papers of Chaim Weizmann*, vol. 1, series B, Papers, August 1898 – July 1931 (New Brunswick, NJ and Jerusalem: Transaction Books and Israel Universities Press, 1983), pp. 70–1.
50 Reinharz, *Chaim Weizmann*, pp. 291–3. Also see pp. 307–10 and p. 493 n. 15 for an important discussion of the different claims about the origins of 'synthetic Zionism'.
51 Shmarya Levin, *The Arena* (New York: Harcourt, Brace, 1932), p. 183.
52 For the debate on the 'Uganda Plan' see Michael Heymann, (ed.), *The Uganda Controversy: Minutes of the Zionist General Council*, 2 vols (Tel Aviv and Jerusalem: Israel Universities Press, Tel Aviv University and the World Zionist Organization/Hassifriya Hazionist, 1977).
53 The letter is reproduced in Herzl, *Zionist Writings*, vol. 2, p. 231.
54 Theodor Herzl, 'Reply', in ibid., p. 234.
55 Ibid., pp. 234–5.
56 Shmarya Levin, *The Arena*, p. 184.
57 Menahem Mendel Ussishkin, *Our Program* (New York: Federation of American Zionists, 1905), pp. 1–2.
58 Ibid., p. 27.
59 Quoted in Jonathan Frankel, *Prophecy and Politics: Socialism, Nationalism, and the Russian Jews, 1862–1917* (Cambridge and New York: Cambridge University Press, 1981), p. 48.

Chapter 4   From a Working Class to a Working Nation

1 Y. H. Brenner, 'Self-criticism', in Arthur Hertzberg (ed.), *The Zionist Idea* (New York: Atheneum, 1969), p. 312.
2 'Ha-interesim shel ha-poalim ve-ha-interesim ha-leumiyim ha-klaliyim – hem haynu hakh.' David Ben-Gurion, 'Ha-pekidut ve-ha-poalim' (Officialdom and the Workers), *Yalkut ha-Ahdut 1907–1919* (Tel Aviv: Am Oved, 1962), p. 174.

3   'The national goal of the working class is the transformation from a working class to a
    working nation. (*Lihiot mi-maamad oved le-am oved zeh yiudo ha-leumi shel maamad
    ha-poalim.*) David Ben-Gurion, 'Hiluf mishmarot' (Changing of the Guards), *Davar*, 15
    January, 1929, p. 2.
4   Karl Marx and Friedrich Engels, *The German Ideology*, in R. C. Tucker (ed.), *The
    Marx-Engels Reader* (New York: Norton, 1972), pp. 136–7.
5   Ibid., p. 137.
6   Nachman (Nahman) Syrkin, 'The socialist Jewish state, 1898', in Marie Syrkin, *Nachman
    Syrkin, Socialist Zionist: A Biographical Memoir with Selected Essays* (New York: Herzl
    Press, 1960), p. 248.
7   Ibid., p. 267.
8   Ibid., p. 284.
9   Nahman Syrkin, 'Call to Jewish youth: 1901', in ibid., p. 303.
10 Ibid., p. 304.
11 Syrkin, 'The socialist Jewish state, 1898', p. 288.
12 On the Bund see, Jonathan Frankel, *Prophecy and Politics: Socialism, Nationalism, and the
    Russian Jews, 1862–1917* (Cambridge: Cambridge University Press, 1981), and Henry J.
    Tobias, *The Jewish Bund in Russia* (Stanford, Calif.: Stanford University Press, 1971).
13 Frankel, *Prophecy and Politics*, p. 140.
14 Quoted in Frankel, p. 322.
15 For a detailed analysis of these events see ibid., ch. 3.
16 Ibid., p. 169.
17 On these various groups see Frankel, *Prophecy and Politics*, chs. 3–7, and Oscar I.
    Janowsky, *The Jews and Minority Rights 1898–1919* (New York: AMS Press, 1966). On
    the ZS see Alexander Guterman, *Ha-Miflgah ha-tsionit-sotsialistit be-russya (S.S.)
    ba-shanim 1905–1906* (The Socialist Zionist Party in Russia in 1905–1906) (Tel Aviv: I. L.
    Peretz Publishing House, 1985).
18 The authoritative study of Borokhov's development is Mattityahu Mintz, *Ber Borokhov:
    Ha-maagal ha-rishon* (Ber Borokhov: The First Circle) (Tel Aviv: Tel Aviv University and
    Ha-Kibbutz ha-Meuhad, 1976).
19 Itzhak Ben-Zvi, 'Labor Zionism in Russia', in J. Frumkin, G. Aronson and A. Goldenweiser
    (eds.), *Russian Jewry 1860–1917* (New York: Thomas Yoseloff, 1966), p. 218. On Poale
    Zion in Russia see Mattityahu Mintz, 'Mifleget ha-poalim ha-sotsial-demokratit ha-yehudit
    poalei tsiyon bein Poltava u-Krakov (The Jewish Social Democratic Workers' Party Poale
    Zion between Poltava and Cracow)', in M. Mintz (ed.), *Veidat Krakov shel mifleget
    ha-poalim ha-sotsial-demokratit ha-yehudit poalei tsiyon be-Russiya August 1907 –
    Teudot* (The Cracow Conference of the Jewish Social Democratic Workers' Party Poale
    Zion in Russia, August 1907 – Documents) (Ramat Aviv: Tel Aviv University, 1979);
    Mattityahu Mintz, 'Introduction', in *Ha-veidah ha-shlishit shel poalei tsiyon be-russiya,
    1917 – Teudot* (The Third Conference of Poale Zion in Russia, 1917 – Documents) (Ramat
    Aviv: Tel Aviv University, 1976).
20 Ber Borochov (Borokhov), 'Our platform', in Ber Borochov, *Class Struggle and the Jewish
    Nation: Selected Essays in Marxist Zionism*, ed. with an introduction by Mitchell Cohen
    (New Brunswick, NJ: Transaction Books, 1984), p. 85.
21 See Borochov's 'The national question and the class struggle', in Borochov, *Class Struggle
    and the Jewish Nation*.
22 'Our Platform', p. 89.
23 Borochov, 'The economic development of the Jewish people', in *Class Struggle and the
    Jewish Nation*, p. 173.
24 'Our Platform', p. 91.
25 Ibid., p. 101.
26 Shlomo Avineri, 'Political and social aspects of Israeli and Arab nationalism', in Eugene
    Kamenka (ed.), *Nationalism* (London: Edward Arnold, 1976), p. 116.

27 Walter Preuss, *The Labour Movement in Israel* (Jerusalem: Rubin Mass, 1965), pp. 40–1.
28 Frankel, *Prophecy and Politics*, p. 366.
29 Berl Katznelson, *My Way to Palestine* (London: Hechalutz/Poale Zion, 1946), p. 26.
30 I summarize from Yosef Gorni, 'Changes in the social and political structure of the Second Aliya between 1904 and 1940', in D. Caspi and G. Yogev (eds.), *Zionism: Studies in the History of the Zionist movement and of the Jewish Community in Palestine*, vol. 1 (Tel Aviv: Massada and Tel Aviv University, 1975), pp. 49–90. The survey was conducted in the late 1930s and early 1940s.
31 David Ben-Gurion, 'Parashat ha-derakhim' (Parting of the Ways), in David Ben-Gurion, *Mi-maamad le-am* (From a Class to a Nation) (Tel Aviv: Am Oved and Keren ha-Negev, 1974 (originally: Tel Aviv: Davar, 1933), pp. 13–14. The occasion was a lecture to the Poale Zion conference in Cleveland, Ohio, November 1915.
32 David Ben-Gurion, 'Matan Erets' (Giving a Land), in *Mi-maamad*, pp. 9–10.
33 'Mikhtav me-erets israel' (Letter from the Land of Israel), in Yehudah Slutsky (ed.), *Poalei Tsiyon be-erets israel 1905–1919: Teudot* (Poale Zion in the Land of Israel 1905–1919: Documents) (Ramat Aviv: Tel Aviv University, 1978), p. 17.
34 'Ha-platformah ha-ramlit (The Ramle Platform)', in ibid., p. 17.
35 'Hatsaat tokhnit' (Proposed Program), in ibid., p. 19.
36 Preuss, *Labor Movement*, p. 41; Slutsky, 'Introduction' in *Poalei tsiyon be-erets israel*, pp. 8–11.
37 Quoted in Yosi Beilin, *Mehiro shel ihud: Mifleget ha-avodah ad milhemet yom ha-kipurim* (The Price of Unity: The Labour Party until the Yom Kippur War) (Israel: Revivim, 1985).
38 Hapoel Hatsair, 'Our Goals', in Paul R. Mendes-Flohr and Yehuda Reinharz (eds.), *The Jew in the Modern World: A Documentary History* (New York and Oxford: Oxford University Press, 1980), p. 445.
39 Beilin, *Mehiro shel ihud*, p. 171.
40 A. D. Gordon, 'Labour', in A. D. Gordon, *Selected Essays* (New York: The League for Labor Palestine, 1938), p. 56.
41 Ibid., p. 58.
42 Franz Oppenheimer, *Cooperative Agricultural Colonization in Palestine* (New York: Federation of American Zionists, 1910), pp. 3–5.
43 Y. Slutsky, 'Introduction' to Y. Slutsky (ed.), *Poalei tsiyon be-erets israel*, p. 9.
44 Ibid., pp. 9–12. Also see chapter 19 in Slutsky's *Mavo le-toldot tnuat ha-avodah ha-israelit* (Introduction to the History of the Israeli Labour Movement) (Tel Aviv: Am Oved, 1973).
45 Rahel Yanait Ben Zvi (Ben-Tsvi), *Coming Home* (New York: Herzl Press, 1964), p. 96.
46 Ber Borokhov, 'Ha-avodah be-erets israel' (The Work in the Land of Israel), in Borokhov's *Ktavim* (Writings), vol. 2 (Tel Aviv: Sifriyat Poalim and Ha-Kibbutz ha-Meuhad, 1958), p. 210. Despite his dogmatism at this time, Borokhov later changed his position to one sympathetic to socialist settlements. See his speech to the third Congress of the Russian Poale Zion in 1917, 'Erets Israel in our program and tactics', in *Class Struggle and the Jewish Nation*.
47 Beilin, *Mehiro shel ihud*, p. 170.
48 Israel Kolatt, 'Zionist Marxism', in Shlomo Avineri (ed.), *Varieties of Marxism* (The Hague: Nijhoff, 1977), pp. 241–2.
49 Anita Shapira, 'Origins of the "Jewish Labor" ideology', *Studies in Zionism*, Spring 1982, p. 106.
50 Arthur Ruppin, 'The Kvutsah', in *Three Decades in Palestine* (Jerusalem: Schocken Books, 1936), pp. 132–3.
51 Karl Marx and Friedrich Engels, 'Preface to the Russian edition of 1882' of the *Manifesto of the Communist Party*, in R. C. Tucker (ed.), *The Marx-Engels Reader* (New York: Norton, 1972), p. 334.

52 Walter Laqueur, *A History of Zionism* (New York: Holt, Rinehart & Winston, 1972), p. 288.
53 David Ben-Gurion, *Zikhronot* (Memoirs), vol. 1 (Tel Aviv: Am Oved, 1976), pp. 66–7.
54 'The Balfour Declaration', in J. C. Hurwitz (ed.), *The Middle East and North Africa in World Politics: A Documentary Record*, vol. 2 (New Haven, Conn., and London: Yale University Press, 1979), p. 106.

Chapter 5   Labour's Road to Dominance I

1 Karl Marx, in Marx and Engels, *The Holy Family*, in Karl Marx and Frederick Engels, *Collected Works*, vol. 4 (New York: International Publishers, 1975), p. 37.
2 There is a historiographical debate on the extent of continuity and discontinuity among the ideological and organizational forms of Labour in the prewar and postwar periods. For a summary and analysis see chapter 1 of Yosef Gorni, *Ahdut ha-Avodah 1919–1930: Ha-yesodot ha-raayoniyim ve-ha-shitah ha-medinit* (Ahdut ha-Avodah 1919–1930: The Ideological Principles and the Political System) (Tel Aviv: Tel Aviv University and Ha-Kibbutz ha-Meuhad, 1973). On the general problems of unification see especially ibid., pp. 21–33; Yonathan Shapiro, *The Formative Years of the Israeli Labour Party: The Organization of Power 1919–1930* (London and Beverly Hills, Calif.: Sage Publications, 1976), pp. 23–36; Shabtai Tevet, *Kinat David: Ben-Gurion ha-tsair* (David's Zeal: The Young Ben-Gurion) (Jerusalem and Tel Aviv: Schocken Books, 1976), pp. 439–67.
3 Tevet, *Kinat David*, p. 439.
4 Gorni, *Ahdut ha-Avodah*, pp. 18–21.
5 Tevet, *Kinat David*, pp. 455–7.
6 Gorni, *Ahdut ha-Avodah*, pp. 28–31.
7 David Ben-Gurion, *Zikhronot* (Memoirs), vol. 1 (Tel Aviv: Am Oved, 1976), p. 112; Anita Shapira, *Berl: The Biography of a Socialist Zionist – Berl Katznelson 1887–1944* (Cambridge: Cambridge University Press, 1984), pp. 85–90.
8 Y. Shapiro, *Formative Years*, pp. 29–30. Also see Gorni, *Ahdut ha-Avodah*, p. 186.
9 Ibid., p. 187.
10 See Israel Kolatt, 'The concept of the Histadrut: emergence and change 1920–1948', in *Labor and Society in Israel* (Tel Aviv: Tel Aviv University Department of Labour Studies and the Histadrut Department of Higher Education, 1973), p. 204.
11 Gorni, *Ahdut ha-Avodah*, p. 188.
12 Minutes of the Ahdut ha-Avodah Central Committee, 14 August, 1921. LA. Also see Y. Shapiro, *Formative Years*, p. 57, which brought this remark to my attention.
13 Ben-Gurion, *Zikhronot*, vol. 1, p. 204.
14 Yosi Beilin, *Mehiro shel ihud: mifleget ha-avodah ad milhemet yom ha-kipurim* (The Price of Unity: The Labour Party until the Yom Kippur War)(Israel: Revivim, 1985), p. 202.
15 David Ben-Gurion, 'Ha-Histadrut ve-ha-miflagah le-ahar ha-ihud (The Histadrut and the Party after Unification)', *Ha-Poel ha-Tsair*, 21 February, 1930.
16 M. S. (Moshe Shertok), 'Ten years of the Histadrut', *Davar (English) Supplement* (henceforth, *Davar Sup.*), 31 December, 1930, p. 2.
17 Y. Shapiro, *Formative Years*, p. 50.
18 Quoted in Shabtai Teveth, *Ben-Gurion and the Palestinian Arabs* (Oxford: Oxford University Press, 1985), p. 41.
19 See the discussion in Y. Shapiro, *Formative Years*, pp. 2–4.
20 Ben-Gurion, *Zikhronot*, vol. 1, pp. 245–6.
21 Ibid., pp. 254–5.
22 Ibid., p. 268.
23 See Y. Shapiro, *Formative Years*, pp. 43–67 and 99.
24 Quoted in Anita Shapira, '"The Left" in the Gdud Ha'avoda (Labor Brigade) and the

Palestine Communist Party until 1928', in D. Caspi and G. Yogev (eds)., *Zionism: Studies in the History of the Zionist Movement and of the Jewish Community in Palestine*, vol. 1 (Tel Aviv: Massada and Tel Aviv University, 1975), p. 130.

25 Anita Shapira, 'Gedud ha-Avodah: a dream that failed', *Jerusalem Quarterly*, 30 (Winter 1984), p. 64.

26 Y. Shapiro, *Formative Years*, pp. 100–1.

27 See the two articles by Anita Shapira cited above, on which I have based this account of the Gdud ha-Avodah, for a discussion of the fate of Elkind and his backers.

28 Walter Laqueur, *A History of Zionism* (New York: Holt, Rinehart & Winston, 1972), pp. 320–1.

29 See D. Weintraub, M. Lissak and Y. Azmon, *Moshava, Kibbutz, and Moshav* (Ithaca, NY, and London: Cornell University Press, 1969), pp. 80–7.

30 David Ben-Gurion, 'On the Histadrut and the parties, Part 1: On the Histadrut platform', *Kuntres*, 2 January 1925, p. 17.

31 David Ben-Gurion, 'Ha-histadrut ha-maamad o federatsiya shel miflagot? (The Histadrut: A Class or a Federation of Parties?), *Kuntres*, 9 January, 1925, p. 5.

32 David Ben-Gurion, 'Ahdut ha-Avodah ve-ha-Histadrut' (Ahdut ha-Avodah and the Histadrut), *Kuntres*, 6 February, 1925, pp. 9–10.

33 Ibid., p. 10.

34 Ibid., p. 11.

35 By the third Congress of the Histadrut (July 1927), its members composed 23.9 per cent of the Palestinian Jewish population. Ben-Gurion, *Zikhronot*, vol. 1, p. 308. According to the statistics of the Zionist Organization, in 1927 there were 147,789 Jews in the country, composing 16.3 per cent of the total population. Of these, there were 34,000 workers, of whom 22,538 were Histadrut members (as opposed to 8,394 members in 1922). *Report of the Executive of the Zionist Organisation submitted to the XVth Zionist Congress at Basle, August 30–September 9 1927* (London: Central Office of the Zionist Organization, 1927), p. 245.

36 Moshe Burstein, *Self-Government of the Jews in Palestine since 1900* (Tel Aviv: Ha-Poel ha-Tsair, 1934), pp. 98–105, 110–12, 119–20.

37 Y. Shapiro, *Formative Years*, p. 140; *Report of the Executive of the Zionist Organisation, 1927*, p. 247; Dan Horowitz and Moshe Lissak, *Origins of the Israeli Polity: Palestine under the Mandate* (Chicago: University of Chicago Press, 1978), p. 20.

38 Beilin, *Mehiro shel ihud*, p. 172.

39 Haim Arlosoroff, 'Milhemet ha-maamadot ba-metsiut ha-erets israelit' (Class War in the Reality of the Land of Israel), in Haim Arlosoroff, *Mivhar ktavim u-firkei haim* (Selected Writings and Chapters of His Life) (Tel Aviv: Am Oved, 1958), pp. 54–5.

40 Ibid., p. 55.

41 Ibid., p. 56.

42 Ibid., pp. 57–8.

43 Ibid., p. 58.

44 Ibid., p. 59.

Chapter 6 Labour's Road to Dominance II

1 Ber Borochov, 'Facing reality', in Ber Bororchov, *Class Struggle and the Jewish Nation: Selected Essays in Marxist Zionism*, ed. Mitchell Cohen (New Brunswick, NJ: Transaction Books, 1984), p. 198.

2 Ezra Mendelsohnn, *Zionism in Poland: The Formative Years, 1915–1926* (New Haven, Conn., and London: Yale University Press, 1981), pp. 256–7.

3 Dan Giladi, 'The economic crisis during the Fourth Aliya (1926–1927)' in D. Caspi and G. Yogev (eds.), *Zionism: Studies in the History of the Zionist Movement and the Jewish*

Community in Palestine, vol. 1 (Tel Aviv: Massada and Tel Aviv University Press, 1975), p. 163.

4   David Ben-Gurion, *Zikhronot* (Memoirs), vol. 1 (Tel Aviv: Am Oved, 1976), p. 335.

5   For a summary of the debates see Giladi, 'The economic crisis during the Fourth Aliya.'

6   N. Tversky, 'Me-asefat ha-vaad ha-poel be-london' (From the Meeting of the General Council in London), *Ha-Poel ha-Tsair*, 33–4 (1927), p. 5.

7   Meir Dizengoff, *Report on Urban Colonisation submitted to the XVth Zionist Congress* (Tel Aviv, 1927), p. 21. ZAL.

8   Yosi Beilin, *Mehiro shel ihud: Mifleget ha-avodah ad milhemet yom ha-kipurim* (The Price of Unity: The Labour Party until the Yom Kipur War) (Israel: Revivim, 1985), p. 169.

9   See Walter Laqueur, *A History of Zionism* (New York: Holt, Rinehart & Winston, 1972), pp. 458–9, and Yonathan Shapiro, *The Formative Years of the Israeli Labour Party: The Organization of Power 1919–1930* (London and Beverly Hills, Calif.: Sage Publications, 1976), p. 73.

10 Chaim Weizmann, 'Earliest impressions of Palestine', in *The Letters and Papers of Chaim Weizmann*, vol. 1, series B, Papers, August 1898–July 1931 (New Brunswick, NJ, and Jerusalem: Transaction Books and Israel Universities Press, 1983), p. 72.

11 Arthur Ruppin, 'A period of crisis', in *Three Decades in Palestine* (Jerusalem: Schocken Books, 1936), p. 153.

12 Ibid., pp.154–5.

13 Ibid., p.157.

14 Ibid., pp. 158–9.

15 See *Report of the Experts submitted to the Joint Palestine Survey Commission*, Boston, Mass., 1 October, 1928. ZAL.

16 'Proceedings of the General Council of the Zionist Organization, Berlin, 19–21 July 1928', *New Judaea*, 31 August, 1928, p. 244.

17 David Ben-Gurion, 'Hiluf mishmarot' (Changing of the Guards), 1, *Davar*, 15 January, 1929, p. 2.

18 David Ben-Gurion, 'Hiluf mishmarot' (Changing of the Guards), 2, *Davar*, 16 January, 1929, p. 2.

19 David Ben-Gurion, 'Ha-mashber ba-tsiyonut u-tnuat ha-poalim' (The Crisis in Zionism and the Workers' Movement), in David Ben-Gurion, *Mi-maamad le-am* (From a Class to a Nation) (Tel Aviv: Am Oved and Keren ha-Negev, 1974), pp. 240–1.

20 For an analysis of the sums involved, see A. Ulitzur, *Ha-hon ha-leumi u-binyan ha-arets* (National Capital and Building the Country) (Jerusalem: Keren Ha-Yesod, 1939), and A. Ulitsur, 'Report on the Capital Invested by Jewish National and Public Funds from 1918–1936', Report to the Jewish Agency, 27 October, 1936, in mimeograph at ZAL. Also see the discussion in chapter 2 of Baruch Kimmerling, *Zionism and Economy* (Cambridge, Mass.: Schenkman, 1983).

21 Ibid., p. xiii.

22 Ben-Gurion, 'Ha-mashber ba-tsiyonut', pp. 241–2. Jews then composed less than 20 per cent of the population of Palestine.

23 See Shapiro, *Formative Years*, p. 191.

24 See Beilin, *Mehiro shel ihud* , pp. 195–6; Haim Arlosoroff, 'Ha-Miflagah ve-ha-histadrut', (The party and the Histadrut), in Haim Arlosoroff, *Mivhar ktavim u-firkei haim* (Selected Writings and Chapters of His Life) (Tel Aviv: Am Oved, 1958), pp. 73–4.

25 Beilin, *Mehiro shel ihud*, pp. 195–7; Laqueur, *A History of Zionism*, p. 317.

26 See Beilin, *Mehiro shel ihud*, p. 209. Beilin argues that these procedures had a critical, and at times very deleterious, impact on the party's ability to act in several important circumstances.

27 David Ben-Gurion, 'Ha-Histadrut ve-ha-miflagah le-ahar ha-ihud' (The Histadrut and the Party after Unification), 2, *Ha-Poel ha-Tsair*, 21 February, 1930, p. 2.

28 Maurice Duverger, *Political Parties* (London: Methuen, 1964), pp. 307–8. Among the

numerous studies concerned with dominance in Israeli politics and political history, see Alan Arian and Samuel H. Barnes, 'The dominant party system: a neglected model of democratic stability', *Journal of Politics*, August 1974; Alan Arian, *Ideological Change in Israel* (Cleveland, Ohio: Case Western Reserve University Press, 1968); Asher Arian, *The Choosing People: Voting Behavior in Israel* (Cleveland, Ohio: Case Western Reserve University Press, 1973); Ariel Levite and Sidney Tarrow, 'The legitimation of excluded parties in dominant party systems: a comparison of Israel and Italy', *Comparative Politics*, April 1983; Shapiro's *Formative Years*, and his 'The end of a dominant party system', in A. Arian (ed.), *The Elections in Israel, 1977* (Jerusalem: Jerusalem Academic Press, 1980).

29   For a study especially preoccupied with this question, see Dan Horowitz and Moshe Lissak, *Origins of the Israeli Polity: Palestine under the Mandate* (Chicago and London: University of Chicago Press, 1978).

30   Duverger, *Political Parties*, p. 307.

31   Marx and Engels, *Manifesto of the Communist Party*, in R. C. Tucker (ed.), *The Marx-Engels Reader* (New York: Norton, 1972), p. 351.

32   Antonio Gramsci, 'Notes on Italian history', in Antonio Gramsci, *Selections from the Prison Notebooks* (New York: International Publishers, 1971), pp. 57–8.

33   Antonio Gramsci, 'The modern prince', in *Selections from the Prison Notebooks*, p. 161.

34   Yosef Gorni, *Ahdut ha-Avodah 1919–1930: ha-yesodot ha-raayoniyim ve-ha-shitah ha-medinit* (Ahdut ha-Avodah 1919–1930: The Ideological Principles and the Political System) (Tel Aviv: Tel Aviv University and Ha-Kibbutz ha-Meutad, 1973), p. 59.

35   Val R. Lorwin, 'Segmented pluralism', *Comparative Politics*, 3, 2, (January 1971), p. 142.

36   Anson Rabinbach, *The Crisis of Austrian Socialism* (Chicago and London: University of Chicago Press, 1983), pp. 26–7; Josef Weidenholzer, 'Red Vienna: a new Atlantis?', in Anson Rabinbach (ed.), *The Austrian Socialist Experiment: Social Democracy and Austro-Marxism 1918–1934* (Boulder, Colo., and London: Westview Press, 1985), p. 208. Also see Frederick C. Engelmann, 'Austria: the pooling of opposition', in Robert Dahl (ed.), *Political Opposition in Western Democracies* (New Haven, Conn., and London: Yale University Press, 1966).

37   Rabinbach, *Crisis*, p. 28.

38   Ibid., pp. 27–8; Peter Marcuse, 'The housing policy of Social Democracy: determinants and consequences', in Rabinbach (ed.), *Austrian Socialist Experiment*, p. 208.

39   Some of the Austrian socialists had ties to the Zionist left. Although Bauer was a champion of assimilation, Max Adler and Julius Braunthal expressed interest in Zionism and admiration for Labour Zionism. In 1931 Adler, his party's most sophisticated philosopher and a leading radical, wrote a foreword for a publication by the Zionist Socialist youth movement, Ha-Shomer ha-Tsair (Young Guard), and two years later he addressed a 25th anniversary meeting of Poale Zion in Vienna. Various party publications occasionally printed articles sympathetic to Labor Zionism. See Jack Jacobs, 'Austrian Social Democracy and the Jewish question in the First Republic', in Rabinbach (ed.), *Austrian Socialist Experiment*, pp. 161–2. Adler's writings were used in Ha-Shomer ha-Tsair internal education. It is worth noting that, influenced by Kant, he rejected orthodox Marxism's hostility to religion. See Leszek Kolakowski, *Main Currents of Marxism*, vol. 2 (Oxford: Oxford University Press, 1981), pp. 282–5.

40   Otto Bauer, 'Socialism and the principle of nationality', in Tom Bottomore and Patrick E. Goode (eds.), *Austro-Marxism* (Oxford: Oxford University Press, 1978), p. 111.

41   Otto Bauer, 'La marche au socialisme', in *Otto Bauer et la révolution*, ed. Yvon Bourdet (Paris: EDI, 1968), p. 94.

42   Friedreich Engels, *The Origin of the Family, Private Property, and the State*, in *The Marx-Engels Reader*, p.655.

43   Otto Bauer, 'La marche au socialisme', *Otto Bauer et la révolution*, p. 87.

44   Karl Marx and Friedrich Engels, *The German Ideology*, in *The Marx-Engels Reader*, p. 151.

45 Marx and Engels, *The Communist Manifesto*, in ibid., p. 337.
46 This argument echoes some of Marx's in *The Eighteenth Brumaire of Louis Bonaparte*. Marx claimed, in his analyses of Bonaparte's coup, that the French state appeared to have stood above an equilibrium of contending class forces, but that the power of Napoleon's nephew rested on an inarticulate class force, the peasantry.
47 Otto Bauer, *The Austrian Revolution* (New York: Burt Franklin, 1925), pp. 244–6. For a very insightful, but harshly critical analysis of Bauer's politics, see Rabinbach's *Crisis*.
48 In the 1919 (first) elections to the Austrian First Republic, the socialists became the country's largest party with 40.8 per cent of the vote. In 1927 they received 42.3 per cent. Like the Labour Zionists, who became Zionism's most powerful force and whose vote was usually around 40 per cent, the Austrian socialists were unable to attain a majority. Mapai, however, was able to attain the status of a dominant party which the Austrians did not.
49 See Rabinbach, *Crisis*, p. 26.
50 See, for example, 'Neum B.G. ba-vikuakh ha-klali' (Ben-Gurion's speech in the general debate)', *Davar*, 14 January, 1934.
51 Yonathan Shapira, *Elit lelo mamshikhim : dorot manhigim ba-hevrah ha-israelit* (An Elite without Successors: Generations of Leaders in Israeli Society) (Tel Aviv: Sifriat Poalim, 1984), p. 28. This short volume is one of the most provocative recent studies of Israeli society and politics.
52 Ibid., pp. 28–31.

Chapter 7 Jabotinsky and the Challenge from the Right I

1 Vladimir Jabotinsky, 'The unknown race', MS, p. 1 in file KA1/JIA. This is a file of manuscripts and manuscript translations of articles by Jabotinsky, some rendered into English by him.
2 See James MacGregor Burns, *Leadership* (New York: Harper Torchbooks, 1978), p. 18.
3 Sidney Verba, 'Comparative political culture', in Lucien W. Pye and Sidney Verba, *Political Culture and Political Development* (Princeton, NJ: Princeton University Press, 1965), p. 247.
4 David Ben-Gurion, *Zikhronot* (Memoirs), vol. 1 (Tel Aviv: Am Oved, 1976), p. 7.
5 Ibid., p. 10.
6 Ibid., p. 7.
7 Yonathan Shapiro, *The Formative Years of the Israeli Labour Party: The Organization of Power 1919–1930* (London and Beverly Hills, Calif.: Sage Publications, 1976), p. 140.
8 David Ben-Gurion, 'Im hatsharat anglia' (With the English declaration), in David Ben-Gurion, *Mi-maamad le-am* (From a Class to a Nation) (Tel Aviv: Am Oved and Keren ha-Negev, 1974), p. 18.
9 Vladimir Jabotinsky, 'Memoirs from my typewriter', in Lucy Dawidowicz (ed.), *The Golden Tradition* (New York: Holt, Rinehart & Winston, 1967), pp. 398–9.
10 Quoted in Joseph Schechtman, *The Jabotinsky Story: Rebel and Statesman*, vol. 1 (New York: Thomas Yoseloff, 1956), p. 49. The biographical data herein is summarized mostly from Schechtman.
11 See Yaakov Shavit, 'Politics and Messianism: the Zionist Revisionist movement and Polish political culture', *Studies in Zionism*, Autumn 1985.
12 Vladimir Jabotinsky, 'Days of mourning', MS, pp. 5–6, KA1/JIA.
13 Vladimir Jabotinsky, 'Affen Pripatchook', *Jewish Herald,* 12 September, 1947, p. 6.
14 Vladimir Jabotinsky and Joseph Trumpeldor, Letter of 14 January, 1917. JIA.
15 Vladimir Jabotinksy, 'Mored or' (Reactionary) in Vladimir Jabotinsky, *Umah ve-hevrah* (Nation and Society) (Jerusalem: Eri Jabotinsky, 1950), p. 101. 'Reactionary' is the title of the manuscript translation of this article in KA1/JIA also.
16 Presumably Jabotinsky meant the Austrians.

17　Jabotinsky, 'Mored or', p. 106.
18　Ibid., p. 107.
19　See 'Raayon Betar' (The Betar idea), especially pp. 313–14, and 'Shaatnez lo alekha' (Don't commit yourself to shaatnez), both in Vladimir Jabotinsky, *Ba-derekh la-medinah* (On the Road to the State) (Jerusalem: Eri Jabotinsky, 1953).
20　Jabotinsky, Letter of 20 February, 1932. JIA. Similarly, he explained in the article 'Affen Pripatchook' that 'It is a pity that we Jews do not pay attention to choral singing. In the Baltic lands, and especially in Estonia, the whole national movement commenced with choral singing, for that is an immensely powerful weapon to develop unity and discipline, and also that social aesthetic which one day, when the [Betar] will become that which it must be, will be known in the Jewish world . . . as Hadar Betari [Betar Pride]', *Jewish Herald*, 12 September, 1947, p. 6.
21　Jabotinsky, Letter of 20 February, 1932. JIA.
22　Vladimir Jabotinsky, 'Truth', (1916), MS, pp. 11–12, KA1/JIA.
23　Vladimir Jabotinsky, 'Manhig' (Leader), in Vladimir Jabotinsky, *Zikhronot ben-dori* (Memoirs of My Contemporary) (Jerusalem: Eri Jabotinsky and Amihai, n.d.), p. 216.
24　Burns, *Leadership*, p. 4.
25　Max Weber, 'The sociology of charismatic authority', in H. H. Gerth and C. Wright Mills (eds.), *From Max Weber* (New York: Oxford University Press, 1974), p. 249.
26　Joseph Schechtman, *The Jabotinsky Story: Fighter and Prophet*, vol. 2 (New York: Thomas Yoseloff, 1961), p. 179.
27　V. Jabotinsky, Letter of 16 June, 1934. JIA.
28　David Ben-Gurion, *Zikhronot* (Memoirs), vol. 2. (Tel Aviv: Am Oved, 1976), p. 186.
29　Ibid., p. 208.
30　Joseph Schechtman and Yehuda Benari, *History of the Revisionist Movement 1925–1930* (Tel Aviv: Hadar, 1970), pp. 220–1.
31　Vladimir Jabotinsky, 'About Cassandra', *The Zionist*, 17 September, 1926, p. 57.
32　Vladimir Jabotinsky, 'National sport', *Jewish Herald*, 12 May, 1939, p. 5.
33　Vladimir Jabotinsky, 'Confidential memorandum to the Zionist Executive, 5/11/22'. JIA.
34　Vladimir Jabotinsky, 'Tsiyon ve-communism' (Zion and communism), in *Ba-derekh la-medinah*, pp. 65–6.
35　Vladimir Jabotinsky, Letter of 22 July, 1935. JIA.
36　Vladimir Jabotinsky, *State Zionism* (New York: Zionist Revisionist Organization of America, n.d.), p. 7.
37　Quoted in Joseph Gorny, *The British Labour Movement and Zionism 1917–1948* (London: Frank Cass, 1983), p. 38.
38　'Report on the 17th Zionist Congress', *New Judaea*, July–August 1931, p. 216.
39　On the consistency of Ben-Gurion's purpose in this regard, see Shabtai Teveth, *Kinat David: Ben-Gurion ha-Tsair* (David's Zeal: The Young Ben-Gurion) (Jerusalem and Tel Aviv: Schocken Books, 1976), p. 420.
40　Vladimir Jabotinsky, 'Ha-smol' (The left), in Vladimir Jabotinsky, *Ba-saar* (In the Storm) (Jerusalem: Eri Jabotinsky, 1959), pp. 15–17.)
41　Schechtman and Benari, *History of the Revisionist Movement*, p. 222.
42　Vladimir Jabotinsky, 'Anahnu ha-"burganim" ' (We the 'bourgeoisie'), in *Zeev Jabotinsky: 11 shanim le-moto* (Zeev Jabotinsky: Eleven Years since His Death) (Tel Aviv: Ha-Histadrut ha-leumit, 1951) pp. 30–1. It appeared originally in Russian in *Rasviet*, 17 April, 1927.
43　Vladimir Jabotinsky, 'Basta!', in *Ba-saar*, pp. 23–5.
44　See V. Jabotinsky, 'Ha-henvani' (The shopkeeper), in *Ba-derekh la-medinah*, pp. 101–6.
45　Jabotinsky, 'Basta!', pp. 27–8.
46　David Ben-Gurion, *Zikhronot* (Memoirs), vol. 4 (Tel Aviv: Am Oved, 1976), pp. 316–17.
47　Vladimir Jabotinsky, 'Pressure without counter-pressure', MS, pp. 1–2, KA1/JIA.
48　Jabotinsky, 'About Cassandra', p. 59.

49 Jabotinsky, Letter of 20 March, 1931. JIA.
50 See Ben-Gurion, *Zikhronot*, vol. 2, pp. 217–19.
51 Otto Kirchheimer, 'Germany – the vanishing opposition', in Robert Dahl (ed.), *Political Opposition in Western Democracies* (New Haven, Conn., and London: Yale University Press, 1966), p. 237.
52 Schechtman, *The Jabotinsky Story*, vol. 2, p. 173.
53 *The Jewish State Party: What It Stands For* (London: Central Committee of the Jewish State Party, n.d.), p. 1.
54 Moshe Shertok, 'The Zionist Congress', *Davar (English) Supplement*, 6 September, 1931, p. 3.
55 See 'The thorny way to unity', *Davar Sup.*, 31 December, 1930, p. 6.
56 Ezra Mendelsohn, *The Jews in East and Central Europe between the Wars* (Bloomington, Ind.: Indiana University Press, 1983), p. 76.
57 Max Weber, 'Politics as a vocation', in Gerth and Mills (eds), *From Max Weber*, p. 78.

Chapter 8   Jabotinsky and the Challenge from the Right II

1   Friedrich Schiller, *On the Aesthetic Education of Man* (New York: Frederick Ungar, 1965), p. 51.
2   V. Jabotinsky, Letter of 20 March, 1931. JIA.
3   David Ben-Gurion, Letter of 20 July, 1931, in David Ben-Gurion, *Letters to Paula* (London: Vallentine, Mitchell, 1971), pp. 56–7.
4   'The Balfour Declaration', in J. C. Hurwitz (ed.), *The Middle East and North Africa in World Politics: A Documentary Record*, vol 2: 1914–45 (New Haven, Conn., and London: Yale University Press, 1979) p. 106.
5   'Jewish majority in Palestine not necessary', Interview with the Jewish Telegraphic Agency, Basle, 3 July, 1931, in *The Letters and Papers of Chaim Weizmann*, vol. 1, series B, Papers, August 1898–July 1931 (New Brunswick, NJ, and Jerusalem: Transaction Books and Israel Universities Press, 1983), p. 642.
6   'Report on the 17th Zionist Congress', *New Judaea*, July–August 1931, p. 210.
7   Anita Shapira, *Berl: The Biography of a Socialist Zionist* (Cambridge: Cambridge University Press, 1984), p. 187.
8   See David Ben-Gurion, *Berurim* (Clarifications) (Tel Aviv: Mapai, 1944), pp. 7–8.
9   David Ben-Gurion, *Zikhronot* (Memoirs), vol. 1 (Tel Aviv: Am Oved, 1976), p. 467.
10 'Report on the 17th Zionist Congress', *New Judaea*, July–September 1931, pp. 210–11.
11 Emanuel Neumann, *In the Arena: An Autobiographical Memoir* (New York: Herzl Press, 1976), p. 100.
12 Ibid., pp. 101–2.
13 Meir Grossman, 'Vladimir Jabotinsky', *New Judaea*, August 1940, p. 180.
14 Moshe Shertok, 'The Zionist Congress', *Davar (English) Supplement* (henceforth, *Davar Sup.*), 6 September, 1931, p. 3.
15 V. Jabotinsky, Letter of 17 August, 1931. JIA.
16 *Report of the Executive of the Zionist Organisation submitted to the XVIII Zionist Congress at Prague, August 21–29, 1933* (London: Central Office of the Zionist Organization, 1933), pp. 36–8.
17 'Decisions of the Revisionist Conference', *New Judaea*, August–September 1932, p. 160. For the Revisionist view of the petition campaign, see V. Jabotinsky, 'The two Revisionist "petitions" ', *Jewish Daily Bulletin*, 12 April, 1935; *Petition submitted to the Permanent Mandates Commission of the League of Nations by the Central Committee of the Union of Zionists-Revisionists in Palestine, 1934* (JIA); *Petition submitted on behalf of the Nessiut(Presidency) of the New Zionist Organisation to the Chairman of the Permanent Mandates Commission of the League of Nations* (London: New Zionist Organization,

1936); 'The World Jewish Petition', *Bulletin* 2, 2nd series (London: Political Department of the World Union of Zionist Revisionists, May 1934).

18   The hostility between the Revisionists and Labour did not prevent the latter from roundly denouncing the decision to bar Jabotinsky. In the English weekly supplement – aimed clearly at British audiences – of *Davar*, the Histadrut daily newspaper, the editors declared: 'The stand of Labour Zionism . . . is poles apart from the Revisionist tenets in their political and especially in their social content. Yet an attempt to close the doors of Palestine to the Revisionist leader would force us to take up arms in defence of his rights. He cannot be denied admission, not only because he is a Palestinian citizen, but because he is a Jew who has fought all his life for the right of Jews to resettle in Palestine his moral claim to consider Palestine of all countries as his fatherland is uncontestable.' 'A citizen's rights', *Davar Sup.*, 2 April, 1930, p. 2.

19   See *Din ve-heshbon. Vaadat ha-hakirah le-hakirat retsah doktor Haim Arlosoroff* (Report of the Commission to Investigate the Murder of Dr. Haim Arlosoroff) (Jerusalem: The Government of Israel, 1985), esp. p. 42.

20   Walter Laqueur, *A History of Zionism* (New York: Holt, Rinehart & Winston, 1972), pp. 361–2.

21   See, for examples, 'Resolutions of the Asefath Ha-nivharim', *New Judaea*, 12 February, 1926, p. 612; Chaim Weizmann, 'The Executive's policy', in 'Report of the Proceedings of the 15th Zionist Congress', *New Judaea*, 23 September, 1927, p. 446; and *The Development of the Jewish National Home in Palestine: Memorandum submitted to His Majesty's Government by the Jewish Agency for Palestine, May 1930* (London: Jewish Agency, 1930), p. 63.

22   *Report of the Executive of the Zionist Organisation submitted to the XIVth Zionist Congress at Vienna, August 18–28 1925* (London: Central Office of the Zionist Organization, 1925), p. 273.

23   Ibid., p. 273.

24   M. S. (Moshe Shertok), 'The labour exchange holds its own', *Davar Sup.*, 18 April, 1930, p. 2.

25   M. S. (Moshe Shertok), 'The Magdiel agreement', *Davar Sup.*, 2 July, 1930, pp. 2–3.

26   David Ben-Gurion, *Tnuat ha-Poalim ve-ha-revisionismus* (The Workers' Movement and Revisionism) (Tel Aviv: The World League for Labour Palestine, 1933), p. 40.

27   For an extensive and insightful study of the problem of Jewish labour see Anita Shapira, *Ha-maavak ha-nikhzav* (The Futile Struggle) (Tel Aviv: Tel Aviv University and Ha-Kibbutz ha-Meuhad, 1977).

28   I summarize from Anita Shapira, 'The debate in Mapai on the use of violence 1932–35', *Zionism,* Spring 1981.

29   Yaakov Goldstein, *Ba-derekh le-hegmoniyah: Mapai – Hitgabshut mediniyutah 1930– 1936* (On the Road to Hegemony: Mapai – The Crystallization of Its Policies 1930–1936) (Tel Aviv: Am Oved/Tarbut ve-Hinukh, 1980), p. 170.

30   Vladimir Jabotinsky, 'Ken, Lishbor' (Yes, Break Them), in V. Jabotinsky, *Ba-saar* (In the Storm) (Jerusalem: Eri Jabotinsky, 1959), pp. 50–1.

31   Ibid., p. 50.

32   Anita Shapira, 'The debate in Mapai', p. 104; A. Shapira, *Berl*, pp. 192–3.

33   Quoted in A. Shapira, 'The debate in Mapai', p. 109.'

34   Golda Meir, *My Life* (New York: G. P. Putnam's Sons, 1975), p. 145.

35   The controversy about Arlosoroff's murder was reignited in the 1980s after the publication of Shabtai Tevet's *Retsah Arlosoroff* (Arlosoroff's Murder)(Jerusalem and Tel Aviv: Schocken Books, 1982) which again raised the spectre of Revisionist guilt. The Israeli government, then under Jabotinsky's successor as Revisionist leader, Premier Menahem Begin, ordered a special commission to investigate the issue. It concluded that the Revisionists were not guilty of the murder and that, given the atmosphere of the 1930s, Mapai was not guilty of a 'blood libel.' See *Din ve-heshbon*, cited above, note 19.

36 Ben-Gurion's Letter of 6 September, 1933 in David Ben-Gurion, *Letters to Paula*, p. 67.
37 See Ben-Gurion's Letters of 2 and 6 September, 1933 in *Letters to Paula*, pp. 66–7.
38 *Resolutions of the 18th Zionist Congress, Prague, August 21 to September 3, 1933 with a Summary Report of the Proceedings* (London: Central Office of the Zionist Organization, 1934), p. 47.
39 Ibid., pp. 37–8.
40 Ibid., p. 38.
41 Ibid., p. 7.

Chapter 9   Terms of Conflict

1 J.W. von Goethe, *Faust: A Tragedy* (New York: Norton, 1976), p. 27.
2 Vladimir Jabotinsky, Letter of 4 November, 1934. JIA.
3 V. Jabotinsky, Letter to Ben-Gurion, 29 October, 1934. JIA.
4 V. Jabotinsky, Letter to Ben-Gurion, 30 March, 1935. JIA.
5 D. Ben-Gurion, Letter to Jabotinsky, 28 April, 1935. Reproduced in full in Yaakov Goldstein and Yaakov Shavit, *Lelo psharot: Heskem Ben-Gurion–Jabotinsky ve-kishlono* (No Compromises: The Ben-Gurion-Jabotinsky Agreement and its Failure) (Tel Aviv: Yariv/Hadar, 1979), p. 146.
6 Ibid., p. 147.
7 Ibid., pp. 147–8.
8 Ibid., pp. 147–8.
9 V. Jabotinsky, Letter to Ben-Gurion, 2 May, 1935. JIA.
10 Meir Grossman, 'Vladimir Jabotinsky', *New Judaea*, August 1940, p. 179.
11 Vladimir Jabotinsky, 'Race and nationality', MS, p. 1. KA1/JIA. The Hebrew version is simply entitled 'Race' (*Gezah*) and lacks the mentioned note. See V. Jabotinsky, *Umah ve-hevrah* (Nation and Society) (Jerusalem: Eri Jabotinsky, 1950), pp. 125–34.
12 Ibid., pp. 1–2.
13 Ibid., 5.
14 Ibid., p. 7.
15 Vladimir Jabotinsky, 'Horoscope', MS, p. 4. KA1/JIA.
16 Jabotinsky, 'Race and Nationality', p. 8.
17 Ibid., p.9.
18 Vladimir Jabotinsky, 'National minority rights', MS, p. 5. KA1/JIA.
19 Vladimir Jabotinsky, 'Mered ha-zkenim' (Revolt of the Old Men)', in *Umah ve-hevrah*, p. 232.
20 Vladimir Jabotinsky, 'Raayon Betar' (The Betar Idea) in V. Jabotinsky, *Ba-derekh la-medinah* (On the Road to the State) (Jerusalem: Eri Jabotinsky, 1953), p. 319.
21 Ibid., p. 320.
22 Vladimir Jabotinsky, 'Al Militarism' (On Militarism) in *Ba-derekh la-medinah*, p. 43.
23 V. Jabotinsky, 'The Jewish state', *Current Jewish Record*, November 1931, p. 22.
24 Ibid., p.20.
25 V. Jabotinsky, 'Mavo le-torat ha-meshek' (Introduction to the Theory of the Economy) in *Umah ve-hevrah*, p. 196.
26 V. Jabotinsky, 'Crisis of the proletariat', MS, pp. 3–6. KA1/JIA. The article is dated 1932. For the Hebrew version see 'Mashber ha-proletarion' in Vladimir Jabotinsky, *Reshimot* (Short Articles) (Tel Aviv: Eri Jabotinsky and Amihai, n.d.), pp. 306–9.
27 V. Jabotinsky, 'Social redemption', manuscript of an article sent to *Our Voice*, January 1935. MS, p. 1. KA1/JIA.J
28 Jabotinsky, 'Crisis of the proletariat', p. 10 (In 'Mashber', pp. 313–14).
29 Ibid.
30 V. Jabotinsky, 'Robot and workman', MS, p. 1. KA1/JIA.

31 Ibid., p. 8.
32 Vladimir Jabotinsky, 'Class questions', MS, p. 4. KA1/JIA.
33 Ibid., p. 9.'
34 V. Jabotinsky, 'Social redemption', p. 3.
35 Vladimir Jabotinsky, 'National arbitration', MS, p. 3. KA1/JIA.
36 Vladimir Jabotinsky, 'Basta!' in *Ba-saar* (In the Storm) (Jerusalem: Eri Jabotinsky, 1959), p. 26.
37 Jabotinsky, 'National arbitration', p. 5.
38 Ibid., pp. 5–9.'
39 See, for example, David Ben-Gurion, *Tnuat ha-Poalim ve-ha-revisionismus (The Workers' Movement and Revisionism)* (Tel Aviv: The World League for Labour Palestine, 1933), p. 12.
40 Weizmann letter to Morris Kentridge, 4 August 1933, *The Letters and Papers of Chaim Weizmann*, series A, vol 16, Letters, June 1933–August 1935 (New Brunswick, NJ, and Jerusalem: Transaction Books and Israel Universities Press, 1978), p. 16.
41 Stephen Wise, 'Why Zionists cannot support Jabotinsky and Revisionism', *New Palestine*, 15 March, 1935, pp. 2–3.
42 Quoted in Howard Morely Sachar, *A History of Israel* (New York: Knopf, 1976), p. 187.
43 See S. William Halpern, *Mussolini and Italian Fascism* (New York: Van Nostrand, 1964), for a useful summary of these policies.
44 'The Charter of Labor', Appendix to Halpern, ibid., p. 129.
45 Quoted in Denis Mack Smith, *Mussolini* (New York: Vintage Books, 1983), p. 150.
46 See J. James Gregor, *Italian Fascism and Developmental Dictatorship* (Princeton, NJ: Princeton University Press, 1979), p. 173.
47 See Gregor, *Italian Fascism*, p. 183.
48 See Mack Smith, *Mussolini*, p. 27.
49 V. Jabotinsky, Letter of 9 December, 1938. JIA.
50 Gregor, *Italian Fascism*, pp. 130–1.
51 Mack Smith, *Mussolini*, p. 119.
52 Ibid., p. 117.
53 Ibid., pp. 88, 140.
54 Ibid., p. 189. Also, at the end of his life, knowing defeat to be at hand, Mussolini speculated – self-servingly as always – on the possibility of a future, more liberal fascism in which the role of the state would be minimal. Ibid., p. 314.
55 Vladimir Jabotinsky, Letter of 4 October, 1933. JIA.
56 Ibid.
57 V. Jabotinsky, 'Jews and Fascism', *Jewish Daily Bulletin*, 11 April, 1935.
58 Ibid.
59 Ibid.
60 Berl Katznelson, 'Eser shnot Ahdut ha-Avodah' (Ten Years of Ahdut Ha-avodah), in *Kitvei Berl Katznelson* (The Writings of Berl Katznelson), vol. 4 (Tel Aviv: Mapai, 1949), pp. 30–1.
61 Ibid., p. 33.
62 David Ben-Gurion, *Jewish Labour* (London: Hechalutz Organization of England, 1935), p. 39.
63 Katznelson, 'Eser shnot . . .' p. 32.
64 David Ben-Gurion, 'Shlihutenu ba-am' (Our Mission in the Nation), in Ben-Gurion, *Mi-maamad le-am* (From a Class to a Nation) (Tel Aviv: Am Oved and Keren ha-Negev, 1974), pp. 195–9.
65 Ben-Gurion, 'Ha-Poel ba-tsiyonut' (The Worker in Zionism), in *Mi-maamad*, p. 252.
66 Ibid., p. 247.
67 Ibid., p. 249.
68 Ben-Gurion, *Tnuat ha-Poalim ve-ha-revisionismus*, p. 39.

69 Ibid., pp. 40–1.
70 Walter Laqueur, *A History of Zionism* (New York: Holt, Rinehart & Winston, 1972), pp. 366–7.
71 For an interesting study of some of the problems of German Jewish integration into the Yishuv, particularly of the intellectuals, see Nusi Sznaider, 'Between past and present: a study of German Jews in Palestine' (Unpublished MA thesis, Faculty of Social Sciences, Tel Aviv University, 1984.)
72 Z. Aharonowitz, *A Decade of Progress: A Review of the Histadrut 1932–1942* (New York: National Committee for Labor Israel, n.d.), pp. 2–3.
73 'Agreement concluded between the Executive of the Zionist Organisation and the World Union of Revisionist Zionists', File 34/4/1A, JIA.
74 The cable is dated 8 November, 1934. *Igrot Berl Katznelson 1930–37* (Correspondence of Berl Katznelson, 1930–37), ed. Anita Shapira and Esther Raizen (Tel Aviv: Am Oved, 1984), p. 159.
75 Itzhak Ben Aharon, 'Remembering Ben Gurion', *Jerusalem Quarterly*, Summer 1980, p. 45.
76 Goldstein and Shavit, *Lelo psharot*, pp. 86–8.
77 Joseph Schechtman, *The Jabotinsky Story: Fighter and Prophet*, vol. 2 (New York: Thomas Yoseloff, 1961), p. 252.
78 Itshak Ben-Aharon, 'Erev ha-veidah' (The Eve of the Convention), *Ha-Poel ha-Tsair*, 21 December, 1934, pp. 4–5.
79 Ibid.
80 Goldstein and Shavit, *Lelo psharot*, pp. 107–8.
81 Ibid., pp. 109–110.
82 Ibid., pp. 111–12. Ben-Gurion provides his own, extensive, account of the entire episode in his *Zikhronot* (Memoirs), vol. 2 (Tel Aviv: Am Oved, 1976), pp. 182–271.
83 Michael Bar-Zohar, *Ben-Gurion* (New York: Delacorte Press, 1978), p. 74.
84 'Al heskemei london ve-ha-masa u-matan im ha-miflagot (sihah im B.G.)' (On the London agreements and the negotiations between the parties (a talk with Ben-Gurion)), *Davar*, 4 January, 1935, p. 1.
85 Summarized from Goldstein and Shavit, *Lelo psharot*, pp. 116–19.
86 Ben-Aharon, 'Erev ha-veidah', p. 5.
87 Ibid.
88 Yonathan Shapiro, *The Formative Years of the Israeli Labour Party* (London and Beverly Hills, Calif.: Sage Publications, 1976), p. 245.
89 Ben-Aharon, 'Erev ha-veidah', p. 5.
90 'Rejection of Labour–Revisionist Agreement', *Palestine Post*, 29 March, 1935, p. 1.
91 See Ben-Gurion's comments at the 'Proceedings of the Zionist General Council Meeting in Jerusalem, March 31, 1935', *New Judaea*, April 1935, p. 106.

Chapter 10 Consolidations

1 D. Ben-Gurion, Letter of 7 October, 1938 in David Ben-Gurion, *Letters to Paula* (London: Vallentine, Mitchell, 1971), p. 188.
2 *Report to the Executive of the Zionist Organisation submitted to the XIXth Zionist Congress at Lucerne, August 20–30 1935* (London: Central Office of the Zionist Organisation, 1935), p. 27.
3 V. Jabotinsky, Letter of 25 March, 1935. JIA.
4 V. Jabotinsky, Letter of 24 April, 1935. JIA.
5 V. Jabotinsky, Letter of 25 March, 1935. JIA.
6 Ibid.

7   Ibid.
8   V. Jabotinsky, Letters of 19 June, 1935 and 7 November, 1935. JIA.
9   V. Jabotinsky, Letter of 19 June, 1935. JIA.
10   V. Jabotinsky, 'A new Zionist organisation: the Revisionist standpoint', Letter to the *London Jewish Chronicle*, 9 August, 1935, p. 18.
11   'Britain target of attack at Congress', *Jewish Daily Bulletin*, 23 August, 1935, p. 3.
12   'Summary of the Congress proceedings', *New Judaea*, September 1935, p. 182.
13   On minimum winning coalitions, see William Riker, *The Theory of Political Coalitions* (New Haven, Conn.: Yale University Press, 1962).
14   D. Ben-Gurion, Letter of 7 September, 1935, in *Letters to Paula*, p. 76.
15   D. Ben-Gurion, Letter of 14 September, 1935, in *Letters to Paula*, pp. 92–3.
16   'Summary of the Congress proceedings', *New Judaea*, September 1935, p. 196.
17   Chaim Weizmann, 'Defense of collective economy', in *The Letters and Papers of Chaim Weizmann*, series B, Papers, vol. 2, December 1931–April 1952 (New Brunswick, NJ, and Jerusalem: Transaction Books, Rutgers University and Israel Universities Press, 1984), p.76.
18   Ibid., p. 77.
19   'Summary of the Congress proceedings', *New Judaea*, p. 174.
20   D. Ben-Gurion, Letter of 10 September, 1935, in *Letters to Paula*, pp. 89–90.
21   Israel Kolatt, 'Ben Gurion: image and greatness', *Dispersion and Unity*, 21/22 (1973–4), pp. 22–3.
22   D. Ben-Gurion, Letter of 7 September, 1935, in *Letters to Paula*, p. 77.
23   V. Jabotinsky, Letter (to Weizmann) of 26 May, 1936, JIA, and David Ben-Gurion, *Zikhronot* (Memoirs), vol. 4 (Tel Aviv: Am Oved, 1976), pp. 316–17.
24   V. Jabotinsky, Letter of 10 July, 1936. JIA.
25   V. Jabotinsky, Letter of 27 January, 1937. JIA.
26   Vladimir Jabotinsky, *The Jewish War Front* (New York: Dial Press, 1942), pp. 53, 72, 76, 78.
27   See David Engel, 'The frustrated alliance: the Revisionist movement and the Polish government in exile, 1939–1945', *Studies in Zionism*, Spring 1986, p. 13.
28   *Evidence submitted to the Palestine Royal Commission, House of Lords, London, February 11th 1937 by M. V. Jabotinsky on behalf of the New Zionist Organization* (London: New Zionist Organization, 1937), pp. 12–13.
29   V. Jabotinsky, Letter of 9 August, 1937. JIA.
30   See his Letter of 9 March, 1939 and his telegrams to Ben-Gurion, Weizmann and Pinhas Rutenberg, 19 May, 1940. JIA
31   V. Jabotinsky, Letter of 22 September, 1939. JIA.
32   On Begin's differences with Jabotinsky, see especially, Sasson Sofer, 'The concept of revolt in Menachem Begin's thought', *Studies in Zionism*, Spring 1986, p. 103.
33   Yosi Beilin, *Mehiro shel ihud: Mifleget ha-avodah ad milhemet yom ha-kipurim* (The Price of Unity: The Labour Party until the Yom Kippur War) (Israel: Revivim, 1985), p. 203.
34   For an analysis of the debate see especially, Eli Sha'altiel, 'David Ben-Gurion on partition, 1937', *Jerusalem Quarterly*, Winter 1979, pp. 38–41.
35   David Ben-Gurion, 'Speech to the Council of the World Union of Zionist Socialist Workers' Parties' (Zurich, 4 August, 1937), *Jerusalem Quarterly*, 10 (1979), pp. 49–51.
36   On Ben-Gurion's attitudes towards the Arabs in this period see especially: D. Ben-Gurion, *Anahnu u-shkheneinu* (We and Our Neighbours) (Tel Aviv: Davar, 1931); D. Ben-Gurion, *My Talks with Arab Leaders* (Jerusalem: Keter, 1972); Shabtai Teveth, *Ben-Gurion and the Palestinian Arabs* (Oxford: Oxford University Press, 1985).
37   For an especially insightful analysis of this change in Ben-Gurion, see Kolatt, 'Ben Gurion: image and greatness', p. 25.
38   On the question of binationalism see Elkana Margalit, 'Binationalism: an interpretation of Zionism 1941–1947', *Studies in Zionism*, October 1981.

39 See Anita Shapira, *Berl: The Biography of a Socialist Zionist* (Cambridge: Cambridge University Press, 1984), p. 324 for a succinct summary of these developments.

40 See *Ha-veidah ha-hamishit shel ha-miflagah bi-khfar vitkin* (The Fifth Conference of the Party at Kfar Vitkin) in *Ahdut ha-Avodah*, December 1942. Ben-Gurion gave a particularly forceful ideological and political statement, 'Shlihut ve-derekh' (Mission and Path), pp. 6–32.

41 'Split in Labour party final', *Palestine Post*, 4 June, 1944, p. 3.

42 'Mapai increased membership', *Palcor*, 27 July, 1944, p. 2.

43 *Palcor*, 9 August, 1944, p. 2.

44 'Histadruth national conference elections', *Palcor*, 9 August, 1944, p. 1, and 'Histadruth strengthened', *Palcor*, 14 August, 1944, p. 3.

45 On Katznelson, see the biography by Anita Shapira noted above. On Siah B, see the study by Yael Ishai, *Siatiyut bi-tnuat ha-avodah: siah bet be-mapai* (Factionalism in the Labour Movement: Siah B in Mapai) (Tel Aviv: Am Oved, 1978).

46 For an analysis of this situation from the perspective of religious workers, see I. Halevy Levin, 'Hapoel Hamizrachi in the political alignment of the Yishuv', *Jewish Horizon*, December 1945.

47 Maurice Duverger, *Political Parties* (London: Methuen, 1964), p. 203.

48 Benjamin Akzin, 'The role of parties in Israeli democracy', in G. Mahler (ed.), *Readings on the Israeli Political System* (Washington, DC: University Press of America, 1982), p. 51.

Chapter 11   *Mamlakhtiyut* I: Of Golden Calves and Messiahs

1 *The Politics of Aristotle*, ed. and tr. Ernest Barker (Oxford: Oxford University Press, 1974), p. 6.

2 *Nationalism: A Report by a Study Group of Members of the Royal Institute of International Affairs* (London: Frank Cass, 1963 (originally Oxford: Oxford University Press, 1939)), p. xviii.

3 Quoted in Yosef Gorni, *Ahdut ha-Avodah 1919–1930: Ha-yesodot ha-raayoniyim ve-ha-shitah ha-medinit* (Ahdut ha-Avodah 1919–1930: The Ideological Principles and the Political System) (Tel Aviv: Tel Aviv University and Ha-Kibbutz ha-Meuhad, 1973), p. 59.

4 'Al heskemei london ve-ha-masa u-matan im ha-miflagot (Sihah im B.G.)' (On the London Agreements and the Negotiations between the Parties (A Talk with Ben-Gurion)), *Davar*, 4 January, 1935, p. 1.

5 David Ben-Gurion, 'Darkenu ba-medinah' (Our Path in the State), in David Ben-Gurion, *Hazon va-derekh* (Vision and Path; henceforth *Hazon*), vol. 3 (Tel Aviv: Mapai; 1952), p. 104.

6 See, for examples, I Kings 20:14 and Esther 8:9.

7 David Ben-Gurion, *Berurim* (Clarifications) (Tel Aviv: Mapai, 1944), pp. 13–14.

8 'The postwar Zionist (Biltmore) program, 11 May 1942', in J. C. Hurwitz (ed.), *The Middle East and North Africa in World Politics: A Documentary Record*, vol. 2: 1914–1945, 2nd edn. (New Haven, Conn., and London: Yale University Press, 1979), p. 597.

9 Ben-Gurion, 'Darkenu ba-medinah', p. 14.

10 Ibid., p. 105.

11 Ibid., pp. 104–6.

12 'Ben Gurion on "Mamlachtiut" ', Interview with Lea Ben Dor, *Jerusalem Post*, 28 May, 1965, p. 10.

13 'The flag and the hymn', *Jerusalem Post*, 1 June, 1953, p. 4.

14 *Divrei ha-knesset* (The Knesset Record), 3 June, 1953 (Jerusalem: Government Printing Office, May – 27 August 1953), p. 1486.

15 'Socialist state 'in our time' is foreseen by P.M.', *Jerusalem Post*, 23 March, 1949, p. 1.

16 Ben-Gurion, 'Darkenu ba-medinah', p. 134.

17 V. Jabotinsky, Letter of 2 May, 1935. JIA.

18 David Ben-Gurion, 'Munahim va-arakhim' (Terms and Values), *Hazut*, 1957, p. 8.

19 Minutes of the Mapai Central Committee, 24 May, 1953, p. 3. LPA.

20 *Divrei ha-knesset*, 3 June, 1953, p. 1485.

21 Ibid.

22 Ibid., p. 1486.

23 'Mapai Council reverses stand on Labour flag and anthem in schools', *Jerusalem Post*, 29 November, 1953, p. 3.

24 David Ben-Gurion, 'Shlihutenu Ba-am', in *Mi-maamad le-am*, p. 195; David Ben-Gurion, *The New Tasks of World Zionism* (London: Zionist Information Office, 1949), p. 3.

25 See Vladimir Jabotinsky, 'Prakim ba-filosofia ha-sotsialit shel ha-tanakh' (Chapters in the Social Philosophy of the Bible)' and 'Raayon ha-yovel' (The Idea of the Jubilee), respectively pp. 183–91 and 173–80 in V. Jabotinsky, *Umah ve-hevrah* (Nation and Society) (Jerusalem: Eri Jabotinsky, 1950).

26 Avraham Avi-hai, *Ben-Gurion, State-Builder* (Jerusalem and New York: Israel Universities Press and John Wiley, 1974), p. 83.

27 Ben-Gurion, 'Darkenu ba-medinah', p. 134.

28 David Ben-Gurion, 'Messianic vision', Speech to the Third World Congress for the Study of Judaism, Jerusalem, 25 July, 1961, in *Ben-Gurion Looks at the Bible* (London and New York: W. H. Allen, 1972), p. 111.

29 David Ben-Gurion, 'Science and ethics: the contributions of Greece, India, and Israel.' Speech at Convocation Honoring David Ben-Gurion at Brandeis University, 3 September 1960. (No pagination). ZAL.

30 *Ben-Gurion Looks Back in Talks with Moshe Pearlman* (London: Weidenfeld & Nicolson, 1965), pp. 231–2.

31 Ben-Gurion, 'Messianic vision', p. 111.

32 David Ben-Gurion, Address to the Opening Session of the 23rd Zionist Congress, Jerusalem, 14 August, 1951, p. 4. CZA, G 12.224.

33 R. J. Zwi Werblowsky, 'Messianism in Jewish history', in H. H. Ben-Sasson and S. Ettinger (eds.), *Jewish Society through the Ages* (New York: Schocken Books, 1973), pp. 30–3.

34 Ibid., pp. 35–6.

35 Ibid., p. 38.

36 Shlomo Avineri, 'Israel in the post-Ben-Gurion era: the nemesis of Messianism', *Midstream*, September 1965, p. 23.

37 Gershom Scholem, 'Toward an understanding of the Messianic idea in Judaism', in Scholem's *The Messianic Idea in Judaism and Other Essays on Jewish Spirituality* (New York: Schocken Books, 1971), p. 35.

38 Ibid.

39 Ibid., p. 36.

40 David Ben-Gurion, 'A new Jew arises in Israel', *Jerusalem Post*, 13 May, 1958.

41 Ben-Gurion, 'Munahim va-arakhim', p. 9. For a translation of this article along with a vigorous critique of this statement, and an exchange between Ben-Gurion and its author, see David Ben-Gurion and Nathan Rotenstreich, 'Israel and Zionism: a discussion', *Jewish Frontier*, December 1957.

42 David Ben-Gurion, 'The state and the future of Zionism', Address at the Zionist General Council in Jerusalem, 25 April, 1950 (Jerusalem: Organization Department and the Executive of the Zionist Organization, 1950), pp. 8–9.

43 David Ben-Gurion, 'Ha-Histadrut ba-medinah' (The Histadrut in the State), in *Ha-Veidah ha-shminit shel ha-Histadrut* (The Eighth Conference of the Histadrut) (Tel Aviv: The Histadrut, 1956), p. 78. LA.

44 Ben-Gurion, 'Munakhim va-arakhim', p. 7.
45 *Our Stand: Program of Mapai* (Tel Aviv: Mapai, 1949), pp. 16–17.
46 See, 'Attack on Titoism opens Mapam parley', *Jerusalem Post*, 31 May, 1951, p. 3; 'Tabenkin: Lenin is no recipe for Israel', *Jerusalem Post*, 3 June, 1951, p. 1; 'Mapam manifesto', *Jerusalem Post*, 8 June, 1951, p. 4.
47 See Numbers 32:31–2 as well as the discussion in Charles S. Liebman and Eliezer Don-Yehiya, *Civil Religion in Israel* (Berkeley, Calif.: University of California Press, 1983), p. 31.
48 David Ben-Gurion, *Medinat Israel ha-mehudeshet* (The Restored State of Israel) (Tel Aviv: Am Oved, 1969), p. 429.
49 'Showdown on flag issue unexpected', *Jerusalem Post*, 26 May, 1953, p. 1.
50 David Ben-Gurion, 'Past and future', Speech to Mapai Central Committee, 20 January, 1955, p. 20. Typed transcript in Ben-Gurion File, ZAL.
51 'Hazit halutsit tahat memshelet poalim' (Pioneer Front instead of a Workers' Government), *La-merhav*, 3 January, 1955, p. 2.
52 'B-G appeals to non-party men to support "pioneering force" ', *Jerusalem Post*, 1 October, 1959, p. 3.
53 See Ben-Gurion, 'Past and future', pp. 1–2.
54 David Ben-Gurion, 'First ones', *Israel Government Yearbook 5723* (1962–3) (Jerusalem, 1963); David Ben-Gurion, *Israel: A Personal History* (New York and Tel Aviv: Funk & Wagnalls and Sabra Books, 1971), chapter 1.
55 David Ben-Gurion, 'Address to the opening session of the 23rd Zionist Congress, Jerusalem, April 14, 1951', p. 4. CZA G 12.224. This praise was not a matter of political expedience, but reflected his true estimation of a man he thought 'even a more profound analyst of Jewish affairs' than Herzl. David Ben-Gurion, *The State and the Future of Zionism*, Address at the Zionist General Council, Jerusalem, 25 April, 1950 (Jerusalem: Organization Department and the Executive of the Zionist Organisation, 1950), p. 10.
56 Ben-Gurion, 'Darkenu ba-medinah', pp. 133–4. Also see 'Ha-Histadrut ba-medinah', pp. 77–78.
57 Ben-Gurion, 'Darkenu ba-medinah', p. 135. For Ben-Gurion's attacks on the left, also see his collection, signed by the pseudonym 'Saba shel Yariv' (Yariv's Grandfather), *Al ha-Communism ve-ha-tsiyonut shel Ha-Shomer ha-Tsair* (On the Communism and the Zionism of Ha-Shomer ha-Tsair) (Tel Aviv: Mapai, 1953).
58 'Attack on Titoism opens Mapam parley', *Jerusalem Post*, 31 May, 1951, p. 3.
59 See for example his remarks on the 'value of the individual' in his speech to the Kfar Vitkin Mapai conference in October 1942, 'Shlihut va-derekh' (Mission and Path), in *Ha-Veidah ha-hamishit shel ha-miflagah bi-Khfar Vitkin* (The Fifth Conference of the Party at Kfar Vitkin), in *Ahdut ha-Avodah*, 406:IV, p. 9.
60 See Ben-Gurion, 'Munahim va-arakhim', p. 7.
61 *Our Stand: Program of Mapai* (Tel Aviv: Mapai, 1949), p. 3.
62 David Ben-Gurion, *Israel: The Tasks Ahead. Statement before the Constituent Assembly of the State of Israel, Tel Aviv, 8 March 1949.* (New York: Israel Office of Information, 1949), p. 6.
63 David Ben-Gurion, 'Signposts: a re-examination of policy', *Jerusalem Post*, 8 June, 1956, p. 5. (in Hebrew in *Davar*, 1 June, 1956.)
64 Ben-Gurion, 'Munahim va-arakhim', p. 7.
65 Zeev Tzahor, 'David Ben-Gurion's attitude toward the diaspora', *Judaism*, Winter 1983, p. 11. Ben-Gurion, we may recall, went to study law in Turkey just a few years after he came to Palestine, and was expelled from the country for the duration of the First World War.
66 Ben-Gurion, 'Munahim va-arakhim', p. 11.
67 David Ben-Gurion, 'Chapters 23–24 from the Book of Joshua', in *Ben-Gurion Looks at the Bible*, p. 194.

68 Ben-Gurion occasionally took this to extremes such as in a lecture he delivered in May 1960 to a somewhat bewildered Israeli Press Guild insisting that on the basis of his own studies he had proved that only 600 people left Egypt with Moses. This led, not surprisingly, to an uproar both among biblical scholars and among the religious parties, one of which presented a no-confidence motion in the Knesset on the grounds of blasphemy. See David Ben-Gurion, 'The Exodus from Egypt', in *Ben-Gurion Looks at the Bible*.

69 David Ben-Gurion, *The State and the Future of Zionism*. p. 73.

70 David Ben-Gurion, Address to the Opening Session of the 23rd Zionist Congress, Jerusalem, 14 August, 1951, p. 7. CZA G 12.224.

71 Ben-Gurion, *The State and the Future of Zionism*, p. 8.

72 David Ben-Gurion, *Israel and Zionism as I See It* (London: Poale Zion, n.d.), p. 25.

73 Ben-Gurion, 'Ha-Histadrut ba-medinah', p. 78.

74 Ibid., p. 72–3.

75 I summarize and distil from Yonathan Shapiro, *Elit lelo mamshikhim* (An Elite without Successors) (Tel Aviv: Sifriyat Poalim, 1984) pp. 33–4.

76 Ibid., p. 34.

77 David Ben-Gurion, 'Uniqueness and destiny', in *Ben-Gurion Looks at the Bible*, pp. 36–7.

78 Ben-Gurion, 'Science and Ethics.'

79 See Michael Keren, *Ben-Gurion and the Intellectuals* (Dekalb, Ill.: Northern Illinois University Press, 1983), pp. 25–6. Keren's valuable study provides the most comprehensive discussion of Ben-Gurion's views of, and obsessions with, science.

80 He declared that 'from Spinoza onward the scientific approach has had a profound impact on our people.' Ben-Gurion, *Israel: A Personal History*, p. xiii.

81 Ben-Gurion, 'Uniqueness and destiny', in *Ben-Gurion Looks at the Bible*, p. 25.

82 Ben-Gurion, 'Science and ethics'.

83 Ibid.

84 'Peres: living in a dangerous era', *Jerusalem Post*, 30 August, 1960, p. 1.

85 Shimon Peres, 'New vistas for Mapai credo', *Jerusalem Post* (Weekend Section), 29 July, 1960, p. II.

86 See Peter Y. Medding, *Mapai in Israel: Political Organisation and Government in a New Society* (Cambridge: Cambridge University Press, 1972), especially pp. 147–53.

87 Shabtai Teveth, *Moshe Dayan* (Boston, Mass.: Houghton Mifflin, 1973), p. 284; 'Young Mapai meets today', *Jerusalem Post*, 16 February, 1951; 'Young Mapai support party policy, ask closer contact', *Jerusalem Post*, 18 February, 1951.

88 Medding, *Mapai*, p. 254.

89 'Barkatt takes issue on Dayan statement', *Jerusalem Post*, 5 April, 1959, p. 3.

90 Lea Ben Dor, 'Dayan takes "hard look" ', *Jerusalem Post*, 18 January, 1959, p. 4.

91 'I talk as I please', Interview with Moshe Dayan, *Jewish Observer and Middle East Review*, 7 November, 1958, p. 13.

92 Moshe Dayan, 'Crisis in pioneering', *Jerusalem Post* (Weekend Section), 25 September, 1959, p. I.

93 Ben Dor, 'Dayan takes "hard look"'.

94 Shimon Peres, 'Israel as a way of life', *Jerusalem Post*, 9 October, 1959.

95 Shimon Peres, 'The next ten years', *Jerusalem Post* (Weekend Section), 23 April, 1958, p. I.

96 Shimon Peres, 'Electoral system and popular democracy', *Jerusalem Post* (Weekend Section), 5 August, 1960, p. I.

97 Peres, 'New vistas'.

98 Shimon Peres, 'Dead symbols and living reality', *Jerusalem Post* (Weekend Section), 21 August 21, 1959, p. I.

99 Peres, 'New vistas'.

100 Ibid.
101 Yosef Almogi, *Total Commitment* (New York and London: Herzl Press and Cornwall Books, 1982), p. 235, and Interview with Yosef Almogi, 3 July, 1983, Haifa.
102 Interview with Shimon Peres, 2 August, 1983, Tel Aviv.
103 See Shimon Peres, 'Ha-Sotsialism he-hadash' (The New Socialism), *Ha-arets*, 14 May, 1982, pp. 13, 17, and Shimon Peres, 'Idan ha-mapekhah ha-shlishit' (Epoch of the Third Revolution), *Ha-arets*, 16 May, 1982, pp. 9, 12.
104 Interview with Shimon Peres, 2 August, 1983, Tel Aviv.
105 Ibid.
106 Ibid. Also see Shimon Peres, 'What Rafi stands for', *Jerusalem Post*, 22 December, 1965, p. 7, for an earlier expression of some of these attitudes.
107 *Our Stand: Program of Mapai* (Tel Aviv: Mapai, 1949), p. 5.
108 'On the moral character of the state of Israel: a debate with David Ben-Gurion', in Paul R. Mendes-Flohr (ed.), *A Land of Two Peoples: Martin Buber on Jews and Arabs* (New York and Oxford: Oxford University Press, 1983), pp. 240–1.

Chapter 12 *Mamlakhtiyut* II: From *Am Oved* to *Am Mamlakhti*

1 *Ben-Gurion Looks Back in Talks with Moshe Pearlman* (London: Weidenfeld & Nicolson, 1965), p. 121.
2 Max Horkheimer and Theodor Adorno, *Dialektik der Aufklärung* (Amsterdam: Querido Verlag, 1947), p. 274.
3 The non-Jewish population grew 67.5 per cent (almost entirely from natural increase).
4 S. N. Eisenstadt, *Israeli Society* (London: Weidenfeld & Nicolson, 1967), pp. 62–4.
5 '200 hurt as police defend Knesset from Herut riot', *Jerusalem Post*, 8 January, 1952, p. 1.
6 'House group votes to suspend Begin', *Jerusalem Post*, 16 January, 1952, p. 1.
7 'Ben-Gurion warns against IZL plot', *Jerusalem Post*, 9 January, 1952, p. 1.
8 Yoram Peri, *Between Battles and Ballots: Israeli Military in Politics* (Cambridge: Cambridge University Press, 1983), pp. 36–8.
9 Ibid., pp. 64–5.
10 This was not just rhetoric: at one point during the 1948 war there was apparently a plot among some Irgun commanders in Jerusalem to attack the IDF headquarters and, with the Stern Group, proclaim 'Free Judaea'. See Peri, *Between Battles and Ballots*, p. 57.
11 David Ben-Gurion, 'The Altalena: statement to the 5th session of the Provisional State Council, 23 June, 1948', in David Ben-Gurion, *Rebirth and Destiny of Israel* (New York: Philosophical Library, 1954), pp. 251–7. For Begin's version, which accuses Ben-Gurion of duplicity in negotiations, see chapters 11 and 12 in Menahem Begin, *The Revolt* (Jerusalem: Steimatzky, n.d.).
12 Anita Shapira, *Mi-piturei ha-rama ad peruk ha-palmah* (The Army Controversy 1948: Ben-Gurion's Struggle for Control, with the Protocol of the Fifth Committee, July 1948) (Tel Aviv: Ha-Kibbutz ha-Meuhad, 1985), p.11.
13 For accounts of these developments see Shapira, *Mi-piturei*, and Peri, *Between Battles and Ballots*.
14 *Our Stand: Program of Mapai* (Tel Aviv: Mapai, 1949), pp. 8–9.
15 R. Murray Thomas, 'The symbiotic linking of politics and education', in R. Murray Thomas (ed.), *Politics and Education* (Oxford and New York: Pergamon Press, 1983), p. 8.
16 It later became the Technion, the Israeli engineering university.
17 For an insightful discussion of these developments, see Moshe Rinott, 'Religion and education: the cultural question and the Zionist movement 1897–1913', *Studies in Zionism*, Spring 1984.

18   Moshe Burstein, *Self-Government of the Jews in Palestine since 1900* (Tel Aviv: Ha-Poel ha-Tsair, 1934), p. 55.

19   'The Mandate for Palestine, 24 July 1922', in J. C. Hurwitz (ed.), *The Middle East and North Africa in World Politics: A Documentary Record*, vol. 2: 1914–1945, 2nd edn (New Haven, Conn., and London: Yale University Press, 1979), p. 308.

20   *Resolutions of the 16th Zionist Congress, Zurich, July 28–August 11 1929* (London: Central Office of the Zionist Organization, 1930), pp. 38–9; Also see Marie Syrkin, 'Education in Israel', *Jewish Frontier*, September 1952, pp. 27–9.

21   According to Syrkin, between 1920 and 1940 about one-eighth of the 3.5 million pounds the Palestine government spent on education went to Jewish schools. Syrkin, 'Education in Israel', p. 27. An internal Jewish Agency Report on the income of the education department of the Vaad Leumi between October 1932 and September 1933 listed the following figures (in Palestine pounds):

From the Jewish Agency	36,968
From the Palestine government	22,222
From PICA (Palestine Jewish Colonization Association)	4,502
From the Yishuv:	
a From the Tel Aviv municipality	21,155
b From town and village councils	5,699
From tuition fees in towns and villages	10,351
From sundries	96
Total	100,993

These figures are taken from A. Ulitzur, 'Report on capital invested by Jewish national and public funds from 1918–1936', Appendix 1, p. 1. Report to the Jewish Agency, 27 October, 1936. Mimeo at ZAL.

22   'The assembly in session', *Davar Sup.*, 18 February, 1931, p. 2.

23   Syrkin, 'Education in Israel', p. 31.

24   Y. Shapiro, *Elit lelo mamshikhim* (An Elite without Successors) (Tel Aviv: Sifriyat Poalim, 1984), p. 67.

25   Burstein, *Self-Government of the Jews*, p. 56.

26   Aharon F. Kleinberger, *Society, Schools, and Progress in Israel* (Oxford: Pergamon Press, 1969), pp. 35–6.

27   The Colonial Office, *The System of Education of the Jewish Community in Palestine: Report of the Commission of Enquiry Appointed by the Secretary of State for the Colonies, 1945* (London: HMSO, 1945), p. 8.

28   Randolph L. Braham, *Israel: A Modern Education System* (Washington, DC: United States Department of Health, Education, and Welfare, 1966), pp. 24–5; Syrkin, 'Education in Israel', p. 31; Kleinberger, *Society, Schools, and Progress*, p. 36. For an extended critical analysis of the General trend's curriculum and its problems see Y. Shapiro, *Elit lelo mamshikhim*, pp. 66–89.

29   *Report of the Executive of the Zionist Organisation submitted to the XVth Zionist Congress at Basle* (London: Central Office of the Zionist Organization, 1927), pp. 377–8.

30   Noah Nardi, *Education in Palestine 1920–1945* (Washington, DC: Zionist Organization of America, 1945), p. 219.

31   Quoted in Nardi, *Education in Palestine*, p. 250 n. 138.

32   See Y. Ron-Polani, 'Hinukh be-ruah tnuat ha-avodah be-avar u-ba-hoveh' (Education in the Spirit of the Labor movement – Past and Present), *Hinukh* March 1969, p. 260, and Nardi, *Education in Palestine*, p. 241.

33   See Judith L. Wolf, 'Selected aspects in the development of public education in Palestine 1920–1946'. (unpublished diss., Boston College, 1981), pp. 256–62.

34   Nardi, *Education in Palestine*, pp. 65–6.

35   Mordecai Halevi, 'Labor education in Eretz Israel' (New York: ZOA Education Department, 1937), p. 3.

36   Moshe Avidor, *Education in Israel* (Jerusalem: World Zionist Organization, 1957), p. 6.
37   Kleinberger, *Society, Schools, and Progress*, p. 121.
38   Naftaly S. Glasman, 'Major planning activities in Israeli education: politically dictated improvisations', *Journal of Educational Thought*, 3, 1 (1969), p. 37.
39   'Education bill gets majority', *Jerusalem Post*, 27 July, 1949.
40   Gerda Luft, 'Politics and education', *Jerusalem Post*, 12 March, 1950.
41   *Din ve-heshbon shel vaadat ha-hakirah be-inyenei ha-hinukh ba-mahanot ha-olim* (Report of the Commission of Inquiry into Education in the Immigrant Camps) (Jerusalem: Government Printing Office, 1950), p. 401.
42   'Knesset approves separate debate on camp disturbances', *Jerusalem Post*, 28 February, 1950, p. 1.
43   Quoted in David Ben-Gurion, *Israel: A Personal History* (New York and Tel Aviv: Funk & Wagnalls and Sabra Books, 1971), p. 386.
44   'State Education Law', *Laws of the State of Israel. Authorised Translation from the Hebrew*. vol. 7, 1952/3. (Jerusalem: Government Printer), p. 113.
45   Ibid., p. 115.
46   Avidor, *Education in Israel*, p. 59.
47   Minutes of the Mapai Central Committee, 17 May, 1954. LPA.
48   Ibid.
49   Ibid., pp. 2–4.
50   Ibid.
51   Ibid., pp. 2–3.
52   Ibid., pp. 2–3.
53   'State education contains essence of Labour movement – Ben-Gurion', *Jerusalem Post*, 5 July, 1953, p. 3.
54   Yitzchak Ben-Aharon, 'Remembering Ben-Gurion', *Jerusalem Quarterly*, Summer 1980, p. 44.
55   David Ben-Gurion, *Medinat Israel ha-mehudeshet* (The Restored State of Israel) (Tel Aviv: Am Oved, 1969), pp. 428–9. The sense of world history expressed by Ben-Gurion is narrow here: the categories of state and nation to which he refers are relatively modern and many peoples were formed into nations and achieved independence in the previous century. Their sense of political self, in terms both of nation and state, therefore also had to undergo difficult and fundamental transformations that, at least in significant cases, may be compared to the Jews. Ben-Gurion tended to speak as if nations and states were not expressions of modern politics, but were eternal and ahistorical categories.
56   Ben-Zion Dinur, 'Hok hinukh mamlakhti', (The State Education Law), in Ben-Zion Dinur, *Arakhim u-drakhim: Beayot hinukh ve-tarbut be-israel* (Values and Paths: Problems of Education and Culture in Israel) (Tel Aviv: Urim, 1958), p. 26.
57   Ibid., p. 31.
58   Ibid., p. 32.
59   Ben-Zion Dinaburg, 'Steps forward in education', *Jerusalem Post*, 21 November, 1952, p. 5.
60   Dinur, 'Hok hinukh mamlakhti', p. 33.
61   See Elad Peled, 'Equality in Israeli educational policy', *Jerusalem Quarterly*, Winter 1984, pp. 19–20. My discussion of these issues is indebted greatly to Elad's thoughtful research.
62   Ibid., p. 22.
63   Ibid., p. 23. Also see the analysis in Elad Peled, 'The hidden agenda of educational policy in Israel: The interrelations between the political system and the educational systems'. (unpublished diss., Columbia University, 1979), pp. 181–3.
64   Peled, 'Equality', p. 23.
65   I say this with qualification because of the tendency of socialists to abstract class the way liberals abstract the individual, and thus often to ignore the issues of ethnicity and nationality.

66 Peled, *Hidden Agenda*, pp. 191–3, and Peled, 'Equality', p. 24.

67 See Naftaly S. Glasman, 'Israel: political roots of two educational decisions', in Thomas (ed.), *Politics and Education*.

68 Naftaly S. Glasman, 'Major planning activities in Israeli education: politically dictated improvisations', *Journal of Educational Thought*, 3, 1 (1969), pp. 29–30.

69 Abba Eban, *An Autobiography* (New York: Random House, 1977), pp. 280–81.

70 Susan Belles, 'The Slow reform', *Jerusalem Post*, 5 May, 1971.

71 See Ben-Gurion, *Medinat Israel ha-mehudeshet*, p. 428.

72 For a retrospective evaluation in this vein see Uzi Ornan, 'Ha-todaah ha-yehudit – hirhurei kfirah' (Jewish Consciousness – Some Reservations), *Ha-Hinukh*, July 1976.

73 Eva Etzioni-Halevy with Rina Shapira, *Political Culture in Israel* (New York and London: Praeger Publishers, 1977), p. 9.

74 Asher Arian, 'Health care in Israel', *International Political Science Journal*, 2 (1981), p. 49.

75 Amitai Etzioni, 'The decline of neo-feudalism: the case of Israel', in Ferrel Heady and Sybil L. Stokes (eds.), *Papers in Comparative Public Administration* (Ann Arbor, Mich.: Institute of Public Administration, the University of Michigan, 1962), p. 237. This is a useful, if rigidly Weberian, analysis of *mamlakhtiyut* as a type of routinization of charisma.

76 Charles S. Liebman and Eliezer Don-Yehiya, *Civil Religion in Israel* (Berkeley, Calif.: University of California Press, 1983), p. 84.

77 Yigal Allon, 'Histadrut and state', *Administration in Israel and Abroad*, 14 (1964), p. 34.

78 Interview with Yosef Almogi, 31 July, 1983, Haifa.

79 Daniel Shimshoni, *Israeli Democracy* (New York: The Free Press, 1982), p. 323.

80 Theoretically all citizens had equality before the law. Israeli Arabs, however, were under military administration until the 1960s and therefore faced numerous restrictions, legally grounded in emergency regulations carried over from the British Mandate. None the less they were able to vote and serve in the Knesset, and did both.

81 Golda Meyerson, 'Identity of interests – Histadrut and state', *Jerusalem Post*, 6 May, 1955, p. 7.

82 See M. Roshwald, 'Political parties and social classes in Israel', *Social Research*, Summer 1956, p. 208.

83 David Ben-Gurion, 'A strong and stable economy needed', *Israel Economic Bulletin*, March (II) 1952, p. 12.

84 David Ben-Gurion, 'Ha-Histadrut ba-medinah.'

85 'Mapai urges nationalization of Histadrut labour exchange', *Jerusalem Post*, 20 November, 1956, p. 4.

86 'Lavon presses nat'l labour exchange plan', *Jerusalem Post*, 7 January, 1956, p. 3.

87 Asher Arian, 'Health care in Israel', *International Political Science Journal*, 2 (1981), pp. 43–4.

88 Yigal Allon, 'Histadrut and State', *Administration in Israel and Abroad*, 14 (1964), p. 35.

89 Shabtai Tevet, 'Shilton be-emtsaut ha-mahalah' (Control by Illness), *Ha-arets*, 3 May, 1957, p. 3.

90 Yair Kotler, 'Mapai neged briut mamlakhtit' (Mapai versus Statist Health), *Ha-arets*, 28 July, 1967, p. 3.

91 Etzioni, 'The decline of neo-feudalism', p. 240.

92 'Lavon urges major reforms in the Histadrut', *Jerusalem Post*, 15 May, 1948, p. 1; 'The Histadrut and the citizen', *Jerusalem Post*, 3 April, 1959, p. 4.

93 Pinhas Lavon, 'Me-hevrat ovdim le-hevrah ovedet' (From a society of workers to a working society), in P. Lavon, *Arakhim u-tmurot* (Tel Aviv: Mifalei tarbut ve-hinukh, 1960), p. 95.

94 Peri, *Between Battles and Ballots*, p. 74.

95 'Right to bargain', *Jerusalem Post*, 25 August, 1960, p. 1. The following November the

Mapai majority in the Histadrut Central Committee suggested, at Lavon's request and after discussions with Ben-Gurion and others, a commission to resolve labor disputes which would have equal representation of the Histadrut, the employers and the 'public.' This was not, however, a compulsory system because disputants would only come to the board voluntarily. Having done so, however, its decisions were to be binding.

96 'Zeev Haring tokef et ha-mamlakhtiyut' (Zeev Haring attacks *Mamlakhtiyut*), *Davar*, 1 September, 1960; 'Histadrut leader hits out at Dayan–Peres group in Mapai', *Jerusalem Post*, 2 September, 1960. Also see *Davar*, 9 August, 1960 and 26 August, 1960 for other arguments by Haring and Dayan on *mamlakhtiyut*.

97 'Lavon warns against "etatism" ', *Jerusalem Post*, 13 December, 1960, p. 3. 'Almogi denies threat of "etatism" ', *Jerusalem Post*, 14 December, 1960, p. 3.

98 See especially the essays by Rotenstreich and Lavon in *Kovets Min ha-Yesod* (Min ha-Yesod Collection) (Tel Aviv: Amikam, 1962).

99 It is worth noting that both Lavon and Rotenstreich had been prominent in Gordonia, a Labour Zionist youth movement founded in the 1920s which was inspired by A. D. Gordon's vision of Jewish Labour and was critical of Marxism.

100 'Socialism within ten years is aim set by Mapai leaders', *Jerusalem Post*, 16 October, 1963, p. 1.

101 However, the extent to which Barkatt's speech used the language of *mamlakhtiyut* to explain the relation of the individual to the state is striking considering the conflict with its advocates. The party, he declared, had to infuse 'state consciousness' in every citizen, adding that 'the separation between society and state should be abolished.' Furthermore, 'The State must forever remain for us the sacred symbol of the fulfilled hopes of past generations and the vision of future generations.' 'Barkatt and Dayan differ over targets of Israeli socialism', *Jerusalem Post*, 17 October, 1963, p. 3.

102 Shlomo Avineri, 'Israel in the post-Ben-Gurion era: the nemesis of Messianism', *Midstream*, September 1965, p. 16.

Conclusion: The Zionist Hedgehog and the Zionist Fox

1 Karl Marx, *Critique of Hegel's 'Philosophy of Right'*, ed. J. O'Malley (Cambridge: Cambridge University Press, 1972), p. 28.

2 Eva Etzioni-Halevy with Rina Shapira, *Political Culture in Israel* (New York: Praeger, 1977), pp. 51–4.

3 Asher Arian, 'Electoral change in a dominant party system', in A. Arian (ed.), *The Elections in Israel 1969* (Jerusalem: Jerusalem Academic Press, 1972), pp. 197–8.

4 Asher Arian and Michal Shamir, 'The primarily political functions of the left–right continuum', in Ernst Krausz (ed.), *Politics and Society in Israel* (New Brunswick, NJ, and Oxford: Transaction Books, 1985), pp. 162–3.

5 Herut only began contesting Histadrut elections in the mid-1960s when the Revisionists decided, after a hiatus of some three decades, to enter into the Labour confederation. Despite the gains of the right, Mapai/Labour always retained its absolute majority there.

6 Arian and Shamir, 'The primarily political functions . .', p. 163.

7 See Yael Yishai, 'Israel's right wing proletariat', in Krausz, *Politics and Society in Israel*.

8 Etzioni-Halevy and Shapira, *Political Culture in Israel*, pp. 40 and 66.

9 Avi Gottlieb and Ephraim Yuchtman-Yaar, 'Materialism, post-materialism, and public views on socioeconomic policy: the case of Israel', in Krausz, *Politics and Society in Israel*, pp. 393–6.

10 This was at the time that Ben-Gurion resigned in order to force out Lavon. See Hanan Kristal, 'Emdot politiot shel ha-itonut ha-yomit ba-"parshat Lavon" ' (Political Positions of the Daily Press in the Lavon Affair), *Medinah, mimshal, vi-hasim beinleumiyim*, Fall 1974, p. 87.

11 Revisionist hostility to the Histadrut and the desire to undermine it were also fundamental to their decision, which was made at the seventh Herut convention. Begin declared there: 'We will get in among those who wish to destroy us and pull the red flag down.' Mark Segal, 'Herut and the Histadrut', *Jerusalem Post*, 25 January, 1963, p. 4.

12 One young Mapai leader, Shulamit Aloni, told a party gathering at the Beit Berl Labour College, 'You older people have left us with a heritage of fanaticism from previous years. We younger people find it difficult to understand why Herut, a legitimate party in this country, could not be taken into account in coalitions and in the Zionist Executive.' 'Relations with Herut aired in Mapai inner circle', *Jerusalem Post*, 1 July, 1962, p. 3.

13 The Revisionist chief, who had been buried in New York after his death in 1940, specified in his will that his remains were not to be transferred, except by order of a sovereign Jewish government. Ever wary of Revisionist exploitation of symbols and pomp, Ben-Gurion apparently felt that his reinterment should not be an act of state, something he thought only appropriate for the remains of Herzl and Baron de Rothschild. However, while still premier, Ben-Gurion did, in July 1960, participate in a memorial ceremony commemorating the 20th anniversary of Jabotinsky's death. He stated at the time that after the 1934 agreements, he felt no personal animus towards his right-wing adversary. 'Jabotinsky memorial gathering marked by an air of conciliation', *Jerusalem Post*, 25 July, 1960, pp. 1, 3. Apparently it was Peres, unbeknown to his mentor, who suggested Jabotinsky's official reinterment. Matti Golan, *Shimon Peres: A Biography* (New York: St Martin's, 1982), p. 125.

14 See Yosef Goell, 'Eshkol urges nation's unity at Herut rally', *Jerusalem Post*, 27 June, 1966, pp. 1, 8.

15 'B-G: Rafi more than Labour movement', *Jerusalem Post*, 29 January, 1967, p. 6; 'B-G would take Herut into Cabinet now', *Jerusalem Post*, 15 February, 1967, p. 8.

16 Yosi Beilin, *Mehiro shel ihud: Mifleget ha-avodah ad milhemet yom ha-kipurim* (The Price of Unity: The Labour Party until the Yom Kippur War) (Israel: Revivim, 1985), p. 41.

17 Ibid., p. 40.

18 Ibid., p. 87.

19 Ibid., p. 87.

20 G. W. F. Hegel, *The Philosophy of Right*, T. M. Knox (Oxford: Oxford University Press, 1967), p. 198.

21 Beilin suggests that this represented a type of paralysis partly due to the union of two parties with substantially different socio-economic outlooks – Ahdut ha-Avodah and Ha-Poel ha-Tsair – in Mapai. See *Mehiro*, pp. 165–6.

22 Of course, I do not imply by this that Ben-Gurion can be classified as a 'Hegelian.'

23 See Anson Rabinbach, *The Crisis of Austrian Socialism* (Chicago and London: University of Chicago Press, 1983).

24 Liebman and Don-Yehiya's suggestive study presents this as a transition from a 'statist' to a 'new' 'civil religion' which emphasized the Bible, the symbols of traditional Judaism (though in secularized guise), Jewish isolation, the Holocaust, and Masada. This is not the place to debate their concept of civil religion; it seems to me that 'belief system' or, more generally, political culture, are preferable terms since 'religion' is just one variant of belief system and belief systems should not be reduced to 'religious' categories, 'civil' or otherwise. They date the 'New Civil Religion' from 1955 when the governing coalition first formulated a 'Jewish Consciousness' programme for Israeli schools. Also, they see the New Civil Religion as closer in spirit to the Likud than to Labour. While, within their framework of analysis, I agree with the latter point, it seems to me that they underestimate the role of Ben-Gurion's messianic and Biblical pronouncements, and especially the extent to which they were intrinsic both to his *mamlakhtiyut* and to the emergence of the so-called New Civil Religion. See Charles S. Liebman and Eliezer Don-Yehiya, *Civil Religion in Israel* (Berkeley, Calif.: University of California, 1983), pp. 124, 136–48, 234.

25 By 1985, 78.6 per cent of Israelis were classified as salaried workers. Asher Arian, *Politics in Israel* (Chatham, NJ: Chatham House, 1985), p. 41.

26 See especially Daniel Bell, *The End of Ideology*, Rev. edn (New York: Collier Books, 1962).

27 Otto Kirchheimer, 'The transformation of the Western European party systems', in Joseph LaPalombara and Myron Weiner (eds.), *Political Parties and Political Development* (Princeton, NJ: Princeton University Press, 1966), pp. 184–7.

28 John Stuart Mill, 'On Liberty', in *The Philosophy of John Stuart Mill*, ed. Marshall Cohen (New York: Modern Library, 1961), p. 246.

29 Isaiah Berlin, 'The hedgehog and the fox', in Isaiah Berlin, *Russian Thinkers* (Middlesex: Penguin Books, 1978), p. 22.

Bibliography

Archives and Libraries

In Israel: the Central Zionist Archives; the Jewish National Library; the Jabotinsky Institute and Archives; *Jerusalem Post* Archives; the Labour Archives and Lavon Institute (Tel Aviv); the Labour Party Archives (Beit Berl). *In Britain*: the Kressel Collection of the Oxford Centre for Postgraduate Hebrew Studies; the Institute of Jewish Affairs of the World Jewish Congress. *In the United States*: the Columbia University Library; the Zionist Archives and Library.

Interviews

Yosef Almogi (3 July, 1983), Itshak Ben-Aharon (2 August, 1985), Arie Eliav (20 July, 1983), Shimon Peres (2 August, 1983), Itshak Rabin (21 July, 1983), Natan Rotenstreich (19 December, 1985).

Newspapers, Journals, Official Publications

Ha-ahdut, Ha-arets, Davar, Davar English Supplement, Divrei ha-Knesset(Knesset Record), *Jewish Daily Bulletin, Jewish Frontier, Jewish Herald, Kuntres, La-merhav, Jewish Chronicle (London), New Judaea, New Palestine, Official Gazette of the Government of Palestine, Palcor, Palestine Post/Jerusalem Post, Ha-Poel ha-Tsair.*

Selected Books and Articles on Zionism and Israeli Politics

Ahad Ha-am, *Essays, Letters, Reminiscences*. Oxford: East and West Library, 1946.
———. *Nationalism and the Jewish Ethic: Basic Writings of Ahad Ha-am*. New York: Schocken Books, 1962.
———. *Selected Essays of Ahad Ha-am*. New York: Atheneum, 1962.
———. *Ten Essays on Zionism and Judaism*. London: Routledge, 1922.
Arian, Asher, *The Choosing People: Voting Behavior in Israel*. Cleveland, Ohio: Case Western Reserve University Press, 1973.
———. 'The dominant party system: a neglected model of democratic stability', *Journal of Politics*, August 1974.
——— (ed.), *The Elections in Israel 1969*. Jerusalem: Jerusalem Academic Press, 1972.
——— (ed.), *The Elections in Israel, 1973*. Jerusalem: Jerusalem Academic Press, 1975.
——— (ed.), *The Elections in Israel, 1977*. Jerusalem: Jerusalem Academic Press, 1980.

—— (ed.), *The Elections in Israel, 1981*. Ramat Aviv: Tel Aviv University/Ramot Publishing, 1983.

——. 'Health care in Israel', *International Political Science Journal*, 2 (1981).

——. *Politics in Israel*. Chatham, NJ: Chatham House, 1985.

Arlosoroff, Haim, *Mivhar ktavim u-firkei haim* (Selected Writings and Chapters of his Life). Tel Aviv: Am Oved, 1958.

Aronoff, M. J., *Power and Ritual in the Israel Labor Party*. Assen/Amsterdam, The Netherlands: Van Gorcum, 1977.

Avi-hai, Avraham, *Ben-Gurion: State-Builder*. Jerusalem and New York: Israel Universities Press and John Wiley, 1974.

Avineri, Shlomo, 'Israel in the post-Ben-Gurion era: the nemesis of Messianism', *Midstream*, September 1965.

——. *The Making of Modern Zionism*. New York: Basic Books, 1981.

——. 'Socialism and Judaism in Moses Hess's *The Holy History of Mankind*', *Review of Politics*, April 1983.

Bar-Zohar, Michael, *Ben-Gurion*. New York: Delacorte Press, 1978.

Beilin, Yosi, *Mehiro shel ihud: Mifleget ha-avodah ad milhemet yom ha-kipurim* (The Price of Unity: The Labour Party until the Yom Kippur War). Israel: Revivim, 1985.

Ben-Gurion, David, *Anahnu u-shkheneinu* (We and Our Neighbors). Tel Aviv: Davar, 1931.

——. *Ben-Gurion Looks at the Bible*. London and New York: W. H. Allen, 1972.

——. *Ben-Gurion Looks Back in Talks with Moshe Pearlman*. London: Weidenfeld & Nicolson, 1965.

——. *Berurim* (Clarifications). Tel Aviv: Mapai, 1944.

——. *Hazon va-derekh* (Vision and Path), 5 vols. Tel Aviv: Mapai, 1951–57.

——. *Israel: A Personal History*. New York and Tel Aviv: Funk & Wagnalls and Sabra Books, 1971.

——. *Letters to Paula*. London: Vallentine, Mitchell, 1971.

——. *Medinat Israel ha-mehudeshet* (The Restored State of Israel). Tel Aviv: Am Oved, 1969.

——. *Mi-maamad le-am* (From a Class to a Nation). Tel Aviv: Am Oved and Keren ha-Negev, 1974.

——. 'Munahim va-arakhim' (Terms and Values), *Hazut*, 1957.

——. *My Talks with Arab Leaders*. Jerusalem: Keter, 1972.

——. *Rebirth and Destiny of Israel*. New York: Philosophical Library, 1954.

——. *Tnuat ha-Poalim ve-ha-revisionismus* (The Workers' Movement and Revisionism). Tel Aviv: The World League for Labour Palestine, 1933.

——. *Zikhronot* (Memoirs), 5 vols. Tel Aviv: Am Oved, 1976–82.

Ben-Zvi, Rahel Yanait, *Coming Home*. New York: Herzl Press, 1964.

Borokhov (Borochov), Ber, *Class Struggle and the Jewish Nation: Selected Essays in Marxist Zionism*, ed. with an introduction by Mitchell Cohen. New Brunswick, NJ: Transaction Books, 1984.

——. *Ktavim* (Writings), 3 vols. Tel Aviv: Ha-Kibbutz ha-Meuhad and Sifriyat Poalim, 1955, 1958, 1966.

Braham, Randolph L., *Israel: A Modern Education System*. Washington, DC: United States Department of Health, Education, and Welfare, 1966.

Burstein, Moshe, *Self-Government of the Jews in Palestine since 1900*. Tel Aviv: Ha-Poel ha-Tzair, 1934.

Chissin (Hissin), Chaim (Haim), *A Palestine Diary: Memoirs of a Bilu Pioneer 1882–1887*. New York: Herzl Press, 1976.

The Colonial Office, *The System of Education of the Jewish Community in Palestine: Report of the Commission of Enquiry Appointed by the Secretary of State for the Colonies, 1945*. London: HMSO, 1945.

The Development of the Jewish National Home in Palestine: Memorandum submitted to His

Majesty's Government by the Jewish Agency for Palestine, May 1930. London: Jewish Agency, 1930.

Din ve-heshbon shel vaadat ha-hakirah be-inyenei ha-hinukh ba-mahanot ha-olim (Report of the Commission of Inquiry into Education in the Immigrant Camps). Jerusalem: Government Printing Office, 1950.

Dinur (Dinaburg), Ben-Zion, *Arakhim u-drakhim: Beayot hinukh ve-tarbut be-israel* (Values and Paths: Problems of Education and Culture in Israel). Tel Aviv: Urim, 1958.

Dizengoff, Meir, *Report on Urban Colonisation submitted to the XVth Zionist Congress by the Director of the Department of Urban Colonisation*. Tel Aviv, 1927.

Eisenstadt, S. N., *Israeli Society*. London: Weidenfeld & Nicolson, 1967.

Etzioni, Amitai, 'The decline of neo-feudalism: the case of Israel', in F. Heady and S. L. Stokes (eds.), *Papers in Comparative Public Administration*. Ann Arbor, Mich.: Institute of Public Administration, University of Michigan, 1962.

Etzioni-Halevy, Eva, with Rina Shapira, *Political Culture in Israel*. New York and London: Praeger Publishers, 1977.

Frankel, Jonathan, *Prophecy and Politics: Socialism, Nationalism, and the Russian Jews, 1862–1917*. Cambridge and New York: Cambridge University Press, 1981.

Goldstein, Yaakov, *Ba-derekh le-hegmoniyah: Mapai – Hitgabshut mediniyutah 1930–1936* (On the Road to Hegemony: Mapai – The Crystallization of Its Policies 1930–1936). Tel Aviv: Am Oved/Tarbut ve-Hinukh, 1980.

———, and Yaakov Shavit, *Lelo psharot: Heskem Ben-Gurion-Jabotinsky ve-kishlono* (No Compromises: The Ben-Gurion-Jabotinsky Agreement and Its Failure). Tel Aviv: Yariv/ Hadar, 1979.

Gorni, Yosef, *Ahdut ha-Avodah 1919–1930: Ha-yesodot ha-raayoniyim ve-ha-shitah ha-medinit* (Ahdut ha-Avodah 1919–1930: The Ideological Principles and the Political System). Tel Aviv: Tel Aviv University and Ha-Kibbutz ha-Meuhad, 1973.

Halpern, Ben, *The Idea of the Jewish State*, 2nd edn. Cambridge, Mass., and London: Harvard University Press, 1969.

Hertzberg, Arthur (ed.), *The Zionist Idea*. New York: Atheneum, 1969.

Herzl, Theodor, *Old–New Land (Altneuland)*. New York: Bloch Publishing, and Herzl Press, 1960.

———. *Complete Diaries*, 5 vols. New York and London: Herzl Press and Thomas Yoseloff, 1960.

———. *The Jewish State*. New York: Herzl Press, 1970.

———. *Zionist Writings: Essays and Addresses*, 2 vols. New York: Herzl Press, 1973, 1975.

Hess, Moses, *Ausgewählte Schriften*, ed. Horst Lademacher. Cologne: Joseph Melzer Verlag, 1962.

Horowitz, Dan, and Moshe Lissak, *Origins of the Israeli Polity: Palestine under the Mandate*. Chicago and London: University of Chicago Press, 1978.

Hurwitz, J. C. (ed.), *The Middle East and North Africa in World Politics: A Documentary Record*, vols 1 and 2. New Haven, Conn., and London: Yale University Press, 1975, 1979.

Jabotinsky, Vladimir, *Ba-derekh la-medinah* (On the Road to the State). Jerusalem: Eri Jabotinsky, 1953.

———. *Ba-saar* (In the Storm). Jerusalem: Eri Jabotinsky, 1959.

———. *Reshimot* (Short Articles). Tel Aviv: Eri Jabotinsky and Amihai, n.d.

———. *Umah ve-hevrah* (Nation and Society). Jerusalem: Eri Jabotinsky, 1950.

———. *Zikhronot ben-dori* (Memoirs of My Contemporary). Jerusalem: Eri Jabotinsky and Amihai, n.d.

Janowsky, Oscar I., *The Jews and Minority Rights 1898–1919*. New York: AMS Press, 1966.

Katznelson, Berl, *Igrot Berl Katznelson 1930–1937* (Correspondence of Berl Katznelson) eds A. Shapira and E. Raizen. Tel Aviv: Am Oved, 1984.

———. *Kitvei Berl Katznelson* (The Writings of Berl Katznelson), vol. 4. Tel Aviv: Mapai, 1949.

———. *My Way to Palestine*. London: Hechalutz/Poale Zion, 1946.

Keren, Michael, *Ben-Gurion and the Intellectuals.* DeKalb, Ill.: Northern Illinois University Press, 1983.

Kleinberger, Aharon F., *Society, Schools, and Progress in Israel.* Oxford: Pergamon Press, 1969.

Kolatt, Israel, 'Ben Gurion: image and greatness', *Dispersion and Unity*, 21/22 (1973–74).

————. 'The concept of the Histadrut: emergence and change 1920–1948', *Labor and Society in Israel.* Tel Aviv: Tel Aviv University Department of Labour Studies and the Histadrut Department of Higher Education, 1973.

————. 'Zionist Marxism', in S. Avineri (ed.), *Varieties of Marxism.* The Hague: Martinus Nijhoff, 1977.

Kovets Min ha-Yesod (Min ha-Yesod Collection). Tel Aviv: Amikam, 1962.

Krausz, Ernst (ed.), *Politics and Society in Israel.* New Brunswick, NJ, and Oxford: Transaction Books, 1985.

Laqueur, Walter, *A History of Zionism.* New York: Holt, Rinehart & Winston, 1972.

Laskov, Shulamit, 'The Biluim: reality and legend (with selected documents)' *Zionism*, Spring 1981.

Levin, Shmarya, *The Arena.* New York: Harcourt, Brace, 1932.

Levite, Ariel, and Sidney Tarrow, 'The legitimation of excluded parties in dominant party systems: a comparison of Israel and Italy', *Comparative Politics*, April 1983.

Liebman, Charles S., and Eliezer Don-Yehiya, *Civil Religion in Israel.* Berkeley, Calif.: University of California Press, 1983.

Mahler, Gregory (ed.), *Readings on the Israeli Political System.* Washington, DC: University Press of America, 1982.

Margalit, Elkanah, 'Binationalism: an interpretation of Zionism 1941–1947', *Studies in Zionism*, October 1981.

Medding, Peter Y., *Mapai in Israel: Political Organisation and Government in a New Society.* Cambridge: Cambridge University Press, 1972.

Mendelsohnn, Ezra, *Zionism in Poland: The Formative Years 1915–1926.* New Haven, Conn, and London: Yale University Press, 1981.

Mintz, Mattityahu, *Ber Borokhov: Ha-maagal ha-rishon* (Ber Borokhov: The First Circle). Tel Aviv: Tel Aviv University and Ha-Kibbutz ha-Meuhad, 1976.

———— (ed.), *Ha-veidah ha-shlishit shel poalei tsiyon be-russiya, 1917 – Teudot* (The Third Conference of Poale Zion in Russia, 1917 – Documents). Ramat Aviv: Tel Aviv University, 1976.

———— (ed.), *Veidat Krakov shel mifleget ha-poalim ha-sotsial-demokratit ha-yehudit poalei tsiyon be-Russiya August 1907 – Teudot* (The Cracow Conference of the Jewish Social Democratic Workers' Party – Poale Zion in Russia, August 1907 – Documents). Ramat Aviv: Tel Aviv University, 1979.

Nardi, Noah, *Education in Palestine 1920–1945.* Washington, DC: Zionist Organization of America, 1945.

Peled, Elad, 'Equality in Israeli educational policy', *Jerusalem Quarterly*, Winter 1984.

————. 'The hidden agenda of educational policy in Israel: The interrelations between the political and the educational systems'. Unpublished diss., Columbia University, 1979.

Peri, Yoram, *Between Battles and Ballots: Israeli Military in Politics.* Cambridge: Cambridge University Press, 1983.

Pinsker, Leo, *Roads to Freedom: Writings and Addresses.* New York: Scopus Publishing, 1944.

Preuss, Walter, *The Labour Movement in Israel.* Jerusalem: Rubin Mass, 1965.

Rabin, Chaim, 'Language revival: colloquialism or pluralism?', *Jewish Frontier*, September 1958.

————. 'The national idea and the revival of Hebrew', *Studies in Zionism*, Spring 1983.

Reinharz, Jehuda, *Chaim Weizmann: The Making of a Zionist Leader.* Oxford: Oxford University Press, 1985.

Rinott, Moshe, 'Religion and education: the cultural question and the Zionist movement 1897–1913', *Studies in Zionism*, Spring 1984.

Ron-Polani, Y., 'Hinukh be-ruah tnuat ha-avodah be-avar u-ba-hoveh' (Education in the Spirit of the Labour Movement – Past and Present), *Hikukh*, March 1969.

Ruppin, Arthur, *Three Decades in Palestine*. Jerusalem: Schocken Books, 1936.

Schechtman, Joseph, *The Jabotinsky Story: Rebel and Statesman* (vol. 1), *Fighter and Prophet* (vol. 2). New York: Thomas Yoseloff, 1956, 1961.

———, and Yehuda Benari, *History of the Revisionist Movement 1925–1930*. Tel Aviv: Hadar, 1970.

Sha'altiel, Eli, 'David Ben-Gurion on partition, 1937', *Jerusalem Quarterly*, Winter 1979.

Shapira, Anita, *Berl: The Biography of a Socialist Zionist – Berl Katznelson 1887–1944*. (Cambridge: Cambridge University Press, 1984.

———. 'The debate in Mapai on the use of violence 1932–1935', *Zionism*, Spring 1981.

———. *Ha-maavak ha-nikhzav* (The Futile Struggle). Tel Aviv: Tel Aviv University and Ha-Kibbutz ha-Meuhad, 1977.

———. *Mi-piturei ha-rama ad peruk ha-palmah* (The Army Controversy 1948: Ben-Gurion's Struggle for Control, with the Protocol of the Fifth Committee, July 1948). Tel Aviv: Ha-Kibbutz ha-Meuhad, 1985.

———. 'Origins of the "Jewish labor" ideology', *Studies in Zionism*, Spring 1982.

Shapiro, Yonathan, *Elit lelo mamshikhim: Dorot manhigim ba-hevra ha-isreaelit* (An Elite without Successors: Generations of Leaders in Israeli Society). Tel Aviv: Sifriyat Poalim, 1984.

———. *The Formative Years of the Israeli Labour Party: The Organization of Power 1919–1930)*. London and Beverly Hills, Calif.: Sage Publications, 1976.

Silberschlag, Eisig (ed.), *Eliezer Ben Yehuda: A Symposium*. Oxford: Oxford Centre for Postgraduate Hebrew Studies, 1981.

Slutsky, Yehudah, *Mavo le-toldot tnuat ha-avodah ha-israelit* (Introduction to the History of the Israeli Labour Movement). Tel Aviv: Am Oved, 1973.

——— (ed.), *Poalei Tsiyon be-erets Israel 1905–1919: Teudot* (Poale Zion in the Land of Israel 1905–1919: Documents). Ramat Aviv: Tel Aviv University, 1978.

Syrkin, Marie, 'Education in Israel', *Jewish Frontier*, September 1952.

———. *Nachman Syrkin, Socialist Zionist: A Biographical Memoir with Selected Essays*. New York: Herzl Press, 1960.

Syrkin, Nachman (Nahman), *Essays on Socialist Zionism*. New York: Young Poale Zion Alliance of America, 1935.

Teveth (Tevet), Shabtai, *Ben-Gurion and the Palestinian Arabs*. Oxford: Oxford University Press, 1985.

———. *Kinat David: Ben-Gurion ha-tsair* (David's Zeal: The Young Ben-Gurion). Jerusalem and Tel Aviv: Schocken Books, 1976.

———. *Moshe Dayan*. Boston, Mass.: Houghton Mifflin, 1973.

Ussishkin, Menahem Mendl, *Our Program*. New York: Federation of American Zionists, 1905.

Ha-Veidah ha-shminit shel ha-histadrut (The Eighth Conference of the Histadrut). Tel Aviv: The Histadrut, 1956.

Vital, David, *The Origins of Zionism*. Oxford: Oxford University Press, 1975.

———. *Zionism: The Formative Years*. Oxford: Oxford Univerity Press, 1982.

Weizmann, Chaim, *The Letters and Papers of Chaim Weizmann*, 25 vols. Jerusalem: Israel Universities Press; Oxford: Oxford University Press; New Brunswick, NJ: Transaction Books; Rehovot, Israel: Yad Weizmann, 1968–1984.

———. *Trial and Error: The Autobiography of Chaim Weizmann*. New York: Schocken Books, 1966.

Wolf, Judith L., 'Selected aspects in the development of public education in Palestine 1920–1946.' Unpublished diss., Boston College, 1981.

Yalkut ha-Ahdut 1907–1919 (Ahdut Anthology). Tel Aviv: Am Oved, 1962.

Glossary

Ahdut ha-Avodah – Literally 'unity of labour', Ahdut ha-Avodah had three manifestations in Zionist/Israeli political history:

a Ahdut ha-Avodah was a labour organization that combined the functions of trade union and political party founded in 1919 by the union of Poale Zion and a 'non-partisan' labour group led by Berl Katznelson. In 1930 it merged with Ha-Poel ha-Tsair to form Mapai.

b Ahdut ha-Avodah was the name taken by the Siah B (Bet) group that split from Mapai to form a new organization in 1944 with Ha-Kibbutz ha-Meuhad. It merged into the Mapam party in 1948.

c Mapam split in 1954 and those who had previously been in Ahdut ha-Avodah and were closely tied to Ha-Kibbutz ha-Meuhad kibbutz federation re-formed Ahdut ha-Avodah. It later merged into the Israel Labour party in 1968.

Aliyah (pl. *aliyot*) – Literally 'ascent', this Hebrew term is used to describe the process of a Jew moving to the Land of Israel. Zionist historiography usually refers to five *aliyot*:

a First Aliyah (1882–1903). About 25,000 immigrants. Mostly eastern European in origins, influenced by the Hibat Zion movement.

b Second Aliyah (1904–14). 20–30,000 immigrants. Dominated by the left, essential in creating the foundations of the Israeli Labour movement.

c Third Aliyah (1919–23). About 35,000 immigrants. Again, brought many socialists and radicals.

d Fourth Aliyah (1924–28). 60–80,000 immigrants. Largely middle class and from Poland.

e Fifth Aliyah (1929–39). 230,000 immigrants. Large influx due to the rise of Nazism and anti-Semitism in Europe.

Asefat ha-Nivharim – The 'Elected Assembly' of Palestinian Jewry, formed 1920. Elections were by proportional representation and party lists. Its executive arm was the *Vaad Leumi* (National Council).

Balfour Declaration – British policy statement supporting the creation of a Jewish national home in Palestine (1917).

Basle Declaration (Programme) – Founding programme of the Zionist Organization (1897) calling for a Jewish home in Palestine secured by public law.

Brit ha-Biryonim – Extremist Revisionist group led by Abba Ahimeir.

British Mandate – League of Nations Mandate under which Britain ruled Palestine 1922–48. One of its terms was facilitating the creation of a Jewish national home.

Betar – Youth movement of the right-wing Revisionist Zionists.

Bilu – Early Russian Zionist group, part of the First Aliyah, advocates of Jewish 'self-labour' in Palestine.

Erets Israel – The Land of Israel (Hebrew).

Etsel – see Irgun Tsvai Leumi.

General Zionism – Essentially a middle-class movement, General Zionists claimed to support Jewish nationalism without appending other 'isms' to it (e.g. socialism). They split into 'General Zionists A' who supported Weizmann's collaboration with the Labour movement and his policies of moderation, and 'General Zionists B' who were opposed to Weizmann and the left and later became the Liberal party of Israel. The Liberals formed an electoral alliance with Herut known as Gahal (1965), which in turn became the major element of the Likud electoral alliance.

Haganah – Mainstream of the Zionist underground forces during the period of the British Mandate. Formed originally by Ahdut ha-Avodah, it was first transferred to the auspices of the Histadrut and then to the Jewish Agency.

Ha-Kibbutz ha-Meuhad – The United Kibbutz Movement, founded in 1927. Itzhak Tabenkin was its spiritual leader. Originally tied to the first Ahdut ha-Avodah and Mapai, it was linked to the later re-formations of Ahdut ha-Avodah.

Ha-Poel ha-Mizrahi – religious Zionist labour party.

Ha-Poel ha-Tsair – Literally 'The Young Worker', a non-Marxist Labour Zionist party opposed to the idea of class struggle and influenced by populism and the ideas of A. D. Gordon. Founded in Palestine in 1905, it published a journal of the same name and later merged with Ahdut ha-Avodah to form Mapai.

Ha-Shomer – Literally 'The Guard', it was a self-defence organization established by Jewish youth in Palestine in 1909.

Ha-Shomer ha-Tsair – Zionist youth movement formed on the eve of the First World War and radicalized in the late 1920s. Marxist–Zionist in orientation, it formed the Ha-Shomer ha-Tsair kibbutz movement (Kibbutz Artsi) in 1927, the Socialist League in 1936 and merged into Mapam in 1948. After Ahdut ha-Avodah split from Mapam in 1954, Mapam remained as a political party affiliated to the Ha-Shomer ha-Tsair kibbutz movement.

Haskalah – Literally 'Enlightenment', a Jewish movement of modernization and Westernization in the late eighteenth and ninteenth centuries. Its followers were called *Maskilim* (sing., *maskil*).

Herut – The 'Freedom' party, founded by the Irgun after the creation of the state of Israel and led by Menahem Begin. Heir to Revisionist Zionism.

Hever ha-Kvutsot – 'Association of Collectives', a kibbutz federation founded in 1928.

Hibat Zion ('Love of Zion') – Proto-Zionist organization founded in Russia in the 1880s. Supported practical Zionism. Followers were called 'Hovevei Zion' (Lovers of Zion).

Histadrut – The General Federation of Jewish Labour in Palestine (later Israel), founded in 1920. It was more than a trade union federation and possessed extensive co-operative economic enterprises composing an important sector of the Yishuv's economy, and an extensive social welfare system. David Ben-Gurion was its first Secretary-General.

Hovevei Zion – see Hibat Zion.

Irgun Tsvai Leumi – Right-wing Zionist underground formed in the 1930s and associated with the Revisionists. Led by Menahem Begin after 1942.

Israel Defence Forces (IDF) – Armed forces of the independent state of Israel, founded in 1948 by the merger of the various Zionist undergrounds.

Jewish Agency – The terms of the British Mandate called for the creation of a Jewish Agency to facilitate the Jewish national home in co-operation with the Mandatory authorities. It was extended in 1929 under a plan designed by Haim Weizmann to make it a partnership of the Zionist Organization and well-to-do non-Zionists in the diaspora who wanted to assist the creation of the national home.

Jewish State Party – Formed in 1933 by a split in the Revisionists. Led by Meir Grossman.

Kibbutz (pl. Kibbutzim) – Literally 'collective'. Communal agricultural settlements established by the Zionist Labour movement.

Knesset – The Israeli parliament. Established 1949.

Labour party – A social democratic party established in 1968 by the merger of Mapai, Ahdut ha-Avodah and Rafi. Formed an electoral alignment with Mapam.

Left Poale Zion – Marxist- and Borokhovist-oriented Zionists who opposed the formation of Ahdut ha-Avodah in 1919.

Liberal Party – see General Zionism.

Likud – Electoral alliance of right-wing parties founded in 1973 and led by Menahem Begin.

Mamlakhtiyut – Derived from *mamlakha* ('kingdom' in Hebrew), this was Ben-Gurion's policy of 'statism', the assertion of state primacy in all aspects of Israeli life.

Mapai – The Israel Workers' party, a democratic socialist party founded 1930, merged into the Labour party in 1968. It dominated Israeli politics for almost the entire period of its existence. Its first leaders were Ben-Gurion, Katznelson and Tabenkin. In the 1960s its leaders were Levi Eshkol, Pinhas Sapir, Golda Meir and Zalman Aran.

Mapam – United Workers' party, founded 1948 by Ha-Shomer ha-Tsair, Ahdut ha-Avodah, and the Left Poale Zion.

Maskilim – see Haskalah.

Mizrahi – Religious Zionist party.

New Zionist Organization (NZO) – Formed 1935 by Jabotinsky to compete with the Zionist Organization.

Palmah – The elite shock troops of the Haganah, closely linked to Ha-Kibbutz ha-Meuhad because Palmah members worked part-time and trained part-time on kibbutzim. Established in 1941 when the German armies were moving across North Africa in the direction of Palestine. The Palmah was dissolved in 1948 and merged into the Israel Defence Forces.

Poale Zion – Socialist Zionist party that developed after the turn of the century. It originally had a Marxist orientation.The Russian branch was dominated by Borokhov. The Palestinian branch was founded in 1905 and dissolved in 1919 with the formation of Ahdut ha-Avodah.

Political Zionism – The Zionism advocated by Herzl. It was strictly political in approach, sought to avoid cultural questions and believed that the key to Zionism's success was in gaining a charter from a great power on behalf of Jewish colonization of Palestine.

Practical Zionism – Associated at first with the Hovevei Zion movement, this approach emphasized the practical tasks of building a Jewish community in Palestine rather than diplomatic efforts to obtain a charter from a big power.

Rafi – Israel Workers' List. Split from Mapai in 1965 led by David Ben-Gurion, Shimon Peres and Moshe Dayan. Merged into the Labour party in 1968, but without Ben-Gurion.

Revisionism – Right-wing, integralist Zionist ideology articulated by Vladimir Jabotinsky. Ultra-nationalist in orientation, the Revisionists claimed that under Weizmann Zionism had betrayed Herzl's legacy and therefore had to be 'revised'. Jabotinsky founded a Revisionist party in 1925 and in 1935 it split from the Zionist Organization to form a competing 'New Zionist Organization'. After Jabotinsky's death in 1940, Revisionism was most forcefully embodied in the Irgun, led by Menahem Begin, and then in the Herut party which he also headed.

Shaatnez – Mixture of wool and cotton forbidden in garments by Jewish tradition. Jabotinsky used the term to describe the mixture of socialism and Zionism advocated by the left.

Siah B (Bet) – Faction in Mapai that split in the 1940s to form Ahdut ha-Avodah with Ha-Kibbutz ha-Meuhad.

Synthetic Zionism – Especially associated with the name of Chaim Weizmann, this Zionism advocated uniting the practical, political and cultural Zionist approaches.

Territorialism – Belief that the Jewish situation required the creation of a state and territorial autonomy in any land available, not necessarily in Palestine.

Uganda Plan – Proposal to Herzl by the British government to create a Jewish home in East Africa.

Vaad Leumi – Literally National Council, the Executive of the Asefat ha-Nivharim.

Yishuv – Literally settlement or community. It refers to the Jewish community of Palestine.

Zionist Organization (ZO) – Also called the World Zionist Organization (WZO). Chief tool of the Zionist movement, founded in 1897 by Herzl at a congress in Basle. It had biennial (at first, annual) congresses (the Zionist Congress) which elected an Actions Committee (the *Vaad ha-Poel*) to function between congresses and a smaller Executive, which functioned something like a Cabinet.

Index